Inauguration and Liturgical Kingship in the Long Twelfth Century

YORK MEDIEVAL PRESS

York Medieval Press is published by the University of York's Centre for Medieval Studies in association with Boydell & Brewer Limited. Our objective is the promotion of innovative scholarship and fresh criticism on medieval culture. We have a special commitment to interdisciplinary study, in line with the Centre's belief that the future of Medieval Studies lies in those areas in which its major constituent disciplines at once inform and challenge each other.

Editorial Board (2021)

Professor Peter Biller, Emeritus (Dept of History): General Editor
Professor Tim Ayers (Dept of History of Art): Co-Director, Centre for Medieval Studies
Dr Henry Bainton: Private scholar
Dr J. W. Binns: Honorary Fellow, Centre for Medieval Studies
Dr K. P. Clarke (Dept of English and Related Literature)
Dr K. F. Giles (Dept of Archaeology)
Dr Holly James-Maddocks (Dept of English and Related Literature)
Dr Harry Munt (Dept of History)
† Professor W. Mark Ormrod, Emeritus (Dept of History)
Dr L. J. Sackville (Dept of History)
Professor Elizabeth M. Tyler (Dept of English and Related Literature): Co-Director, Centre for Medieval Studies
Dr Hanna Vorholt (Dept of History of Art)
Professor J. G. Wogan-Browne (English Faculty, Fordham University)

All enquiries of an editorial kind, including suggestions for monographs and essay collections, should be addressed to: The Academic Editor, York Medieval Press, Department of History, University of York, Heslington, York, YO10 5DD (E-mail: pete.biller@york.ac.uk)

Details of other York Medieval Press volumes are available from Boydell & Brewer Ltd.

Inauguration and Liturgical Kingship in the Long Twelfth Century

Male and Female Accession Rituals in England, France and the Empire

Johanna Dale

THE UNIVERSITY *of York*

YORK MEDIEVAL PRESS

© Johanna Dale 2019

All rights reserved. Except as permitted under current legislation
no part of this work may be photocopied, stored in a retrieval system,
published, performed in public, adapted, broadcast,
transmitted, recorded or reproduced in any form or by any means,
without the prior permission of the copyright owner

The right of Johanna Dale to be identified as
the author of this work has been asserted in accordance with
sections 77 and 78 of the Copyright, Designs and Patents Act 1988

First published 2019
Paperback edition 2021

A York Medieval Press publication
in association with The Boydell Press
an imprint of Boydell & Brewer Ltd
PO Box 9, Woodbridge, Suffolk IP12 3DF, UK
and of Boydell & Brewer Inc.
668 Mt Hope Avenue, Rochester, NY 14620–2731, USA
website: www.boydellandbrewer.com
and with the
Centre for Medieval Studies, University of York

ISBN 978 1 903153 84 0 hardback
ISBN 978 1 903153 98 7 paperback

A CIP catalogue record for this book is available
from the British Library

The publisher has no responsibility for the continued existence or accuracy of
URLs for external or third-party internet websites referred to in this book, and
does not guarantee that any content on such websites is, or will remain, accurate or
appropriate

Contents

	List of Illustrations	vi
	Acknowledgements	viii
	List of Abbreviations	x
	Timeline	xi
	Genealogies	xii
	Introduction	1
1	Liturgical Texts: The Spoken Word and Song	26
2	Liturgical Rituals: Rubrication and Regalia	68
3	Who and Where? Actors, Location and Legitimacy	105
4	What and When? Consecration and the Liturgical Calendar	130
5	Royal Titles, Anniversaries and their Meaning: The Charter Evidence	159
6	Seal Impressions and Christomimetic Kingship	191
	Conclusion	215
	Appendix 1: Editions and Manuscripts of the Selected *Ordines*	225
	Appendix 2: Prayer Formulae Incipits	229
	Appendix 3: Tables of Ritual Elements in the *Ordines*	232
	Appendix 4: Brief Descriptions of Royal and Imperial Seals and *Bullae*	239
	Bibliography	255
	Index of Biblical References	285
	General Index	286

Illustrations

Plates

Plate 1. Thirteenth-century *laudes*: Cambridge, Trinity College MS B.11.10, fol. 108r–109v
Reproduced by kind permission of the Master and Fellows of Trinity College Cambridge 62

Plate 2. The Reichsschwert (so-called Sword of St Maurice)
Reproduced by kind permission of the KHM-Museumsverband 86

Plate 3. The 'Coronation Miniature' from the Gospels of Henry the Lion: Wolfenbüttel, Herzog-August-Bibliothek, MS Guelf. 105 Noviss. 2°, fol. 171v
Reproduced by kind permission of the Herzog-August-Bibliothek Wolfenbüttel 96

Plate 4. Coronation of the Virgin: Eton College MS 177, fol. 7v
Reproduced by kind permission of the Provost and Fellows of Eton College 100

Plate 5. The wedding feast of Henry V and Matilda of England: Cambridge, Corpus Christi College MS 373, fol. 95v
Reproduced by kind permission of the Master and Fellows of Corpus Christi College, Cambridge 125

Plate 6. Henry VI's diploma for the citizens of Constance
Reproduced by kind permission of The Constance Rosgartenmuseum 186

Genealogies

Genealogy 1. Simplified Genealogy of the Norman and Plantagenet Kings, 1066–1272 xii

Genealogy 2. Simplified Genealogy of the Capetian Kings, 1060–1270 xiii

Genealogy 3. Simplified Genealogy of the Salian Kings and Emperors, 1024–1125 xiv

Genealogy 4. Simplified Genealogy of the Staufen and Welf Kings and Emperors, 1125–1250 xv

Tables

Table 1. Distribution of Prayers in the Royal Ordines 41

Table 2. Distribution of Prayers in the Imperial Ordines 42

Illustrations

Table 3. Frequency of the Occurrence of Prayers in the Royal and
Imperial Ordines   43

Table 4. Details from the Ritual of Anointing in the Royal Ordines   74

The author and publishers are grateful to all the institutions and individuals listed for permission to reproduce the materials in which they hold copyright. Every effort has been made to trace the copyright holders; apologies are offered for any omission, and the publishers will be pleased to add any necessary acknowledgement in subsequent editions.

Acknowledgements

Since David du Croz and Richard Markham first introduced me to medieval history as a teenager, I have had the benefit of exceptional teachers and mentors. Elisabeth van Houts has been a source of inspiration and encouragement for the past fifteen years. In Nicholas Vincent I had a most stimulating and intellectually ambitious doctoral supervisor who coupled high expectations with a welcome sense of fun – thank you Nick. I am grateful to Jörg Peltzer for inviting me to spend a semester as part of his research group in Heidelberg, enabling me to experience the venerable traditions of German academia. Colleagues in Cambridge, Norwich, Heidelberg, London, and further afield, have shared work, ideas and advice (and often tea, wine, and friendship). Space precludes the detailing of all but the greatest of my professional debts. These are owed to Helen Hunter, Jonathan Lyon, Thomas Smith, Danica Summerlin, Max Wemhöner, Björn Weiler, and, in particular, to Levi Roach and Alice Taylor, both of whom have helped me far more than can reasonably be demanded by the bonds of *amicitiae*. Caroline Palmer of Boydell & Brewer greeted this project with enthusiasm and has remained enthusiastic, supportive and, above all, patient. Rebecca Cribb has guided me through the production process with efficiency and good humour.

This book would not have been possible without the support of the School of History at the University of East Anglia, where the award of an Arts and Humanities Research Council studentship facilitated my escape from a windowless office in Bayswater. Cambridge University Library and the German Historical Institute in London have provided much-needed access to German-language materials. I have also benefitted from the libraries of two of the jewels in the crown of the University of London: the Warburg Institute and the Institute of Historical Research. Through its seminar programme and common room the IHR has provided me with an invaluable intellectual community too. In supporting my return to work on a part-time basis following the birth of my son, the British Academy has enabled me to balance professional and personal lives in a manner not often afforded to early career academics. I am extremely thankful to have such an enlightened sponsor and to Claire Morley at UCL History for taking care of the administrative side of things.

That I am a medievalist is largely a result of stubbornness. However, that I am an historian at all is due to my family. My (invariably mispronounced) German Christian name points to the influence of another culture and history on an otherwise quintessentially English upbringing. My grandmother, Rita Hodge (née Lüdecke) and her best friend, Gisela Herwig, met during the Second World War when both were interned as enemy aliens on the Isle of

Acknowledgements

Man. That they had lived through the momentous events of the twentieth century, which I learned about at school, fascinated me. While my chronological focus has shifted, my commitment to considering English and German history together is a testament to their enduring influence. My parents, Billie and Gerard, have fostered my curiosity and been ever ready to show an interest in my work (particularly before breakfast). My siblings, with whom I first enjoyed Monty Python, have also been a source of support for over three decades. In the final stages of research and writing, Sebastian and Rex have accompanied me on much needed head-clearing walks along the River Crouch. My greatest debt in the writing of this book, however, is owed to my husband Julian, skipper of Blue Owl. Without his support and encouragement, I would never have returned to academia, nor stuck it out long enough for this book to see the light of day, nor, more importantly, would I have had so much fun over the last fifteen years. For, as Ratty rightly declares in *The Wind in the Willows*, 'there is nothing – absolutely nothing – half so much worth doing as simply messing about in boats.'

This book is produced with the generous assistance of a grant from Isobel Thornley's Bequest to the University of London.

Abbreviations

CdS	Corpus des sceaux français du Moyen Age
HBS	Henry Bradshaw Society
MGH Const.	*Monumenta Germaniae Historica Constitutiones et acta publica imperatorum et regum*
MGH DD	*Monumenta Germaniae Historica Diplomata*
MGH Fontes Iuris	*Monumenta Germaniae Historica Fontes Iuris Germanici antiqui in usum scholarum separatim editi*
MGH Ldl	*Monumenta Germaniae Historica Libelli de lite imperatorum et pontificum*
MGH LL	*Monumenta Germaniae Historica Leges (in Folio)*
MGH SS	*Monumenta Germaniae Historica Scriptores (in Folio)*
MGH SS rer. Germ.	*Monumenta Germaniae Historica Scriptores rerum Germanicarum in usum scholarum separatim editi*
MGH rer. Germ. N.S.	*Monumenta Germaniae Historica Scriptores rerum Germanicarum, Nova series*
MIÖG	*Mitteilungen des Instituts für Österreichische Geschichtsforschung*
OMT	Oxford Medieval Texts
RHF	*Recueil des historiens des Gaules et de la France*
RS	Rolls Series
SHM	Sources d'histoire médiévale

Timeline

Reigning Kings and Popes

Date	England	France	Germany	Popes & *Antipopes
1050	Edward (1042–66)	Philip I (1059–1108)	Henry IV (1056–1105)	Leo IX (1049–54) Victor II (1055–7) Stephen IX (1057–8) *Benedict X (1058–9)
	William I (1066–87)			Nicholas II (1058–61) Alexander II (1061–73) *Honorius II (1061–4) Gregory VII (1073–85) *Clement III (1080–1100)
	William II (1087–1100)			Victor III (1086–7) Urban II (1088–99) Paschal II (1099–1118)
1100	Henry I (1100–35)	Louis VI (1108–37)	Henry V (1105–25)	*Theodoric (1100–01) *Albert (1101) *Silvester IV (1105–11) Gelasius II (1118–19)
			Lothar III (1125–37)	*Gregory VIII (1118–21) Calixtus II (1119–24) Honorius II (1124–30)
	Stephen (1135–54)	Louis VII (1137–80)	Conrad III (1138–52)	*Celestine II (1124) Innocent II (1130–43) *Anacletus II (1130–8) *Victor IV (1138) Celestine II (1143–4) Lucius II (1144–5)
1150			Frederick I (1152–90)	Eugenius III (1145–53) Anastasius IV (1153–4)
	Henry II (1154–89)			Hadrian IV (1154–9) Alexander III (1159–81) *Victor IV (1159–64) *Paschal III (1164–8) *Calixtus III (1168–78)
		Philip II (1180–1223)		*Innocent III (1179–80) Lucius III (1181–5)
	Richard I (1189–99)		Henry VI (1190–97)	Urban III (1185–7) Gregory VIII (1187–91) Clement III (1187–91)
1200	John (1199–1216)		Philip of Swabia (1198–1208) Otto IV (1198–1215)	Celestine III (1191–8) Innocent III (1198–1216) Honorius III (1216–27)
	Henry III (1216–72)	Louis VIII (1223–26) Louis IX (1226–70)	Frederick II (1215–50)	Gregory IX (1227–41) Celestine IV (1241) Innocent IV (1243–54) Alexander IV (1254–61) Urban IV (1261–4)

xi

Genealogies

Genealogy 1 *Simplified Genealogy of the Norman and Plantagenet Kings, 1066–1272*

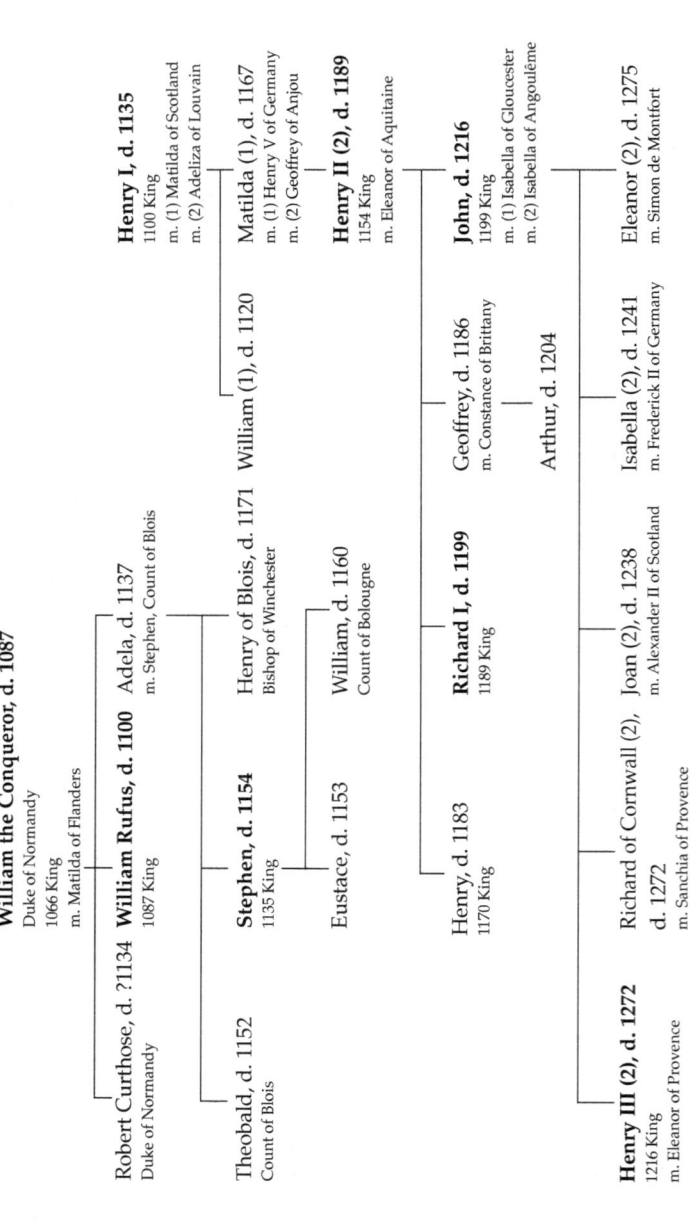

Genealogy 2 *Simplified Genealogy of the Capetian Kings, 1060–1270*

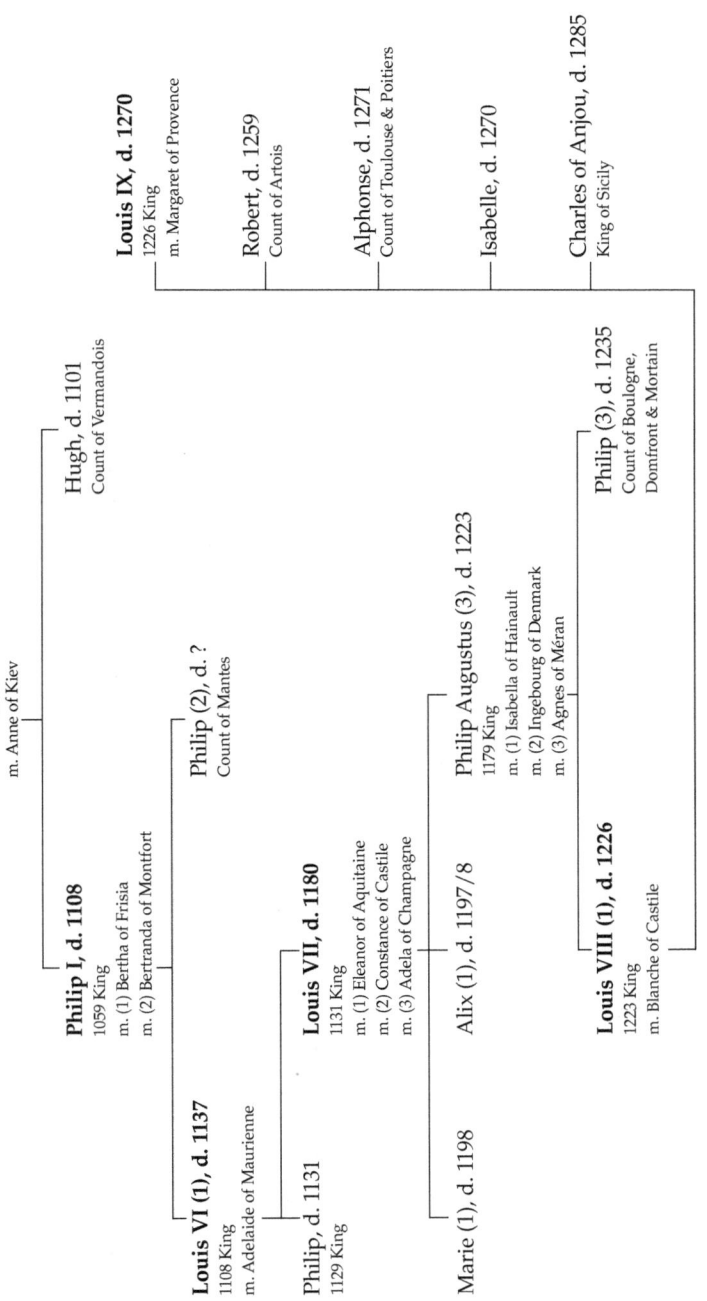

Genealogy 3 *Simplified Genealogy of the Salian Kings and Emperors, 1024–1125*

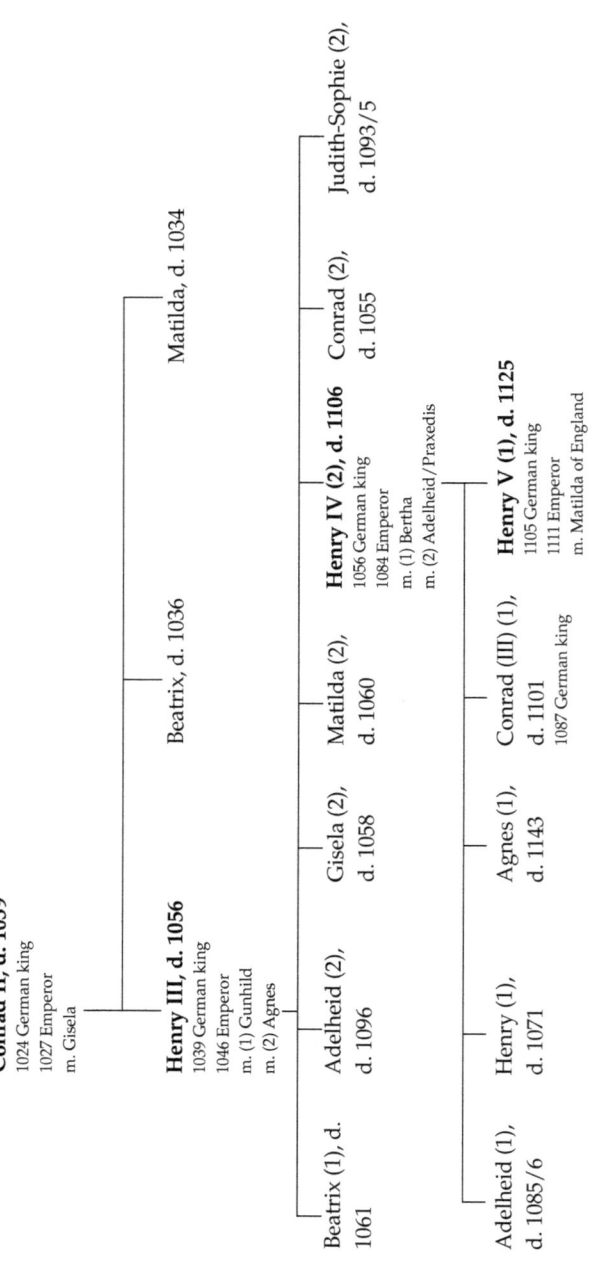

Genealogy 4 *Simplified Genealogy of the Staufen and Welf Kings and Emperors, 1125–1250*

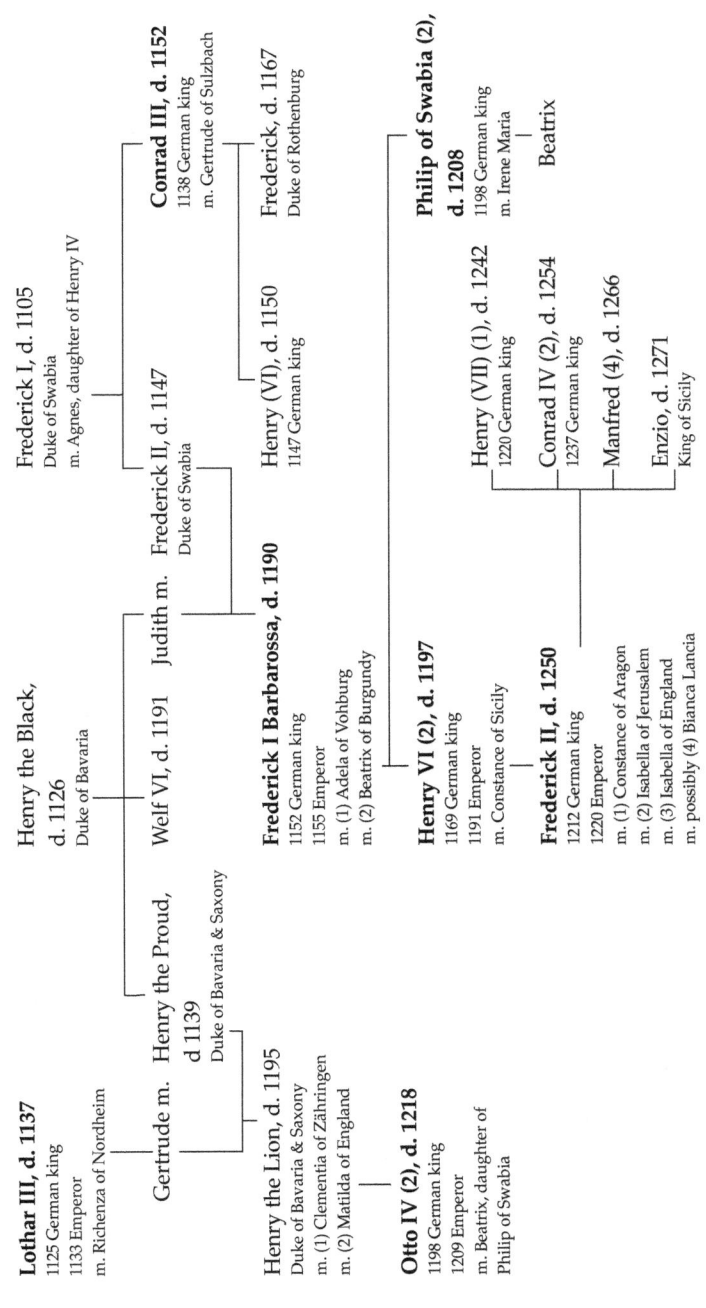

Introduction

In 1975, in typically surreal fashion, the British comedy group Monty Python parodied that staple of medieval entertainment: Arthurian legend. In one scene, our hero approaches two peasants. One, inexplicably named Dennis and unaware of Arthur's identity, objects to the fact that Arthur automatically treats him as an inferior. Arthur justifies his haughty behaviour by replying that he *is* king. This does little to ameliorate Dennis's disgruntlement. At this point Dennis's female companion exclaims that she did not vote for Arthur to be king. 'You don't vote for kings', Arthur retorts incredulously. The peasant woman then asks how Arthur became king and he explains that the Lady of the Lake presented him with the sword Excalibur, signifying by divine providence that he should be king. This is too much for Dennis, who interjects with the memorable line that 'strange women lying in ponds distributing swords is no basis for a system of government. Supreme executive power derives from a mandate from the masses, not from some farcical aquatic ceremony.' In the inauguration ceremonies investigated in this book, swords played a prominent role, though they were bestowed on the monarch by men of the cloth rather than lake-dwelling fairies. The assent of the clergy and people was also a feature of medieval inaugurations, though twelfth-century kings could hardly have been described as having a mandate from the masses. Rather, the relevance of this scene from *Monty Python and the Holy Grail* to the subject matter of this book lies in the similarity between the impertinent peasants' approach to King Arthur and the manner in which modern scholars have approached high medieval kingship.

While focusing on the rituals of royal and imperial inauguration, this book aims to contribute to a much wider debate about the nature of kingship in what has come to be seen as a transitional period. Like Dennis and his female companion, modern scholars have often assumed the inevitability of the modern secular state so that the liturgical trappings of high medieval kingship, particularly in England, have been treated simply as the 'froth on top of serious government'.[1] Inherent to the paradigm of modern state formation is the assumption that the sacrality of monarchy, and the spell of its divine providence, at some point wanes. Although the moment of desacralization has been identified differently in the three countries considered in this book, all three historiographical traditions have bought in to this paradigm. The fact that the three national traditions have each moulded the paradigm

---

[1] T. Reuter, 'The Making of England and Germany, 850–1050: Points of Comparison and Difference', in *Medieval Polities and Modern Mentalities*, ed. J. L. Nelson (Cambridge, 2006), pp. 284–99 (p. 294).

to fit their own histories is instructive and indicates the necessity of taking a comparative approach to this topic. As Ludger Körntgen has argued, the juxtaposition between German monarchy supposedly being stripped of its sacrality by the popes in the late eleventh and early twelfth centuries and the alleged strengthening of the sacrality of the French monarchy in the thirteenth century requires explanation.[2] Bringing England in to this comparison adds another dimension to the study. For the Anglo-Norman and Angevin rulers of England are not considered to have been stripped of sacrality by the popes, but instead to have had no more need for such religious frivolity, thanks to their precocious administrative abilities and the development of the English common law.

In 1995, in an influential essay, Geoffrey Koziol wrote that, 'between the sacred liturgies of pontifical kings and the political theatre of statist monarchs lies the twelfth century, whose political rituals we understand scarcely at all'.[3] This book is an attempt to better understand the image of monarchy as projected in the political rituals of the twelfth century and it aims to do so by loosening the chains that have bound the subject matter to interpretations that focus on secularization and modernization. This is not to deny that the exercise of kingship changed markedly in this period, in which professionalization and institutionalization went hand in hand. Nor is it to deny that there were very real differences in the way in which kings in England, France and the Empire ruled their domains. It is to argue, however, that we should be more comfortable with the discrepancy between the image and reality of high medieval kingship. For Koziol, the fact that the twelfth-century monarchs of England and France continued to avow the political morality of the Carolingians whilst developing sophisticated administrative machinery appears problematic, and the continuity of twelfth-century political liturgies appears 'unexpected' against the backdrop of ecclesiastical reform. Koziol concludes that the continuity of these liturgies demonstrates that the Investiture Controversy had a minimal impact on political liturgy in England and France.[4] Putting the impact of ecclesiastical reform to one side for a moment, there remains an apparent tension between the continuity of liturgy and the development of administrative apparatuses and growing legal sophistication.

However, as Janet L. Nelson has convincingly argued, it is modern historians rather than medieval kings and their subjects who find the idea of the

---

[2] L. Körntgen, '"Sakrales Königtum" und "Entsakralisierung" in der Polemik um Heinrich IV.', in *Heinrich IV.*, ed. G. Althoff, Vorträge und Forschungen 69 (Ostfildern, 2009), pp. 127–60 (p. 129).

[3] G. Koziol, 'England, France and the Problem of Sacrality in Twelfth-Century Ritual', in *Cultures of Power: Lordship, Status and Power in Twelfth-Century Europe*, ed. T. N. Bisson (Philadelphia, 1995), pp. 124–48 (p. 124).

[4] Ibid., p. 126.

synchronicity of liturgy and law problematic. As she points out, throughout the Middle Ages, 'liturgy as a form of political communication ... coexisted with law rather than competing with it'.[5] Likewise, it is modern historians who have seen administration as anathema to liturgy. Timothy Reuter once memorably commented that 'nobody wants bureaucracies and the other tedious apparatus of modern government; they have them forced on them when the old extensive methods fail'.[6] Bureaucracy is often necessary, but it seldom sets the pulse racing and even more infrequently provided the ideological wellspring from which the image of high medieval monarchy was drawn. Thus, the continuity of liturgical rituals that this study uncovers should be seen as neither 'unexpected' nor anachronistic. That they have previously been so interpreted owes much to modern periodization. As John Watts has emphasized in his comparative history of European polities in the fourteenth and fifteenth centuries, the subdivision of the Middle Ages into 'early', 'high' and 'late' has profoundly influenced approaches to its study.[7] For Watts the consequences of this relevant to his period are that the later Middle Ages have tended to be seen as a time of decline and transition, in which the institutions and cultural forms that flourished in the high Middle Ages gradually disintegrated, a characterization he questions. In doing so he highlights how the period known as the 'high' Middle Ages is in many ways considered the high point of the medieval period. It is the age of national and papal monarchies, chivalry, the Crusades, and witnessed prodigious growth in royal, civil, ecclesiastical and educational institutions. It is thus also set apart from the 'early' period, with few scholars working on topics spanning widely across the millennial division.[8]

Given the assumption of difference, it is thus unsurprising that sacral kingship, seen as characteristic of the Carolingians and the Ottonians, should be considered to have no place in the brave new world of the twelfth century. The questions early medievalists ask of their sources no longer seem relevant in an age of administration and institutional and legal development. Many of the approaches taken in this book will be familiar to those working on earlier centuries. What novelty there is in my analysis lies in applying these approaches to evidence from the eleventh to the thirteenth centuries. In

---

[5] J. L. Nelson, 'Liturgy or Law: Misconceived Alternatives?', in *Early Medieval Studies in Memory of Patrick Wormald*, ed. S. Baxter et al. (Aldershot, 2009), pp. 433–50 (p. 441).

[6] T. Reuter, 'The Medieval German *Sonderweg*? The Empire and Its Rulers in the High Middle Ages', in *Medieval Polities and Modern Mentalities*, ed. J. L. Nelson (Cambridge, 2006), pp. 388–412 (p. 403).

[7] J. Watts, *The Making of Polities: Europe, 1300–1500* (Cambridge, 2009), p. 10.

[8] Particularly in England, where serious study of the period pre-1066 requires additional language capabilities. By contrast, the *Habilitation* system, in which scholars are encouraged to pursue a second research project from a different period to their doctorate, means this is less true of German medievalists.

doing so it becomes clear that, while Carolingian political morality did not continue unchanged into the later period, it was adapted and reinterpreted and this dynamic process ensured the enduring relevance of liturgy to the political culture of the high medieval period. Indeed, it will be shown that medieval images of kingship continued to be shaped by liturgy, even as Richard fitz Nigel was writing his *Dialogus de Scaccario*, in which he described the workings of the Exchequer, that institution of administrative kingship *par excellence*.[9]

Kingship in Comparison

Comparison is, as Michael Borgolte has stressed, a fact of life. As soon as man recognizes that he is not alone in the world, he begins comparing himself to others.[10] This is true on an individual and group level, and in both it is often in comparison with others that ideals, identities and self-perceptions are formed. For Borgolte, founder of the Institut für vergleichende Geschichte Europas im Mittelalter at the Humboldt-Universität in Berlin, a comparative approach to the Middle Ages is the only effective method for writing European medieval history.[11] He emphasizes the plurality of European history, arguing that a canonistic and definitive history of Europe cannot be written without imposing an artificial unity on the history of a richly varied continent, a danger that can be averted with a comparative methodology.[12] British historians, working in a country where the modern European project has recently been rejected, might well view with scepticism Borgolte's rallying cry to make Europe a prominent research theme, when, as Borgolte himself admits, Europe was not an idea with much currency in the medieval period.[13] Replacing multiple national teleologies with a single European teleology is certainly not an attractive proposition. However, comparing in a European context does offer the opportunity to dismantle national schools

---

[9] *Dialogus de Scaccario, and Constitutio Domus Regis*, ed. E. Amt and S. Church (Oxford, 2007).

[10] M. Borgolte, 'Mediävistik als vergleichende Geschichte Europas', in *Mediävistik im 21. Jahrhundert: Stand und Perspektiven der internationalen und interdisziplinären Mittelalterforschung*, ed. H.-W. Goetz and J. Jarnut (Munich, 2003), pp. 313–23 (p. 313).

[11] Ibid., p. 321.

[12] Ibid., p. 322; Borgolte's textbook gives an indication of his approach to the writing of medieval European history: M. Borgolte, *Europa entdeckt seine Vielfalt 1050–1250* (Stuttgart, 2002).

[13] M. Borgolte, 'Perspektiven europäischer Mittelalterhistorie an der Schwelle zum 21. Jahrhundert', in *Das europäische Mittelalter im Spannungsbogen des Vergleichs: Zwanzig internationale Beiträge zu Praxis, Problemen und Perspektiven der historischen Komparatistik*, ed. M. Borgolte (Berlin, 2001), pp. 13–27 (p. 14). See also K. Oschema, *Bilder von Europa im Mittelalter* (Ostfildern, 2013).

Introduction

of historiography, and does not automatically demand the construction of a monolithic European school in their stead. This is certainly not Borgolte's aim and taking a European perspective is not the British historian's equivalent of Westminster politicians surrendering power to Brussels-based technocrats.

This study of royal inauguration in England, France and Germany must be placed in a European context but not mistaken as representing a European norm. It is a comparison in a very traditional form in that it seeks parallels and distinctions between different geographic regions in the same time period.[14] In addition to this synchronic method, one could compare the same phenomena in different time periods, a diachronic comparison, or, rather than comparing elements of a shared culture as in this book, compare elements in a transcultural context.[15] However, a synchronic comparison has been preferred in this study for several reasons. Escaping from national teleologies and cultural solipsism, a major aim of this study, is one of the key advantages of a synchronic comparison. As Chris Wickham has argued, without geographical comparison we end up with 'a Europe – a world – of islands, with no relation to each other … Worse, these insularities in nearly every case match up with national teleologies, the study in each country of the historical reasons why We are special, better than – or at least different from – the Others'.[16] Synchronic comparison thus provides the opportunity to study shared cultural phenomena and to question orthodoxies implicit in national historiographies. This study is, for the most part, limited to the three kingdoms of England, France and Germany. The reasons for this are partly pragmatic. There is more than enough medieval evidence and modern literature for the timeframe which the pressures of modern academia allowed to be dedicated to this project. But more than this: in current scholarship, far too many hasty and casual contrasts are drawn between monarchs in England and France and their counterparts in the Empire, so that a trilateral study is urgently needed.[17]

---

[14] As d'Avray has commented, 'for most people, comparative history means this sort of comparative history'. D. L. d'Avray, 'Comparative History of the Medieval Church's Marriage System', in *Das europäische Mittelalter im Spannungsbogen des Vergleichs: Zwanzig internationale Beiträge zu Praxis, Problemen und Perspektiven der historischen Komparatistik*, ed. M. Borgolte (Berlin, 2001), pp. 209–22 (p. 220).

[15] In typically ambitious fashion, David d'Avray illustrated the potential of all three methods within the scope of a single essay: d'Avray, 'Comparative History of the Medieval Church's Marriage System'.

[16] C. Wickham, 'Problems in Doing Comparative History', in *Challenging the Boundaries of Medieval History: The Legacy of Timothy Reuter*, ed. P. Skinner, Studies in the Early Middle Ages 22 (Turnhout, 2009), pp. 5–28 (p. 6).

[17] As Levi Roach has pointed out, casual comparisons often rely heavily on secondary literature with insufficient attention paid to historiographical traditions so that we 'run the risk of comparing proverbial apples and oranges'. L. Roach, 'Penance, Submission and *deditio*: Religious Influences on Dispute Settlement in Later Anglo-Saxon England (871–1066)', *Anglo-Saxon England* 41 (2012), 343–71 (p. 345).

It would certainly be desirable, as a further step, to extend the comparison to include other kingdoms.[18] Where it has been possible to look outside of these three kingdoms, which in many ways can be understood as the cultural heirs to the Carolingian empire, the results are illuminating.[19] However, there is much to be said for first establishing what similarities and differences might exist within these 'core' kingdoms, before extending the comparison to those on the cultural 'periphery' or even kingdoms from different cultural spheres.[20] Inauguration has often, as the result of the influence of anthropology on historical methodologies, been the subject of transcultural comparison. While the influence of anthropological and sociological methodologies has undoubtedly opened up new avenues for comprehending medieval sources, such approaches should not be stretched too far.[21] For transcultural comparison to be meaningful the parameters must be carefully considered. Beyond conceptual frameworks, there is little of value to a historian to be found in comparing medieval kingdoms with pre-modern village societies. Historical comparison requires context. It cannot skip blithely between cultures and centuries without diminishing its power to explain complex phenomena that are rooted in time and place.[22] Intra-cultural comparisons are perhaps less eye-catching, but they are a necessary antidote to the assumption of homogeneity which is implicit in so many transcultural studies. To take an example relevant to this research, we must first uncover if the anointing of

---

[18] Borgolte argues that it is better not just to concentrate on neighbouring lands, but to cast the comparative net wider. Borgolte, 'Perspektiven europäischer Mittelalterhistorie', p. 23.

[19] The three kingdoms are treated as such in J. L. Nelson, 'Kingship and Empire', in *The Cambridge History of Medieval Political Thought c.350–c.1450*, ed. J. H. Burns (Cambridge, 1988), pp. 211–51.

[20] For a consideration of the core-periphery model and its application to medieval contexts see R. Bartlett, 'Heartland and Border: The Mental and Physical Geography of Medieval Europe', in *Power and Identity in the Middle Ages: Essays in Honour of Rees Davies*, ed. H. Pryce and J. Watts (Oxford, 2007), pp. 23–36; As Jörg Peltzer has pointed out, it is not always easy to differentiate between intra- and transcultural comparisons. J. Peltzer, 'Introduction', in *Princely Rank in Late Medieval Europe: Trodden Paths and Promising Avenues*, ed. T. Huthwelker, J. Peltzer and M. Wemhöner (Ostfildern, 2001), pp. 11–25 (p. 13).

[21] For the tension between historical methodologies and the social sciences inherent in comparative history see P. Baldwin, 'Comparing and Generalizing: Why All History is Comparative, Yet No History is Sociology', in *Comparison and History: Europe in Cross-National Perspective*, ed. D. Cohen and M. O' Connor (New York, 2004) pp. 1–22.

[22] Although such comparisons are undoubtedly thought provoking, it is not the job of the historian, but the anthropologist, to compare sixteenth-century English Protestantism, fourteenth-century Javanese Hinduism and nineteenth-century Moroccan Islam as in C. Geertz, 'Centers, Kings and Charisma: Reflections on the Symbolics of Power', in *Culture and its Creators: Essays in Honor of Edward Shils*, ed. J. Ben-David and T. N. Clark (Chicago, 1977), pp. 150–71.

Introduction

kings as part of the inauguration ceremonies in the 'core' of England, France and Germany was understood in the same way, before we can nonchalantly compare anointed kings with those on the cultural 'periphery' who were not anointed, or who sought the right of anointing in the course of the thirteenth century. A comparison between anointed and non-anointed kings within Latin Christendom assumes homogeneity. We must first establish whether such homogeneity existed.[23]

The comparison of medieval kings within Latin Christendom has a long history. As Bernd Schneidmüller has pointed out, German historians of the nineteenth and twentieth centuries were far from the first to compare Germany to neighbouring France and draw the conclusion that Germany was not flattered by the comparison.[24] As early as the 1140s, Suger of Saint-Denis constructed a negative image of the Salian king Henry V, in comparison to whom the Capetian Louis VI could be presented as the most Christian king (*rex christianissimus*). Even the manner in which the kings were made could be compared by contemporaries. Schneidmüller highlights Matthew Paris's report of an embassy sent from Louis IX of France to Frederick II of Germany. Louis's men were not what one might describe as diplomatic, asserting that their king, from a long line of royal blood, was surely superior to an emperor, who had merely earned his position through election.[25] Modern historians have tended to agree with Louis's envoys (and Monty Python's King Arthur), but as Schneidmüller explains, medieval commentators did not always concur.[26] The elective element of German kingship could engender

---

[23] Which is not to say that if such a comparison is carefully structured it cannot bear fruit. Janet Nelson's essay comparing inaugurations in the Western and Eastern Empires is an example of a successful comparison of this kind: J. L. Nelson, 'Symbols in Context: Rulers' Inauguration Rituals in Byzantium and the West in the Early Middle Ages', in *The Orthodox Churches and the West*, ed. D. Baker, Studies in Church History 13 (Oxford, 1976), pp. 97–119.

[24] B. Schneidmüller, 'Außenblick für das eigene Herz. Vergleichende Wahrnehmung politischer Ordnung im hochmittelalterlichen Deutschland und Frankreich', in *Das europäische Mittelalter im Spannungsbogen des Vergleichs: Zwanzig internationale Beiträge zu Praxis, Problemen und Perspektiven der historischen Komparatistik*, ed. M. Borgolte (Berlin, 2001), pp. 315–38 (pp. 315–16).

[25] '*Credimus enim dominum nostrum regem Galliae, quem linea regii sanguinis provexit ad sceptra Francorum regenda, excellentiorem esse aliquo imperatore, quem sola provehit electio voluntaria*'. Matthew Paris, *Chronica Majora*, ed. H. R. Luard, 7 vols., RS 57 (London, 1872–80), III, 626.

[26] German electoral kingship has been the subject of a huge quantity of scholarship. For an introduction to the topic see J. Rogge, *Die deutschen Könige im Mittelalter: Wahl und Krönung* (Darmstadt, 2006). The best treatment in English, which rejects the idea that electoral kingship was necessarily harmful to the development of Germany, remains J. Gillingham, 'Elective Kingship and the Unity of Medieval Germany', *German History* 9 (1991), 124–35; Björn Weiler has rightly questioned how rigid the electoral process was in this period: B. K. Weiler, 'Suitability and Right: Imperial Succession and the Norms of Politics in Early Staufen Germany', in *Making and*

pride, as is clear in Otto of Freising's description of the election of Frederick Barbarossa, in which Otto portrayed election as indicative of the special rank of the Empire.[27]

Modern scholars have, like their medieval predecessors, at times looked outside of their respective countries to compare elements of kingship and government in England, France and Germany. However, while early medievalists tend to travel unencumbered through the breadth of the Carolingian Empire, high medievalists often end their journeys at the imagined borders of incipient nation states, despite the fact that, as Robert Bartlett has shown, Europe after 1000 was marked by greater internal integration and homogeneity based on increased mobility and cross-regional contacts.[28] British historical scholarship thus becomes more insular at the precise moment at which the history of the continent becomes increasingly interconnected. This insularity has ensured that high medieval comparisons have tended to be bilateral. Due both to patterns of foreign language learning in Britain and the possession by English kings of lands in modern-day France, Anglo-French comparisons have vastly outnumbered those dealing with England and the Empire in Anglophone scholarship. Recent work on aspects of kingship in England and the Empire by Alheydis Plassmann, Björn Weiler and David Warner stands out against a backdrop of scholarship that is Anglo-French in outlook.[29] Marc Bloch laid modern foundations for comparisons between English and French kingship with his highly influential book on the royal touch, written in 1924 and translated into English

---

Breaking the Rules: Succession in Medieval Europe, c.1000–c.1600, ed. F. Lachaud and M. Penman (Turnhout, 2008), pp. 71–86.

[27] Schneidmüller, 'Außenblick für das eigene Herz', p. 331. It should be recognised, however, that Otto stressed the elective element as a way of justifying the passing over of Conrad III's young son Frederick of Rothenburg. See K. Görich, *Friedrich Barbarossa: Eine Biographie* (Munich, 2011), pp. 93–107; J. P. Niederkorn, 'Zu glatt und daher verdächtig? Zur Glaubwürdigkeit der Schilderung der Wahl Friedrich Barbarossas (1152) durch Otto von Freising', *MIÖG* 115 (2007), 1–9; G. Althoff, 'Friedrich von Rothenburg: Überlegungen zu einem übergagenen Königssohn', in *Festschrift für Eduard Hlawitschka zum 65. Geburtstag* (Kallmünz, 1993), pp. 307–16.

[28] R. Bartlett, *The Making of Europe: Conquest, Colonization and Cultural Change, 950–1350* (Princeton, 1993).

[29] A. Plassmann, 'The King and His Sons: Henry II's and Frederick Barbarossa's Succession Strategies Compared', *Anglo-Norman Studies* XXXVI (2014), 149–66; B. K. Weiler, 'The King as Judge: Henry II and Frederick Barbarossa as Seen by Their Contemporaries', in *Challenging the Boundaries of Medieval History: The Legacy of Timothy Reuter*, ed. P. Skinner (Turnhout, 2009), pp. 115–40; B. K. Weiler, *Kingship, Rebellion and Political Culture: England and Germany, c.1215–c.1250* (Basingstoke, 2007); B. K. Weiler, *Henry III of England and the Staufen Empire, 1216–1272* (Woodbridge, 2006); D. A. Warner, 'Comparative Approaches to Anglo-Saxon and Ottonian Coronations', in *England and the Continent in the Tenth Century: Studies in Honour of Wilhelm Levison (1876–1947)*, ed. D. Rollason, C. Leyser and H. Williams, Studies in the Early Middle Ages 37 (Turnhout, 2010), pp. 275–92.

Introduction

in 1973.³⁰ Aspects of comparative Anglo-French kingship have been elucidated by Hollister and Baldwin, Hallam, and Vincent, amongst others.³¹ It is the existence of this backdrop that makes this trilateral comparison possible.

While a trilateral comparison between England, France and Germany is possible, it is also, as with most attempts at comparison, not unproblematic. There are three main hurdles to overcome, the historiographical, the empirical, and the need to identify things that are meaningful to compare.³² It is due to the need to compare like with like that this study has crystallized around the practice of royal and imperial inauguration.³³ In doing so it engages with a tradition which has focused on the development of the inauguration ritual through time and particularly on the elaboration of liturgical texts.³⁴ However, although informed by this important body of scholarship, my aim is not to reconstruct the ritual or trace its changes, but rather to uncover how it was understood in the three realms and whether it can be interpreted as evidence for the continuation of liturgical kingship in this period. Inevitably the three hurdles are connected, and another reason for the focus on inauguration is the availability of comparable sources in the three realms. Timothy

---

³⁰ M. Bloch, *Les rois thaumaturges: études sur le caractère surnaturel attribué à la puissance royale particulièrement en France et en Angleterre* (Strasbourg, 1924); M. Bloch, *The Royal Touch: Sacred Monarchy and Scrofula in England and France*, trans. J. E. Anderson (London, 1973).

³¹ C. W. Hollister and J. W. Baldwin, 'The Rise of Administrative Kingship: Henry I and Philip Augustus', *The American Historical Review* 83 (1978), 867–905; E. M. Hallam, 'Royal Burial and the Cult of Kingship in France and England, 1060–1330', *Journal of Medieval History* 8 (1982), 359–80; N. Vincent, 'King Henry III and the Blessed Virgin Mary', in *The Church and Mary*, ed. R. N. Swanson, Studies in Church History 39 (Woodbridge, 2004), pp. 126–46; N. Vincent, 'Twelfth and Thirteenth-Century Kingship: An Essay in Anglo-French Misunderstanding', in *Les idées passent-elles La Manche? Savoirs, representation, pratiques (France-Angleterre, Xe–XXe siècles)*, ed. J.-P. Genêt and F.-J. Ruggiu (Paris, 2007), pp. 21–36.

³² Wickham, 'Problems in Doing Comparative History'.

³³ Choosing the appropriate units for comparison (i.e. nations, regions, institutions) and what/whom to compare are two of the chief difficulties in structuring a comparison. See H.-G. Haupt and J. Kocka, 'Comparative History: Methods, Aims, Problems', in *Comparison and History: Europe in Cross-National Perspective*, ed. D. Cohen and M. O'Connor (New York, 2004), pp. 23–40 (pp. 26–7); There has been some debate about whether using the nation as a unit of comparison unnecessarily privileges the nation-state thereby always confirming the nation's significance. As a major aim of this study is to question national historiographical narratives nations, or better kingdoms, are the appropriate unit. For a flavour of this debate see G. Sluga, 'The Nation and the Comparative Imagination', in *Comparison and History: Europe in Cross-National Perspective*, ed. D. Cohen and M. O'Connor (New York, 2004), pp. 103–14 and P. Ther, 'Beyond the Nation: The Relational Basis of a Comparative History of Germany and Europe', *Central European History* 36 (2003), 45–73.

³⁴ This body of scholarship will be considered at length in the first chapter.

Reuter, in an essay on the development of England and Germany in the early medieval period, highlighted the fact that a world seen through the rich narrative sources found in Germany 'is bound to look different from one which is seen through law-codes and sparse narrative sources'.[35] For the period under consideration here, it can hardly be surprising that kings viewed through the lens of administrative documents appear different from those viewed through narrative sources. In this book source types that are common to all three realms are considered, predominantly liturgical texts, charters and narrative accounts. This is not to deny that there were real differences between how kings in England, France and Germany exercised their power, but to investigate how the nature of the power they wielded was understood.

The final hurdle, that of historiography, is again closely linked to the issue of source material. The relative wealth of surviving medieval administrative material from both England and later France has, with few exceptions, ensured the triumph of the 'Manchester' over the 'Münster' school of history, so that state and constitution take precedence over 'ritual' or 'pneuma'. As a result, kingship in these countries has often been characterized as 'administrative' or 'law-centred', in opposition to the 'liturgical' kingship of an earlier period. By contrast, historians of the Empire, lacking the detailed administrative records of their English and French counterparts, exploit the anthropological approaches successfully used by early medievalists to compose an image of kingship concerned more with human behaviour than with institutions. A historiographical tradition, in which Germany is presented as exceptional in the light of prevailing Anglo-French norms, has thus been accentuated by the availability of different types of source material. Chris Wickham has suggested how to deal with these issues, emphasizing that, if we wish to take a comparative approach, we need to master the primary sources 'to see whether they can give us the comparative elements that the historiography denies us' and to gain an understanding of the institutional and historiographical contexts in which historians in different countries carry out their research.[36] These contexts mould the approaches of historians, who are encouraged to engage with issues considered crucial in the tradition in which they work. These issues vary between countries, regions and even individual universities. Before turning to the sources themselves, in the spirit of intense disbelief advocated by Wickham, we must first take time to understand the historiographical traditions in which these differing ideas of medieval kingship have been nurtured.

---

[35] Reuter, 'The Making of England and Germany, 850–1050', p. 295.
[36] Wickham, 'Problems in Doing Comparative History', p. 9.

Introduction

Monarchy, State Formation and Sacral Kingship

The study of medieval monarchy has, in all three countries studied in this book, been embedded within wider narratives of modern state formation. The high medieval period has been seen as a particularly important moment on the path to modern statehood in England and France, given that it witnessed the birth of a number of institutions that are part of the apparatus of the modern state. A famous expression of this linear development is found in Joseph Strayer's *On the Medieval Origins of the Modern State*, which concentrates on the English and French realms.[37] That Germany remained peripheral to Strayer's argument is indicative of historical and historiographical difference and of the German nation's special path, or *Sonderweg*, to modern statehood. Yet, perhaps precisely because of high medieval Germany's lack of state-like characteristics, historians of medieval Germany have been no less in thrall to the idea of the state. Indeed, Bernd Schneidmüller has commented that the medieval Empire's lack of state-like characteristics can still feel like an affliction to German medieval historians in the twenty-first century.[38]

Putting to one side debates about the appropriateness of the terminology of statehood for describing medieval polities, there remains a problem with the broad paradigm of modern state formation for our study.[39] It has ensured that, in addition to the exercise of monarchical power in its economic, military and judicial manifestations, conceptions of kingship have also tended to be examined through a teleological lens, with the assumption of an inevitable trend towards secular rulership. In Germany and France, the epoch defining moments of 1077 and 1789 respectively ensured the 'desacralization' of monarchy. In England, there was no humiliation by the pope or guillotine blade required to cut sacral monarchy down to size – instead the spell gradually waned during the long twelfth century as administrative and legal structures grew increasingly sophisticated. To a certain extent, all three historiographical traditions are variations on the same theme. However, in their treatment of the high Middle Ages they differ markedly and these differences must be understood before we can undertake a comparative analysis. The scarcely credible juxtaposition between the alleged continuation of sacral monarchy in France well into the eighteenth century and its disappearance in Germany and England six centuries earlier requires explanation, as does the

---

[37] J. R. Strayer, *On the Medieval Origins of the Modern State* (Princeton, 1970).
[38] Schneidmüller, 'Außenblick für das eigene Herz', p. 316.
[39] For a flavour of this debate see: S. Reynolds, 'The Historiography of the Medieval State', in *Companion to Historiography*, ed. M. Bentley (London, 1997), pp. 117–38; R. R. Davies, 'The Medieval State: The Tyranny of a Concept?', *Journal of Historical Sociology* 16 (2003), 280–300; S. Reynolds, 'There were States in Medieval Europe: A Response to Rees Davies', *Journal of Historical Sociology* 16 (2003), 550–5.

fact that different explanations for its loss are proffered for those two realms: popes for one and pipe rolls for the other.

For the purposes of this study the French tradition, in which sacral kingship is considered to have carried on unchanged throughout the period, is the least problematic. As Nicholas Vincent has elucidated, French historians have been concerned with the growth of a post-Carolingian strong monarchy and with trying to explain why this centralized monarchy came to grief in the French Revolution.[40] In the exact period in which English and German historians see sacral monarchy as disappearing, it is considered to have strengthened under the Capetians, particularly during the reign of Louis IX.[41] Vincent has compared Jacques Le Goff's biography *Saint Louis* with Maurice Powicke's book *King Henry III and the Lord Edward*. He contrasts Powicke's study, which he characterizes as conveying a vivid sense of the court and political elite, but little in the way of a personal portrait of the king, with Le Goff's focus on the personal, psychological and intellectual life of his subject.[42] For Vincent this pronounced difference of portrayal is illustrative of two things; the dissimilarity in the materials at the disposal of the two authors and the disparity in the questions English and French historians are attempting to answer. As Vincent pithily concludes, 'English historians, tempted to ask when and if King Alfred actually burned the cakes, like French historians inclined to ask what the theoretical cakes may have symbolized, are frequently bewildered by one another's absurdities.'[43]

French approaches to kingship have been flavoured by social theory, with theoretical and philosophical approaches provoking more interest than institutional development. Indeed, it is Americans, particularly Joseph Strayer and John Baldwin, who have been, in the past century, most interested in the development of the French medieval state.[44] Baldwin has focused on the administrative elaborations of a French king in his work on Philip Augustus, combining with C. Warren Hollister to draw links between France and England.[45] That the English king Henry I (1100–35), considered in their

---

[40] Vincent, 'Twelfth and Thirteenth-Century Kingship', p. 28.

[41] See for example, J. Le Goff, *Saint Louis* (Paris, 1996); M. C. Gaposchkin, *The Making of Saint Louis: Kingship, Sanctity and Crusade in the Later Middle Ages* (Ithaca, 2008); M. Cohen, *The Sainte-Chapelle and the Construction of Sacral Monarchy: Royal Architecture in Thirteenth-Century Paris* (Cambridge, 2015).

[42] Vincent, 'Twelfth and Thirteenth-Century Kingship', p. 25.

[43] N. Vincent, 'The Pilgrimages of the Angevin Kings of England 1154–1272', in *Pilgrimage: The English Experience from Becket to Bunyan*, ed. C. Morris and P. Roberts (Cambridge, 2002), pp. 12–45 (p. 32).

[44] Strayer's interest in the development of the state was surely connected to his interest in the contemporary American state. For his CIA career see N. Cantor, *Inventing the Middle Ages: The Lives, Works and Ideas of the Great Medievalists of the Twentieth Century* (New York, 1991), pp. 261–2.

[45] J. W. Baldwin, *The Government of Philip Augustus: Foundations of French Royal Power in the Middle Ages* (Berkeley, 1986); Hollister and Baldwin, 'The Rise of Administrative Kingship'.

Introduction

jointly-authored article on the rise of administrative kingship, died almost nine decades before Philip Augustus (1179–1223) is demonstrative of a real difference in source material in the two countries. The first English pipe roll survives from the reign of Henry I, an outlying indication of a later richness of administrative material that is unmatched in France or Germany. Rather than royal finances, it is royal image that has interested recent historians of French kingship. From explications of seal iconography and royal charters to those of chronicles and liturgical texts, manifestations of royal power rather than its financial underpinning have shone through.[46] Moreover, there is another school that has had perhaps as much influence on French approaches to kingship: that found at Saint-Denis, where Abbot Suger laid the foundations for a tradition of historical writing that emphasized the sacrality of the Capetian kings.[47]

Neither England nor Germany possesses an equivalent to the ambitious Abbot of Saint-Denis, who built Capetian kingship into the very masonry of his abbey church. Certainly monarch-centred narratives survive from all three realms, but those from England and Germany are haphazard survivals and part of no grand scheme, in stark contrast to the French *Grandes Chroniques*.[48] While German historians exploit narrative sources, English historians remain less enamoured with this type of historical record, preferring the clarity and precision of administrative documents to the opaque inexactitude of chronicle accounts. Discussing James Campbell's 'maximalist' interpretation of the Anglo-Saxon state, Reuter characterizes his dismissal of the importance of hunting, praying and court ceremony for royal government as being 'a variant of one of the standard tropes of English medievalists: narrative sources unreliable, back to the archives'.[49] As the archives are those of central government, the insights which they yield relate to central government. Thus, central government continues to take centre stage in historical explanations. As Reuter has elucidated, 'English political medievalists are peculiarly state-fixated: the importance of the state in our history becomes self-reinforcing, so that the real substance is seen to lie in administrative practice and innovation rather than in the relations between the members of the political community.'[50] Modern Anglophone writing on kingship thus continues to revolve around

---

[46] See particularly Bedos-Rezak's work on seals, Gasparri, Guyotjeannin and Parisse on charters, Le Goff and Bonne on liturgy. The work of these historians will be discussed in more detail in later chapters; details are in the bibliography.

[47] See the various essays in P. L. Gerson, ed., *Abbot Suger and Saint-Denis* (New York, 1986) and L. Grant, *Abbot Suger of Saint-Denis: Church and State in Early Medieval France* (London, 1998).

[48] On the lack of historical accounts of the Plantagenet kings see Nicholas Vincent, 'The Strange Case of the Missing Biographies: The Lives of the Plantagenet Kings of England 1154–1272', in *Writing Medieval Biography: Essays in Honour of Professor Frank Barlow*, ed. D. Bates, J. Crick and S. Hamilton (Woodbridge, 2006), pp. 237–57.

[49] Reuter, 'The Making of England and Germany, 850–1050', p. 294.

[50] Ibid.

the traditional and overlapping themes of legal and administrative elaboration. This central point is cemented by the continuity of English institutions, which allows Paul Brand, while dispensing with the anachronisms apparent in the work of an earlier generation of legal historians, quite happily to discuss the role of Henry II in the creation of the English Common Law as if Henry were a member of one of the modern Inns of Court.[51] Central government and its records continue to attract sustained attention, an entirely understandable phenomena given that a single year's pipe roll contains enough content for an entire PhD thesis.[52] The seam of governmental records in England runs deep and continues to be mined by a number of scholars, including David Carpenter and Nicholas Vincent. Carpenter has, in effect, established his own school on the Strand, with a number of his former students making important contributions to the study of English government in the twelfth and thirteenth centuries.[53]

David Carpenter and Nicholas Vincent are both, however, well aware that there was more to medieval kingship than administrative procedures and, indeed, that bureaucratic documents can in fact shed light on diverse aspects of kingship.[54] Vincent, in particular, has pioneered an alternative approach to the Plantagenet kings, arguing that they should not be seen as a profane and violent equivalent to the holy and pacific Capetians.[55] However, serious engagement with liturgical and narrative sources still remains outside the remit of most historians of English kingship, who pay little more than lip-service to factors that cannot be firmly grounded in the archives. As Geoffrey Koziol has pointed out,

---

[51] P. Brand, 'Henry II and the Creation of the English Common Law', in *Henry II: New Interpretations*, ed. C. Harper-Bill and N. Vincent (Woodbridge, 2007), pp. 215–41. By contrast John Gillingham is unconvinced that Henry II was personally involved in the judicial developments of his reign: J. Gillingham, 'Conquering Kings: Some Twelfth-Century Reflections on Henry II and Richard I', in *Warriors and Churchmen in the High Middle Ages: Essays Presented to Karl Leyser*, ed. T. Reuter (London, 1992), pp. 163–78 (pp. 164–71).

[52] See for example that of R. Cassidy, 'The 1259 Pipe Roll' (unpublished PhD thesis, King's College London, 2012).

[53] For example, A. Jobson, ed., *English Government in the Thirteenth Century* (Woodbridge, 2004); B. L. Wild, 'Royal Finance Under King Henry III, 1216–72: The Wardrobe Evidence', *Economic History Review* 65 (2012), 1380–402; N. Barratt, 'The Revenue of King John', *English Historical Review* 111 (1996), 835–55; N. Barratt, 'Finance and the Economy in the Reign of Henry II', in *Henry II: New Interpretations*, ed. C. Harper-Bill and N. Vincent (Woodbridge, 2007), pp. 242–56.

[54] For example, Carpenter examines a list surviving from the Wardrobe of Henry III to illuminate aspects of royal ideology in D. A. Carpenter, 'The Burial of King Henry III, the Regalia and Royal Ideology', in his *The Reign of Henry III* (London, 1996), pp. 427–62.

[55] E.g. Vincent, 'King Henry III and the Blessed Virgin Mary'; Vincent, 'The Pilgrimages'.

Introduction

D. C. Douglas writing of William the Conqueror, Judith Green writing of Henry I, and W. L. Warren writing of Henry II all dutifully reiterate the traditional beliefs articulated in Carolingian and Ottonian sources: that kings ruled in the image of God and the Old Testament rulers of Israel and that the great ceremony for communicating this typology was royal anointing. Yet when these historians get down to the real business of Norman and Angevin kingship, they describe feudal levies, financial exactions, and judicial reform, with not another word about pontifical kings.[56]

These factors *are* all characteristic of the practice of power by the Norman and Angevin kings, but feudal levies, taxation and law did not develop at the expense of liturgical ceremonial, which continued to provide an ideological basis for English kingship.

Although rulers of the high medieval Empire lacked the administrative sophistication of their French and English counterparts, the law has been seen as offering the Staufer rulers an alternative foundation of power. However, in contrast to the English experience, law has not been understood to have gradually eroded liturgy, instead Roman law filled the vacuum caused by the demise of sacral kingship during the course of the Investiture Controversy.[57] In German historiography, the critical moment is considered to have occurred in 1077 when Henry IV, seeking to depower the opposition of his enemies within the German kingdom, sought the forgiveness of Gregory VII at Canossa. In choosing to subtitle his popular history of these events 'The Disenchantment of the World', Stefan Weinfurter deliberately invoked Max Weber's modernization paradigm, reminding us once again of the extent to which concepts of kingship have been viewed through the lens of an inevitable path to modernity and secular rulership.[58] In seeing Canossa as a turning point (*Wende*) in medieval German history Weinfurter is part of

---

[56] Koziol, 'England, France and the Problem of Sacrality', p. 124.
[57] H. Appelt, 'Friedrich Barbarossa und das römische Recht', *Römische Historische Mitteilungen* 5 (1962), 18–34; J. Fried, *Die Entstehung des Juristenstandes im 12. Jahrhundert: Zur sozialen Stellung und politischen Bedeutung gelehrter Juristen aus Bologna und Modena* (Cologne and Vienna, 1974), pp. 46–56; G. Koch, *Auf dem Wege zum Sacrum Imperium. Studien zur ideologischen Herrschaftsbegründung der deutschen Zentralgewalt im 11. und 12. Jahrhundert* (Cologne, 1972); T. Struve, 'Die Stellung des Königtums in der politischen Theorie der Salierzeit', in *Die Salier und das Reich*, ed. S. Weinfurter, 3 vols. (Sigmaringen, 1991), III, 217–44; T. Struve, 'Die Salier und das römische Recht: Ansätze zur Entwicklung einer säkularen Herrschaftstheorie in der Zeit des Investiturstreites', *Akademie der Wissenschaften Mainz: Abhandlung der Geistes- und Sozialwissenschaftlichen Klasse* 5 (1999), 7–89; T. Struve, 'Die Rolle des römischen Rechts in der kaiserlichen Theorie vor Roncaglia', in *Gli inizi del diritto pubblico: L'età de Frederico Barbarossa: legislazione e scienza del diritto*, ed. G. Dilcher and D. Quaglioni (Bologna, 2007), pp. 71–99; B. Töpfer, 'Tendenzen der Entsakralisierung der Herrscherwürde in der Zeit des Investiturstreites', *Jahrbuch für Geschichte des Feudalismus* 6 (1982), 164–71.
[58] S. Weinfurter, *Canossa: Die Entzauberung der Welt* (Munich, 2006).

Inauguration and Liturgical Kingship

a long tradition, the classic statement being Anton Mayer-Pfannholz's 1933 essay *'Die Wende von Canossa'*.[59] As will be discussed below, this tradition has recently started to be questioned and it is this new wave of German scholarship that has inspired many of the approaches taken in this book. However, before moving on to these new approaches it is imperative to understand why the issue of sacrality has been so dominant in German academic discourse concerning kingship.

In his seminal work *The King's Two Bodies*, Ernst Kantorowicz discussed the famous frontispiece of the late tenth-century Aachen Gospels, in which a ruler, presumed to be Otto III, is presented in striking similarity to contemporary depictions of Christ in majesty.[60] Kantorowicz is far from alone in identifying the purest expression of Christomimetic kingship in the lavish liturgical books of the Ottonian era and it is entirely understandable that the dazzling products of the scriptoria of the Ottonian *Reich* have inspired such sustained interest in the image of Ottonian sacral kingship.[61] However, there is another reason for this focus on the imagery of Ottonian power: a perceived lack of bureaucratic sophistication on the part of royal government. In the absence of a state apparatus the rulers' sacral aura attained increased significance as a way of holding the Ottonian polity together, and while the idea of a rigid imperial-church system (*Reichskirchensystem*) no longer dominates, a close bond with the church has continued to be seen as essential to the propagation of the Ottonian image.[62] Anticipating the fracturing of the relationship, Tilman Struve described this reliance on ecclesiastical cooperation as a 'structural weakness' in Ottonian theocratic rulership.[63] Thus, when the events of the late eleventh century 'shook the world' the tremors were sufficient to

---

[59] A. Mayer-Pfannholz, 'Die Wende von Canossa: Eine Studie zum Sacrum Imperium', *Hochland* 30 (1933), 385–404.

[60] E. Kantorowicz, *The King's Two Bodies: A Study in Mediaeval Political Theology*, 2nd edn (Princeton, 1997), pp. 61–78.

[61] H. Hoffmann, *Buchkunst und Königtum im ottonischen und frühsalischen Reich*, 2 vols. (Stuttgart, 1986); U. Kuder, 'Die Ottonen in der ottonische Buchmalerei: Identifikation und Ikonographie', in *Herrschaftsrepräsentation im ottonischen Sachsen*, ed. G. Althoff and E. Schubert, Vorträge und Forschungen 46 (Sigmaringen, 1998), pp. 137–234; H. Mayr-Harting, *Ottonian Book Illumination: An Historical Study*, 2 vols. (London, 1991); S. Weinfurter, 'Sakralkönigtum und Herrschaftsbegründung um die Jahrtausendwende: Die Kaiser Otto III. und Heinrich II. in ihren Bildern', in *Bilder erzählen Geschichte*, ed. H. Altrichter (Freiburg im Breisgau, 1995), pp. 47–104.

[62] T. Reuter, 'The "Imperial Church System" of the Ottonian and Salian Rulers: A Reconsideration', in *Medieval Polities and Modern Mentalities*, ed. J. L. Nelson (Cambridge, 2006), pp. 325–54; R. Schieffer, '"Mediator cleri et plebis": Zum geistlichen Einfluß auf Verständnis und Darstellung des ottonischen Königtums', in *Herrschaftsrepräsentation im ottonischen Sachsen*, ed. G. Althoff and E. Schubert, Vorträge und Forschungen 46 (Sigmaringen, 1998), pp. 345–61; G. Isabella, 'Das Sakralkönigtum in Quellen aus ottonischer Zeit: unmittelbarer Bezug zu Gott oder Vermittlung durch die Bischöfe', *Frühmittelalterliche Studien* 44 (2010), 137–52.

[63] Struve, 'Die Salier und das römische Recht', p. 7.

bring the whole edifice of sacral kingship tumbling down.[64] It was not until the later twelfth century that Frederick Barbarossa was, with recourse to Roman law, able to re-burnish the image of monarchy to some degree.

The debates surrounding Canossa and the demise of sacral kingship embody the broader modernization and desacralization paradigm in microcosm and reflect Germany's experience of state formation. David Warner wrote of what he called the 'Presumption of Ottonian Success', which, in the context of the medieval German *Sonderweg* assumed that the Ottonian rulers had begun the construction of a coherent and integrated German state before the later Salian and Staufer rulers oversaw its failure.[65] Once again, the problem of a teleological approach that explains the development of modern states as being related to the loss of the sacral resources of the monarch rears its head. As sacral kingship has been seen as such an important element in Ottonian success it is inevitable that its weakening becomes a major explanation for the later failure of Salian and Staufer power, as Ludger Körntgen has pointed out.[66] However, hand-in-hand with anthropologically inspired approaches to the reality of Ottonian rule, associated above all with Gerd Althoff and his adherents, the image of Ottonian sacral kingship has been re-examined.[67] This exploration has stripped the image of Ottonian sacral kingship of some of its mystique and, as a result, the later Salian and Staufer rulers now appear less overshadowed by the comparison.

The events at Canossa have also been subject to reassessment, a re-evaluation that has been given fresh impetus by the provocative contributions of Johannes Fried.[68] While Stefan Weinfurter came to maintain that the word 'Canossa' stands for a whole process of change in the late eleventh and early twelfth century, the idea of Canossa as a turning point, whether in its broad or narrow interpretation, has also begun to be questioned.[69] In 2010 Hartmut Hoffmann published an article in *Deutsches Archiv* under the

---

[64] The image of Canossa as an earthquake was invoked in the name of a high-profile exhibition: C. Stiegemann and M. Wemhoff, ed., *Canossa 1077 – Erschütterung der Welt: Geschichte, Kunst und Kultur am Aufgang der Romanik*, 2 vols. (Munich, 2006).

[65] D. A. Warner, 'Reading Ottonian History: The "Sonderweg" and Other Myths', in *Challenging the Boundaries of Medieval History: The Legacy of Timothy Reuter*, ed. P. Skinner, Studies in the Early Middle Ages 22 (Turnhout, 2009), pp. 81–114 (pp. 95–101).

[66] Körntgen, '"Sakrales Königtum" und "Entsakralisierung"', p. 134.

[67] See, in particular, G. Althoff, *Spielregeln der Politik im Mittelalter: Kommunikation in Frieden und Fehde* (Darmstadt, 1997) and G. Althoff, *Family Friends and Followers: Political and Social Bonds in Early Medieval Europe*, trans. C. Carroll (Cambridge, 2004).

[68] J. Fried, 'Der Pakt von Canossa: Schritte zur Wirklichkeit durch Erinnerungsanalyse', in *Die Faszination der Papstgeschichte: Neue Zugänge zum frühen und hohen Mittelalter*, ed. W. Hartmann and K. Herbers (Cologne, 2008), pp. 133–98; J. Fried, *Canossa: Entlarvung einer Legende: eine Streitschrift* (Berlin, 2012).

[69] S. Weinfurter, 'Canossa als Chiffre: von den Möglichkeiten historischen Deutens',

title 'Canossa – eine Wende?', a play on the title of Mayer-Pfannholz's 1933 study.[70] In it Hoffmann rejected the paradigm of the demise of sacral kingship after 1077, concluding forcefully that kingship was neither 'desacralized' nor 'demystified'.[71] Arnold Angenendt, Franz-Reiner Erkens and Ludger Körntgen have also advocated this view.[72] For Erkens, the late eleventh century saw a more modest modification in the concept of sacral kingship within the *Reich* and he points to the fact that many of the elements of sacral kingship found pre-1077 are evident in the twelfth century too.[73] Importantly he also argues that rather than providing an alternative secular basis for Staufen kingship, Roman law actually strengthened ruler sacrality.[74]

Throughout his important book on sacral conceptions of kingship found in Ottonian and early Salian art and historiography Ludger Körntgen argues for the need to contextualize this evidence fully.[75] It is thus of no surprise that two of his contributions to the debates surrounding Canossa focus closely on properly contextualizing two types of source material. Firstly, he has looked at the so-called *Streitschrifte* and argued that the polemical tracts associated with Henry IV should not be understood as some kind of coherent defence of royal sacrality, but rather as specific responses to specific papal attacks.[76] He

---

in *Canossa: Aspekte einer Wende*, ed. W. Hasberg and H.-J. Scheidgen (Regensburg, 2012), pp. 124–40.

[70] H. Hoffmann, 'Canossa – eine Wende?', *Deutsches Archiv* 66 (2010), 535–69.

[71] 'In einer Welt, die unter dem Motto *Fides quaerens intellectum* stand, war das Königtum nicht "entsakralisiert" und schon gar nicht "entzaubert".' Hoffmann, 'Canossa – eine Wende?', p. 568.

[72] A. Angenendt, 'Vor und nach Canossa: rex et sacerdos', in *Canossa: Aspekte einer Wende*, ed. W. Hasberg and H.-J. Scheidgen (Regensburg, 2012), pp. 141–50; F.-R. Erkens, *Herrschersakralität im Mittelalter: Von den Anfängen bis zum Investiturstreit* (Stuttgart, 2006); F.-R. Erkens, 'Der "pia Dei ordinatione rex" und der Krise sakral legitimierter Königsherrschaft in spätsalisch-frühstaufischer Zeit', in *Vom Umbruch zur Erneuerung?: Das 11. und beginnende 12. Jahrhundert. Position der Forschung* (Munich, 2006), pp. 71–101; Körntgen, '"Sakrales Königtum" und "Entsakralisierung"'; L. Körntgen, 'Der Investiturstreit und das Verhältnis von Religion und Politik im Frühmittelalter', in *Religion und Politik im Mittelalter: Deutschland und England im Vergleich* (Berlin, 2013), pp. 89–115; L. Körntgen, 'Herrscherbild im Wandel – Ein Neuansatz in staufischer Zeit?', in *BarbarossaBilder: Entstehungskontexte, Erwartungshorizonte, Verwendungszusammenhänge*, ed. K. Görich and R. Schmitz-Esser (Regensburg, 2014), pp. 32–45.

[73] Erkens, 'Der "pia Dei ordinatione rex"', p. 85.

[74] Ibid., pp. 92–7.

[75] L. Körntgen, *Königsherrschaft und Gottes Gnade: Zu Kontext und Funktion sakraler Vorstellungen in Historiographie und Bildzeugnisse der ottonisch-frühsalischen Zeit* (Berlin, 2001).

[76] The *Streitschrifte* have seen sustained scholarly interest. For a flavour of this see I. S. Robinson, *Authority and Resistance in the Investiture Contest: The Polemical Literature of the Late Eleventh Century* (Manchester, 1978); and A.-L. Schroll and E. Reversi, ed., *Brief und Kommunikation im Wandel: Medien, Autoren und Kontexte in den Debatten des Investiturstreits* (Cologne, 2016).

argues that the Investiture Controversy precipitated such a huge outpouring of texts that it is easy to gain the misguided impression that the key issue in the conflict was the religious legitimation of kingship, whereas in fact it was much more about the concrete issue of Henry IV's ability to rule and the justness of Gregory VII's actions against him.[77] For Körntgen the Investiture Controversy is thus a moment of discontinuity rather than a turning point or moment of desacralization.[78] In a second contribution Körntgen questions whether a change in the way rulers were depicted in art can be seen as a manifestation of changes in conceptions of kingship.[79] Specifically, he considers the disappearance of images of rulers from liturgical manuscripts and the development of the more historical ruler imagery associated with the later Salians and Staufer. He argues that this change cannot simply be attributed to the demise of sacral kingship, but needs to be considered in far broader cultural-historical horizons, particularly taking into account changes in aesthetics and commemoratory practices across the high Middle Ages.

Körntgen also questions the very concept of 'sacral kingship', drawing attention to how nebulous it is and how imprecisely it has been used by historians of medieval Germany.[80] He is not the first to recognize the problem: Karl Leyser, for example, in 1979 expressed his misgivings at using the word 'sacral' to describe the kingship of the Ottonians, though for Leyser the very imprecision of the word was beneficial as he felt anointing alone could not explain the numinous aura of the Ottonian emperors and that the word 'sacral' encapsulated both ecclesiastical/liturgical aspects and more mystical attributes.[81] However, if the concept of sacral kingship is so amorphous, does it not lose its explanatory power? This is the argument of Jens Engels, an historian of the French Revolution (the key moment of 'desacralization' in French history), who has criticized the use of the concept of 'sacral kingship' by historians.[82] He points out that the concept is employed in a variety of ways by ethnologists, sociologists, historians and anthropologists so that there is no consensus as to what 'sacral kingship' actually entails. The term has become a meaningless catch-all phrase to encompass all the aspects of old-style monarchy that do not make sense to the modern rational mind.[83] Building on Engels's work, Körntgen writes of the 'universal explanatory power' (*universale Erklärungspotenz*) of the demise of sacral kingship as a key feature in the development of modern states, so that complex political,

---

[77] Körntgen, '"Sakrales Königtum" und "Entsakralisierung"', pp. 137–55.
[78] Ibid., p. 159.
[79] Körntgen, 'Herrscherbild im Wandel'.
[80] Körntgen, '"Sakrales Königtum" und "Entsakralisierung"', pp. 133–4.
[81] K. Leyser, *Rule and Conflict in an Early Medieval Society: Ottonian Saxony* (London, 1979), p. 75.
[82] J. I. Engels, 'Das "Wesen" der Monarchie? Kritische Anmerkungen zum "Sakralkönigtum" in der Geschichtswissenschaft', *Majestas* 7 (1999), 3–39.
[83] Engels, 'Das "Wesen" der Monarchie?', p. 8.

social and economic factors pale into insignificance.[84] Bearing this in mind, the term 'liturgical kingship' has been preferred throughout this book in place of the opaque and loaded term 'sacral kingship'. The term 'liturgical kingship' emphasizes the fact that this study is concerned with the interaction between monarchy and liturgy, and the impact (or not) of the ecclesiastical reform movement on this interaction. In its precision, the term can also help to break the spell of the desacralization paradigm, for the king's relationship with liturgical ceremonial was but one facet of kingship. It must not be seen as standing in opposition to bureaucratic or legal sophistication or any of the other complex political, social and economic developments which characterized the long twelfth century and which, from our modern vantage point, have been considered to denote progress towards the secular state.

Inauguration and Liturgical Kingship in the 'Long' Twelfth Century

The practice of royal and imperial inauguration forms the focal point of this study. Inauguration supplies the clearest evidence of liturgical kingship in this period and for it sufficient source materials and secondary literature are available for the different realms. My study concentrates on the creation of the kings of France, England and Germany and the inauguration of the emperor. It does not encompass an investigation into the myriad additional king-making events within the Empire, such as the German kings being made monarchs of Lombardy or Burgundy, nor the making of sub-kings such as that of Bohemia. However, while inauguration provides the central pillar of the investigation, the aim here is not to delineate every detail of the ceremony and its development, an approach that has been taken many times before. Indeed, the longevity of the ritual has made it particularly attractive to historians taking (national) teleological approaches. This can be seen in Richard Jackson's valuable edition of the 'French' *ordines*, in which he openly admits that a number of the texts cannot really be designated as 'French' at all.[85] Andreas Büttner's study of the evolution of inauguration in the late-medieval German kingdom is a further example of the developmental method.[86] Rather than seeking the roots of later developments the twelfth-century evidence will be assessed on its own terms.

A comparative approach necessitates the drawing of defined boundaries. The central period under consideration in this book is the twelfth century. As alluded to above, the twelfth century is often considered a transitional period

---

[84] Körntgen, '"Sakrales Königtum" und "Entsakralisierung"', p. 133.
[85] *Ordines Coronationis Franciae: Texts and Ordines for the Coronation of Frankish and French Kings and Queens in the Middle Ages*, ed. R. A. Jackson, 2 vols. (Philadelphia, 1995–2000).
[86] A. Büttner, *Der Weg zur Krone: Rituale der Herrschererhebung im spätmittelalterlichen Reich*, 2 vols. (Ostfildern, 2012).

Introduction

in terms of medieval kingship and also the key period in which German development diverged from the Anglo-French model.[87] Having given its name to a renaissance, the twelfth century is also considered a transitional period in a more general sense.[88] Periodizations are, however, often unsatisfactory and periods of stability or change rarely fit neatly into a framework organized by centuries. Thus historians are now accustomed to talk of the 'long' twelfth century, in recognition of the fact that the aspects seen as characteristic of this era can be identified both before 1100 and after 1200. Unfortunately, there exists no scholarly consensus as to how long the 'long' twelfth century actually was, as Thomas Noble has recently pointed out.[89] In this study I follow Reuter in seeing the years between about 1070 and about 1220/30 as of particular significance for the transformation of monarchical power.[90] These 150 years thus form the focal point of my enquiries, but at times it is necessary to trespass earlier or later, for the reigns of kings do not helpfully align with scholarly constructs. This points to another possible approach to periodization, which would be to pick two important events and study the period in between them. This is the kind of periodization that characterizes the English Middle Ages as having run from the Battle of Hastings to the Battle of Bosworth Field. For one country such a pragmatic approach can be justified, especially given that few historians stick rigidly to such boundaries as 1066 or 1485, recognizing that it is rare even for such canonical dates to delineate moments of complete change.[91] In a study of three different countries, however, attempting to periodize using 'epoch defining' events would be misguided; there would be little coherence in a study running, for example, from 1066 to 1245 (the year in which Frederick II was deposed by

---

[87] As Reuter wrote in an important comparative essay, it was the during the 'long' twelfth century that, 'if ever, the train was missed: if it had been caught, then perhaps the retarding of the [German] nation and hence the coming too late of state-formation on a national basis, might have been averted'. T. Reuter, 'All Quiet Except on the Western Front? The Emergence of Pre-modern Forms of Statehood in the Central Middle Ages', in *Medieval Polities and Modern Mentalities*, ed. J. L. Nelson (Cambridge, 2006), pp. 432–58 (p. 435).

[88] The idea of the twelfth century as a period of renaissance was first advanced by Charles Homer Haskins in his *The Renaissance of the Twelfth Century* (Cambridge, MA, 1927). On the legacy of this concept see the discussion in T. F. X. Noble, 'Introduction', in *European Transformations: The Long Twelfth Century*, ed. T. F. X. Noble and J. van Engen (Notre Dame, 2012), pp. 1–16 (pp. 2–5).

[89] Noble, 'Introduction', p. 4.

[90] Reuter, 'All Quiet', p. 435.

[91] As Len Scales recently commented while discussing the scope of his study on German identity,'it will also be necessary fairly regularly to step back beyond the book's terminal dates … Assessing the role of an institution which claimed the heritage of the Roman Caesars cannot set off from a standing start in the time of the last Staufer'. L. Scales, *The Shaping of German Identity: Authority and Crisis, 1245–1414* (Cambridge, 2012), p. 4.

an ecclesiastical assembly at Lyon). Instead this study encompasses a period in which concepts of kingship in the three realms had distinct similarities, from the mid-eleventh century, by which time monarchs in all three realms had adopted the Christomimetic image of an enthroned king on their seals, to the mid-thirteenth century, at which point inauguration liturgies, which had hitherto displayed little in the way of 'national' characteristics, began to diverge.

The comparative approach chosen for this study also demands the assessment of comparable primary sources. The three major types of sources that have been consulted in the writing of this book are liturgical texts, narrative texts and charter evidence, each of which forms the central focus of a pair of chapters. The boundaries between such categories are, indubitably, permeable. The texts of charters, for example, are sometimes only known to us from their inclusion in a chronicle, and it is not always apparent whether a given text should be categorized as being narrative or liturgical in nature. These pragmatically chosen categories do, however, allow differing methodological approaches to be applied to source material that is available from all three realms. In any case, the chapters are not hermetically sealed off from one another. Where relevant, liturgical texts are cited to support arguments drawn from narrative sources, and charter evidence to confirm insights gained from reading liturgical texts. In addition to this borrowing between the three major source types considered, additional evidence has been consulted where appropriate, with material culture and visual evidence playing an important role throughout the book.

Chapters 1 and 2 thus focus on the liturgy of the consecration ceremony itself. Although early medievalists have studied consecration liturgy with great intensity, it has received considerably less attention in the high medieval period. Liturgies themselves tend to become fossilized. As a result, the high medieval *ordines* are sometimes regarded as a relic from the past with little contemporary relevance. The problematic nature of liturgical texts, which cannot meaningfully be subjected to study by traditional source criticism techniques, has contributed to their neglect. The first chapter of my study of the *ordines* begins with a discussion of the history of liturgical scholarship and then presents a methodology that embraces the problematic nature of these texts. Instead of struggling to trace borrowings and to assign dates to different texts (approaches that have dominated the study of consecration liturgy), I take a pragmatic approach, making a virtue of the consecration liturgy's atemporal nature and wide diffusion. Approaching the texts in this way allows me, in the following chapter, to tease out a conceptual link between the sacraments of consecration and marriage, which demonstrates the richness and depth of the imagery inherent in these texts. This chapter, which includes a consideration of rubrication and items of regalia, illustrates that fossilization of prayer formulae did not lead to petrification in interpretation. Recognizing that the consecration liturgy was no outdated relic, but instead was subject to

Introduction

lively debate and reinterpretation, makes explicit its continued relevance in the high Middle Ages.

Narrative evidence takes centre stage in the middle segment of the book in which I analyse descriptions of royal consecration in chronicles and annals. As these descriptions are often brief, historians have overlooked their importance. I argue, beginning with the banalities, that the cursory nature of such descriptions highlights the elements of consecration considered to be of most relevance by contemporaries. These were who was involved, what happened and where and when an inauguration took place. Accordingly, Chapter 3 is concerned with the participants in an inauguration ceremony and the places chosen for inauguration ceremonies, two elements closely linked to ideas of legitimacy. In Chapter 4 the vocabulary used to describe inauguration is examined, as are the dates chosen for royal and imperial inauguration. It shall be demonstrated that the very choice of words for the making of a king ('coronation', 'consecration', 'inauguration', etc.) is of fundamental significance if we are to understand what these processes singly and collectively involved. Taking inspiration from German scholars who have noted the coincidences between the great events of imperial history and the more important dates in the liturgical calendar, I apply this particular insight to royal acts outside the German kingdom. Recognizing that dates were recorded with reference to saints' days and feasts of the church, has enabled me to mine a rich seam of liturgical symbolism that has hitherto remained buried.

The final component of the book is an interdisciplinary study of charter evidence, in which textual content, physical appearance and seal iconography are all examined. Although Anglophone scholars might be surprised to find charters and seals discussed in a study of liturgical kingship, their relevance to this theme has long been noted by continental scholars. Accordingly, Chapter 5 opens with a discussion of approaches taken to charter scholarship in England, France and Germany, a consideration of methodological issues and an exposition of the need to examine medieval charters holistically, rather than concentrating solely on their textual content. This chapter therefore focuses on protocols and eschatacols in royal charters, considering their textual content, and visual and physical appearance. A document's authenticity is its most important characteristic and, as will be demonstrated, the manner in which kings guaranteed this authenticity frequently referred back to the ceremony in which they had been made monarch. This point is made manifest in the seals and bulls used by the monarch and the concluding chapter thus offers an investigation of seal iconography.

This explication of seal iconography points to the potential of visual and material sources to contribute to the study of liturgical kingship. A numismatic analysis lies beyond the scope of this monograph, but as a widely seen medium with marked iconographic similarities to seal design, a comparative study of coinage in the three realms would certainly be worthwhile. The omission of a comprehensive discussion of manuscript imagery might strike the reader as surprising, given that Ottonian (and to a lesser extent Anglo-Saxon) manuscript art has been seen as the *locus classicus* of early medieval liturgical kingship.[92] However, both a lack images of inauguration and also methodological issues prevent the integration of manuscript miniatures into this study. It is amazing how few surviving manuscript miniatures actually depict inauguration. The wonderful miniature of Henry VI's imperial inauguration from Peter of Eboli's *Liber ad honorem Augusti*, which adorns the cover of this book, is entirely unique in the way in which it depicts, on a single folio, a number of rituals, which together make up the inauguration rite. Moreover, many of the images that have been labelled 'coronation miniatures' (or similar) by scholars do not actually depict the act of inauguration itself. While images of monarchs receiving crowns from the hand of God, or being depicted enthroned and crowned between bishops, surely are relevant to ideas of liturgical kingship they cannot easily be integrated into a study with a tight focus on the moment of inauguration. Such images are particularly difficult to include in a comparative study because of the diverse manuscript contexts in which they survive. As Ludger Körntgen has argued in an essay in which he considers ruler imagery in German manuscripts, the idea that one can straightforwardly compare images in liturgical manuscripts with those in manuscripts containing chronicles and histories is highly problematic.[93] Thus both the rarity of manuscript miniatures, which can actually confidently be considered to depict an inauguration, and also the diversity of the contexts in which these rare images are found cautions against integrating them into a comparative study of the type attempted here.

The preference for German (and to a lesser extent French) methodologies should not be interpreted as the author considering them inherently superior to Anglophone scholarship. The prioritizing of continental approaches is determined by the source material. Comparative history necessitates comparing the comparable. The type of documents that have fascinated historians of English kingship are simply not available for all three realms. Thus, English approaches cannot possibly be projected onto German evidence. By contrast, types of evidence exploited by German historians do abound in England, and hitherto have been only superficially used. In taking a different approach to high medieval English kingship, by placing it in a European perspective and assessing it through the lens of alternative historiographical traditions, this study has the aim of stimulating debate about the nature of kingship in England. Historians of English kingship are blessed with a diversity of sources of which it has been possible to consult only a limited number in the

---

[92] See above note 61 and R. Deshman, '*Christus rex et magi reges*: Kingship and Christology in Ottonian and Anglo-Saxon Art', *Frühmittelalterliche Studien* 10 (1976), 367–405.

[93] Körntgen, 'Herrscherbild im Wandel', pp. 36–7.

Introduction

course of this project. It is my contention, however, that the picture provided by chronicles and liturgical texts can complement that which can be drawn from the records of central government. These records contain information such as when the king paid for the 'Te Deum' to be sung, how much was spent on food for a feast, or what items were held in the royal wardrobe. These concrete facts provide a unique opportunity to assess the accuracy of the image projected in more ephemeral sources.[94] When English scholars take the tube to Kew to consult the documents of royal administration, they should take with them not just a knowledge of the bewildering technical language of the pipe rolls. They should also carry a Missal.

---

[94] The potential of this kind of approach has been demonstrated by a number of scholars: L. Kjær, 'Food, Drink and Ritualised Communication in the Household of Eleanor de Montfort, February to August 1265', *Journal of Medieval History* 37 (2011), 75–89; B. L. Wild, 'The Empress's New Clothes: A Rotulus Pannorum of Isabella, Sister of King Henry III, Bride of Emperor Frederick II', *Medieval Clothing and Textiles* 7 (2011), 2–31; P. Webster, *King John and Religion* (Woodbridge, 2015).

1
Liturgical Texts: The Spoken Word and Song

In February 1111 Henry V's plan to receive imperial coronation was thrown into disarray when Pope Paschal II refused to crown him emperor unless he first renounced episcopal investiture. Following a tumultuous meeting at St Peter's on 12 February, Henry took the pope and a number of his cardinals captive. He held them until he had exhorted a privilege allowing him to continue investing bishops with a ring and staff. This privilege (soon after dubbed a *pravilegium* or 'bad law') was formally confirmed during Henry's imperial inauguration, which took place on 11 April. Some details of this ceremony were recorded by David Scottus, bishop of Bangor, who was apparently present as an imperial chaplain.[1] His original account does not survive, but versions of it were incorporated into the anonymous Latin *Kaiserchronik* (c.1114) and, with significantly more detail, by William of Malmesbury into his *Gesta regum Anglorum*.[2] According to William, David reported that

> the king was received at the Silver Gate by the bishops and cardinals and the whole clergy of Rome, and the prayer contained in the ordinal being begun by the bishop of Ostia ... he was taken to the middle of the Rota, and there was the recipient of a second prayer from the bishop of Porto, as the Roman ordinal prescribes. They then took him with litanies to the shrine of the Apostles, and there the bishop of Ostia anointed him between the shoulders and on the right arm. Next he was taken by the Holy Father to the altar of the same Apostles, and there the pope himself set the crown upon his head, and he was consecrated emperor. After the crowning a mass of the Lord's Resurrection was celebrated, in which before making his communion our lord the pope gave a privilege to the emperor with his own hand.[3]

---

[1] On David's role at the imperial court see F. Hausmann, *Reichskanzlei und Hofkapelle unter Heinrich V. und Konrad III.* (Stuttgart, 1956), pp. 310–19.

[2] *Frutolfi et Ekkehardi chronica necnon anonymi chronica imperatorum*, ed. F.-J. Schmale and I. Schmale-Ott (Darmstadt, 1972), pp. 254–61; William of Malmesbury, *Gesta regum Anglorum*, ed. M. Winterbottom, R. M. Thomson and R. A. B. Mynors, 2 vols., OMT (Oxford, 1998), I, 765–71.

[3] William of Malmesbury, *Gesta regum Anglorum*, pp. 766–9: 'Et in Argentea Porta receptus est rex ab episcopis et cardinalibus et toto clero Romano, et cepta oratione quae in ordine continetur ab Hostiensi episcopo, quoniam Albanus deerat a quo debuisset|dici si adesset, ad mediam rotam ductus est; et ibi recepit secundam orationem a Portuensi episcopo, sicut precipit Romanus ordo. Deinde duxerunt eum cum letaniis usque ad confessionem apostolorum, et ibi unxit eum Hostiensis episcopus inter scapulas et in bracho dextro. Post haec a domino Apostolico ad

In his report David twice mentions an *ordo*, which in the second instance is described as *romanus*. These references are to a liturgical text for imperial inauguration. David has described a number of elements of this rite, including several prayers and the pre-eminent acts of unction and coronation.

The following two chapters are concerned with such liturgical texts, that were written for the inauguration of kings and emperors during this period. Once described by Kantorowicz as 'a magic thicket of prayers, benedictions, and ecclesiastical rites', their mystical status was long maintained by successive generations of liturgical scholars, whose use of impenetrable terminology ensured that many politically orientated historians did not engage with either their work or the texts they worked on.[4] Even the names given to these texts by earlier generations of liturgical scholars can cause confusion with, for example, the *ordo* for royal inauguration contained within the *Romano-Germanic Pontifical* also being known as the 'Ottonian *Ordo*' and the 'Mainz *Ordo*'.[5] Possibilities to get lost in this dense thicket certainly abound, but if we do not allow ourselves to be spooked by its magical aura, and follow new paths beaten by a growing number of current scholars of liturgy, it can be traversed with the acquisition of merely a few scratches.[6] Like all liturgies, those for royal and imperial inauguration are composed of a number of prayers, blessings and rubrics describing ritual actions. These building blocks could be brought together in a variety of ways, and augmented with both new material and material from other liturgical ceremonies.

The texts as we find them are, however, not full records of what would have been said, sung and done in an inauguration ceremony. They provide only a framework, and the performance of a ceremony would have required recourse to other sources. This phenomenon can be witnessed in church services to this day. If we take, as an example, a modern Roman Catholic wedding ceremony, the 'Order of Service', often printed specially for the occasion, assimilates material from a number of sources. To the outline of the marriage service are added readings from the Bible and hymns from a hymn book. The bride and groom can also decide whether they want a mass

---

altare eorundem apostolorum deductus et ibidem, imposita sibi corona, ab ipso Apostolico in imperatorem est consecratus. Post impositam coronam missa de resurrectione Domini est celebrata, in qua ante communionem domnus Apostolicus privilegium imperatori propria manu dedit.'

[4] As Gathagan has commented, 'the study of medieval sacraments has traditionally fallen to that rarefied breed of historian, the liturgist'. L. L. Gathagan, 'The Trappings of Power: The Coronation of Mathilda of Flanders', *Haskins Society Journal* 13 (1999), 21–39 (p. 21).

[5] Alternative names by which the different texts are known are included in Appendix 1.

[6] Early medievalists have led the way here, see Yitzhak Hen's useful survey: Y. Hen, 'Key Themes in the Study of Early Medieval Liturgy', in *T&T Clark Companion to Liturgy*, ed. A. Reid (London, 2015), pp. 73–92.

as part of the ceremony. Medieval liturgical inauguration texts exhibit similar properties. In the same way that contemporary Roman Catholic marriage ceremonies comprise a collection of prayers, promises, readings and hymns that together stress the solemnity of matrimony in the eyes of the Church, so too did the prayers, promises and rituals associated with royal and imperial inauguration emphasize the solemnity of these most sacred of occasions for high medieval kings and emperors.

Janet Nelson has rightly stressed that 'successive recensions of *ordines* ought not to be treated like set texts in a Political Ideas course. Liturgy is not the place to look for polemic, and though political ideas can be found in the *ordines*, they are of the most general, uncontentious and normative kind.'[7] With Nelson's warning ringing in our ears, in this chapter I present a methodology that embraces the problematic nature of liturgical texts and seeks a way to integrate inauguration *ordines* into a comprehensive comparative study of images of kingship in England, France and the Empire. To this end, a brief history of the inauguration rite in the early medieval period, and the development of the modern study of the *ordines*, is in order. Following a discussion of the problems that arise in examining liturgical texts, the mechanism for the comparison and selection of texts to be compared will be set out and justified. The comparison itself makes manifest the many similarities between the rites, not just the three royal rites, but also the close correlation between royal and imperial liturgy. Where imperial liturgy diverges from royal tradition this is due to the participation of the pope. It will also be made apparent that papal influence did not extend to the royal liturgies. The focus of this chapter is the words spoken and sung by participants in an inauguration ceremony. The component ritual acts and performative elements of the liturgy will be considered in the following chapter.

The genesis of the inauguration ritual, which by Carolingian times had developed to include a ritual crowning and anointing, is shrouded in uncertainty.[8] The ritual of crowning corresponded to Byzantine practice and the tradition of crown wearing had a long ancestry reaching back through the traditions of ancient Rome and Hellenistic monarchy to the Persian emperors of the sixth century BC. The Byzantine ceremony, however, did not include

---

[7] J. L. Nelson, 'The Rites of the Conqueror', *Anglo-Norman Studies* IV (1982), 117–32 (p. 122).

[8] In the period under consideration in this book initially only the German kings and emperors, and the kings of France and England were anointed. Then, on the establishment of the kingdoms of Jerusalem in 1100 and Sicily in 1130 their kings were granted the right of unction. Aragon received unction in 1204, Navarre in 1257 and Scotland in 1329. Some of the Norman princes of southern Italy were also anointed. See E. Kantorowicz, *Laudes Regiae: A Study in Liturgical Acclamations and Medieval Ruler Worship* (Berkeley, 1942), p. 162; R. Schieffer, 'Die Ausbreitung der Königssalbung im hochmittelalterlichen Europa', in *Die mittelalterliche Thronfolge im europäischen Vergleich*, ed. M. Becher, Vorträge und Forschungen 84 (2017), pp. 43–79.

anointing, and thus another source for this rite must be sought.⁹ The earliest non-biblical reference to royal unction appears in the *Historia Wambae* of Julian of Toledo, who describes the death of King Recceswinth in 672 and the election and later anointing of King Wamba. Roger Collins has argued that Julian's purpose in writing the *Historia* was to defend the right of Toledo to anoint the new king.¹⁰ That Julian desired to defend such a right suggests that inaugural anointing at Toledo was an established practice in seventh-century Visigothic Spain; however, following this mention, the trail goes cold. Our next firm evidence for royal unction is provided by Pippin's anointing at Soissons in 751 and again by Pope Stephen at Saint-Denis in 754, although Achim Hack has argued that unction must have been part of Merovingian inaugural ceremonial before 751.¹¹ Richard Jackson posits that the rite could have come to Gaul via Spain, but given the obvious Old Testament model for such an act (provided by Samuel's anointing of Saul and David), he points out that it is also possible that the rite could have been generated independently.¹²

Writing in 1928, Eduard Eichmann argued that royal anointing was adopted from the episcopal rite.¹³ However, as Arnold Angenendt has since pointed out, when Pippin was anointed in 751 episcopal anointing was unknown in the Gallic church and thus, despite parallels between the rites, a straightforward borrowing from the episcopal rite seems unlikely.¹⁴ Angenendt favours the explanation of Walter Ullmann, that the introduction of royal unction was linked to baptismal anointing: just as the newly baptized was reborn in Christ, so too was the newly anointed king.¹⁵ In contrast, C.

---

⁹ We should perhaps heed Kantorowicz's warning that we should not just assume a Byzantine origin for everything, because 'a continuous taking, giving, and returning is significant of the relations between Byzantium and the West'. Kantorowicz, *Laudes Regiae*, p. 28. For the differences between Western and Byzantine inauguration see Nelson, 'Symbols in Context'. The different theories for the genesis of royal anointing are helpfully summarized in A. Hack, 'Zur Herkunft der karolingischen Königssalbung', *Zeitschrift für Kirchengeschichte* 110 (1999), 170–90 (pp. 170–6).

¹⁰ R. Collins, 'Julian of Toledo and the Royal Succession in Late Seventh-Century Spain', in *Early Medieval Kingship*, ed. P. H. Sawyer and I. Wood (Leeds, 1977), pp. 30–49 (p. 45).

¹¹ Hack, 'Zur Herkunft der karolingischen Königssalbung', pp. 177–89.

¹² *Ordines Coronationis Franciae*, ed. Jackson, I, 23; M. J. Enright, *Iona, Tara, and Soissons: The Origin of the Royal Anointing Ritual* (Berlin, 1985) suggests an Irish origin for royal anointing, but this work has been critically received.

¹³ E. Eichmann, *Königs- und Bischofsweihe* (Munich, 1928).

¹⁴ A. Angenendt, 'Rex et Sacerdos: Zur Genese der Königssalbung', in *Tradition als historische Kraft: Interdiziplinäre Forschungen zur Geschichte des früheren Mittelalters*, ed. N. Kamp and J. Wollasch (Berlin, 1982), pp. 100–18 (p. 100).

¹⁵ A. Angenendt, 'Rex et Sacerdos', p. 101; W. Ullmann, 'Schranken der Königsgewalt im Mittelalter', *Historisches Jahrbuch* 91 (1971), 1–21 (pp. 7–10). On the sacrament of baptism in the Middle Ages see A. Angenendt, *Kaiserherrschaft und Königstaufe* (Berlin and New York, 1984), pp. 21–91; P. Cramer, *Baptism and Change in the Early Middle Ages* (Cambridge, 1993).

A. Bouman rejects this baptismal link, claiming that inaugural anointing had no basis in the baptismal anointing of Clovis by Remigius (St Rémi) in 496, an incident prominently noticed by Gregory of Tours.[16] But it would be unwise to leap to so categorical a rejection. Mary Garrison and Janet Nelson have both highlighted a symbolic affiliation to post-baptismal confirmation anointing, a practice that was established in Rome in the fifth century, was next attested in Anglo-Saxon England, and was thereafter re-exported to the Continent by St Boniface.[17] As Garrison has commented, 'it is impossible to say whether the witnesses to a royal anointing would have been struck by their king's relationship to the kings of Israel or by the ceremony's resemblance to a new-fangled and sometimes controversial addition to baptism'.[18] Garrison also suggests that despite the clear typological link to the Old Testament, royal anointing had a Roman dimension, evidenced by the author of the *Annales Mettenses priores*, who associated the papal anointing of Pippin with his elevation to the status of *patricius*.[19]

Given these varying, yet uncertain hypotheses, a multi-casual explanation for the origin of royal anointing is perhaps the most satisfactory conclusion we can draw. Whether or not Hack is right to assert that unction must already have been part of Merovingian ceremonial, his careful reading of the sources makes clear that contemporary accounts of the event did not stress its novelty.[20] In this late eighth-century context, royal unction apparently made sense to contemporaries, who would have had a multiplicity of reference points. They could have made a variety of overlapping connections between royal liturgy and other liturgical practices, such as baptismal and post-baptismal unction, not to mention biblical models in the form of Old Testament royal and priestly anointing. Looking beyond the origins of the rite, parallels between episcopal and royal inauguration liturgies remain striking and certainly could have influenced the interpretation of both rites in the period under consideration in this book, as will be discussed in subsequent chapters.

The earliest surviving liturgical texts relating to royal inauguration shed little light on the genesis of the rite. In his edition of the French *ordines*, Richard Jackson includes four texts dating from before 900. These cannot be described as *ordines* proper, but rather are collections of royal blessings.

---

[16] C. A. Bouman, *Sacring and Crowning: The Development of the Latin Ritual for the Anointing of Kings and the Coronation of an Emperor before the Eleventh Century* (Groningen, 1957), p. x.

[17] M. Garrison, 'The Franks as the New Israel? Education for an Identity from Pippin to Charlemagne', in *The Uses of the Past in the Early Middle Ages*, ed. Y. Hen and M. Innes (Cambridge, 2002), pp. 114–61 (p. 138); J. L. Nelson, 'The Lord's Anointed and the People's Choice: Carolingian Royal Ritual', in her *The Frankish World 750–900* (London, 1996), pp. 99–132 (p. 110).

[18] Garrison, 'The Franks as the New Israel?', p. 138.

[19] Ibid.

[20] Hack, 'Zur Herkunft der karolingischen Königssalbung', pp. 177–80.

Liturgical Texts: The Spoken Word and Song

Jackson stresses that his *Ordo* I, taken from the Sacramentary of Gellone, from c.790–800, is the earliest surviving liturgical formula associated with inauguration ceremonial, but that this is a chance survival and that the formulae contained within it must all have existed in earlier collections.[21] Of the four prayer formulae in this sacramentary, three reappear in later royal *ordines* from England, France and Germany, and also in the imperial *ordines*.[22] The royal texts in the Sacramentary of Angoulême (Jackson's *Ordo* II) are the earliest texts that specifically state they are for use in an inauguration ceremony and are the earliest witness to the prayer formula *prospice omnipotens Deus*, which reappears in all the *ordines* traditions. While the earliest texts associated with royal inauguration hail from the Frankish kingdom, Janet Nelson has compellingly argued that the earliest surviving royal inauguration *ordo* is of Anglo-Saxon origin and that the earliest surviving Frankish *ordo*, that for the marriage and inauguration of Judith, was largely drawn from the Anglo-Saxon Leofric *Ordo*.[23]

That the Leofric *Ordo* makes no allowance for a crowning within the inauguration ceremony must be significant in understanding the coming together of the twin elements of crowning and anointing. Bouman asserted, but frustratingly failed to provide evidence, that before the ninth century there existed an understanding that kings were anointed but not crowned, and emperors crowned but not anointed.[24] This assertion is perhaps supported by the Leofric *Ordo*, but in any case, anointing had been included in the imperial coronation by 816.[25] Both crowning and anointing were first certainly combined in a royal *ordo*, based on the Leofric text, for the marriage of the Frankish princess Judith to King Æthelwulf of the Anglo-Saxons on 1 October 856, during which she was also made queen.[26] They remained united in all succeeding western *ordines*. This early interweaving of Anglo-Saxon and Frankish traditions, on the marriage of a Frankish princess to an Anglo-Saxon king, exemplifies the common liturgical vocabulary of the earliest inauguration *ordines*.[27] The Judith *Ordo* is the first of four *ordines* that

---

[21] *Ordines Coronationis Franciae*, ed. Jackson, I, 51.
[22] Ibid., I, 52–4.
[23] J. L. Nelson, 'The Earliest Surviving Royal *Ordo*: Some Liturgical and Historical Aspects', in *Authority and Power: Studies on Medieval Law and Government Presented to Walter Ullmann on his Seventieth Birthday*, ed. B. Tierney and P. Linehan (Cambridge, 1980), pp. 29–48; This *ordo* has been published as part of the missal bearing the same name: *The Leofric Missal*, ed. N. A. Orchard, 2 vols., HBS 114 (Woodbridge, 2002), II, 429–32.
[24] Bouman, *Sacring and Crowning*, p. ix.
[25] Ibid., p. x.
[26] *Ordines Coronationis Franciae*, ed. Jackson, I, 73–9.
[27] On the context of this marriage see P. Stafford, 'Charles the Bald, Judith and England', in *Charles the Bald: Court and Kingdom*, ed. M. T. Gibson and J. L. Nelson, 2nd edn (Aldershot, 1990), pp. 139–53.

Inauguration and Liturgical Kingship

can all be assigned to specific historical events. All four are considered the work of Hincmar of Reims. As Julie Ann Smith has commented, 'the reign of Charles the Bald was remarkable for its proliferation of liturgical rites, largely through the assiduous creativity of Archbishop Hincmar, liturgist *par excellence*'.[28] In addition to that for the marriage and coronation of Judith, Hincmar also composed *ordines* for the anointing and coronation of Charles the Bald's wife Ermentrude on 25 August 866, the inauguration of Charles himself as king of Lorraine on 9 September 869, and the inauguration of Louis the Stammerer on 8 December 877.[29] Unfortunately our level of information about the composition and deployment of these early *ordines* is the exception rather than the rule; the subsequent development and usage of inauguration liturgies is significantly less clear.

In his introduction to a collection of essays entitled *Coronations*, Janos Bak provides a historiographical sketch of the development of the study of *ordines*, tracing the development of the discipline back to the nineteenth-century German constitutional historian Georg Waitz.[30] Given the lack of a recent edition of the German *ordines*, *ordines* scholars still often cite Waitz's *Die Formeln der deutschen Königs- und der römischen Kaiser- Krönung vom zehnten bis zum zwölften Jahrhundert*, published in 1872, as a source for the German rite.[31] Bak saw this German tradition initiated by Waitz as splitting into three strands; firstly under Percy Ernst Schramm, who looked at medieval coronations in the context of the symbolism of kingship, secondly under Walter Ullmann, who investigated medieval political and legal theory, and thirdly via Ernst Kantorowicz, who developed the concept of 'political theology'.[32] Even in the patriotic haze of the nineteenth century, Waitz had recognized that few nationalist elements could be identified in the *ordines*.[33] This was reflected in the work of his successors, such as Schramm, who did not confine himself to the study of the *ordines* in Germany, but instead ranged widely across Europe, even offering an English translation of the history of the English coronation to coincide with the succession of King George VI to the British throne in 1937.[34]

---

[28] J. A. Smith, 'The Earliest Queen-Making Rites', *Church History* 66 (1997), 18–35 (p. 24).
[29] *Ordines Coronationis Franciae*, ed. Jackson, I, 80–123.
[30] J. M. Bak, 'Introduction: Coronation Studies – Past, Present, and Future', in *Coronations: Medieval and Early Modern Monarchic Ritual*, ed. J. M. Bak (Berkeley, 1990), pp. 1–15. Waitz's most famous work was an eight-volume constitutional history of Germany published between 1844 and 1878.
[31] G. Waitz, *Die Formeln der deutschen Königs- und der römischen Kaiser-Krönung vom zehnten bis zum zwölften Jahrhundert* (Göttingen, 1872).
[32] A phrase Kantorowicz deployed in the subtitle of his best-known work: Kantorowicz, *The King's Two Bodies*.
[33] Waitz, *Die Formeln*, p. 3.
[34] P. E. Schramm, *A History of the English Coronation*, trans. L. G. W. Legg (Oxford, 1937).

Events in twentieth-century Europe ensured the diffusion of the German tradition, as Ernst Kantorowicz, after his initial enthusiasm subsided, became dissatisfied with the ruling National Socialists and left Germany, via Oxford, for the United States in 1938.[35] In the same year, following the *Anschluss*, Walter Ullmann fled from Austria to England and after the war secured a fellowship at Cambridge. In England, Ullmann's former doctoral student Janet Nelson has been at the forefront of the study of inauguration liturgy in the early medieval period, and Ullmann also encouraged George Garnett to examine the *ordines*.[36] In Germany, an interest in inauguration liturgy endured in the work of Carl Erdmann and Reinhard Elze, a member of the *Monumenta* and former student of Schramm, who edited the imperial *ordines* and has published several articles on the topic.[37] In the 1980s and 1990s, Richard Jackson, an American, completed his work on the French coronation in the later medieval period and edited the entire corpus of the French *ordines*.[38]

The development of the study of inauguration *ordines* has been highly influenced by anthropological approaches and increasingly by a more nuanced understanding of the nature of liturgical texts. Scholars of liturgy continually stress the special nature of liturgy and how it is inappropriate to use the traditional techniques of *Quellenkritik* as favoured by Schramm.[39] Not only does liturgy have a tendency to fossilization, but it was formulated from a limited selection of repetitive formulae, which makes attempts to trace borrowings and developments challenging. Hence Nelson's warning that succeeding versions cannot be dissected to discover the development of political ideas. As demonstrated by the disagreement between Garnett and Nelson over which

---

Schramm's other contributions to the study of royal and imperial inauguration liturgy included P. E. Schramm, 'Die *Ordines* der mittelalterlichen Kaiserkrönung: Ein Beitrag zur Geschichte des Kaisertums', *Archiv für Urkundenforschung* 11 (1930), 285–390; P. E. Schramm, '*Ordines*-Studien II: Die Krönung bei den Westfranken und den Franzosen', *Archiv für Urkundenforschung* 15 (1938), 4–55.

[35] On Kantorowicz's complicated response to the rise of National Socialism see M. Ruehl, '"In this Time without Emperors": The Politics of Ernst Kanotorowicz's *Kaiser Friedrich der Zweite* Reconsidered', *Journal of the Warburg and Courtauld Institutes* 63 (2000), 187–242. On his life and career see the contributions in R. L. Benson and J. Fried, ed., *Ernst Kantorowicz: Erträge der Doppeltagung Institute for Advanced Study Princeton / Johann Wolfgang Goethe-Universität Frankfurt*, Frankfurter Historische Abhandlungen 39 (Stuttgart, 1997).

[36] J. L. Nelson, 'Rituals of Royal Inauguration in Early Medieval Europe' (unpublished PhD dissertation, University of Cambridge, 1967); G. Garnett, *Conquered England: Kingship, Succession, and Tenure, 1066–1166* (Oxford, 2007), p. vii.

[37] C. Erdmann, *Forschungen zur politischen Ideenwelt des Frühmittelalters*, ed. F. Baethgen (Berlin, 1951); *Die Ordines für die Weihe und Krönung des Kaisers und der Kaiserin*, ed. R. Elze, *MGH Fontes Iuris* 9 (Hannover, 1960).

[38] R. A. Jackson, *Vive le roi: History of the French Coronation from Charles V to Charles X* (Chapel Hill, 1984); *Ordines Coronationis Franciae*, ed. Jackson.

[39] Bouman, *Sacring and Crowning*, p. 55.

recension of the English *ordines* was used at the inauguration of William the Conqueror, attempting to tie liturgical texts to actual ceremonial usage is fraught with difficulty.[40] Jackson rightly cautions against using descriptions from other sources to try to associate an *ordo* with a particular inauguration, pointing out that such descriptions would have been written after the event and that an author might have had a copy of an *ordo* in front of him, but not necessarily the *ordo* that was used.[41] Royal and imperial inauguration rites often survive in manuscripts that can never possibly have been used for an actual ceremony but which might have been available to a monastic chronicler. *Ordines* tend to survive in pontificals, which are books containing the orders of service for sacraments administered by bishops or popes.[42] Given that the text in a pontifical was not binding on those leading the ceremonies, it seems impossible to uphold Schramm's distinction between 'received' and 'not-received' *ordines*. Moreover, manuscript evidence suggests older texts could be mined for information, thus continuing to shape the ceremony long after the words were originally transferred from pen to parchment.[43]

As Jackson comments of the so-called Ratold *Ordo*, that originated *c*.980, 'the number of surviving twelfth-century manuscripts ... strongly suggest that this *ordo* was consulted for the coronations [in France] in that century, although there is no way of determining the degree to which each ceremony adhered to the model'.[44] In this pronouncement the archetypal nature of liturgical texts is highlighted. By making a virtue of this quality we can examine inauguration liturgy not with the aim of teasing out nuanced changes to the texts over time, but as a stockpile of images of liturgical kingship. As a comparison makes explicit, the idealized character of liturgy was not confined to one text, such as the Ratold *Ordo*, but is evident across geographical and temporal divides. Not only are German and French *ordines* derived from a common Frankish source, but the English *ordines* were also subject to continental influence and in turn exerted influence on French and German practice. Indeed, designating an *ordo* as coming from a particular country can be far from straightforward, as Jackson acknowledges in his edition of the French *ordines*, suggesting that a transnational approach to the topic is in any case more appropriate than a narrow national investigation.[45]

---

[40] G. Garnett, 'The Third Recension of the English Coronation *Ordo*: The Manuscripts', *Haskins Society Journal* 11 (1998), 43–71; Nelson, 'The Rites of the Conqueror'.

[41] *Ordines Coronationis Franciae*, ed. Jackson, I, 34. Here echoing similar points made by Reinhard Elze in his edition of the imperial *ordines*: *Die Ordines*, ed. Elze, p. xxiv.

[42] A number of politically charged imperial rites also survive in papal bulls, but these are exceptional.

[43] *Ordines Coronationis Franciae*, ed. Jackson, I, 34.

[44] Ibid., I, 30.

[45] He states, 'a number of texts in the present edition should also be included in editions of German royal or Anglo-Saxon/English *ordines*'. *Ordines Coronationis Franciae*, ed. Jackson, I, 11.

Liturgical Texts: The Spoken Word and Song

Although an in-depth study of the development and elaboration of these rites, not to mention the links between different 'national' traditions remains a scholarly desiderata, that is not the purpose of this book, which focuses on the interpretation of, rather than the construction of, inauguration rituals.

The number of manuscript witnesses of the *ordines* of each of the three kingdoms varies enormously, and although the *ordines* are mostly available in printed editions, the editorial standards applied are far from identical. Only the imperial and French *ordines* have been edited in coherent editions, and even these are not without their problems.[46] These editions have been thoroughly consulted, but there remains a danger that the ready availability of the imperial and French *ordines* may lead to an imbalance in the comparison with the German and English *ordines*. Another issue is how to deal with the difference between the inauguration *ordines* included in the Vogel and Elze edition of the compilation known as the *Romano-Germanic Pontifical* (PRG), compiled from only nine of over forty surviving manuscripts, and the *ordo* included in the H. A. Wilson edition of the Pontifical of Magdalen College, in which only the reading of this one manuscript is presented. The difference between editions of an entire pontifical, such as that from Magdalen College, in which the inauguration *ordo* is presented in the context of a complete liturgical handbook, and Jackson's edition of the French *ordines*, in which they have been divorced from their liturgical setting, present further problems. Given such differences in editorial practice, any precise comparison between the texts is impossible without an in-depth investigation of hundreds of manuscripts, a task beyond the scope of this study. Not only the nature of liturgy, but the myriad attempts of modern scholars to edit liturgical texts suggest that we should adopt a flexible and general approach to inauguration liturgy, if we wish to understand how contemporaries understood this event in this period.

A closer look at the problems of the PRG edition, comprehensively exposed by Henry Parkes, makes clear both the extent of the liturgy's malleability and the dangers inherent in attempting to fit such flexible and adaptable texts between the rigid covers of a modern scholarly edition.[47] The modern edition of the PRG radiates conformity and exactitude whereas the medieval texts are in reality discordant and irregular. Indeed, Vogel and Elze recognized that the PRG actually contains three recensions of the royal inauguration *ordo*: a short recension and two variants of a longer recension. But in consistency with

---

[46] *Die Ordines*, ed. Elze; *Ordines Coronationis Franciae* ed. Jackson. Jackson structured his edition of the French *ordines* to complement the approach taken by Reinhard Elze in his pioneering edition of the imperial *ordines* for the *MGH*. Jackson makes his editorial decisions explicit and includes all the texts. In contrast Elze repeatedly refers back to the text of other *ordines* and does not include all manuscript variants.

[47] H. Parkes, *The Making of Liturgy in the Ottonian Church: Books, Music and Ritual in Mainz, 950–1050* (Cambridge, 2015).

the rest of their edition these are presented as variant readings of the same *ordo*.[48] As Parkes has commented, although the texts for royal coronation (and episcopal ordination) exist in different states in different groups of PRG manuscripts, editorial practice 'actively subdues' such important distinctions.[49] In selecting which texts to compare, I have thus had to make a number of pragmatic decisions, to overcome the problems with the modern editions, the problems with precisely dating texts and the problems of designating an *ordo* as coming from a particular country. Although in choosing texts I have sought to identify a representative sample from all three realms and from across the period, I am aware of the limitations of the material and the subjectivity of these decisions. These texts are highly problematic, but at the same time absolutely fundamental to understanding the liturgical resonances inherent in images of medieval kingship. Despite their difficulties they demand examination.

Selecting texts from the English kingdom is the simplest task, because only three recensions of *ordines* have been identified by scholars as being in use before c.1250: the Leofric *Ordo*, and the so-called Second and Third Recensions. The Third Recension was most probably in use for the majority of the period under consideration and possibly, according to Janet Nelson, for the entire period.[50] George Garnett, however, has contested the assertion that the Third Recension was used for the inauguration of William the Conqueror.[51] Due to the uncertainty Garnett sows here, the Second Recension has also been considered. Garnett and the late John Brückmann, who also worked on the manuscripts of the Third Recension, agree that it survives in seven manuscripts, but they do not agree on the relationship between these manuscripts, six of which are from the twelfth century with one dating from the early fourteenth century. Neither of them have put forward a definitive reading of the *ordo*.[52] Brückmann divided the manuscripts into three groups, according to whether they contained what he termed 'early' or 'later' versions of the *ordines* for a king and a queen.[53] In addition to highlighting the different

---

[48] *Le pontifical romano-germanique du dixième siècle*, ed. C. Vogel and R. Elze, 3 vols. (Vatican City, 1963–72), III, 24.

[49] H. Parkes, 'Questioning the Authority of Vogel and Elze's *Pontifical romano-germanique*', in *Understanding Medieval Liturgy: Essays in Interpretation*, ed. S. Hamilton and H. Gittos (Farnham, 2016), pp. 75–101 (p. 81).

[50] Nelson, 'The Rites of the Conqueror'.

[51] Garnett, 'The Third Recension'.

[52] J. Brückmann, 'English Coronations, 1216–1308: The Edition of the Coronation *Ordines*' (unpublished PhD thesis, University of Toronto, 1964); J. Brückmann, 'The *Ordines* of the Third Recension of the Medieval English Coronation Order', in *Essays in Medieval History Presented to Bertie Wilkinson*, ed. T. A. Sandquist and M. R. Powicke (Toronto, 1969), pp. 99–115.

[53] Brückmann, 'The *Ordines* of the Third Recension', pp. 109–12. That is, one group contained the early *ordo* for a king and the later *ordo* for the queen, another group

modes of diffusion for the male and female *ordines*, such a division of the Third Recension manuscripts into 'early' or 'later' versions again raises questions about the extent to which we can precisely define *ordines* texts. That there are several surviving versions of the *ordo* reminds us that the subsequent grouping of liturgical texts into recensions does not imply complete conformity. However, as Shane Bobrycki has commented of early medieval liturgy, we should not be too nominalist about these texts, demanding that every version be seen as distinct.[54] The texts of the Third Recension certainly form a coherent group. The accessibility of the manuscript copies of the Third Recension has allowed a number of them to be consulted in the flesh.[55] Unfortunately a comprehensive examination of all the hundreds of manuscripts containing inauguration texts has been beyond the scope of this project.

For the *ordines* of the French kings and the German kings and emperors I have been reliant on published texts and online manuscript repositories. From Jackson's edition of the French *ordines* I have chosen to consult the Ratold *Ordo* (composed c.980 but, as has already been alluded to, frequently consulted in the twelfth century), and three further *ordines* identified by Jackson as composed in France in this period. These are the Royal *Ordo* in Cologne Dombibliothek, MS 141, the *Ordo* of Saint-Bertin and the *Ordo* of 1200. The *Ordo* of 1200 is the first of a series of French *ordines* for which the place of origin is certain. It was written at Reims, and one of the two surviving manuscripts remained in the coronation cathedral at Reims until the French Revolution.[56] The 'Frenchness' of the other two *ordines* is less clear: the Cologne manuscript contains a combination of texts from the PRG and the Ratold *Ordo*, while the *Ordo* of Saint-Bertin is a variant of the 'German' *ordo* contained within the PRG.[57] The impossibility of assigning a nationality to the Cologne *ordo* is once again suggestive of the shared liturgical traditions of these medieval kings. This text survives in only two manuscripts. The first, from which it takes its name, originated in the first half of the eleventh century. The second manuscript (now Bamberg Staatsbibliothek, MS Msc. Lit. 56) dates from the fourteenth century. The most likely place of origin for the text was in the diocese of Cambrai, but as Jackson has made clear, this does not make assigning it a nationality any easier:

---

the late *ordo* for a king and the early *ordo* for a queen and his final group the early *ordines* for a king and a queen.

[54] S. Bobrycki, 'The Royal Consecration *Ordines* of the Pontifical of Sens from a New Perspective', *Bulletin du centre d'études médiévales d'Auxerre* 13 (2009), 131–42 (p. 131).

[55] I have viewed the following manuscripts of the Third Recension: Cambridge, Trinity College. MS B. II. 10; Cambridge University Library, MS EE. II. 3; London, British Library, MS Cotton Claudius A. III; London, British Library, MS Cotton Tiberius B. VIII.

[56] *Ordines Coronationis Franciae*, ed. Jackson, I, 248.

[57] *Ordines Coronationis Franciae*, ed. Jackson, I, 201, 240.

Cambrai was under imperial control in the eleventh century, and its bishops were appointed by the emperor, so one could argue that the *ordo* was not composed in France and does not belong to the sequence of French *ordines*. On the other hand, is it not far more important that Cambrai was a suffragan of Reims and that the bishop of Cambrai and Arras from 1012–1051 was Gerard I, nephew of Adelbéron, archbishop of Reims, making direct influence from Reims very possible when the *ordo* was composed?[58]

The link between Cambrai and Reims at the time the manuscript was written added to the fact that the text was previously unedited prompted Jackson to include the *ordo* in his edition of French texts. In this study, which is not concerned with the development of national rites, the *ordo*'s statelessness is of little concern.

For evidence of the German tradition I have consulted the three recensions contained within the PRG edition of Vogel and Elze, in conjunction with texts presented by Erdmann and Waitz.[59] As discussed above, the PRG edition is not without its problems. It does, however, provide a representative edition of inauguration texts circling within the Empire in the high medieval period. In his edition of the imperial inauguration rite Elze presents eighteen texts originating before *c*.1250. From these texts I have selected five *ordines* that reflect the growing complexity of the imperial ceremony and the increasing influence of the pope. These are the imperial *ordo* in Cologne Dombibliothek, MS 141, the two *ordines* attributed to Cencius, later Pope Honorious III, the so-called Staufen *Ordo* and a final *ordo* originating in the papal curia at the beginning of the thirteenth century. That the Cologne manuscript contains both a royal and imperial rite, not to mention an inauguration rite for a queen, suggests a close relationship between royal and imperial texts.

Having selected the texts, a final issue remains: how to compare texts that differ in length and detail. For example, some *ordines* include the full texts of prayers, others only the incipits. The rubrication can be brief and cursory or lengthy and detailed. Some texts include musical elements and integrate the mass into the *ordo*. By contrast others provide no detail of the antiphons to be sung and make no allowance for a mass. Some male inauguration texts are associated in a manuscript with texts for the inauguration of a queen or empress, while a number of texts envisage the inauguration of king and queen, or emperor and empress, in the same text. The traditional way of presenting *ordines* for comparison in an abbreviated form neglects these divergences between different texts and is for this reason an unsatisfactory technique to use when comparing a dozen diverse texts. To overcome this issue a pragmatic approach has been adopted here, breaking the *ordines*

---

[58] *Ordines Coronationis Franciae*, ed. Jackson, I, 202.
[59] Erdmann, *Forschungen zur politischen Ideenwelt des Frühmittelalters*, pp. 83–91; Waitz, *Die Formeln*.

down into their constituent parts, thus enabling like aspects to be directly compared. The *ordines* analysed, and the editions of these texts that have been consulted, are summarized in Appendix 1.

The Spoken Word: Prayers and Promises

An examination of prayer formulae contained within the twelve selected *ordines* drives home the extent of their shared liturgical vocabulary. For example, although there are a total of 181 prayers contained within the selected *ordines* relating to male inauguration these are drawn from only fifty discrete prayer formulae. In other words, on average each prayer appears in around three or four different *ordines*. This picture is reinforced by considering the nine *ordines* that contain prayers associated with female inauguration. A total of thirteen distinct prayer formulae are used a total of forty-seven times, giving us a similar average of each prayer formula appearing in between three and four different *ordines*. Of course, such an overview disguises the fact that some prayers appear only once. Others appear again and again in both the royal and imperial *ordines*, some only in the royal *ordines*, and others only in the imperial *ordines*.

In order to analyse the prayer formulae in the twelve *ordines*, I have assigned each distinct formula an alphanumeric code. These numbers in no way assign precedence to prayer formulae in terms of the direction in which copying occurred but are purely a device to enable clearer analysis. In assigning numbers minor variants of the same prayer formula have been given the same number and more major variants different numbers.[60] Variations and adaptions from, for example, an Anglo-Saxon to Frankish or from a royal to imperial context, will be discussed separately. Male and female prayers have been numbered independently as have prayers signalled as being from the mass. This is due to the fact that not all the selected *ordines* contain female or mass elements and this would not be clear without making it explicit in the coding system.[61] Prayers for female inauguration need to be considered as more than just a subset of prayers used for male inauguration,

---

[60] Variations in spelling have been ignored as have changes in word order and other minor embellishments or elaborations of less than a sentence or two. Where significant new material has been introduced into a prayer this has been given a separate code. K22, for example, combines prayers K18 and K15 and includes a small amount of original material. In some *ordines* a number of the longer prayers have been divided into several shorter prayers with rubrics making this explicit. In order to avoid giving a misleading impression of novelty, I have not assigned these short prayers their own codes. In all cases of this phenomenon the entire text of the longer prayer is included in the *ordo*.

[61] The division of mass formulae from those for inauguration is not perfect due to inconsistent rubrication across the twelve *ordines*.

especially given the complex relationship between male and female inauguration. In this system, male prayers are distinguished with a K, female with a Q, and prayers from the mass with an M. The numbers assigned to distinct prayer formulae can be found in Appendix 2, which comprises an index of prayer incipits. The alphanumeric designations are then used to provide three tables. Tables 1 and 2 show the distribution of the prayers in the different *ordines* in the position in which they appear in the respective liturgies. The frequency with which individual prayers are used and whether they appear in royal or imperial liturgies is indicated in Table 3.

The prayer formulae that make up the *ordines* are full of such generalized phrases as 'in this kingdom' ('in hoc regno'), with no qualifying adjective making clear which realm is being referred to. Indeed the very incipits of the *ordines* exemplify this. The French *Ordo* of 1200, for example, begins, 'here begins the *ordo* for the benediction of the king, when he is newly elevated to the kingdom by the clergy and people'.[62] In agreement with the incipits of the remaining six royal *ordines* under consideration, our text provides no indication as to which kingdom the clergy and people belong. Some of the *ordines* do make reference to particular kingdoms, but these references are not always straightforward. The second English recension, for example, includes several references to its Anglo-Saxon context. In the prayer (K4), which precedes the anointing, reference is made to the 'kingdom of the English and Saxons' ('regnum Anglorum vel Saxonum') and to the throne and sceptre of the English and Saxons.[63] Later in the *ordo*, in prayer K17, there is a reference to 'Gregory, apostle of the English' ('Gregorius Anglorum apostolicus').[64] By contrast, references to the Anglo-Saxon kingdom and the apostle of the English do not appear in the third English recension, which instead only includes one geographical reference in a prayer (K15) asking that the king be honoured 'above all the kings of Britain' ('pre cunctis regibus Britannie').[65] The same prayer formula appears in the PRG devoid of any geographical qualifier as, 'honour him above all the kings of the peoples' ('honorifica eum pre cunctis regibus gentium').[66]

Perhaps surprisingly the references to an Anglo-Saxon kingdom were to have more influence on the development of inauguration liturgy on the continent than in England, demonstrating once again the extent of the shared liturgical model from which the *ordines* of all three realms sprang. This was a model that was not constrained by the boundaries of kingdoms. The prayers in which the references to the Anglo-Saxon kingdom and St Gregory are contained (K4 and K17) were assimilated into the Ratold *Ordo*, with the continental

---

[62] *Ordines Coronationis Franciae*, ed. Jackson, I, 250: 'incipit ordo ad benedicendum regem, quando novus a clero et populo sublimatur in regnum'.
[63] *English Coronation Records*, ed. L. G. W. Legg (London, 1901), p. 16.
[64] Ibid., p. 20.
[65] Ibid., p. 35.
[66] *Le pontifical romano-germanique*, ed. Vogel and Elze, I, 250.

Table 1 *Distribution of Prayers in the Royal Ordines*

English		German Royal	German/French	French		
Second	*Third*	*PRG*	*Cologne 141*	*Ratold*	*Saint-Bertin*	*Ordo of 1200*
K1	K4	K33	K33	K1	K33	K33
K2	K22	K34	K34	K2	K34	K34
K3	K23	K35	K35	K3	K35	K35
K4	K24	K22	K1	K4	K22	K22
K5	K25	K4	K2	K5	K23	K23
K6	K7	K23	K3	K6	K26	K24
K7	K26	K24	K4	K7	K38	K25
K8	K27	K25	K5	K8	K10	K36
K9	K28	K36	K6	K9	K31	K26
K10	K29	K26	K7	K10	K16	K4
K11	K30	K7	K31&K8	K11	K11	K7
K12	K12	K27	K9	K12	K39	K27
K13	K13	K31	K28	K13	K37	K31
K14	K31	K16	K11	K14	K32	K16
K15	K14	K37	K37	K15	K19	K37
K16	K15	K32	K13	K16		K32
K17	K16	K19	K14	K17	M6	K19
K18	K32		K15	K18	M7	
K19	K19	M6	K16	K19	M9	M6
K20		M7	K17	K20*		M7
K21	Q6	M8	K22	K21*		M8
	Q7	M9	K19			M9
Q1	Q8			M1		M11
Q2	Q1	Q6	M6	M2		M12
Q3	Q2	Q7	M7	M3*		M13
Q4	Q3	Q8	M10	M4*		
Q5	Q9	Q9	M9	M5*		Q6
	Q4					Q7
M1	Q10		Q6	Q11		Q8
M2	Q5		Q7	Q1		Q10
M3			Q8	Q2		Q12
M4			Q2	Q3		
M5			Q5	Q4		
			Q4	Q5		
			Q10			
* not in all MSS			Q1			

Table 2 *Distribution of Prayers in the Imperial Ordines*

Cologne 141	Cencius I	Cencius II	Staufen	Roman Curia
K40	K44	K44	K44	K44
K23	K23	K23	K23	K23
K26	K42	Q6	K45	K45
K41	K7	K42	K46	K48
K42	K43	K7	K42	K46
K43		Q7	K7	K42
M14		Q8	M14	K7
		K8	M15	M14
		K9	M16	M15
		K10	K43	M16
		K11	K47	K43
		K43	Q13	K25
		Q13		K49
		K14		K50
		K15		K27
		M14		K43
				Q6
				Q7
				Q8
				Q10

scribes copying the *ordo* responding to these references in a variety of ways. Of the twenty manuscripts consulted by Jackson, eleven contain a reference to the royal throne and sceptre of the 'Saxons, Mercians and Northumbrians' ('Saxonum, Merciorum Nordan Himbrorumque').[67] In one manuscript the sentence has been changed to read 'of the Franks' ('Francorum'), in two others to read 'of the Franks, Burgundians and Aquitanians' ('Francorum, Burgundiorum, Aquitanorum').[68] In the final three manuscripts presented by Jackson, no kingdoms are mentioned. In asking for the intercession and

---

[67] *Ordines Coronationis Franciae*, ed. Jackson, I, 181.
[68] *Ordines Coronationis Franciae*, ed. Jackson, I, 181. The reference to Franks, Burgundians and Aquitanians has been considered by Elizabeth Brown. E. A. R. Brown, '"Franks, Burgundians, and Aquitanians" and the Royal Coronation Ceremony in France', *Transactions of the American Philosophical Society* 82 (1992), 1–189.

Liturgical Texts: The Spoken Word and Song

Table 3 *Frequency of the Occurrence of Prayers in the Royal and Imperial Ordines*

Prayer	Royal	Imperial	Total	Prayer	Royal	Imperial	Total
K1	3	–	3	K41	–	1	1
K2	3	–	3	K42	–	4	4
K3	3	–	3	K43	–	5	5
K4	6	–	6	K44	–	3	3
K5	3	–	3	K45	–	2	2
K6	3	–	3	K46	–	2	2
K7	6	3	9	K47	–	1	1
K8	3	1	4	K48	–	1	1
K9	3	1	4	K49	–	1	1
K10	3	1	4	K50	–	1	1
K11	4	1	5	Q1	4	–	4
K12	3	–	3	Q2	4	–	4
K13	4	–	4	Q3	3	–	3
K14	4	1	5	Q4	4	–	4
K15	5	1	6	Q5	4	–	4
K16	7	–	7	Q6	4	2	6
K17	2	–	2	Q7	4	2	6
K18	2	–	2	Q8	4	2	6
K19	7	–	7	Q9	2	–	2
K20	2	–	2	Q10	3	1	4
K21	2	–	2	Q11	1	–	1
K22	5	–	5	Q12	1	–	1
K23	4	4	8	Q13	–	2	2
K24	3	–	3	M1	2	–	2
K25	3	1	4	M2	2	–	2
K26	4	1	5	M3	2	–	2
K27	3	1	4	M4	2	–	2
K28	2	–	2	M5	2	–	2
K29	1	–	1	M6	3	–	3
K30	1	–	1	M7	4	–	4
K31	5	–	5	M8	3	–	3
K32	4	–	4	M9	4	–	4
K33	4	–	4	M10	1	–	1
K34	4	–	4	M11	1	–	1
K35	4	–	4	M12	1	–	1
K36	2	–	2	M13	1	–	1
K37	4	–	4	M14	–	4	4
K38	1	–	1	M15	–	2	2
K39	1	–	1	M16	–	2	2
K40	–	1	1				

protection of the saints, Gregory has been transformed from the apostle of the English to the 'apostle of the Angels' ('Angelorum apostolicus').[69]

In the differing reactions of scribes and copyists one can perhaps detect an ambivalent attitude to these Anglo-Saxon references. One certainly gains the impression that 'national' allusions were not of particular importance in the *ordines*. Some scribes thought to make the reference relevant to a new context, but the majority did not. Janet Nelson has advanced a semiotic explanation for the presence of these references in French *ordines*, when they had no contemporary political relevance, stating that, 'long after the topical reference to Anglo-Saxon hegemonial rulership had been forgotten, the solemn copying out of these time-honoured words in French manuscripts signified the profound respect of the later middle ages for ritual tradition, precisely observed. The medium itself had become the message.'[70] That the medium had become the message does not, however, mean that the message had remained static. Moreover, that a scribe working in a monastic scriptorium copied a text exactly does not mean that the text was ever used in that precise form in practice. Not only was the text not binding on the archbishop overseeing an inauguration ceremony, but many of these manuscripts were unsuitable for use or consultation for an actual ceremony. This demonstrates once again the dangers of trying to use such liturgical texts to make specific historical points.

That some prayers are found in both royal and imperial *ordines* is indicative of the similarity in the conception of the office of king and that of emperor. The imperial *ordo* Cencius II provides a clear example of the relationship between royal and imperial anointing in its presentation of a prayer (K23) that appears in ten of the twelve selected *ordines* and that was already included in the earliest text identified by Jackson. The rubric tells us that the celebrant should say the prayer *Deus ineffabilis auctor mundi*, 'etc. just as in the unction of a king' ('et cetera sicut in unctione regis').[71] With this assertion it is made explicit that imperial and royal anointing are concomitant rituals. The correlation between royal and imperial unction is made clear by the presence of the prayer most closely associated with anointing, *Deus dei filius ihesus christus dominus noster qui a patre oleo exultationis unctus est* (K7), in six out of seven of the royal *ordines* and four out of five of the imperial *ordines*. A number of female *ordines*, such as that in the PRG, were intended for the inauguration of a queen or an empress, showing a similar flexibility in the use of the female *ordines*. Furthermore, the adaptation of oaths from the royal ceremony to the imperial ceremony provides additional evidence for the close relationship between royal and imperial ceremonies. The *Ordo* of Saint-Bertin, a royal *ordo*,

---

[69] *Ordines Coronationis Franciae*, ed. Jackson, I, 188.
[70] J. L. Nelson, 'Ritual and Reality in the Early Medieval *Ordines*', in *Politics and Ritual in Early Medieval Europe* (London, 1986), pp. 329–39 (p. 333).
[71] *Die Ordines*, ed. Elze, p. 40.

includes a promise, which is incorporated in slightly different forms in the imperial *ordines* Cencius I and Cencius II:

Saint-Bertin: 'I N. in the name of Christ promise, pledge and vow in the presence of God and St Peter the apostle, to be the protector and defender of this Roman Church in all useful things, in as much as I shall be supported by divine assistance, according to my understanding and ability'.[72]

Cencius I: 'In the name of Christ I, emperor N., promise, pledge and vow in the presence of God and St Peter, to be the protector and defender of this Roman Church in all useful things, in as much as I shall be supported by divine assistance, according to my understanding and ability'.[73]

Cencius II: 'In the name of our Lord Jesus Chris, I, king and future emperor of the Romans N., promise, pledge, vow and swear on these Gospels in the presence of God and St Peter the apostle in fidelity to you N. vicar of St Peter the apostle and to your canonically appointed successors, to be henceforth the protector and defender of this holy Roman Church and your person and of your successors in all useful things, in as much as I shall be supported by divine assistance, according to my understanding and ability, without deceit or evil trickery. Thus God and this holy Gospel help me'.[74]

Apart from the absence of the word 'apostolo' and some changes of word order, the promises in Cencius I and the Saint-Bertin *Ordo* are very similar. However, there is one important difference. The promise in Cencius I explicitly mentions the office of the promise maker: he is an *imperator*. This small discrepancy is again evidence of the ease with which the same inauguration prayers and promises could be used in both a royal and an imperial context with little need for alteration. Indeed, the difference between the promises in the two imperial *ordines* is much greater than between Saint-Bertin and

---

[72] *Ordines Coronationis Franciae*, ed. Jackson, I, 243: 'Ego N. in nomine Christi promitto, spondeo atque polliceor coram Deo et beato Petro apostolo, me protectorem ac defensorem esse huius Romanae ecclesiae in omnibus utilitatibus, in quantum divino fuero fultus adiutorio, secundum scire meum et posse'.

[73] *Die Ordines*, ed. Elze, p. 23: 'In nomine Christi promitto, spondeo atque polliceor ego N. imperator coram Deo et beato Petro, me protectorem atque defensorem esse huius sancte Romane ecclesie in omnibus utilitatibus, in quantum divino fultus fuero adiutorio, secundum scire meum ac posse'.

[74] Ibid., p. 37: 'In nomine domini nostri Iesu Christi. Ego N. rex et futurus imperator Romanorum promitto, spondeo, polliceor atque per hec evangelia iuro coram Deo et beato Petro apostolo tibi N. beati Petri apostoli vicario fidelitatem tuisque successoribus canonice intrantibus, meque amodo protectorem ac defensorem fore huius sancte Romane ecclesie et vestre persone vestrorumque successorum in omnibus utilitatibus, in quantum divino fultus fuero adiutorio, secundum scire meum ac posse, sine fraude et malo ingenio. Sic me Deus adiuvet et hec sancta evangelia'.

Cencius I. In Cencius II the promise has been significantly elaborated and in it the difference in office between king and emperor is stressed. The monarch being inaugurated makes the promise as 'king and future emperor of the Romans'. The reason for this emphasis on the difference between the offices is made clear by considering the other additions to the promise. The promise is no longer being made solely in the presence of God and St Peter, but to a named pope and his successors. Likewise it is not just the Church of Rome that will be protected and defended, but also the pope and his successors. The elaboration of the promise in this way points to the fact that whereas there is one leading man, the king, in royal inauguration, in the imperial inauguration there were two actors, the emperor and the pope, sharing the stage and competing for the limelight.

Promises feature in some form in all of the royal *ordines* under consideration. Although the PRG edition makes no mention of an oath, a number of PRG manuscripts from the eleventh and twelfth centuries do include one. The coronation oath has been intensively studied in an English context and understood as forming an integral part of early English law.[75] It has been closely linked to the English practice of issuing 'coronation' charters, with the 'Coronation Charter' of Henry I being seen as a specific application of the general three-fold oath clause found close to the beginning of both the second and third recensions of the English *ordines*.[76] By his oath the king-elect promised three things: firstly to protect the peace of the Church and the Christian people, secondly to prevent rapacity and iniquities and, finally, to ensure just and merciful judgments. When the king-elect had finished uttering the oath the congregation responded 'Amen'. In the Third Recension, the role of the congregation is further elaborated. They are asked by one of the bishops if they wish to submit themselves to such a prince and leader and to obey his commands. They respond 'we wish and submit'.[77] Oath and acclamation here belong together. This relationship between oath and acclamation in the English *ordines* suggests that we should look more closely at the process by which the oath was administered or scrutinized. In *ordines* lacking a traditional stand-alone oath, this process is often closely associated with the congregation giving their consent. The interrogation is perhaps best understood as a type of structured promise or oath in which the king-elect makes similar general promises to those found in the oaths of the English and German *ordines*. Indeed the

---

[75] See amongst others H. G. Richardson, 'The English Coronation Oath', *Transactions of the Royal Historical Society* 4th s. 23 (1941), 129–58; H. G. Richardson, 'The English Coronation Oath', *Speculum* 24 (1949), 44–75; P. Stafford, 'The Laws of Cnut and the History of Anglo-Saxon Royal Promises', *Anglo-Saxon England* 10 (1981), 173–90; *Die Gesetze der Angelsachsen*, ed. F. Liebermann, 3 vols. (Halle, 1903–16), I, 215–17.

[76] R. Foreville, 'Le sacre des rois anglo-normands et angevins et le serment du sacre (XI–XIIe siecles)', *Anglo-Norman Studies* I (1978), 49–63 (p. 57). See Chapter 5 for a consideration of charters associated with inauguration.

[77] *English Coronation Records*, ed. Legg, p. 31.

interrogation concludes with a short promise in five of the nine manuscripts consulted in the production of the PRG edition. In all nine manuscripts interrogation is immediately followed by the metropolitan asking those present whether they wish to accept such a prince as their ruler.

Unlike the English oath, which was taken close to the beginning of the ceremony, the oath found in manuscripts of the German *ordines* was spoken following the new king's enthronement and before the kiss of peace.[78] This occurs in the same position in the ceremony as the oath envisaged in eighteen manuscripts containing the Ratold *Ordo* and in the *Ordo* of 1200.[79] This placement of the oath is important. In the English tradition the oath was sworn before the king was made and is associated with his acceptance as king by the congregation, whereas in the German tradition, once an oath was added to the liturgy in the late eleventh or early twelfth century, it was sworn after the king's position had already been formalized. In this respect, the German oath could perhaps be seen as the royal equivalent of the practice envisaged in the three detailed imperial *ordines*, of swearing an oath to the Romans (*sacramentum / iuramentum Romanis*) on Monte Mario following the completion of the ceremony and its ensuing festivities.[80] As in the later imperial *ordines*, this concluding oath does not replace interrogation or an oath earlier in the ceremony. In the imperial tradition this oath is in addition to an oath sworn to the pope near the beginning of the ceremony. When an oath appears in the PRG tradition it does not replace the customary interrogation earlier in the ceremony.[81] The similarity in the function of interrogation and oath-swearing in the *ordines* cautions against any attempt precisely to define different spoken elements in liturgical texts or to assign enhanced legal significance to particular elements.

The musicologist Nancy van Deusen has described the Book of Psalms as a stockpile of phrases used as building blocks in the construction of hymns and chants.[82] This metaphor can be expanded to designate the contents of the books of the Old Testament as building material for the fabrication of prayer

---

[78] See Andreas Büttner for details of manuscripts containing the oath and a summary of previous German scholarship on the topic. Büttner, *Der Weg zur Krone*, I, 108–11.

[79] The oath found in the Ratold *Ordo* is, with the exception of small textual variations, identical to that found in the English tradition. The text of the German oath is, on the contrary, completely independent from the English oath.

[80] *Die Ordines*, ed. Elze, pp. 47, 69, 87.

[81] This is the case in, for example, Cologne Dombibliothek, MS 139, in which the interrogation appears on fol. 23v and the king swears an oath before the altar on fol. 37v. Both interrogation and oath were incorporated into the early fourteenth century Aachen *Ordo*. This *ordo* is reproduced in *Constitutiones Regum Germaniae*, ed. G. H. Pertz, *MGH LL* 2 (Hannover, 1837), pp. 384–93. On the dating see Büttner, *Der Weg zur Krone*, I, 126–42.

[82] N. van Deusen, 'Laudes Regiae: In Praise of Kings, Medieval Acclamations, Liturgy and the Ritualization of Power', in *Procession, Performance, Liturgy and Ritual*, ed. N. van Deusen (Ottawa, 2007), pp. 83–118 (p. 84).

formulae. The *ordines* are rich in biblical references, and these references are not confined to biblical precedents for the anointing of kings. Indeed, only prayer formula K24, found in the English Third Recension, the PRG and the *Ordo* of 1200, draws a parallel between the anointing of the hands of the monarch with Samuel's anointing of David as king.[83] The remaining seven *ordines* include references to David, but not explicitly to his anointing.[84] Given that Old Testament anointing has often been cited as the origin of the medieval practice of inaugural anointing, it is remarkable that the majority of the *ordines* considered here make no reference to it in their prayer formulae.[85] However, the Old Testament provides more than a narrow Davidic model for the monarch. Although he is the figure most frequently referred to, David appears in conjunction with his son Solomon and earlier leaders of the Israelite people, including most often Abraham, Moses and Joshua. Nelson commented of the anointing of Pippin in 751 that, 'it was not a precise situational model, but a more general one that the Frankish clergy found in the Old Testament. The typological link existed not only between Carolingian and Davidic kingship and between reformed Frankish and Levite priesthood, but between the whole Frankish *gens* and the people of Israel.'[86] To take Nelson's point further, if we identify the *populus* of the *ordines* with the Israelite people, we can then understand the biblical allusions, not only to the kings David and Solomon, but also to other non-royal Israelite rulers.[87]

These leaders are presented in succession, implying that the monarch is not just a new David, but has inherited a tradition of rulership. The way in which the leaders are often presented in a list is reminiscent of an Old Testament genealogy, emphasizing the idea that a broad typological link

---

[83] 'Unguantur manus iste de oleo sanctificato unde uncti fuerunt reges et prophete sicut Samuel David in regem.' This wording is taken from the English Third Recension. *English Coronation Records*, ed. Legg, p. 32.

[84] An antiphon in several of the *ordines* recalls Zadok and Nathan anointing Solomon. See below p. 55.

[85] One prayer form (K41) in the earliest imperial *ordo* considered here, alludes to biblical anointing and then only in a general context, not specifically linked to David: 'unde unxisti sacerdotes reges et prophetas'. *Die Ordines*, ed. Elze, p. 22.

[86] J. L. Nelson, 'Inauguration Rituals', in her *Politics and Ritual in Early Medieval Europe* (London, 1986), pp. 283–307 (p. 291).

[87] C. M. Kauffmann argues that identifying with the Israelites was a peculiar trait of the Anglo-Saxons and that the Carolingians confined their Old Testament allusions to their kings. As Mary Garrison's article makes clear, however, identifying with the Israelites was also a trait of the Carolingians. Moreover, as George Molyneaux has recently argued, claims that the Anglo-Saxons saw themselves as God's elect above other peoples owes more to post-Reformation attitudes than evidence from the Anglo-Saxon period. Rather than national particularism, identification with Israel was associated with all Christian people. C. M. Kauffmann, *Biblical Imagery in Medieval England 750–1550* (London, 2003), p. 36; Garrison, 'The Franks as the New Israel?', p. 120; G. Molyneaux, 'Did the English Really Think They Were God's Elect in the Anglo-Saxon Period?', *Journal of Ecclesiastical History* 65 (2014), 721–37.

Liturgical Texts: The Spoken Word and Song

is being made. In the 1970s, David Dumville highlighted the importance of genealogies in the construction of kingship.[88] More recently, C. M. Kauffmann has pointed to the genealogy of King Æthelwulf, who traced his ancestry via Woden to the patriarchs of Genesis.[89] The use of such genealogical devices, which in the Bible extend into the New Testament as well, in the form of the *Liber generationis*, the opening of Matthew's Gospel in which Christ is described as a son of David and of Abraham (Matthew 1. 1), is indicative of the desire to place the monarch in the narrative of biblical and salvation history.[90] The most common combination of Old Testament figures in the *ordines* is that of Abraham, Moses, Joshua, David and Solomon, sometimes augmented with Gideon and Samuel, which appears in prayer formulae K4 and K23. Prayer formula K4 makes clear the composite model provided by these Israelite leaders, asking that God bless the king and, linking five qualities desired in a king to the five different Old Testament figures referenced:

> Provide, we beseech you with our humble prayers, and always multiply the gifts of your blessings and the power of your right hand upon this servant of yours, whom in suppliant devotion we choose as king and, strengthened by the faithfulness of aforementioned Abraham, trusting with the gentleness of Moses, fortified with the courage of Joshua, exalted by the humility of David, and adorned with the wisdom of Solomon, let him be pleasing to you.[91]

Both Philippe Buc and Markus Saur have highlighted the fact that the Old Testament includes many anti-monarchical themes.[92] In presenting the monarch not solely as a successor to biblical kings, but also to the non-royal leaders of Israel, such as Abraham or Moses, the idea of kingship as a negative institution is glossed over in the *ordines*. This is made more explicit in the references to Gideon, in the English Third Recension, the PRG, the *Ordo* of 1200 and all the imperial *ordines*. When he was offered the kingship, Gideon declined (Judges 8. 22–3).

---

[88] D. N. Dumville, 'Kingship, Genealogies and Regnal Lists', in *Early Medieval Kingship*, ed. P. H. Sawyer and I. Wood (Leeds, 1977), pp. 72–104.
[89] Kauffmann, *Biblical Imagery*, p. 36.
[90] The *Liber generationis* was the Gospel reading on the Feast of the Nativity of Mary. See below p. 145.
[91] This wording is from the English Third Recension. *English Coronation Records*, ed. Legg, p. 31: 'Respice quesumus ad preces humilitatis nostre et super hunc famulum tuum quem supplici devotione in regem eligimus benedictionum tuarum dona multiplica eumque dextere tue potentia semper et ubique circunda quatinus predicti Abrahe fidelitate firmatus Moysi mansuetudine fretus Iosue fortitudine munitus Dauid humilitate exaltus Salomonis sapientia decoratus'.
[92] P. Buc, *L'ambïguité du livre* (Paris, 1994), p. 28; M. Saur, 'Königserhebung im antiken Israel', in *Investitur- und Krönungsrituale: Herrschaftseinsetzungen im kulturellen Vergleich*, ed. M. Steinicke and S. Weinfurter (Cologne, 2005), pp. 29–42 (p. 29).

One biblical king not mentioned in the *ordines* is Saul. His omission is highly significant. Although Samuel's anointing of David is invoked in the prayer associated with anointing the monarch's hands, David was not the first king to receive unction from Samuel. This distinction belonged to Saul. I Samuel 8 recounts how Samuel's sons, Joel and Abijah, were incapable of providing military leadership against the Philistines, leading the Israelites to demand that instead a king rule over them. This request angered the Lord, who saw it as a rejection of his kingship and he told Samuel to warn the Israelites about the rights of the king who would reign over them. Samuel repeated the Lord's warning to the people, making clear that the king would be a tyrant and would exploit them. The Israelites refused to listen to Samuel and continued to demand a king. Shortly thereafter Samuel anointed Saul as king by taking a phial of oil and pouring it over Saul's head (I Samuel 10. 1).[93] Saul's reign was not a great success. He quarrelled with Samuel, disobeyed the Lord's orders and was eventually rejected by the Lord (I Samuel 15. 23), who sent Samuel to anoint David as Saul's successor (I Samuel 16. 1–14). Saul's elevation to the kingship is depicted as the introduction of tyranny. It is therefore unsurprising there is no reference to it in the *ordines*.

Other figures who are presented together in several of the *ordines* are the patriarchs Abraham, Isaac and Jacob. They appear as a group in the prayer *Prospice omnipotens deus* (K25). Julie Ann Smith has analysed this prayer to demonstrate that the biblical language used here stresses the fertility of the king in a way that mirrors the language used in the Judith *Ordo*.[94] She points out that the invocation 'may the Lord give him dew from heaven and richness from earth and an abundance of grain, wine and oil' is taken from Isaac's blessing upon Jacob in Genesis 27. 28–9.[95] The appearance of this trio of patriarchs creates a chain in which the monarch is implicitly a link, and to which his offspring will also belong. The dynastic element in this reference to the patriarchs is made more explicit in the prayer *Deus ineffabilis auctor mundi* (K23), which appears in slightly variant forms in nine of the twelve selected *ordines*. In it God is described as having 'chosen a king to profit the world from the loins (*ex utero*) of your faithful friend our patriarch Abraham'.[96] This reference to the womb or belly of Abraham reinforces Smith's point that 'the blessings of abundance and richness which are called down upon the new queen are no different from those requested for kings or for the Old Testament exemplars'.[97]

---

[93] The account of Saul's elevation to the kingship is contradictory, with three different versions included in the Old Testament. See Saur, 'Königserhebung im antiken Israel', pp. 31–2.

[94] Smith, 'The Earliest Queen-Making Rites', p. 26.

[95] Ibid., p. 26.

[96] This wording is taken from the English Third Recension. *English Coronation Records*, ed. Legg, p. 32: 'ex utero fidelis amici tui patriarche nostri Habrahe preelegisti regem seculis profuturum'.

[97] Smith, 'The Earliest Queen-Making Rites', p. 27.

Liturgical Texts: The Spoken Word and Song

An examination of the Old Testament figures invoked in the female inauguration *ordines* makes clear that the blessings for men and women are not only basically the same, but are actually two complementary blessings that make reference to each other: they are two sides of the same coin. In the prayer *Omnipotens sempiterne deus fons et origo totius bonitatis* (Q6), which appears in six of the nine female inauguration *ordines*, reference is made to the wives of the three patriarchs: 'and that she be one with Sarah and Rebecca, Leah and Rachel and happy and fortunate women and she might merit to rejoice and multiply in the fruit of her womb'.[98] Leah, Jacob's first wife, is not included in the prayer in the English Third Recension and neither Leah nor Rachel are found in the Ratold *ordo*, which does not include the prayer itself. Broadly speaking, these biblical exemplars for a queen or empress are good wives. As Brigette Kasten has highlighted, although the church fathers provided a number of possible allegorical interpretations for these Old Testament women, the themes of marriage and motherhood were what they were most strongly associated with in the Carolingian *ordines*.[99] In her examination of the earliest queen-making rites, Smith stresses the strong nuptial overtones in the Ermentrude *Ordo* (of 866), but asserts in a footnote that 'the bridal element of the Hincmar rites did not persist in the later queen-making *ordines*'.[100] The continued reference to Sarah, Rebecca, Leah and Rachel in the later *ordines* undermines this assertion and the strong typological link between marriage and female inauguration will be discussed in the following chapter.

Two further biblical figures feature in the prayer formulae of the female *ordines*: Judith and Esther.[101] Smith has discussed their appearance, pointing to the appropriateness of the biblical Judith appearing in the *ordo* composed for the Frankish Judith. But she inexplicably asserts that the Judith *Ordo* 'is the only queen-making *ordo* known which makes reference to this Old Testament queen. The biblical Judith is never again invoked as a model for queenly behaviour.'[102] This is incorrect; Judith continues to appear in the female inauguration *ordines*, in fact in all of the seven female *ordines* that

---

[98] This wording is taken from the *ordo* in Cologne MS 141. *Ordines Coronationis Franciae*, ed. Jackson, I: 214: 'et una cum Sara atque Rebecca, Lia et Rachel beatis reverendisque feminis fructu uteri sui fecundari seu gratulari mereatur'.

[99] B. Kasten, 'Krönungsordnungen für und Papstbriefe an mächtige Frauen im Hochmittelalter', in *Mächtige Frauen? Königinnen und Fürsten im europäischen Mittelalter (11.–14. Jahrhundert)*, ed. C. Zey, Vorträge und Forschungen 81 (Ostfildern, 2015), pp. 249–306 (pp. 256–60).

[100] Smith, 'The Earliest Queen-Making Rites', p. 34, n. 78.

[101] Judith and Esther were already seen as suitable models for queenship before they appear in the Judith *Ordo*. In the 830s Hrabanus Maurus presented biblical commentaries on the two women to the Empress Judith, second wife of Louis the Pious. See M. B. de Jong, 'Exegesis for an Empress', in *Medieval Transformations: Texts, Power, and Gifts in Context*, ed. E. Cohen and M. B. de Jong (Leiden, 2001), pp. 69–100.

[102] Smith, 'The Earliest Queen-Making Rites', p. 26.

make biblical allusions. Judith's beheading of the Assyrian king Holofernes (Judith 13. 8–10), and the subsequent victory of the Israelites over their former oppressors could perhaps be seen as a female counterpart to David's defeat of Goliath (I Samuel 17. 49–51) and thus Israel's defeat of the Philistines. Smith is also mistaken in describing Judith as a biblical queen. She is not designated as royal in the Old Testament. Perhaps her inclusion really did rest on the name of the queen, Judith, for whom the original *ordo* was composed.[103] Esther, in contrast, was a *bona fide* queen who, having found favour with King Assuerus, had the royal diadem placed on her head (Esther 2. 17). The importance of Esther as a biblical role-model lies in her intercession with King Assuerus to save the Israelite people.[104] As John Carmi Parsons, amongst others, has demonstrated, intercession with the king was an important queenly role, and one that enabled queens to exercise a degree of power.[105] Like Judith, Esther continued to be invoked as a model for queenly behaviour, and not solely in the inauguration *ordines*. As Lois Huneycutt has highlighted, Aelred of Rievaulx described Henry I's wife, Matilda of Scotland, as 'another Esther in our time'.[106] Moreover, correspondence between the queen and Anselm of Canterbury suggests that Matilda herself was aware of the biblical exemplar named in the inauguration *ordines*. Huneycutt comments that 'her threat to throw off her royal robes and tread them underfoot closely parallels the language of Queen Esther's contempt for her own royal robes'.[107]

The Sung Word: Antiphons, Responsories, Litanies and Laudes

The *ordines* provide a one-dimensional view of the musical content of inauguration ceremonies. Indeed the two earlier imperial *ordines* make no allowance for chanting or the singing of antiphons or responsories within the liturgy. The

---

[103] This echoes de Jong's observation that, although Hrabanus Maurus re-dedicated his commentary on Esther to Emperor Lothar's wife Irmingard, following a friendly meeting in 841, his commentary on Judith was not included in his homage to Irmingard: de Jong, 'Exegesis for an Empress', p. 73.

[104] On the use of Esther as a role-model for queenly behaviour in the high Middle Ages, with a focus on England, see L. L. Huneycutt, 'Intercession and the High Medieval Queen: The Esther Topos', in *Power of the Weak: Studies on Medieval Women*, ed. J. Carpenter and S.-B. MacLean (Champaign, IL, 1995), pp. 126–46.

[105] J. C. Parsons, 'The Queen's Intercession in Thirteenth-Century England', in *Power of the Weak: Studies on Medieval Women*, ed. J. Carpenter and S.-B. MacLean (Champaign, IL, 1995), pp. 147–77; J. C. Parsons, 'The Intercessionary Patronage of Margaret and Isabella of France', *Thirteenth Century England* VI (1997), 145–56; For the early medieval Empire see S. Gilsdorf, *The Favor of Friends: Intercession and Aristocratic Politics in Carolingian and Ottonian Europe* (Leiden, 2014), pp. 114–24.

[106] L. L. Huneycutt, *Matilda of Scotland: A Study in Medieval Queenship* (Woodbridge, 2003), p. 6.

[107] Ibid., p. 83.

ordines in which musical information is included contain only brief incipits. Other types of manuscripts, including antiphonaries and graduals, would have been consulted to provide the music and a full text of the antiphons, hymns and chants. This point is important, because it drives home the extent to which an *ordo* as contained within a pontifical does not present the entire ceremony. The musical information contained within the *ordines* can be divided into three groups. The first includes normal elements of the mass, such as the *graduale*, which denotes the chant or hymn used in the liturgical celebration of the Eucharist, and the *Kyrie Eleison*, also a regular component of the mass. These elements are mainly found in the later imperial *ordines*, and their presence here is surely a product of the fact that these *ordines* are significantly more elaborate and specific. Because they are generic to the mass and not specific to the inauguration ceremony, and because not all the *ordines* are integrated into a mass text, they will not be considered here. The second group comprises the specific antiphons, chants and hymns, where they are designated by their incipits, rather than generically as, for example, an antiphon or an introit. The final group is composed of two genres that have long been recognized to be closely linked: litanies and *laudes*.[108] In a discussion of the *laudes*, Nancy van Deusen declares 'music, using time and motion as its material makes leadership and rulership plain. Music makes abstractions ... concrete and substantial.'[109] The analysis offered here is confined to the textual fabric of the liturgy, but, as van Deusen's assertion makes clear, the text does not tell the whole story.

Of the ten incipits that appear in the selected *ordines*, only one incipit is found in both royal and imperial liturgies. This is the incipit *ecce mitto angelum meum*, which is found in four of the royal *ordines* and all three of the later imperial *ordines*.[110] Kantorowicz thought this referred to a verse from Malachi, and indeed Malachi 3. 1, 'behold I send my angel, and he shall prepare the way before my face', was used as an antiphon, most frequently for the Wednesday of the second week of Advent, a not particularly significant liturgical day.[111] If one only consulted the imperial *ordines*, Kantorowicz's assertion would be tenable. However, the PRG *ordo* makes explicit that we are dealing with a *responsorium* and this text provides the *versu: Israel si me audieris*.[112] The incipit

---

[108] E. H. Kantorowicz, 'Ivories and Litanies', *Journal of the Warburg and Courtauld Institutes* 5 (1942), 56–81 (p. 61). For an introduction to the form, origins, insular and continental diffusion of litanies and their subsequent influence on other liturgical forms, such as the *laudes* see M. Lapidge, *Anglo-Saxon Litanies of the Saints*, HBS 106 (Woodbridge, 1991), pp. 1–61.

[109] van Deusen, '*Laudes Regiae*: In Praise of Kings', p. 116.

[110] It appears in the PRG, Royal *Ordo* in Cologne MS 141, Saint-Bertin *Ordo*, *Ordo* of 1200, Cencius II, Staufen *Ordo*, and the *Ordo* from the Roman Curia.

[111] Kantorowicz, *Laudes Regiae*, p. 75; CANTUS: A database for Latin Ecclesiastical Chant: <http://cantusdatabase.org/node/375840> [accessed 18 October 2016]: 'ecce mitto angelum meum qui praeparabit viam tuam ante faciem tuam'.

[112] *Le pontifical romano-germanique*, ed. Vogel and Elze, I, 247.

most probably thus refers to the following responsory: 'behold I will send my angel, who shall go before you and always protect you. Take notice of me and hear my voice and I will be an enemy to your enemies and will afflict them that afflict you and my angel will precede you.'[113] This comes not from Malachi but is adapted from Exodus 23. 20–3, and the link to Exodus is confirmed by the responsory verse, which also reflects the language of Exodus 23. 22. This responsory alludes to the observation of Old Testament law and, strengthened by the mention to Israel, reflects the biblical references of the prayer formulae, which were not confined to references to biblical kings, but which numbered patriarchs amongst their list of role models. It could be argued that the incipit *ecce mitto angelum meum* in the imperial *ordines* could refer to the antiphon, based on Malachi 3. 1, and that the same incipit in the royal *ordines* to the responsory based on Exodus 23. 20–3. However, the identical position of the incipit in the royal and imperial *ordines* counsels against this interpretation. More significantly, far from being associated with an ordinary liturgical day, the responsory based on Exodus 23. 20–2 was sung on the Fourth Sunday of Lent, otherwise known as Laetare Sunday.[114] This important feast, with its triumphal introit, was far better suited to providing musical elaboration to the inauguration *ordines*.[115]

Importantly the phrase *ecce mitto angelum meum* also appears in several places in the New Testament.[116] In the synoptic Gospels this scriptural phrase is seen as foretelling the appearance of John the Baptist, himself the herald of Christ's advent. Mark's Gospel opens with a conflation of scriptural references (Exodus 23. 20; Malachi 3. 1 and Isaiah 40. 3), which Mark attributes to Isaiah and interprets as prophesizing the coming of John the Baptist (Mark 1. 1–3). John then proclaims that a man greater than he shall come and that this man will baptize with the Holy Spirit rather than with water (Mark 1. 7–8). Jesus's baptism by John follows this proclamation (Mark 1. 9–11). In Matthew and in Luke the allusion to an angel preparing the way is found not in the description of Christ's baptism in the River Jordan, instead this scriptural reference is deployed by Christ himself to describe the Baptist to the messengers John had sent to him asking if he was the awaited Messiah (Matthew 11. 10; Luke 7. 27). In both royal and imperial liturgies the singing of *ecce mitto angelum meum* is prescribed right at the beginning of the inauguration. In the case of the royal rite it takes place as the king-elect processes,

---

[113] CANTUS: <http://cantusdatabase.org/node/381260> [accessed 18 October 2016]: 'ecce mitto angelum meum qui praecedat te et custodiat semper observa et audi vocem meam et inimicus ero inimicis tuis et affligentes te affligam et praecedet te angelus meus'.

[114] Ibid.

[115] The importance of *Laetare* Sunday is discussed in Chapter 4.

[116] On the relationship between the Old and New Testaments see H. de Lubac, *Medieval Exegesis: Volume I, The Four Senses of Scripture*, trans. M. Sebanc (Grand Rapids, 1998), pp. 225–67.

surrounded by clerics, to the doorway of the church, at which he is received by the officiating archbishop. In the imperial rite it is also sung as part of the initial procession. As in the New Testament, in the liturgy this scriptural reference prefigures the coming of the Lord's anointed, on whom the Holy Spirit will descend as part of his consecration.[117]

The royal and later imperial *ordines* have no other musical incipits in common, reflecting, perhaps, papal influence on the composition of the later imperial liturgies. One incipit, in particular, reinforces the idea of the specificity of the imperial *ordines*. All three of the detailed imperial *ordines* include the incipit *Petre amas me*.[118] This phrase refers to John 21. 15 and to Jesus giving St Peter charge over his flock and probably refers to either the antiphon or responsory 'Peter love me, feed my lambs, you know O Lord that I love you', which were sung on a number of Petrine feasts.[119] The attraction to the papacy of including a reference to Peter's supremacy over the church, and by extension to the supremacy of his successors as bishops of Rome, is transparent. It is equally apparent that such an allusion would find no place in the royal rite. *Petre amas me* emphasizes the role of the pope in the inauguration of the emperor. Again we discern that, in contrast to the royal liturgy, the imperial liturgy is a script with two main actors, and the message in the inclusion of this reference to Petrine superiority is obvious: the pope is the lead actor, with the emperor playing only a secondary role.

In the investigation of prayer formulae it was noted that only three of the royal *ordines* referred to the anointing of David, a fact that seems remarkable given the obviousness of this Old Testament model for royal inauguration. When we also consider the musical elements of the *ordines*, however, further references to Old Testament royal anointing come to light. Three of the royal *ordines* – the second English recension, the Royal *Ordo* in Cologne MS 141 and the Ratold *Ordo* – include the antiphon based on I Kings 1. 45: 'Zadok the priest and Nathan the prophet anointed Solomon as king in Gihon and the happy ones approaching said the king lives in eternity'![120] This means that when sung elements are examined in addition to spoken words, six out of seven of the royal

---

[117] The model of John baptizing Christ was central to Byzantine inauguration practices. I. Ševčenko, 'Ernst H. Kantorowicz (1895–1963) on Late Antiquity and Byzantium', in *Ernst Kantorowicz: Erträge der Doppeltagung Institute for Advanced Study, Princeton/ Johann Wolfgang Goethe-Universität, Frankfurt*, ed. R. L. Benson and J. Fried, Frankfurter Historische Abhandlungen 39 (Stuttgart, 1997), pp. 274–87 (pp. 286–7).
[118] *Die Ordines*, ed. Elze, pp. 38, 63, 73.
[119] Antiphon: CANTUS: <http://cantusdatabase.org/node/377717> [accessed 18 October 2016]: 'Petre amas me, pasce oves meas, tu scis domine quia amo te'; Responsory: CANTUS: <http://cantusdatabase.org/node/384337> [accessed 18 October 2016]: 'Petre amas me tu scis domine quia amo te pasce oves meas'.
[120] *English Coronation Records*, ed. Legg, p. 17; *Ordines Coronationis Franciae*, ed. Jackson, I, 183, 207: 'unxerunt Salomonem Sadoch sacerdos et Nathan propheta regem in Gion et accedentes laeti dixerunt vivat rex in aeternum alleluia'.

ordines do actually make reference to Old Testament anointing. It is important that the inaugurations of both David and Solomon serve as models, because it is again clear that the *ordines* do not just contain a narrow Davidic paradigm, but a composite one. Moreover, Philippe Buc has discussed the transmission of the throne from David to Solomon, describing it as the good succession *par excellence* due to the fact that David both organized the ceremonial and arranged the participants.[121] David's participation could be used to argue that a reigning king himself could choose his successor.[122] Such an interpretation might be attractive to kings seeking to champion the hereditary nature of their power at the expense of any elective elements, as in the twelfth-century Empire. Thus, while the role of the priest Zadok and prophet Nathan are emphasized in this antiphon, it should not be understood as a straightforward acknowledgement of priestly superiority in the inauguration ceremony.

The *Te deum*, which was sung on major feast days such as Easter, Pentecost and Ascension, features in all seven of the royal *ordines* under consideration, but does not appear in any of the imperial liturgies.[123] The incipit *domine salvum fac regem*, which appears in four royal *ordines*, appears to be a straightforward use of a phrase found in Psalm 19. 9 and is clearly appropriate in the context of a royal inauguration.[124] The same phrase is found in one imperial *ordo*, the Staufen *Ordo*, where it appears as part of a spoken prayer (K45) rather than a sung anthem.[125] Elizabeth Danbury has studied this phrase in the context of its later use as a royal motto under Henry VI of England and his successors.[126] Following its translation into the vernacular, the phrase 'God save the king' became the best known of all English language royal acclamations and was eventually incorporated into the national anthem that is still in use today. Although it does not appear in any of the English *ordines* under consideration here, Danbury pointed to its inclusion in other European *ordines* and in English church liturgy. The phrase is incorporated into several services in the Use of Sarum. It can be found in the weekday mass (except between Easter and the first Sunday of Trinity), in some daily offices and on several ceremonial occasions.[127] A manuscript from Cambrai, written between *c*.1230–*c*.1250, includes an antiphon with a very similar incipit: 'Lord save the kingdom and king, you

---

[121] Buc, *L'ambïguité du livre*, p. 330.

[122] Ibid., p. 331.

[123] Kantorowicz has suggested that the *laudes* began to be sung as part of the inauguration ceremony due to inaugurations taking place on the days they were already customarily sung. The same reasoning could be applied to the singing of the *Te Deum*. Kantorowicz, *Laudes Regiae*, p. 83.

[124] The *ordines* in question are those found in the PRG, Cologne MS 141, the *Ordo* of Saint-Bertin and the *Ordo* of 1200.

[125] *Die Ordines*, ed. Elze, p. 64.

[126] E. Danbury, '"Domine Salvum Fac Regem": The Origin of "God Save the King" in the Reign of Henry VI', *The Fifteenth Century* X (2011), 121–42.

[127] Ibid., pp. 132–3.

Liturgical Texts: The Spoken Word and Song

who gather your flock to the joy of the crown.'[128] This antiphon, which appears on fol. 429r of Cambrai, Bibliothèque municipale, MS 38, is to be sung on the feast of the Crown of Thorns, newly established in France following Louis IX's purchase of the crown for a staggering 135,000 *livres* in 1239.[129] If these incipits are indeed related, it suggests that the liturgy for the Crown of Thorns could have been influenced by the inauguration ceremony, and that hearing this antiphon on the feast of the Crown of Thorns would perhaps have reminded listeners of the royal inauguration.[130] Having the Crown of Thorns placed on his head at the dedication of the Sainte-Chapelle was just one of a number of ways in which Louis utilized this Christological relic to enhance his kingship. As Meredith Cohen has argued, the chapel itself was designed to 'publicly broadcast the notion of sacral kingship' and this idea was reinforced by a liturgical programme that extended well beyond the chapel walls.[131]

The remaining five incipits each appear in no more than two *ordines*, suggesting, perhaps, that when it came to musical elements the *ordines* exhibited a degree of independence from one another.[132] The antiphons *firmetur manus tua*, based on Psalm 88. 14–15 and *confortare et esto vir*, based on I Kings 2. 2–3, have an English origin. The second appears only once in a continental *ordo*, in the so-called Ratold *Ordo*. It does not appear in the other texts for royal inauguration in France or the Empire. With the exception of the English Second Recension and the Ratold *Ordo*, the remaining royal *ordines* envisage the singing of a litany near the beginning of the ceremony while the king lay prostrate before the altar. In the English Second Recension and Ratold *Ordo* the *Te deum* was sung at this juncture. The royal *ordo* in Cologne MS 141 and the English Third Recension give no details as to the content of the litany, whereas the PRG and *Ordo* of Saint-Bertin relate that the litany should include the twelve apostles and the same number of martyrs, confessors and virgins.[133]

---

[128] CANTUS: A database for Latin Ecclesiastical Chant: <http://cantusdatabase.org/node/125307> [accessed 9 August 2013]: '<u>salvum fac</u> o <u>domine</u> regnum atque <u>regem</u> qui coronae gaudio tuum ditas gregem'.

[129] See E. Guerry, *Crowning Paris: King Louis IX, Archbishop Cornut, and the Translation of the Crown of Thorns*, Transactions of the American Philosophical Society (Philadelphia, forthcoming).

[130] On the liturgy for this feast see J. Blezzard, S. Ryle and J. Alexander, 'New Perspectives on the Feast of the Crown of Thorns', *Journal of the Plainsong and Mediaeval Music Society* 10 (1987), 23–47 (pp. 32–8); Cohen, *The Sainte-Chapelle and the Construction of Sacral Monarchy*, pp. 167–9.

[131] Cohen, *The Sainte-Chapelle*, pp. 4, 12.

[132] It is likely that, where not specified, antiphons and other musical elements were adopted from the liturgy for the day on which an inauguration occurred. A useful primer on the structure of the liturgical offices, using the example of Saint Louis of France, is provided in Gaposchkin, *The Making of Saint Louis*, pp. 93–7.

[133] *Ordines Coronationis Franciae*, ed. Jackson, I, 242: 'ceteris in choro letaniam breviter psallentibus, id est XII apostolos ac totidem martyres, confessores et virgines'; *Le pontifical romano-germanique*, ed. Vogel and Elze, I, 248.

The *Ordo* of 1200 stands alone in providing the full text of the litany to be sung at this point. It begins by beseeching Christ to hear, before invoking Mary and the three archangels, Michael, Gabriel and Raphael. It then continues to mention individually the twelve apostles, then twelve martyrs, twelve confessors and twelve virgins.[134] In other words, in its detail it conforms to the pattern outlined in the PRG and *Ordo* of Saint-Bertin. This is not, however, to suggest that the litany transmitted in the *Ordo* of 1200 was that which was universally used. Although there were only twelve apostles, there were many more martyrs, confessors and virgins to choose from when composing a litany. This particular litany includes six confessor saints closely associated with Reims. These saints, Remigius, Sixtus, Sinicius, Rigobert, Maurilius and Eutropia, are found in the litany to be sung in the ceremony for the dedication of a church in one of the two surviving manuscripts containing this *ordo* and were included in all but two of the succeeding French inauguration *ordines*.[135]

The later imperial *ordines* include the chanting of a variety of *laudes*, an element that is absent from the published editions of the *ordines* in England, France and Germany.[136] However, before we see these facts as evidence of differences between the royal and imperial rite, or between different national traditions, we need to consider the manuscript transmission of litanies and *laudes*. As Kantorowicz outlined, the *laudes* were usually placed separately as a special song, perhaps on the fly-leaves of a manuscript, or within a liturgical manuscript, but without a set place in the service.[137] Given that the *laudes* were sung on a number of occasions, not just at inaugurations but on major church feasts, not including them within an *ordo* is understandable in that it saved copying them out a number of times in the same manuscript. Again we see the limitations of the liturgical texts with which we work, for we cannot conclude that litanies were a peculiar Frankish inclusion and that the singing of the *laudes* was confined to imperial ceremonies. Indeed, the survival of *laudes* texts naming William the Conqueror and his queen Matilda of Flanders makes clear that the *laudes* were also an important part of the inauguration ceremony in other realms.[138]

That *laudes* were first included in an *ordo* for the consecration of a pope should alert us to the reason for the inclusion of *laudes* in the later, elaborate, imperial *ordines*.[139] Their inclusion in those *ordines*, which originated at the papal curia, is evidence of a papal desire to provide complete *ordines*

---

[134] *Ordines Coronationis Franciae*, ed. Jackson, I, 252–3.
[135] Ibid., I, 248.
[136] On the singing of the *laudes* in the Hohenstaufen Empire see J. Dale, 'Inauguration and Political Liturgy in the Hohenstaufen Empire, 1138–1215', *German History* 34 (2016), 191–213 (pp. 202–7).
[137] Kantorowicz, 'Ivories and Litanies', p. 62.
[138] On these *laudes* see Gathagan, 'The Trappings of Power'.
[139] Benedict of St Peter's included a form of *laudes papales* in a rite for the pope. Kantorowicz, 'Ivories and Litanies', p. 63.

for imperial inauguration. By prescribing, amongst other things, the exact form of the *laudes* to be sung at the imperial inauguration any *spielraum* was removed from the liturgical *ordo*.[140] The inclusion of the *laudes*, in addition to the increased elaboration of these later imperial *ordines*, needs to be seen in the context of a wider twelfth-century drive towards the codification of both liturgical and non-liturgical ritual at the papal curial. As Susan Twyman has demonstrated in her study of the papal *adventus* at Rome in the twelfth century, the compilations in which such liturgical texts are found are unprecedented in the manner in which they incorporate the public and popular as well as the private and sacred elements of the ritual associated with papal accession.[141] This is also true of the imperial consecration, where, as we will see in the following chapter, the liturgical texts include detailed information about events that take place both within St Peter's and in the wider environment of Rome itself. By looking at the form of the *laudes* included in the three different imperial *ordines* it is possible to identify a change in papal approach. In the Cencius II *ordo* the *laudes* are included in full, following the crowning of the emperor and empress. We learn that they were also sung after the ceremony outside St Peter's and at San Lorenzo fuori le Mura, presumably using the same text.

Laudes in Cencius II

Exaudi Christe
Domino nostro C. a Deo decreto summo pontifici et universali pape vita (×3)
Exaudi Christe
Domino nostro a Deo coronato magno et pacifico imperatori vita et victoria (×3)
Exaudi Christe
Domine nostre .N. eius coniugi excellentissime imperatrici vita (×3)
Exaudi Christe
Exercitui romano et theutonico vita et victoria (×3)

Salvator mundi	Resp: Tu illos adiuva (×3)
Sancta Maria	Resp: Tu illos adiuva (×3)
Sancte Michael	Resp: Tu illos adiuva (×3)
Sancte Gabriel	Resp: Tu illos adiuva (×3)
Sancte Raphael	Resp: Tu illos adiuva (×3)
Sancte Petre	Resp: Tu illos adiuva (×3)
Sancte Paule	Resp: Tu illos adiuva (×3)
Sancte Iohannes	Resp: Tu illos adiuva (×3)
Sancte Gregori	Resp: Tu illos adiuva (×3)
Sancte Maurici	Resp: Tu illos adiuva (×3)

---

[140] Elze has seen these more prescriptive twelfth-century texts as evidence of papal attempts to remove the opportunity for improvisation. *Die Ordines*, ed. Elze, p. xii.
[141] S. Twyman, *Papal Ceremonial at Rome in the Twelfth Century*, HBS Subsidia 4 (Woodbridge, 2002), pp. 23–4.

Sancte Mercuri   Resp: Tu illos adiuva (×3)
Christus vincit, Christus regnat, Christus imperat (×3)
Spes nostra   Resp: Christus vincit
Salus nostra   Resp: Christus vincit
Victoria nostra   Resp: Christus vincit
Honor nostra   Resp: Christus vincit
Gloria nostra   Resp: Christus vincit
Murus noster inexpugnabilis   Resp: Christus vincit
Laus nostra   Resp: Christus vincit
Triumphus noster   Resp: Christus vincit
Ipsi laus honor et imperium per immortalia secula seculorum.[142]

The pope and emperor appear together in these *laudes*, and although the pope is acclaimed first, this priority is perhaps counterbalanced by the inclusion of an empress. Importantly the emperor is described as *a deo coronatus*. This phrase was used in the *laudes* from at least as early as the inauguration of Charlemagne in 800, and could also be used to describe saints who had obtained the crown of martyrdom.[143] The wording is significant as it implies that the emperor received his crown, and hence power, directly from God. The pope might appear above the emperor in the *laudes* hierarchy, but he is not the source of the emperor's authority. The tricolon *Christus vincit, Christus regnat, Christus imperat*, which is included in the *laudes* in Cencius II, is normally considered to be the chant's most distinctive element. It is this tricolon that differentiates the *laudes* from a litany of saints. Instead of the penitential spirit of a litany the *Christus vincit* chant imbues the *laudes* with a jubilant character.[144] A consideration of the *laudes* contained within the two later imperial *ordines* demonstrates the extent to which the papal curia sought to undermine the association presented in the *laudes* between the emperor, God and Christ.

Laudes *in the Staufen* Ordo

Exaudi Christe
Domino N. invictissimo Romanorum imperatori et semper augusto salus et
    victoria (×3)
Salvator mundi   Resp: Tu illum adiuva (×3)
Sancta Maria   Resp: Tu illum adiuva (×2)
Sancte Michael, Sancte Gabriel, Sancte Raphael,

---

[142] *Die Ordines*, ed. Elze, pp. 45–6.
[143] The phrase was recorded in both the *Life* of Pope Leo and in the Fulda *Reichsannalen*: B. Opfermann, *Die liturgischen Herrscherakklamationen im Sacrum Imperium des Mittelalters* (Weimar, 1953), p. 21. The multiplicity of ideas inherent in the action of crowning is discussed in the following chapter.
[144] Kantorowicz, *Laudes Regiae*, p. 14.

Sancte Iohannes Baptista
Sancte Petre, Sancte Paule, Sancte Andrea,
Sancte Stephane, Sancte Laurenti, Sancte Vincenti,
Sancte Silvester, Sancte Leo, Sancte Gregori,
Sancte Benedicte, Sancte Basili, Sancte Saba,
Sancta Agnes, Sancta Cecilia, Sancta Lucia.
Kyrieleyson   Resp: Christeleyson
Kyrieleyson.[145]

The *laudes* in the *ordo* from the Roman Curia are almost identical. The only disparity is that they lack the *Christeleyson* response.[146] The divergence between these two forms of the *laudes* and the *laudes* in Cencius II is striking. The emperor is no longer described as crowned by God, but is styled instead *semper augustus*, like an ancient Roman emperor. The *Christus vincit* tricolon has been completely eradicated; Christ no longer rules through the emperor. The repetitive *Christus vincit* response has also fallen by the wayside, and instead the list of saints has more of the characteristics of a penitential litany. Perhaps most importantly the pope has ceased to be acclaimed in the *laudes*. His absence is not meant to imply imperial independence, but is a symptom of the development of a specific *laudes papales* for acclaiming the pope. H. E. J. Cowdrey commented 'by their exclusive concentration upon either pope or emperor, these high medieval *laudes* illustrate the post-Gregorian tension between the *sacerdotium* and the *regnum* as the constituent elements of Christian society'.[147] They certainly illustrate post-Gregorian tension between the pope and the emperor, but it is necessary to consider non-imperial *laudes* before drawing general conclusions.

Although *laudes* are most often to be found apart from royal inauguration *ordines*, one manuscript of the Third Recension of the English rite does contain *laudes*, thus allowing us to examine them as part of the inauguration liturgy. That they are included in only one of the seven surviving manuscripts of the English Third Recension is again indicative of the fact that such liturgical *ordines* tended to provide a framework for the ceremony, rather than to specify the contents of a ceremony in its entirety, as was the case in the later imperial *ordines*. The manuscript in question is a pontifical that was written in the diocese of Canterbury in the twelfth century and is now MS B. II. 10 in the library of Trinity College, Cambridge. In contrast to the imperial *ordines*, that include the *laudes* in the middle of the ceremony, the *laudes* in the Trinity manuscript come after the *ordo* for the king and before that of the queen (Plate 1).

---

[145] *Die Ordines*, ed. Elze, pp. 67–8.
[146] Ibid., pp. 82–3.
[147] H. E. J. Cowdrey, 'The Anglo-Norman *Laudes Regiae*', *Viator* 12 (1981), 37–78 (p. 46).

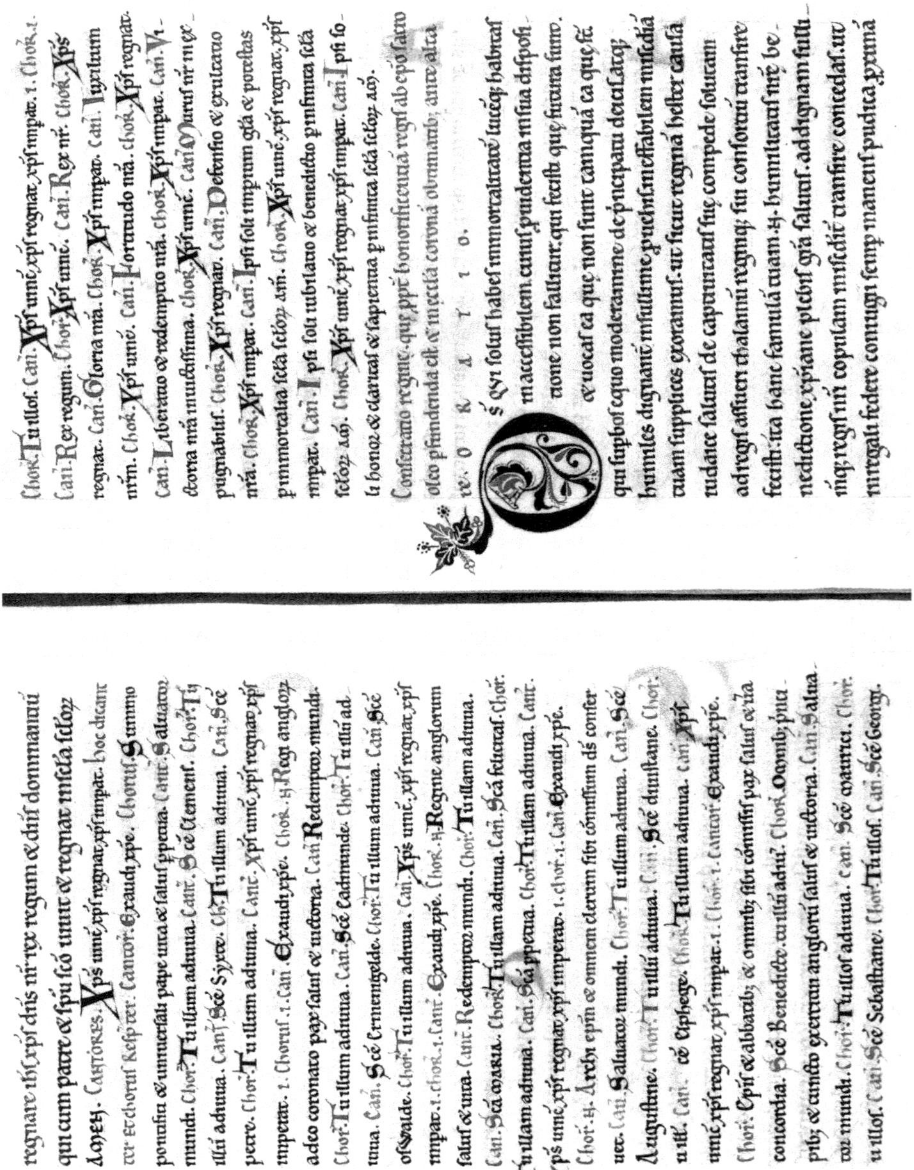

Plate 1. Thirteenth-century *laudes*: Cambridge, Trinity College MS B.11.10, fol. 108r–109v

Trinity laudes
Christus vincit, Christ regnat, Christus imperat (×3)
Exaudi Christi (×3)
Summo pontifici et universali pape vitae et salus perpetua
Salvator mundi   *Resp*: Tu illum adiuva
Sancte Clemens   *Resp*: Tu illum adiuva
Sancte Syxte   *Resp*: Tu illum adiuva
Sancte Petre   *Resp*: Tu illum adiuva
Christus vincit, Christus regnat, Christus imperat
Exaudi Christi
.N. Regi anglorum a deo coronato pax salus et victoria
Redemptor mundi   *Resp*: Tu illum adiuva
Sancte Eadmunde   *Resp*: Tu illum adiuva
Sancte Ermenigelde   *Resp*: Tu illum adiuva
Sancte Oswald   *Resp*: Tu illum adiuva
Christus vincit, Christus regnat, Christus imperat
Exaudi Christi
.N. Regine anglorum salus et vita
Redemptor mundi   *Resp*: Tu illam adiuva
Sancta Maria   *Resp*: Tu illam adiuva
Sancta Felicitas   *Resp*: Tu illam adiuva
Sancta Perpetua   *Resp*: Tu illam adiuva
Christus vincit, Christus regnat, Christus imperat
Exaudi Christi
.N. Archiepiscopum et omnem clerum sibi commissum deus conservet
Salvator mundi   *Resp*: Tu illos adiuva
Sancte Augustine   *Resp*: Tu illos adiuva
Sancte Dunstane   *Resp*: Tu illos adiuva
Sancte Elphege   *Resp*: Tu illos adiuva
Christus vincit, Christus regnat, Christus imperat
Exaudi Christi
Episcopis et abbatibus et omnibus sibi commissis pax salus et vita concordia
Sancte Benedicte   *Resp*: Tu illos adiuva
Omnibus principibus & cuncto exercitui anglorum salus et victoria
Salvator mundi   *Resp*: Tu illos adiuva
Sancte Maurici   *Resp*: Tu illos
Sancte Sebastiane   *Resp*: Tu illos
Sancte Gregori   *Resp*: Tu illos
Christus vincit, Christus regnat, Christus imperat
Rex regum   *Resp*: Christus vincit
Rex noster   *Resp*: Christus regnat
Gloria noster   *Resp*: Christus imperat
Auxilium nostram   *Resp*: Christus vincit
Fortitudino nostra   *Resp*: Christus regnat

Inauguration and Liturgical Kingship

Liberatio et redemptio nostra   *Resp*: Christus imperat
Victoria nostra invictissima   *Resp*: Christus vincit
Murus noster inexpugnabilis   *Resp*: Christus regnat
Defensio et exultatio nostra   *Resp*: Christus imperat
Ipsi soli imperium gloria et potestas per immortalia secula seculorum Amen
Christus vincit, Christus regnat, Christus imperat
Ipsi soli iubilatio et benedicto per infinita secula seculorum   Amen
Christus vincit, Christus regnat, Christus imperat
Ipsi soli honor et claritas et sapientia per infinita secula seculorum   Amen.[148]

These twelfth-century English *laudes* give no indication of a post-Gregorian tension between *sacerdotium* and *regnum*. They follow the traditional pattern of the Gallo-Frankish *laudes*, as outlined by Cowdrey.[149] They open with the characteristic *Christus vincit* tricolon, and then seek heavenly aid for the terrestrial hierarchy, with the pope at its pinnacle. The tricolon is repeated between each rank in the hierarchy. Following the pope, the king and queen are acclaimed, then come the archbishops and clerics, the bishops and abbots and, finally, the barons and the whole army. The *laudes* conclude with a celebration of the victorious Christ, into which the *Christus vincit* chant is liberally mixed. It is worth stressing that this manuscript originated in the diocere of Canterbury. The relationship between the English king and archbishop of Canterbury was often strained during the twelfth century. These *laudes* do not, however, reflect the bitterness that led to several archbishops, most famously Thomas Becket, spending years in exile. Instead we find a text in which the pope, king, queen and archbishop are all fêted. The triumphant *Christus vincit* tricolon abounds, and the king is described as *a deo coronatus*. In the Trinity *laudes*, unlike those emanating from the papal curia, *regnum* and *sacerdotium* are presented in harmony. The *laudes* contained within the inauguration *ordines* thus suggest that the pope heavily influenced the imperial liturgy, but that this influence did not stretch to royal ceremonial.

The Trinity *laudes* can be used to raise one final issue. Although typically papal saints are petitioned for the pope, the saints called upon for the king and archbishop have, with one exception, an undeniably English character. For the king, three royal saints, St Edmund, St Ermengild and St Oswald, are invoked. In referencing Oswald, a seventh-century Northumbrian king martyred in battle against the pagan Mercians, and Edmund, king of East Anglia from 855 until his martyrdom at the hands of the Vikings in 869/70, the newly consecrated king is placed firmly in the tradition of English Christian kingship.[150] The inclusion of Ermengild, a sixth-century Visigothic

---

[148] Cambridge, Trinity College, MS B.11.10, fols. 108v–109r.
[149] Cowdrey, 'The Anglo-Norman *Laudes Regiae*', pp. 44–5.
[150] On veneration of St Oswald in the late eleventh and early twelfth centuries see D. Rollason, 'St Oswald in Post-Conquest England', in *Oswald: Northumbrian King to*

prince whose cult was popularized by Gregory the Great in his *Dialogues*, is rather more puzzling.[151] His invocation can perhaps be explained by the fact that this saint is found in close proximity to both Oswald and Edmund in the litany found in a Gallican psalter written at Exeter in the late eleventh century.[152] Although written in the West Country, this litany, surviving in a manuscript now in the British Library, is one of the longest surviving litanies of saints from Anglo-Saxon England and Lapidge has suggested it represents an act of scholarly compilation rather than local devotion.[153] The similarity of the Visigothic saint's name to another English royal saint, the rather obscure saintly princess Ermenilda, might also be relevant to explaining his inclusion. Ermenilda was the niece of the better-known royal founder of Ely abbey, St Etheldreda, and, following the death of her husband Wulfhere of Mercia, she followed in her aunt's footsteps by becoming abbess of the foundation.[154]

For the archbishop of Canterbury three of his saintly predecessors, Augustine, Dunstan and Alphege (Ælfheah), are called upon.[155] By referencing Augustine, a Benedictine monk sent to England by Pope Gregory the Great in 597, these *laudes* connect the present archbishop to the first holder of his see. At first overshadowed by other saints, including the pope who sent him to England, interest in Augustine grew, especially at Canterbury, during the eleventh century. In 1091 his body was translated into the church of St Augustine's Abbey and a cycle of works was written for the occasion by Goscelin of Saint-Bertin.[156] Dunstan, archbishop from 960 until his death in 988, was seen as a model for the interaction between the archbishop and

European Saint, ed. C. Stancliffe and E. Cambridge (Stamford, 1995), pp. 164–77. On St Edmund's cult in the same period see T. Licence, 'The Cult of St Edmund', in *Bury St Edmunds and the Norman Conquest*, ed. T. Licence (Woodbridge, 2014), pp. 104–30.

[151] Gregory the Great, *Dialogus* III.31.
[152] Now London, British Library, MS Harley 863.
[153] Lapidge, *Anglo-Saxon Litanies*, p. 74.
[154] Susan Ridyard has comprehensively discussed the origins and diffusion of the cult of royal saints at Ely. See. S. J. Ridyard, *The Royal Saints of Anglo-Saxon England: A Study of West Saxon and East Anglian Cults* (Cambridge, 1988), pp. 176–210.
[155] This trio of saints is also invoked in the *laudes regiae* found in the Cosin gradual (Durham University Library, Cosin V. v. 6), which was copied at Christ Church soon after the Norman Conquest and sent to Durham between 1083 and 1096. In the two sets of *laudes* found in Worcester, Cathedral Library, F. 160, written *c.*1230, Augustine has been replaced by Thomas Becket. P. Lendinara, 'Forgotten Missionaries: St Augustine of Canterbury in Anglo-Saxon and Post-Conquest England', in L. Lazzari, P. Lendinara and C. di Sciacca ed., *Hagiography in Anglo-Saxon England: Adopting and Adapting Saints' Lives into Old England Prose (c.950–1150)*, ed. L. Lazzari, P. Lendinara and C. di Sciacca (Barcelona, 2014), pp. 365–497 (pp. 422–3).
[156] On veneration of Augustine and the 1091 translation see Lendinara, 'Forgotten Missionaries'; R. Sharpe, 'The Setting of St Augustine's Translation, 1091', in *Canterbury and the Norman Conquest: Churches, Saints and Scholars, 1066–1109*, ed. R. Eales and R. Sharpe (London, 1995), pp. 1–13.

the king and officiated at the coronation of King Edgar at Bath in 973.[157] Alphege, who was canonized soon after his death at the hands of Vikings in 1012, had himself, when archbishop, vigorously promoted Dunstan's cult.[158] During his archiepiscopate Dunstan's feast was prominent at Canterbury. As Alan Thacker has shown, it was supplied with twelve lessons for the offices and also prominently presented in a calendar probably written at Canterbury Cathedral between 988 and 1012.[159] After initial doubts as to the categorization of Alphege's death as martyrdom, Archbishop Lanfranc (1070–89) promoted his cult and Alphege's shrine was rebuilt in the early twelfth century during Anselm's reign as archbishop (1093–1109), demonstrating a lively interest in the saint at the probable time of the composition of these *laudes*.[160] Although the prayer formulae and rubrics of the inauguration *ordines* tend not to exhibit 'national' characteristics, in the composition of *laudes* saints appropriate to the setting could be chosen. We have seen that this is also true of the litany transmitted as part of the French *Ordo* of 1200. The *ordines*, for the most part, present a royal liturgy for England, France and Germany that shows little 'national' variation. These royal liturgical texts provided a framework for a ceremony that could be adapted to particular circumstances. While the image of kingship projected in the *ordines* was to a large extent shared across all three realms, the invoking of local saints reminds us that this shared outline could be coloured in different ways.

This investigation into spoken and sung words in the *ordines* has underscored Janet Nelson's point, that what we find in the *ordines* are ideas 'of the most general, uncontentious and normative kind'.[161] The prayers urge the king to be faithful like Abraham, mild like Moses, brave like Joshua, humble like David and wise like Solomon, thus providing a composite Old Testament image of kingship. We have also seen that, to a large extent, royal and imperial rites shared this biblical vocabulary. However, in the development of the oath in the imperial *ordines*, in the musical accompaniment, which explicitly associated the pope with St Peter, and, perhaps most obviously in the rewriting of the imperial *laudes*, the potential of these ideas to be contentious can be glimpsed. The following chapter will examine how the evidence gleaned from increasingly sophisticated rubrics

---

[157] On Dunstan's close cooperation with King Edgar see N. P. Brooks, 'The Career of St Dunstan', in *St Dunstan: His Life, Times and Cult*, ed. N. Ramsey, M. Sparks and T. Tatton-Brown (Woodbridge, 1992), pp. 1–24 (pp. 18–22).

[158] A. R. Rumble, 'From Winchester to Canterbury: Ælfheah and Stigand – Bishops, Archbishops and Victims', in *Leaders of the Anglo-Saxon Church from Bede to Stigand*, ed. A. R. Rumble (Woodbridge, 2012), pp. 165–82 (p. 168).

[159] A. Thacker, 'Cults at Canterbury: Relics and Reform under Dunstan and his Successors', in *St Dunstan: His Life, Times and Cult*, ed. N. Ramsey, M. Sparks and T. Tatton-Brown (Woodbridge, 1992), pp. 221–45 (pp. 222–3).

[160] Rumble, 'From Winchester to Canterbury', pp. 172–3.

[161] Nelson, 'The Rites of the Conqueror', p. 122.

points to papal attempts to suppress some of the general and normative ideas found in the *ordines*. It will also demonstrate how these ideas could be reinterpreted as part of royal attempts to reassert a Christomimetic image of kingship.

2
Liturgical Rituals: Rubrication and Regalia

The previous chapter focused on spoken and sung elements in the *ordines*. As we have seen in the context of litanies of saints, such chants, prayers and oaths were associated with ritual acts, in the case of litanies with prostration before the altar. In this chapter, the focus will be on the ritual acts themselves and on items of regalia involved in the myriad mini-rituals, which together made up the inauguration ceremony. It has been noted that prayer formulae in the *ordines* remained relatively static from the ninth century to the end of the period under consideration here. This is not to say, however, that monarchical inauguration did not evolve after the Carolingian age. To reveal these changes we need to consider another aspect of the *ordines*: their rubrication. As Jackson has commented, 'it is the rubrics that change most of all, and it is primarily in them that one must seek the changing perceptions of medieval kingship'.[1] To take Jackson's point further, mutable rubrics had the effect of making static prayer formulae dynamic. They altered the context in which the prayers were to be understood, allowing innovative materials to be woven from traditional threads. A discussion of rubrics and regalia must thus refer to their associated prayer formulae. As changing rubrics could alter the interpretation of century-old prayers, so too could changing cultural contexts alter the perception of the entire rite. Thus, the chapter concludes with a discussion of the female *ordines* and makes the tentative suggestion that the well-documented growth of Marian devotion in the twelfth century enabled a strengthening of the king's Christomimetic image.

Rubrication

The most striking contrast in rubrication is that found between, on the one hand, the three later imperial *ordines* (Cencius II, The Staufen *Ordo* and the *Ordo* of the Roman Curia) and, on the other, the remaining royal and imperial *ordines*. These three imperial *ordines* outline the ritual elements in the imperial inauguration ceremony with a considerably higher level of complexity than in any of the other *ordines* under consideration. The specificity of these imperial *ordines* explains their elaboration, at least in part. Unlike the royal *ordines*, which, as discussed in the previous chapter, are not country specific and make no mention

---

[1] *Ordines Coronationis Franciae*, ed. Jackson, I, 35.

of a particular inauguration church or celebrant, these three imperial *ordines* are full of detail about St Peter's and Roman topography, and the actions of the pope and other named episcopal celebrants. In the royal *ordines* the focus is on the monarch, in the imperial *ordines* there is a dual focus. This is made explicit even in the incipit to Cencius II: 'Here begins the Roman ordo for the blessing of the emperor, when he receives the crown from the lord pope in the cathedral of Saint Peter the apostle before the altar of Saint Maurice'.[2] The reference to the altar of St Maurice appears, at first glance, to be innocent enough. On further examination, however, the inclusion of this detail in an *ordo* written at the papal curia and copied by a future Pope, can be shown to be symptomatic of tensions between papal and imperial power.[3] For the consecration of the emperor had previously taken place in front of the altar of St Peter and the change of location of imperial unction to an altar in a side aisle is clearly demonstrative, as Ernst Kantorowicz recognized, of a downgrading of the imperial ceremony.[4]

A brief glance at the tables grouped together in Appendix 3 makes immediately apparent the difference in length and complexity of the three later imperial *ordines* in stark contrast to the earlier imperial *ordines* and to a lesser extent the royal *ordines*. Whereas the royal *ordines* have between fourteen and twenty-two distinct ritual acts (including those related to queens), the later imperial *ordines* have between twenty-nine and thirty-six (including those related to empresses). The jump from Cencius I to Cencius II is particularly pronounced, suggesting that the increasing specificity of the imperial *ordines* was no organic process of accretion, but rather a deliberate attempt by the papal curia to fix the details of the ceremony. Whereas royal *ordines* continued to provide flexible model texts that could be adapted to circumstances, the later all-encompassing and rigid imperial *ordines* ensured that the primacy of the pope within the event was permanently secured. A symptom of this tendency is to be found in the fact that these later imperial *ordines* go into great detail about acts that took place outside of the walls of St Peter's. A number of the royal *ordines* include a procession from palace to church without going into much detail. They tell us only that

---

[2] *Die Ordines*, ed. Elze, p. 36: 'Incipit ordo romanus ad benedicendum imperatorem, quando coronam accipit a domino papa in basilica beati Petri apostoli ad altare sancti Mauritii'. Cf. unspecific royal initial rubric cited above p. 40.

[3] The *ordines* Cencius I and II are transmitted in the *Liber Censuum* of Cencius, later Pope Honorius III (1216–27). Earlier historians dated the *ordo* Cencius II to the early eleventh century, more recently Elze has dated it to the first half of the twelfth century, a dating I have accepted: R. Elze, 'Der Liber Censuum des Cencius (Cod. Vat. lat. 8486) von 1192 bis 1228', in *Päpste – Kaiser – Könige und die mittelalterliche Herrschaftssymbolik: Ausgewählte Aufsätze*, ed. B. Schimmelpfennig (London, 1982), pp. 251–70.

[4] Kantorowicz, *Laudes Regiae*, p. 143; W. Ullmann, *The Growth of Papal Government in the Middle Ages: A Study in the Ideological Relation of Clerical to Lay Power* (London, 1955), pp. 253–61.

two bishops were to lead the king to the church in a procession carrying the gospel, unnamed relics, crosses and incense.[5] In the royal *ordines* all other action is envisaged as taking place within a church. In the later imperial *ordines* prominent symbolic acts are described that take place outside St Peter's both before and after the act of consecration itself. The importance of these acts will be discussed presently. Relevant in this context is the papal desire to fix even the non-liturgical elements of an inauguration. Cencius II includes details about the feast to be held following the inauguration. It is well known that such feasts were features of royal inauguration, but such non-liturgical minutiae are not to be found in royal *ordines* of this period.

These later imperial *ordines* contain a wealth of information about the participants involved in the inauguration and the sites, both within and outside St Peter's, at which particular acts should take place. This is quite different from the royal *ordines*, which are full of general designations such as 'bishop' or 'metropolitan' with no further qualifying words. For instance, the Third Recension of the English *ordines* does not specify that it is the archbishop of Canterbury that is to anoint the king, and the Saint-Bertin *Ordo*, while making clear that several celebrants were involved, refers generally to 'one of the bishops, ('unus episcoporum') saying one prayer and 'another bishop' ('alius episcopus') the following prayer.[6] Even the earlier, considerably briefer and less specific, imperial *ordines* mention that it was the cardinal bishop of Ostia that anointed the emperor and all imperial *ordines* also mention other celebrants by name. These are the cardinal bishops of Albano and Porto, who say prayers over the emperor elect shortly after his entry to St Peter's. These three Lateran bishops, of Ostia, Porto and Albano, also took part in the consecration of the pope.[7] However, in imperial inauguration the focus is very much on the pope's role rather than the actions of the bishops. As Walter Ullmann long ago recognized, the climax of the imperial inauguration was the coronation, in which 'the pope's function is ... brought into clearest possible relief'.[8] In addition to supplying information about the celebrants, the later imperial *ordines* include precise information about where exactly acts should take place. In the Staufen *Ordo*, for example, we are told that the Bishop of Albano speaks his prayer 'in front of the silver door', and the Bishop of Porto within St Peter's 'in the middle of the rota'.[9] A number of different altars within St Peter's are also mentioned. In addition to the

---

[5] The *ordines* including this information are those in the PRG, Cologne Dombibliothek, MS 141, Saint-Bertin and the *Ordo* of 1200.

[6] *English Coronation Records*, ed. Legg, pp. 32–3; *Ordines Coronationis Franciae*, ed. Jackson, I, 243.

[7] The Bishop of Ostia had consecrated the pope since 336. Ullmann, *The Growth of Papal Government*, p. 226.

[8] Ibid.

[9] *Die Ordines*, ed. Elze, pp. 63–4: 'ante ipsam portam argenteam'; 'in medio rote'.

altar of St Peter where the emperor is crowned by the pope, and the altar of St Maurice where he is anointed by the bishop of Ostia, Cencius II also has a number of acts taking place at the altar of St Gregory. Outside of St Peter's, other Roman churches and sites are also referred to in all three texts.

Comparing ritual acts common to the royal and imperial *ordines* highlights the manner in which the participation of the pope skews the focus away from the elect towards the celebrant in the imperial context. A kiss of peace is included in all but one of the royal *ordines* under consideration here, with only the English Second Recension making no mention of this act, which in all other cases was envisaged as taking place near the conclusion of the inauguration.[10] Unsurprisingly, given their brevity, we find no mention of a kiss in the cursory imperial texts in Cologne MS 141 or in Cencius I. A kiss of peace is, however, included in the Staufen *Ordo* and in the *Ordo* of the Roman Curia, where it similarly takes place near the conclusion of the ceremony, after the emperor has made an offering of gold to the pope.[11] A kiss of peace appears in Cencius II in a different context, which will be described in the following paragraph. The kiss of peace is a ritual in which participants assume a degree of equality. It does not exalt one participant above another and instead acts as a clear sign of mutual respect.[12] The kiss of peace is the only kissing ritual found in the royal *ordines*. In contrast, the imperial *ordines* contain a number of other acts in which kissing features, and in these acts the pecking order of the participants is made apparent.

Before the emperor elect even entered St Peter's he had first to kiss the feet of the pope, who waited outside the church of St Maria in Turri, seated at the top of the steps, thereby emphasizing his higher position. In the Staufen *Ordo* and the *Ordo* of the Roman Curia the kissing of the pope's feet is immediately followed by the emperor offering the pope 'as much gold as will be pleasing to him'.[13] As with the kiss of peace envisaged later in the ceremony in these two *ordines*, kissing and gold go hand in hand. Following this gift of gold the pope responds with a kiss and an embrace.[14] This kiss does not thus appear to be the mutual kiss of peace but a kiss given as a sign that the pope accepts the submission and gifts of the emperor elect.[15] Cencius II differs from the two

---

[10] As can be seen from the first two tables of Appendix 3 the exact position varies slightly.

[11] *Die Ordines*, ed. Elze, pp. 68, 83.

[12] The importance and widely understood meaning of this ritual was clearly demonstrated in the course of the dispute between Henry II of England and Thomas Becket. T. Reuter, '*Velle Sibi Fieri in Forma Hac*: Symbolic Acts in the Becket Dispute', in *Medieval Polities and Modern Mentalities*, ed. J. L. Nelson (Cambridge, 2006), pp. 167–90 (pp. 182–3).

[13] *Die Ordines*, ed. Elze, p. 62: 'aurum quantum sibi placuerit'.

[14] Ibid.

[15] This embrace is perhaps a simplified version of the enfolding under the pope's mantle as found in Cencius II.

later *ordines* in that, following the kissing of feet, the emperor elect swears the oath and is then asked three times by the pope if he would like to be at peace with the church, to which the elect responds 'I wish it'. The pope then declares that he gives the elect peace 'just as the Lord gave to his disciples'.[16] This is a bestowal of peace in which the pope assumes the role of Christ and the elect one of his disciples, rather than the mutual kiss of peace. The kiss itself is one-sided and by kissing the elect on the forehead, chin and cheeks the pope forms a cross.[17] The pope then asks the elect three times whether he would like to be a 'son of the church' ('filius ecclesie'), to which the elect thrice responds in the affirmative. The visual manifestation of this adoption is that the emperor elect is enfolded under the mantle of the pope and kisses the pope on the breast.[18] The actions of the pope and emperor elect are far from symmetrical. On the contrary, these kissing rituals make clear that the relationship of pope to emperor is like that of Christ to his disciples or a father to his son.

Although the selected *ordines* vary greatly in detail and length, all twelve describe the two most important ritual acts: anointing and crowning, and in all cases they appear in that order. Even so, these two ritual acts vary across the *ordines* in important ways. Significantly, the manner in which the emperor was anointed has been seen as exemplifying the downgrading of anointing within the imperial inauguration, in which, as noted above, coronation by the pope had become the central rite. In a famous letter of 1204, Innocent III delineated the differences between royal and episcopal anointing and used these divergences to argue for the superiority of bishops over kings.[19] Writing to the Bulgrian primate, the archbishop of Trnovo, about anointing within the Roman church, he declared,

> Moreover, a difference between the unction of bishops and princes is assigned, because the head of the bishop is consecrated with chrism whereas the arm of the prince is anointed with oil, in order to make clear how great the difference is between the authority of the bishop and the power of the prince.[20]

---

[16] *Die Ordines*, ed. Elze, p. 37: 'sicut Dominus dedit discipulis suis'.
[17] Ibid.
[18] See Walter Ullmann's analysis of the adoption in Ullmann, *The Growth of Papal Government*, p. 257.
[19] This passage is cited by almost all scholars concerned with liturgy or coronation. See for example Erdmann, *Forschungen zur politischen Ideenwelt*, p. 71; Kantorowicz, *The King's Two Bodies*, pp. 319–20; Ullmann, *The Growth of Papal Government*, p. 227.
[20] *Die Register Papst Innocenz' III.*, ed. O. Hageneder, A. Sommerlechner and H. Weigl, 13 vols. (Vienna, 1964–2015), VII, 11; Innocent's letter was incorporated into the first book of the *Liber Extra* of Pope Gregory IX (tit. XV, cap. I). *Corpus Iuris Canonici*, ed. E. A. Friedberg and A. L. Richter, 2 vols. (Leipzig, 1881), II, 131–4: 'Refert autem inter pontificis et principis unctionem, quia caput pontificis crismate consecratur, brachium vero principis oleo delinitur, ut ostendatur, quanta sit differentia inter auctoritatem pontificis et principis potestatem'.

As Carl Erdmann long since recognized, there are two issues at stake here, firstly the type of oil used and secondly the part of the body anointed. He noted that according to the *ordo* Cencius I, the emperor was not anointed on the head, but on the right arm and between the shoulders, and with *oleum exorcitatum* rather than with chrism.[21] This manner of anointing appears in all the imperial *ordines* under consideration here. Erdmann argued that the distinction between oil and chrism was not as clear-cut as Innocent III suggested, but this view is refuted by Ullmann who stressed that there are three types of oil used in liturgical contexts and that the differences must be recognized.[22] In any case it is apparent that in the context of imperial inauguration the pope could ensure a lower grade of oil was used and that the emperor was not anointed on the head. The extent to which Innocent's argument can be extended to monarchs in general is, however, questionable. Kings might well exert a pressure over their archbishops that an emperor could not exert over the pope. In this context Koziol's observation that prelates 'were more likely to dispute their own rights of precedence in a king's ceremonies than to dispute the sanctity the ceremonies conferred', is pertinent.[23]

The type of oil used in royal inauguration is a rather vexing problem as the words employed to describe the oil used rarely conform to the three categories delineated by Ullmann. As Table 4 makes clear, a variety of words were used to describe the oil, with only the royal *ordo* in Cologne MS 141 specifying that *oleum exorcitatum* be used.[24] This oil has the function of driving out evil spirits and purifying, and was the type used in the imperial inauguration.[25] The majority of *ordines* do not stipulate which type of oil was used, preferring vague qualifiers such as 'sacred', 'holy' or the oil 'of anointing'. I would suggest that such opaque descriptions do not categorically rule out the use of chrism in royal anointing and indeed that this vagueness reflects once again the flexibility of the royal *ordines* in this period. Moreover, at least two copies of the English Third Recension do make mention of chrism, albeit in addition to, rather than instead of, *oleum sanctificatum*. These are the versions found in the pontifical Claudius III and the unpublished manuscript copy in Cambridge, Trinity College, MS B. 11. 10.[26] In these texts, which

---

[21] Erdmann, *Forschungen zur politischen Ideenwelt*, p. 71.

[22] The three types were, following Ullmann, 1) the *cleum infirmorum*; 2) the *oleum catechumenorum* or *exorcitatum*; and 3) chrism. Ullmann, *The Growth of Papal Government*, p. 227.

[23] Koziol, 'England, France and the Problem of Sacrality', p. 127.

[24] *Ordines Coronationis Franciae*, ed. Jackson, I, 207.

[25] In the imperial *ordo* contained within Cologne Dombibliothek, MS 141 *oleum sanctum* is described as being used in the imperial context.

[26] London, British Library, MS Cotton Claudius A. III contains three fragmentary pontificals from the tenth, eleventh and twelfth centuries respectively. It is an artificial composition, probably compiled by Robert Cotton himself. The pontifical

Table 4 Details from the Ritual of Anointing in the Royal Ordines

		English			German	German/French
		Second	Third	PRG		Cologne 141
King	Type of Oil	oleum	oleum sanctificatum/ chrisma	oleum sanctificatum		oleum exorcizatum
	Place of anointing	not specified	hands	hands		not specified
			head, breast, shoulders & elbows	head, breast, shoulders & elbows		
Queen	Type of oil	oleum sacri unguinis	oleum sanctum/ sacrum	sacrum oleum		oleum sanctum
	Place of anointing	head	not specified	not specified		head

		French			
		Ratold Ordo	Saint-Bertin	Ordo of 1200	
King	Type of Oil	oleum/oleum sanctificatum	oleum sanctum	oleum sanctificatum	
	Place of anointing	head, breast, shoulders & elbows	feet, shoulders & elbows	head, breast, shoulders & elbows	
				hands	
Queen	Type of oil	oleum ungui	no female *ordo*	sacrum oleum	
	Place of anointing	head		not specified	

both originated at Christ Church Canterbury in the twelfth century, the oil is described as 'sanctified' in the rubric describing the anointing of the hands. Following a prayer oil is mentioned again in the second stage of anointing: 'afterwards let his breast and shoulders and the joints of both his arms be anointed with the aforementioned oil, and with the same let a cross be made on his head and afterwards with chrism'.[27] Although papal teaching might have forbidden the use of chrism in royal inauguration, the Trinity *ordo* suggests that chrism continued to be used in practice in the context of the anointing of the head. We know from other sources that the kings of France, with their Holy Ampoule, and the kings of England, continued to be anointed with chrism in their inauguration ceremonies.[28] It is possible that the German kings were too. The 1246 inventory of the regalia held at Trifels contains a tantalizing reference to balsam (*den balsam*).[29] Balsam was mixed with oil to make chrism and was significantly more expensive than the oil with which it was mixed.

Table 4 also makes apparent the variety of body parts anointed in the royal *ordines*. Schramm attributed the most surprising reference to the anointing of the monarch's feet in the two surviving manuscripts of the *Ordo* of Saint-Bertin to a copyist mistaking the word 'breast' (*pectus*) for the word 'feet' (*pedes*).[30] Given that the anointing of feet appears in no other inauguration rite this seems likely, as does the fact that *pedes* occurs here in combination with anointing of the shoulders and arm joints. The trio of breast, shoulders and arm joints occur together in four of the six remaining royal rites.[31] The second English recension, and the royal *ordo* in the Cologne manuscript, simply state that the king is anointed, without specifying where. With the exception of the Saint-Bertin *Ordo*, the remaining four *ordines* stipulate that the head should be anointed, along with the breast, shoulders and arm joints. Although the pope, chief celebrant in the imperial inauguration, could ensure that emperors were no longer anointed on the head, it is apparent that liturgical

---

fragment known as Claudius III (fols. 19r–29v) contains only an *ordo* written in a hand associated with Christ Church Canterbury c.1090–1150. See *The Claudius Pontificals*, ed. D. H. Turner, HBS 97 (Woodbridge, 1970).

[27] Cambridge, Trinity College, MS B. 11. 10, fol. 106r: 'Postea vero pectus et scapule ambeque compages brachiorum ipsius unguantur de supradicto oleo et de eodem crux fiat super caput eius et postea de crismate'.

[28] For the development of the legend of Clovis's baptism by St Remigius and the later connection drawn between this event and a relic at Reims that became known as the Holy Ampoule see F. Oppenheimer, *The Legend of the Ste. Ampoule* (London, 1953).

[29] *Mittelalterliche Schatzverzeichnisse I: von der Zeit Karls des Großen bis zur Mitte des 13. Jahrhunderts*, ed. B. Bischoff (Munich, 1967), p. 99.

[30] Schramm, '*Ordines*-Studien II', p. 40; *Ordines Coronationis Franciae*, ed. Jackson, I, 244.

[31] It is possible, but unlikely, that anointing on the feet is an allusion to the biblical story of Jesus having oil poured over his feet, which is recorded in Luke 7. 36–50 and John 12. 1–8.

texts for royal inauguration continued to state that the king's head would be anointed. This is vividly illustrated in one of the miniatures of the thirteenth-century manuscript containing the French *Ordo* of 1250. This manuscript contains the only surviving witness to a text compilation that, in the view of Jackson, 'was perhaps hastily – and certainly poorly – put together from four sources slightly before 1250'.[32] Rather than for its text, which is so garbled that it could never have been used to carry out an inauguration, this *ordo* is important for its cycle of images, including a miniature of a king kneeling before an altar and being anointed on the forehead.[33] Moreover, it is apparent that Innocent's pronouncement that kings should not be anointed on the head was known by at least one thirteenth-century English ecclesiastic. The Cambridge, Trinity College manuscript of the Third Recension, itself dating from the twelfth century, contains a marginal gloss in a thirteenth-century hand next to the rubric for the anointing of the breast, shoulders, arm-joints and head. It reads, 'yet Innocent III says in his work on sacred unction that the king ought not be anointed on his head, but instead on his lower arm, shoulder or upper arms'.[34] Here papal pronouncements and royal practice evidently diverged.

The third English recension, the PRG, and the *Ordo* of 1200, also include a separate rubric and prayer for the anointing of hands.[35] This type of anointing played a central role in priestly consecration, following its introduction into the ordination rite in Carolingian times.[36] Thus, in these *ordines* the king is both anointed on the head, like a bishop, and on the hands, like a priest.[37] These manifest parallels with ecclesiastical practice make clear that liturgical texts continued to enable kings in England, France and the Empire to associate their kingship with episcopal and sacerdotal qualities. In a study of the early medieval *ordines* Janet Nelson cautioned against reading too much into the similarity between episcopal and royal consecration rites, arguing that likenesses between elements in the rites 'might be attributed to a trend in liturgical technique rather than to some ideologically motivated direct

---

[32] *Ordines Coronationis Franciae*, ed. Jackson, I, 341.

[33] The images from this important manuscript are reproduced along with commentary in J. Le Goff et al., *Le sacre royal à l'époque de Saint Louis* (Paris, 2001); The manuscript, Paris, Bibliothèque nationale de France, MS lat. 1246, is also viewable online: <http://gallica.bnf.fr/ark:/12148/btv1b10506563t/f1.image.r=1246> [accessed 23 November 2017].

[34] Cambridge, Trinity College, MS B. 11. 10, fol. 106r: 'dicit tamen Innocentius III in tit. de sacra unctione quod rex non debet inungi in capite, sed in brachio, humero vel armis'.

[35] *English Coronation Records*, ed. Legg, p. 32; *Le pontifical romano-germanique*, ed. Vogel and Elze, I, 242; *Ordines Coronationis Franciae*, ed. Jackson, I, 256.

[36] Cramer, *Baptism and Change*, p. 142.

[37] In priestly consecration the anointing of hands is linked to ideas about purity. Garrison, 'The Franks as the New Israel?', p. 135.

borrowing from the episcopal to the royal rite'.[38] There remains a disjuncture, however, between the intentions of the early medieval liturgists, who originally composed these rites, and the way in which they were interpreted, both at the time and in later centuries. The very least we can say is that, as the liturgical rites developed, parallels between them continued. In the late medieval empire an unusual, and slightly comic ritual, was introduced into both royal and episcopal rites. It subsequently appeared as part of papal inauguration and in the inauguration of abbots and abbesses. The first king to partake of this ritual, which involved sitting on the main altar for the entire duration of the *Te deum*, was possibly Henry VII, following his election at Frankfurt in November 1308.[39] Certainly his successor Louis IV of Wittelsbach sat on the altar at his royal inauguration, as did almost every successive ruler until Joseph I in 1690.[40] From the mid-fourteenth century, high-ranking imperial bishops also sat on the altar as part of their inaugurations. This could be, as Nelson suggested for the earlier period, simply liturgical trend, but ideologically motivated borrowing from one rite to others, in this case from the royal to the episcopal and papal rites, remains a possible explanation. In any case, as remains true to this day, adoption or rejection of changing fashions is seldom ideology free. The incorporation of sitting on the altar into episcopal and papal rites points to a desire for the consecration of prelates not to be overshadowed by royal rites. Surely the large audience at these theatrical festivities would have made a connection between the unusual sight of grown men sitting on an altar. Likewise, the secular and ecclesiastical nobles that constituted the audience for both episcopal and royal consecration would quite probably have been struck by the similarity between episcopal and royal unction.

The rubrics for female inauguration exhibit a similar diversity with respect to anointing. The two earlier imperial *ordines* do not include female inauguration, and of the three later *ordines*, two mention female unction. In both Cencius II and the *Ordo* of the Roman Curia, the empress is anointed on the breast. Of the six royal *ordines* that include queenly anointing, three do not specify where. The remaining three specify the head. Given the sex of the anointed, it perhaps makes more sense to see queenly anointing as symbolic of baptism rather than seeking parallels with episcopal consecration. In other words, the same act, anointing on the head, could convey alternative

---

[38] Nelson, 'Ritual and Reality', p. 334.

[39] On Henry VII's election see Büttner, *Der Weg zur Krone*, I, 276–83; On the phenomenon in general see A. Schmidt, *'Bischof bist Du und Fürst': Die Erhebung geistlicher Reichsfürsten im Spätmittelalter – Trier, Bamberg, Augsburg* (Heidelberg, 2015), pp. 413–34; M. A. Bojcov, 'Warum pflegten deutsche Könige auf Altären zu sitzen?', in *Bilder der Macht in Mittelalter und Neuzeit: Byzanz – Okzident – Rußland*, ed. O. G. Oexle and M. A. Bojcov (Göttingen, 2007), pp. 243–314.

[40] Schmidt, *'Bischof bist Du und Fürst'*, p. 414.

meanings in differing contexts. Perhaps we can go further and suggest that the act of anointing on the head could convey multiple meanings in the same context. For, queenly anointing on the head suggests, as Garrison highlighted, that a link between baptismal and royal anointing, whether male or female, should not be categorically denied. In any case, it is apparent that despite papal moves to downgrade the status of the emperor at the imperial inauguration, exemplified by his anointing between the shoulders and right arm, the popes could not prevent kings and queens in England, the Empire or France from being anointed on the head.

Regalia

Many of the ritual acts in the *ordines* involved the handing over of items of regalia, and it is to these acts and objects that our attention shall now turn. To understand the meanings of these objects we shall need to consider the rubrics that describe their handing over, and the prayers that accompany their concession. At times material evidence will also aid the analysis. However, the following is not an attempt to trace the story of genuine historical items of regalia, as was the aim of Schramm and his acolytes.[41] Rather than taking the inventorizing antiquary approach of earlier *Insignienforscher*, the focus here is on how the *ordines* present these objects and what their presence in the inauguration liturgy can tell us about images of medieval kingship.[42] It will be suggested that, in all three realms, the resonances intrinsic to types of insignia were of as much importance as specific objects themselves.

While there are historical items of regalia, such as the Holy Ampoule in France, that are associated with the rite of anointing, no mention is made of objects associated with anointing in any of our *ordines*, and the Holy Ampoule itself first appears in a French *ordo* dating from the late thirteenth century.[43] Alongside anointing, the highest-ranking ritual in both royal and imperial inauguration was the coronation, in which the king or emperor received an item of headgear from an archbishop or pope. The crown has come to be seen as the symbol of monarchy *par excellence*, with the word 'crown' being used to designate a monarch's realm and the survival of individual crowns, such as the Reichskrone in Vienna, ensuring a plethora of studies concerning the history and meaning of particular crowns.[44] Particularly in the Empire, the historical insignia, and especially the crown, have been

---

[41] Schramm, *Herrschaftszeichen und Staatssymbolik*.

[42] Jürgen Petersohn has characterized Schramm's approach thus. J. Petersohn, 'Über monarchische Insignien und ihre Funktion im mittelalterlichen Reich', *Historische Zeitschrift* 266 (1998), 47–96 (p. 47).

[43] *Ordines Coronationis Franciae*, ed. Jackson, II, 387.

[44] See Arno Mentzel-Reuters for an updated study of the Reichskrone and its

seen as fundamental to the transfer of power. In Reuter's words, the regalia 'had to represent the abstract notion of the kingdom in Germany precisely because there was no institutional core round which a transpersonal view of the state could condense'.[45] More recently Jürgen Petersohn has suggested that the focus of German scholarship on the individual objects that make up the *Reichskleinodien* has been misleading.[46] Rather than thinking in terms of 'genuine' and 'false' items of insignia, Petersohn argues that a king required *a* crown, not necessarily *the* Reichskrone.[47] It has perhaps been historiographical trends, rather than historical reality, that has driven the idea that the insignia were comparatively more important in a German context.[48] As will be seen, the *ordines* themselves are concerned with generic symbols rather than with specific physical or historical entities. They make, with one exception, no allowance for specific objects.

The language of the *ordines* makes it difficult even to determine the type of headgear referred to. As with the type of oil used in the anointing, the liturgical language lacks the precision modern scholars crave. In the royal *ordines* the word used to describe the headwear imposed is crown (*corona*), whereas in four of the five imperial *ordines* the emperor is crowned with a diadem (*diadema*). The diadem, originally a purple and white ribbon, can be traced back to ancient Persia and was worn habitually by Constantine, thus cementing its association with Christian imperial power.[49] The rubrication of the *ordines* certainly suggests that this distinction was recognized. But a consideration of the variant of prayer form K43 associated with the imperial coronation in the *Ordo* of the Roman Curia raises some doubt about this: 'Receive the sign of glory, the diadem of the kingdom, the crown of the empire, in the name of the Father and the Son and the Holy Spirit'.[50] Here the diadem is a royal attribute and the crown associated with imperial power. It thus seems clear that vocabulary could be used flexibly and that we need to exercise caution in making distinctions and assigning meaning based on vocabulary alone. The variability of the vocabulary must partly stem from the influence of biblical language on the *ordines*. The Old and New Testaments

---

use. A. Mentzel-Reuters, 'Die goldene Krone: Entwicklungslinien mittelalterlicher Herrschaftssymbolik', *Deutsches Archiv* 60 (2004), 135–82.

[45] Reuter, 'The Making of England and Germany, 850–1050', p. 291.

[46] J. Petersohn, *"Echte" und "falsche" Insignien im deutschen Krönungsbrauch des Mittelalters?*, Sitzungsberichte der wissenschaftlichen Gesellschaft an der Johann-Wolfgang-Goethe-Universität Frankfurt am Main 30 (Stuttgart, 1993).

[47] Petersohn provides a useful table summarizing his findings concerning the use, or lack thereof, of the 'Reichskrone' in German royal coronations from 1198 to 1486. Ibid., p. 119.

[48] Ibid., p. 101.

[49] E. Twining, *European Regalia* (London, 1967), p. 7.

[50] *Die Ordines*, ed. Elze, p. 77: 'Accipe signum glorie, diadema regni, coronam imperii, in nomine Patris et Filii et Spiritus sancti'.

were composed over several centuries and by multiple authors, making it inevitable that words would not be used consistently across time. If the composer of a prayer formula borrowed a biblical phrase, the choice of word to use had already been made for him. In the case of the formula above, a clear biblical parallel for both *corona* and *diadema* being deployed in the same sentence is provided by Isaiah 62. 3, which declares: 'you will be a crown of glory in the hand of the Lord and a diadem of the kingdom in the hand of your God'.[51]

The flexibility of the biblically influenced vocabulary of the *ordines* is made clear when considering another item of regalia. A *virga* is normally considered to be a short rod, in contrast to a *sceptrum*, a longer sceptre. However, prayer formula K14, which appears in four royal and two imperial *ordines*, confirms that such a definite distinction cannot always be made. Following the delivery of the sceptre in the Ratold *Ordo*, for example, the prayer begins, 'receive the sceptre of royalty, the emblem of power, the rod of rule, the rod of virtue, with which you yourself might rule well'.[52] In the PRG, the delivery of the sceptre and staff (*baculum*) is followed by the prayer (K16), 'receive the rod of virtue and equity' ('accipe virgam virtutis atque aequitatis').[53] In terms of biblical borrowings, Psalm 109 supplies the expression *virgam virtutis* and Hebrews 1. 8 the phrase *virgam aequitatis*.[54] The combination of rubrics and prayers makes clear that these words, *sceptrum*, *baculum* and *virga*, could be used interchangeably and that it is not possible to assign meaning to these items of regalia, as a child colouring by numbers assigns a colour based on a number. In any case, as Sandy Heslop has pointed out, the rod cannot be understood purely as an item of royal regalia. As will be argued below, the multiple meanings inherent in such items need to be recognized more fully in an attempt to uncover high medieval images of kingship.[55]

After the crown, the item of insignia that appears most often in the *ordines* is the sword, which is included in all the royal *ordines*, and in the three later imperial *ordines*.[56] Prayer formula K27, which appears following the bestowal of the sword in four of the royal *ordines*, makes clear that this sword

---

[51] 'eris corona gloriae in manu Domini et diadema regni in manu Dei tui'.
[52] *Ordines Coronationis Franciae*, ed. Jackson, I, 187: 'accipe sceptrum regiae potestatis insigne, virgam scilicet rectam, virgam virtutis, qua te ipsum bene regas'.
[53] *Le pontifical romano-germanique*, ed. Vogel and Elze, I, 256.
[54] Psalm 109. 2, 'virgam virtutis tuae emittet Dominus ex Sion dominare in medio inimicorum tuorum'; Hebrews 1. 8, 'ad Filium autem thronus tuus Deus in saeculum saeculi et virga aequitatis virga regni tui'.
[55] T. A. Heslop, 'The Virgin Mary's Regalia and Twelfth-Century English Seals', in *The Vanishing Past: Studies of Medieval Art, Liturgy and Metrology Presented to Christopher Hohler*, ed. A. Borg and A. Martindale (Oxford, 1981), pp. 53–63 (pp. 55–9).
[56] Although not included in the cursory early imperial *ordines*, the handing over of a sword is first evidenced in an imperial inauguration of 823. Ullmann, *The Growth of Papal Government*, p. 157.

is a gift from the Church to be used for the protection of the Church. The king is exhorted to, 'receive the sword ordained by God for the defence of the holy church of God, from the hands of the bishops, although unworthy'.[57] Prayer formula K10, which appears in the remaining three royal *ordines* makes similar demands of the recipient, who should protect the 'fortress of God' ('castra Dei') with the help of 'the most unconquerable triumphant Lord our Jesus Christ'.[58] The prayers associated with the handing over of the sword that appear in the three later imperial *ordines* are all found in the royal *ordines*. Cencius II has two prayers associated with the sword, K10 and K11, a pairing that is also found together in the English Second Recension, in the Ratold *Ordo* and in the *Ordo* of Saint-Bertin.[59] The Staufen *Ordo*, and that from the Roman Curia, make use of prayer K27. In the Staufen *Ordo* only a short incipit is given.[60] In contrast, in the *Ordo* from the Roman Curia the entire prayer is written out with a small alteration to suit the papal context in which it was to be used.[61] This *ordo* is also the only one whose rubrics go into any detail about the handing over of the sword. Here it is apparent that prayer and rubric complement one another.

Small though it is, the change made to prayer K27 in the *Ordo* from the Roman Curia is nevertheless telling. Instead of merely accepting the sword from the hands of the bishop, the emperor is exhorted to accept the sword 'taken up by our hands from over the body of blessed Peter'.[62] The 'our' in question here is the pope, successor of St Peter, to whose body he refers. The superior position of the pope as the supplier of the sword is thereby stressed through this minor alteration to the prayer formula.[63] The alteration is, however, significantly magnified by the accompanying rubrics, which describe the pope's role and explain the reference to the body of St Peter. There is some confusion in the *ordo* about whether the sword should be given before or after the coronation and the handing over of the sceptre and orb.[64]

---

[57] This wording is from the English Third Recension. *English Coronation Records*, ed. Legg, p. 34: 'accipe gladium per manus episcoporum, licet indignas ... in defensionem sancte Dei ecclesie divinitus ordinatum'.

[58] This wording is from the English Second Recension. Ibid., p. 18: 'invictissimi triumphatoris domini nostri Ihesu Christi'.

[59] In the *Ordo* of Saint-Bertin the order appears confused and following the first prayer associated with the sword comes the concession of the ring and sceptre, before the second sword-related prayer. *Ordines Coronationis Franciae*, ed. Jackson, I, 244–5.

[60] *Die Ordines*, ed. Elze, p. 67.

[61] Ibid., p. 80.

[62] Ibid., p. 80: 'desuper beati Petri corpore sumptum per nostras manus'.

[63] Ullmann suggests that the idea that the emperor should protect the pope can also be seen in the manner of his anointing on the right arm and between the shoulder blades, which 'symbolizes the sanctification of the physical support and protection of the head'. The head in this case being the pope himself. Ullmann, *The Growth of Papal Government*, p. 228.

[64] Following the bestowal of the sword comes a rubric which reads 'sed sciendum est,

Leaving this problem to one side, the rubrics inform us that the pope is seated before the altar of St Peter and on a higher level ('in supereminenti specula') than the emperor-elect, with this position underlining the pope's superiority.[65] He then ascends to the altar and picks up the unsheathed sword. It is in this literal sense that the emperor receives a sword assumed from above the body of St Peter.[66] The pope carries this sword, which is described as embodying the command of the whole empire ('coram intelligens imperii totius') and continues to hold it while speaking the prayer.

At the conclusion of the prayer, the pope girds the emperor with the sword while repeating a phrase taken from Psalm 44. 4, which had already been invoked in the prayer: 'gird thy sword upon thy thigh, O thou most mighty'. This phrase is, however, expanded to stress that it is not through use of the sword that those consecrated conquer kingdoms, but through faith.[67] In this context it is manifest that faithfulness to the pope, as much as to God, is demanded.[68] This is underlined by the actions that follow. Though there is some confusion over whether the emperor is now crowned, the rubrics prescribe that he should take the sword out of its scabbard and brandish it three times with manly vigour before immediately re-sheathing the sword.[69] The triple brandishing symbolizes that the sword is to be used in the name of the Trinity, cementing the message transmitted in the prayer formula, that this sword is to be used for the defence of the Church. Further to emphasize this point the emperor is, in the following rubric, described as having been made a 'miles beati Petri'. This is a sword to be brandished to protect the Church, under the command of St Peter and his successors. Through the minor change made to the prayer formula, the papal addition to the reference to Psalm 44, and the actions described in the rubrics, the handing over of the sword in the *Ordo* of the Roman Curia becomes a ritual action that once again, makes explicit that the position of the pope is superior to that of the emperor. This *ordo* can be seen as reflecting papal interpretations of the Gelasian 'two

---

quod in aliquibus libris primo datur gladius, postea diadema'. The coronation and handing over of sceptre and orb are subsequently repeated in the text. *Die Ordines*, ed. Elze, p. 80.

[65] This phrase is adopted from the papal metaphor of the 'speculum pastoralis' employed by Innocent III in a number of *arengae* and referencing Jeremiah 31. 21. See N. Vincent, 'Stephen Langton, Archbishop of Canterbury', in *Étienne Langton, prédicateur, bibliste, théologien*, ed. L.-J. Bataillon et al., Bibliothèque d'histoire culturelle du Moyen Âge 9 (Turnhout, 2010), pp. 51–126.

[66] Cf. the image of an unsheathed sword on the altar in the *Ordo* of 1250. Paris, Bibliothèque nationale de France, MS lat. 1246, fol. 17r: <http://gallica.bnf.fr/ark:/12148/btv1b10506563t/f43.image.r=1246> [accessed 23 November 2017]

[67] 'sancti non in gladio, sed per fidem vicerunt regna'. *Die Ordines*, ed. Elze, p. 80.

[68] See below pp. 151, 157 for Psalm 44 in a royal context.

[69] 'eximit eum de vagina, viriliterque ter illum vibrat et vagine continuo recommendat'. *Die Ordines*, ed. Elze, p. 81.

Liturgical Rituals: Rubrication and Regalia

swords' theory, which had played a central role in the polemical writings of both papal and imperial partisans during the Investiture Controversy.[70]

The three prayers associated with the handing over of the sword (K10, K11 and K27) are representative of the symbolism to be found in the prayers associated with other items of regalia. Rather than assigning specific items specific meanings, similar exhortations are associated with a variety of items. Thus, just as prayer K27 dictates that the sword is to be used to establish equity ('per eundem vim aequitatis exerceas'), the prayer normally associated with the giving of the sceptre, formula K16, tells us that the rod is a sign of virtue and equity ('virgam virtutis atque aequitatis'). In the same way in which prayer K27 claims that the sword should be used to curse and destroy the enemies of the church ('nec minus sub fide falsos quam Christiani nominis hostes execreris et destruas'), another prayer (associated with the giving of the ring in both the English second recension and the Ratold *Ordo*), prayer formula K8, makes similar associations for the ring so that it is made to sound as much of a weapon as a sword, indeed Walter Ullmann memorably described the ring in the *ordines* as having the function of a knuckle-duster.[71] By accepting the ring, the seal of holy faith, the king will increase in power and learn to 'repel enemies, destroy heretics, unite believers, and join together in the preservation of the catholic faith'.[72] Thus the individual items of regalia can be seen to encapsulate a number of virtues. As a result it is inadvisable either to assign fixed meanings to individual items or to assume that meanings, once assigned, remained fixed.[73] Only by admitting the fluctuations in interpretation of different items of regalia, rather than stubbornly assuming immutable meanings, can we hope to understand the ideas at stake here.

As noted above, it is, with one exception, impossible to identify actual historical items of regalia in the *ordines*. Petersohn has rightly warned, that it would be folly to take the general descriptors found in the *ordines*, such as *corona regni* and *corona imperii*, and to conclude that they corresponded to a specific

---

[70] I. S. Robinson, *The Papacy, 1073–1198: Continuity and Innovation* (Cambridge, 1990), pp. 296–9; R. L. Benson, 'The Gelasian Doctrine: Uses and Transformations', in *La notion d'autorité au Moyen Âge: Islam, Byzance, Occident*, ed. G. Makdisi, D. Sourdel and J. Sourdel-Thomine (Paris, 1982), pp. 13–44 (pp. 24–36). See also W. Levison, 'Die mittelalterliche Lehre von den beiden Schwertern', *Deutsches Archiv* 9 (1952), 14–42.

[71] W. Ullmann, *Principles of Government and Politics in the Middle Ages* (London, 1966), pp. 181–2.

[72] This wording is from the English Second Recension. *English Coronation Records*, ed. Legg, p. 18: 'hostes repellere, hereses destruere, subditos coadunare, et catholice fidei perseverabilitati conectere'.

[73] Two of the imperial *ordines*, the Staufen and Roman Curia *ordines*, include the handing over of the imperial orb (*pomum aureum*), an item of regalia that is not found in the royal *ordines*, despite the fact that the kings of Germany and England were depicted with orbs on their seals.

crown, as has occasionally been attempted in German scholarship.[74] David Carpenter too has cautioned against trying to trace the history of any particular English coronation crown because, 'crowns could be altered and, in any case, most kings had several of various shapes and sizes'.[75] Indeed, it is likely that several crowns were used on the very day of a king or emperor's inauguration. Towards the conclusion of the inauguration ceremony, the newly consecrated monarch swapped his cumbersome coronation crown for something rather more suitable for wearing in procession, while feasting or, indeed, while riding a horse around Rome.[76] Not only the *ordines*, but also the absence of material evidence, cautions against attributing too much significance to historical items of regalia used during the inaugurations of kings and emperors in this period.

The notable exception here comes from the *ordo* Cencius II. Following the conclusion of the mass, the count of the palace approaches the emperor and removes his liturgical footwear. He then proceeds to dress the emperor with the imperial greaves and the spurs of St Maurice ('calcaria sancti Mauricii').[77] It is surely no coincidence that spurs associated with St Maurice should appear in this *ordo*, which in its opening rubric also mentions the saint by name. As noted above, this *ordo* is the first to suggest that the emperor's anointing should take place before the altar of St Maurice rather than that of St Peter.[78] This link suggests that his subsequent mention in relation to spurs might also be for the benefit of the pope rather than the emperor. That this is the case is further implied by the actions of the emperor and pope following the bestowal of the spurs. The emperor and pope are led to waiting horses and the emperor holds the stirrup for the pope as he mounts his horse.[79] The pope, also crowned, then rides at the head of a procession, followed by the emperor and behind him the empress. These events are a clear symbolic

---

[74] Petersohn, 'Über monarchische Insignien', p. 52.

[75] Carpenter, 'The Burial of King Henry III, the Regalia and Royal Ideology', p. 444.

[76] Roger of Howden, for example, reports that Richard I swapped his coronation crown for a lighter one before the ensuing feast. Roger of Howden, *Chronica magistri Rogeri de Houedene*, ed. W. Stubbs, 4 vols., RS 51 (London, 1870), III, 12. The swapping of crowns is beautifully illustrated in a miniature in the *Ordo* of 1250, which is reproduced as plate 15 in Le Goff et al., *Le sacre royal à l'époque de Saint Louis*; Paris, Bibliothèque nationale de France, MS lat. 1246, fol. 42r: <http://gallica.bnf.fr/ark:/12148/btv1b10506563t/f93.image.r=1246> [accessed 23 November 2017].

[77] *Die Ordines*, ed. Elze, p. 46.

[78] See above p. 69.

[79] Both Lothar III and Frederick Barbarossa performed this service, with Lothar III also taking the reins and leading Innocent II's horse when they met at Liege in 1131. B. Schneidmüller, 'Canossa – Das Ereignis', in *Canossa 1077 – Erschütterung der Welt: Geschichte, Kunst und Kultur am Aufgang der Romanik*, ed. C. Stiegemann and M. Wemhoff (Munich, 2006), pp. 36–46 (p. 45). For German kings fulfilling the office of *strator* for the pope see A. T. Hack, *Das Empfangszeremoniell bei mittelalterlichen Papst-Kaiser-Treffen* (Cologne, 1999), pp. 504–40.

presentation of the pope's position above the emperor. As with the bestowal of the sword in the *Ordo* from the Roman Curia, dressing the emperor with the spurs of St Maurice is designed to make clear that his military powers are to be used to serve the pope.

The Holy Lance, known by at least the mid-thirteenth century as the lance of St Maurice, was one of the most important items of regalia in the Empire, but had no role to play in either the royal or imperial inauguration ceremony. The lance, *Sante Mauricien sper*, is included in the 1246 inventory from Trifels, in which mention is also made of three golden spurs.[80] The spurs are not, however, associated with the saint and neither are the two swords, described in the inventory as having scabbards decorated with precious stones.[81] This general description could fit many surviving medieval swords, including the blade known to posterity as the sword of St Maurice (Plate 2). This sword was probably used during the inauguration of Otto IV in Aachen in 1198, and can be dated to between 1198 and 1218 due to the fact that the pommel displays the Welf arms on one side and the royal arms on the other.[82] Setting aside its later erroneous association with St Maurice, the decoration on the guard of the sword offers a tantalizing insight into the language of the royal inauguration ceremony in Germany at the beginning of the thirteenth century. The guard is engraved on both sides, with the side displaying the Welf arms bearing the legend + C(H)RISTVS . VINCIT . C(H)RISTVS . REIGNAT . CHRIST(VS) INPERAT.[83] The side displaying the royal arms bears a shortened version of this tricolon: + C(H)RISTVS . VINCIT . C(H)RISTVS . REINAT.

The significance of this triumphant tricolon and its subsequent removal from the *laudes* included in the Staufen *Ordo* being a manifestation of post-Gregorian tension between the pope and emperor was emphasized in the previous chapter.[84] There are no known manuscript copies of the *laudes* surviving from the German kingdom after *c*.1100, a fact that has been seen as indicative of the desacralization of German kingship.[85] However, if we compare the situation to England, where only one *laudes* text survives from the twelfth century, integrated into the *ordo* in the Cambridge, Trinity College manuscript, and only two from the thirteenth century, both in the same Worcester antiphonary, it is apparent that the survival of these *laudes*

---

[80] *Mittelalterliche Schatzverzeichnisse*, ed. Bischoff, p. 100.
[81] Ibid: 'Zwey swert mit zweyn scheiden, gezieret mit edelem gesteyne'.
[82] M. Schulze-Dörrlamm, *Das Reichsschwert*, Römisch-germanisches Zentralmuseum Forschungsinstitut für Vor- und Frühgeschichte 32 (Sigmaringen, 1995); Petersohn, *"Echte" und "falsche" Insignien*, pp. 74–82.
[83] The unusual spelling might hint to the place of the sword's origin. Schulze-Dörrlamm, *Das Reichsschwert*, p. 27.
[84] See above, pp. 58–66.
[85] Kantorowicz, *Laudes Regiae*, p. 97; Cowdrey, 'The Anglo-Norman *Laudes Regiae*', p. 46.

Inauguration and Liturgical Kingship

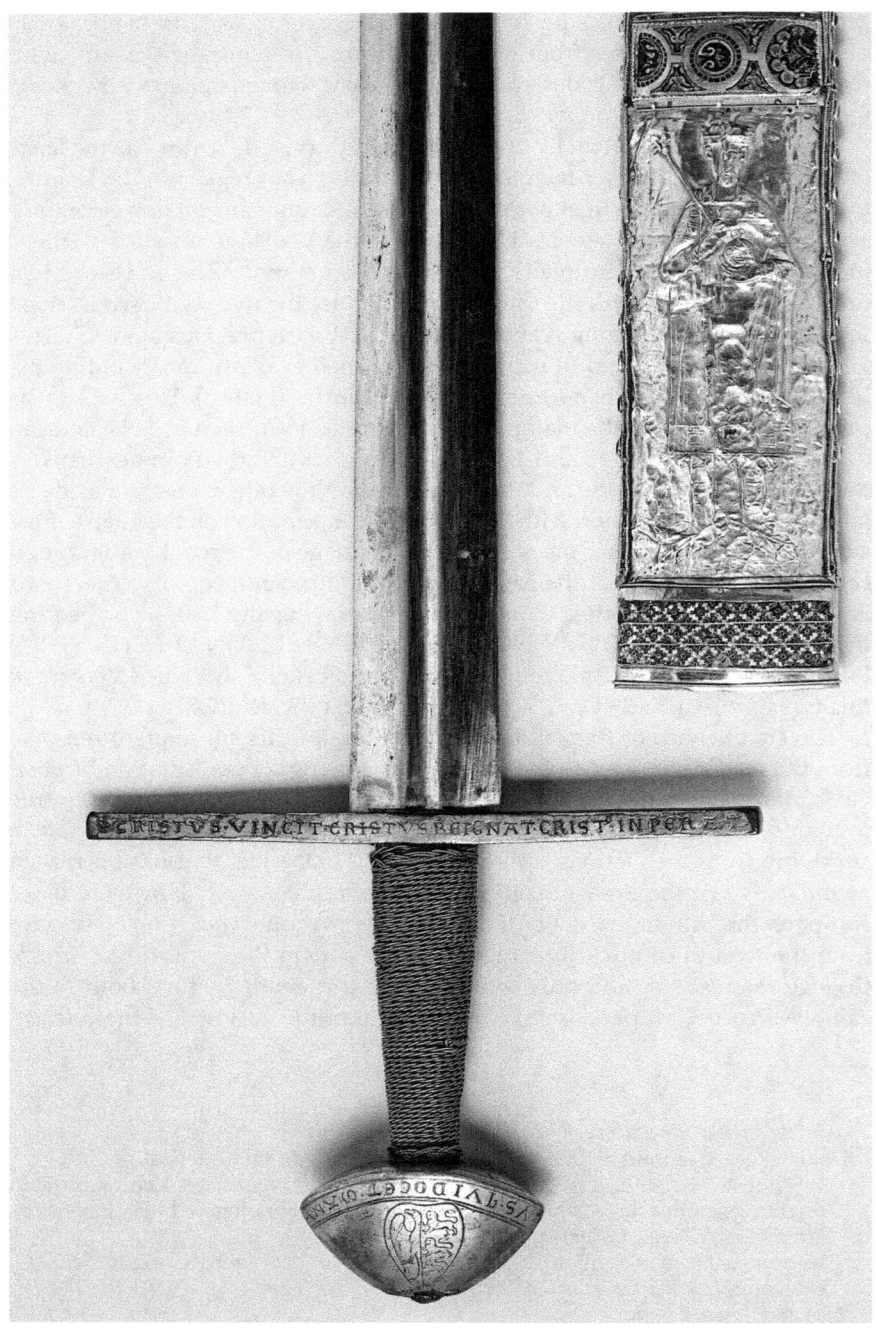

Plate 2. The Reichsschwert (so-called sword of St Maurice)

texts is extremely rare.⁸⁶ Often written on fly-leaves, and probably also on rolls, the texts themselves were surely frequent victims of damage or rebinding. The rarity of their survival tells us little of how frequently they were recited. In England, despite the scarcity of surviving *laudes* formulae, we know from payments to the king's chaplains recorded in the chancery and exchequer rolls that the *laudes* were very frequently recited, certainly several times a year on significant liturgical days. The fact that the defining *laudes* tricolon, absent from the *laudes* in the Staufen *Ordo*, was engraved on the guard of a sword belonging to a German king dating to a century after the last manuscript copy of the text is significant. It suggests that in a royal context the *laudes* did not suffer the same fate that they had in the context of imperial inauguration ceremonies. On the contrary, the German kings probably continued to use the *laudes* to associate their rule with the victorious Christ.

Royal Marriage

All the queens inaugurated in England, France and the Empire in the period under consideration in this book were queens by virtue of their marriage. While Matilda of England claimed the English throne in her own right she was never, as is well known, consecrated queen of England, whereas she had been crowned and anointed in Mainz in 1110 in anticipation of her marriage to Henry V of Germany. There exists, then, a concrete link between royal marriage and inauguration and this relationship is not just with the female rite. As we shall see in chapter 3, if a king was not already married on his accession to the throne he often took the opportunity to be crowned for a second time at his spouse's inauguration, thus referencing back to his own transformation to the royal dignity. If a king had a spouse before he commenced his reign, a joint-inauguration was most often the order of the day. The queen thus had an important role to play in legitimizing the king's position at these pre-eminent moments of royal ceremonial, which also sought to project dynastic legitimacy on to existing or hoped for royal successors. However, in addition to the more tangible benefits of queenly participation, the conceptual connections between marriage and inauguration also had the potential to strengthen ruler sacrality. Latent in the inauguration liturgies from the time of their original composition, twelfth-century developments in Marian devotion had the potential to reinvigorate nuptial and coronation imagery within the female rite. In the realm of ideology, as in reality, female inauguration reflected on the image of the king.

---

[86] The Worcester antiphonary is now Worcester Cathedral Library, MS F. 160. Cowdrey, 'The Anglo-Norman *Laudes Regiae*', p. 66.

Inauguration and Liturgical Kingship

Only two items of regalia, the crown and the ring, regularly appear in female inauguration *ordines*. One of the twenty manuscripts consulted by Jackson in his edition of the Ratold *Ordo* is unique in that it includes the handing over of a sceptre in the inauguration of the queen.[87] This manuscript, now Siena, Biblioteca Comunale degli Intronati, MS G. V. 12, is a pontifical from Tyre dating to the first decade of the thirteenth century. It has understandably been associated with the inauguration of the Latin monarchs of Jerusalem.[88] The addition of the sceptre, considered to represent broadly the exercise of justice, is perhaps indicative of the frequency with which queens ruled in their own right in the Holy Land.[39] A crown appears in all of the six royal and three imperial *ordines* that include an *ordo* for a queen or empress. As was the case with items of regalia found in the male *ordines*, it is seldom possible to identify particular material crowns as having been used in specific realms or contexts. Indeed, few queenly crowns survive from the pre-Investiture Controversy period. In his study of queenly inauguration in the early Middle Ages, Gunther Wolf was only able to identify two surviving queenly crowns, one belonging to the Lombard queen Theodelinde (*c*.575–627), now kept in the cathedral treasury at Monza, and the second associated with the Empress Kunigunde (*c*.975–1040) and now in the treasury of the Munich Residenz.[90]

Four of the six queenly *ordines* include a ring. A ring is also found in all male royal *ordines*, with the exception of the English Second Recension, but only in Cencius II in an imperial context. Beyond the monarchical context, a ring played an important role in episcopal consecration, one that was the subject of much debate during the Investiture Controversy. Given the oft-noted links between the rites of episcopal and royal consecration this is surely significant. Of connected importance is the nuptial association inherent in rings and their use in the marriage mass. Indeed, in the *ordo* for the consecration of a bishop included in the PRG edition, the prayer associated with investiture with the ring describes it as a ring of faith and a symbol of God's bride, here it does not have the function of a knuckle-duster as in the kingly inauguration rites.[91] In her study of female *ordines* Brigitte Kasten asserts that

---

[87] *Ordines Coronationis Franciae*, ed. Jackson, I, 196.

[88] H. E. Mayer, 'Das Pontificale von Tyrus und die Krönung der lateinischen Könige von Jerusalem: zugleich ein Beitrag zur Forschung über Herrschaftzeichen und Staatssymbolik', *Dumbarton Oaks Papers* 21 (1967), 213–30.

[89] For the importance of queens in the Crusader states see B. Hamilton, 'Women in the Crusader States: The Queens of Jerusalem (1100–1190)', in *Medieval Women*, ed. D. Baker (Oxford, 1978), pp. 143–74. Queens were often depicted with sceptres on their seals. See Appendix 4.

[90] G. Wolf, 'Königinnen-Krönungen des frühen Mittelalters bis zum Beginn des Investiturstreits', *Zeitschrift der Savigny-Stiftung für Rechtsgeschichte: Kanonistische Abteilung* 76 (1990), 62–88 (p. 62).

[91] *Le pontifical romano-germanique*, ed. Vogel and Elze, I, 109: 'annulum fidei, scilicet

the crown symbolizes different qualities in a queenly and kingly context. For the queen the crown stands for her morality and virtue, whereas for the king it is a symbol of his ruler attributes such as glory and justness.[92] However, the fact that the same prayer is associated with male and female coronation in a number of the *ordines* cautions against this interpretation.[93] As suggested above, however, assigning fixed meanings to items of regalia, and particularly to crowns, even when recognizing differing contexts, might well obscure other competing or complimentary readings. Although we tend to think of the crown as the symbol of monarchy *par excellence*, and as an abstraction that comes to embody the state, it is also found in a nuptial context. Given developments in iconography associated with growing devotion to the Virgin Mary in the twelfth century, the potential of the intertwining of royal and nuptial symbolism to strengthen the Christological claims of terrestrial kings deserves consideration.

A thread running through the analysis of the *ordines* is the relationship between male and female inauguration. From our consideration of the prayer formulae it became clear that the male inauguration prayer references to Abraham, Isaac and Jacob were complemented by the prayers in the female inauguration *ordines*, in which their wives, Sarah, Rebecca, Leah and Rachel, were also invoked. With relation to the musical content of the *ordines* it is noticeable that the *laudes* in the imperial *ordo* Cencius II and the English Third Recension included the acclamation of the empress or queen, whereas the later imperial *laudes* lack any reference to an empress. In the rubrication we see that, in some *ordines*, female inauguration was incorporated into the same *ordo* as male inauguration. In other *ordines* the participation of a queen or empress is not envisaged and a separate *ordo* is provided. Richard Jackson commented that 'the liturgy was frozen in time because its prayers and benedictions came, almost without exception, from the Carolingian age'.[94] However, while he is undoubtedly correct to describe the prayer formulae as 'frozen in time' such a judgement cannot be extended to the liturgy in its entirety as an examination of the changing dynamic between the male and female inauguration *ordines* demonstrates.

The rites for king- and queen-making were inextricably linked, due to the very fact that a queen most often merited her inauguration by virtue of her relationship to a king. This is made clear in a manuscript of the Third Recension of the English *ordines*, now in the Cambridge University Library, from which we learn that the queen is anointed for the king's honour. The *ordo* opens with the words: 'here begins the consecration of the queen, who

---

signaculum quatenus sponsam Dei'.
[92] Kasten, 'Krönungsordnungen für und Papstbriefe', p. 255.
[93] K30 and Q9 are, with minor variants, the same prayer and are found in three royal liturgies: one male and two female.
[94] *Ordines Coronationis Franciae*, ed. Jackson, I, 35.

on account of honouring the king is imbued on the head with holy oil by the bishop'.[95] This incipit echoes the assertion of William of Poitiers that William the Conqueror did not wish to rush his coronation as king of England as 'if God granted this honour, he wished to be crowned with his spouse'.[96] Although events dictated that William was crowned king on 25 December 1066, without Matilda being present (she was consecrated a few years later at Pentecost 1068) his desire for a double inauguration is striking.[97] In an imperial context, the participation of the emperor-elect's wife had become the norm following the dual inauguration of Otto I and Adelheid of Italy in 962. Before the mid-tenth century the inauguration of the emperor's wife seems to have been rather haphazard.[98] Sometimes the emperor's wife was crowned empress, but seldom in a joint ceremony. Between 962 and 1220, however, an imperial coronation only took place without an empress when the emperor-elect was unmarried (in 967, 996, 1111, 1185, 1209). In these cases, where possible, spouses were crowned subsequently.[99] There is evidence to suggest that the participation of a spouse could be at the instigation of the emperor elect. An entry in the papal registers dated 28 August 1220 records that Honorius III granted Frederick II's request that his wife Constance be crowned empress alongside him.[100] This dual imperial consecration took place on 22 November 1220. That Constance's participation was specifically requested by Frederick is indicative of the importance of spouses to the construction of royal and imperial power.

Smith has highlighted the nuptial language in the Carolingian *ordines* for the inaugurations of Judith and Ermentrude, but she suggests that these elements were no longer present in the so-called Erdmann *Ordo*, which formed the basis of the Anglo-Saxon and West Frankish queen-makings of the tenth and eleventh centuries.[101] In fact, these later *ordines* adopted many

---

[95] Cambridge University Library, MS EE. II. 3, fol. 90r: 'Incipit consecratio regine que propter honorificentiam regis ab episcopo sacro oleo super verticem perfundenda est'.

[96] *The Gesta Guillelmi of William of Poitiers*, ed. R. H. C. Davis and M. Chibnall, OMT (Oxford, 1998), p. 148: 'si Deus ipsi hunc concedit honorem, secum velle coniugem suam coronari'.

[97] See Elisabeth van Houts's nuanced discussion of William's desire to be crowned with his wife in E. M. C. van Houts, 'Cnut and William: A Comparison' (forthcoming).

[98] C. Zey, '"Imperatrix, si venerit Romam...": Zu den Krönungen von Kaiserinnen im Mittelalter, *Deutsches Archiv* 60 (2004), 3–52 (p. 5).

[99] Ibid., p. 31.

[100] Vatican City, Archivio Segreto Vaticano, Registra Vaticana 11, fol. 14v: 'gratanter accepimus quod karissimam in Christo filiam nostram Constantiam illustrem reginam coniugem tuam precum nostrarum intuitu tecum ducis ut et ipsa tecum suscipiat imperialis glorie diadema'. I am grateful to Thomas W. Smith for this reference.

[101] Smith, 'The Earliest Queen-Making Rites', p. 34 n. 78; *Ordines Coronationis Franciae*, ed. Jackson, I, 142–53.

of the biblical allusions of the *ordines* for Judith and Ermentrude, and such allusions make it clear that the female inauguration rites remained in direct dialogue with those for a king. A closer look at the vocabulary of the prayer formulae makes clear one important facet of this dialogue. Prayer K23, from the male *ordines*, talks of a king being brought forth from the belly ('ex utero') of Abraham. In the complementary female prayer (Q6), it is hoped that the queen might merit, like Sarah, Rebecca, Leah and Rachel, to rejoice in the fruits of her womb ('fructus uteri'). The implication of the use of the word *uterus* is self-evidently linked to the production of an heir, which was, in the succinct words of John Carmi Parsons, the 'guarantee of the integrity and continuity of the realm'.[102]

This focus on an heir highlights the dynastic ambitions behind the increasing interweaving of male and female inauguration rites. Raising the status of queenly inauguration by associating it more closely with the inauguration of the king was a way of emphasizing the hereditary aspect of kingship. Indeed, Franz-Reiner Erkens has explained the consecration of Ermentrude in 866, over twenty years after her marriage to Charles the Bald, as an attempt to produce another son, given that two had chosen the religious life, others had died in childbirth and his sons Charles and Louis both suffered from physical disabilities.[103] This dynastic aspect was undoubtedly significant. However, such practical benefits do not exclude the possibility of more ephemeral advantages in the sphere of monarchical imagery too. In her study of English queenship in the late Middle Ages, Joanna Laynesmith emphasized the way in which the queen's role explicitly legitimized kingship through constructing a Christ-like image for the king, which drew on marriage ideology and Marian symbolism.[104] As an example she points to the civic pageantry that greeted Margaret of Anjou's arrival in London in 1445, following her marriage to Henry IV and in anticipation of her coronation. Given Laynesmith's insight, and the work of other scholars showing the increasing importance of Mary as a model for queenship, growing devotion to the Virgin in the twelfth century must be taken into account as we seek to understand how inauguration liturgies could be reinterpreted.[105] While dynastic considerations were as relevant in 1445 as in 866, the Marian allusions of 1445 had no resonance

---

[102] J. C. Parsons, 'Introduction: Family, Sex, and Power: The Rhythms of Medieval Queenship', in *Medieval Queenship*, ed. J. C. Parsons (Stroud, 1994), pp. 1–14 (p. 4).

[103] F.-R. Erkens, '"Sicut Esther Regina": Die westfränkische Königin als *consors regni*', *Francia* 20 (1993), 15–38 (p. 28).

[104] J. L. Laynesmith, *The Last Medieval Queens: English Queenship 1445–1503* (Oxford, 2004), p. 30.

[105] The potential of, and ambiguities inherent in, Mary as a queenly model come through in many of the contributions in A. J. Duggan, ed., *Queens and Queenship in Medieval Europe* (Woodbridge, 1997). See Duggan's introductory comments on the subject, pp. xvi–xvii.

in the ninth century. We should not allow the apparent timelessness of the liturgy to blind us to the different contexts in which it was used.

In identifying changes in the interpretation of inauguration liturgies our investigation is once again hampered by the very nature of the texts and the manuscripts in which the *ordines* survive. Pontificals were comprehensive liturgical books, in which a multiplicity of rites was assimilated and whose contents are grouped by type.[106] The first surviving text that contains both a male and female inauguration ceremony is the so-called Erdmann *Ordo*, composed c.900. The appearance of these texts together led scholars to suggest that the *ordo* must have been composed for a specific joint coronation. However, Jackson has rejected this, pointing out that no meaning can be read into the inauguration rites for kings and queens appearing side by side in a pontifical, and that scholars 'have been led astray by a simple succession of texts in liturgical manuscripts'.[107] Jackson is absolutely right to counter attempts to tie the Erdmann *Ordo* to a particular historical event, but setting out his argument so forcefully perhaps leads him to dismiss too hastily the evidence in later *ordines*.

For example, Jackson has described the inclusion of elements from the marriage ceremony in the *Ordo* of 1200 as a 'peculiarity', arguing that while there remains a possibility the text could have been deliberately designed this way, it is more likely to be the result of scribal error.[108] In the *ordo*, which survives in two manuscripts, the inauguration of the king is followed by mass and then by the inauguration of the queen.[109] Once the queen has been blessed, anointed and crowned the reading from Ephesians 5. 22–33 and the Gospel reading from Matthew 19. 3–11 normally found in the marriage ceremony follow. That the *missa ad nuptiis* is the next ceremony found in the manuscript has led Jackson to conclude that these readings probably belong to the wedding mass rather than the inauguration rite. However, following the marital offertory and communion chant, a puzzling prayer appears. It seems to link back to the inauguration rite, in that in mentions a king, a crown and unction, the reference to anointing being particularly out of place in a nuptial context. The prayer (Q12) begins with the familiar words *deus tuorum corona fidelum*, which is found at the start of a prayer associated with both male and female coronation (K30 and Q9), before continuing in a unique form that I have not found elsewhere, either in an inauguration or a marriage

---

[106] That is, similar status-changing rites, such as the consecration of a bishop and the consecration of an abbot, tend to appear in succession in pontificals.

[107] *Ordines Coronationis Franciae*, ed. Jackson, I, 143.

[108] Ibid., I, 249.

[109] Jackson designates the manuscripts *A* Reims, Bibliothèque municipale, MS 343 and *B* Besançon, Bibliothèque municipal, MS 138. In his view *B* was copied from *A*, probably with an eye for use as a number of abbreviated words have been expanded. *B* also included the sections related to marriage, as does the *Ordo* of 1250. *Ordines Coronationis Franciae*, ed. Jackson, I, 248–9.

liturgy.[110] The uniqueness of the prayer suggests it is not necessarily a simple copyist's error.

The *Ordo* of 1200 is, admittedly, exceptional in the extent of the assimilation of marriage liturgy, and does suggest a degree of confusion, but also that we should examine more closely the relationship between male and female *ordines* in the manuscripts. Of the royal liturgies, all but the Saint-Bertin *Ordo* have associated female *ordines*. Jackson's argument about the simple succession of texts in a liturgical manuscript seems to hold in these cases. The female inauguration text normally follows that of the male. In the Cambridge, Trinity College manuscript (of the third English recension), the *laudes*, mentioning both a king and queen, are sandwiched between the male and female inauguration texts. In the Cologne manuscript, the sequence is male royal, male imperial, female royal. However, by the time of the composition of the three later imperial rites, female inauguration appears to have been integrated into the male rite. The *ordo* Cencius II assumes participation of a queen throughout, and, while neither the Staufen *Ordo* nor the *Ordo* of the Roman Curia assume a queen will be present, if a queen is to be inaugurated as well, her inauguration as empress is allowed for within the single rite. As we have seen, this reflects the historical reality that, if already married, the German king's spouse was always raised to the imperial dignity in conjunction with him. In the light of these integrated imperial *ordines*, and imperial practice, the *Ordo* of 1200 might be seen as less of an exception.

In chapter 1, references to Sarah, Rebecca and Rachel were linked to their status as exemplary wives. It is unsurprising, therefore, to find that nuptial resonances are found elsewhere in the *ordines*, particularly in association with coronation. Prayer formula Q13, which appears in five of the royal inauguration rites and two of the imperial rites, references the eternal bridegroom in a prayer following the coronation of the queen:

> Receive the crown of royal superiority, which is placed on your head by the hands, unworthy though they are, of the bishops, so that just as you shine forth outwardly wreathed with gold and gems, so too on the inside strive for the gold of wisdom and the gems of virtues, so that after the setting

---

[110] Ibid., I, 267: 'Deus tuorum corona fidelium, qui quos ad regnum vocas, in misericordia et miseratione coronas, hunc corone plenitudinem tue benedictionis digneris infundere, ut per istam unctionem et nostram benedictionem sanctificetur et in insigne regni habeatur, quatinus eius impositione famulus tuus rex noster insignitus, cetere plebi tue emineat, et memor desponsationis et honoris a te sibi collati, ita tibi devotus existat, ut in diebus suis iusticia et habundantia pacis oriatur, et ad ianuam paradisi de manu tua qui es rex regum coronam regni celestis percipere mereatur'.

of this age you might, with the prudent virgins, prevail to join the eternal bridegroom our Lord Jesus Christ.[111]

The earthly 'crown of royal superiority' thus prefigures the queen's salvation on her entry to the celestial kingdom where she will be united with the heavenly bridegroom. This is made clear by the reference to 'prudent virgins', which recalls the parable of the ten virgins who awaited the bridegroom (Matthew 25. 1–13). The five prudent virgins took spare oil for their lamps, whereas the five foolish virgins omitted to and had to go to fetch more at the crucial moment, missing the arrival of the betrothed couple. As a result, only the prudent virgins, who are often depicted crowned in manuscript miniatures, gained entry to the wedding celebration.[112] In this parable, as in the parable found in Matthew 22. 1–14, the wedding feast symbolizes the kingdom of heaven thus entwining nuptial and royal imagery with salvation.

This link between a crown and the eternal bridegroom is symptomatic of a depth of symbolism that has been obscured by the very language used to describe monarchical inauguration. The custom of describing the inauguration of a monarch as a 'coronation' has not only implied the precedence of that ritual act over the act of unction in the making of a king, but it has also smothered the term with royal associations, thus suffocating alternative senses. Madeline Caviness has stressed that medieval symbols cannot be decoded without recognizing the multiple layers of meaning assigned to sacred symbols.[113] She points to the widespread twelfth-century tradition of exegesis that constructed several levels of meaning including the physical, the allegorical and the moral or tropological.[114] It is thus apparent that we cannot take the crown as an object to be a purely royal symbol, nor assume that the word 'crown' was used exclusively to designate either an object or a realm. This is a significant point because, as we shall see in chapter 4, the increasing use of words associated with crowning and coronation to describe the entire inauguration rite has been seen as evidence for desacralization. This is due to modern word associations rather than medieval ones, when crowns were understood to be the regalia of saints as well as of monarchs.

---

[111] This wording is taken from the English Third Recension. *English Coronation Records*, ed. Legg, pp. 38–9: 'Accipe coronam regalis excellentie que licet ab indignis episcoporum tamen manibus capiti tuo imponitur unde sicut exterius auro et gemmis redimita enites. Ita et interius auro sapientie virtutumque gemmis decorari contendas. Quatinus post occasum huius seculi cum prudentibus virginibus sponso perenni domino nostro Ihesu Christo valeas adherere'.

[112] J. M. Dye, 'The Virgin Mary as *Sponsa* c.1100–c.1400' (unpublished PhD thesis, University College London, 2001), pp. 202–3.

[113] M. H. Caviness, 'Reception of Images by Medieval Viewers', in *A Companion to Medieval Art: Romanesque and Gothic in Northern Europe*, ed. C. Rudolph (Oxford, 2006), pp. 65–85 (p. 71). See also de Lubac, *Medieval Exegesis*.

[114] Ibid.

In the same way that we should not narrow our understanding of the material evidence by assuming the use of only one coronation crown in this period, we should also not confine ourselves to understanding the crown as an abstraction with purely royal associations. Indeed, as Cecilia Gaposchkin has pointed out, coronation and crown-wearing 'had nothing to do with king-making in the biblical context (the crucial bit was unction), and most crowns (*corona*) and diadems (*diadema*) of scripture referred not to temporal rule but to salvation'.[115] The variety of surviving material crowns and the myriad potential meanings of the crown as a symbol were made explicit by Schramm in his 1955 essay on crowns in the early Middle Ages. As he astutely commented, one of the reasons the history of crowns is so complicated is that in the Bible they do not just feature as items of headwear worn by Old Testament kings and high priests, for the word *corona* is also often used metaphorically.[116] The allegorical depth of meaning inherent in the crown as a symbol makes the interpretation of coronation imagery far from straightforward. This is illustrated by the continuing debates about the meaning of the crowns in the famous 'coronation miniature' found in the Gospel book produced for Henry the Lion in the late twelfth century (Plate 3).[117] Scholars have argued that the crowns demonstrate the Lion's royal aspirations, his piety and desire for salvation, or could be a type of nuptial imagery.[118] Scholarly consensus on how to interpret this image seems unlikely, and it is hard not to concur with Bernd Schneidmüller's assertion that the medieval miniaturist perhaps better understood the meaning of a golden crown than modern theologizing viewers.[119]

Earlier, I referred to the fact that not only kings and queens, but also bishops received a ring during their consecrations. So too did nuns, whose rings were described in some contemporaneous liturgies in similar terms to a bishop's ring, as being a 'ring of faith, sign of the holy spirit, that you are called the

---

[115] Gaposchkin, *The Making of Saint Louis*, p. 108.

[116] P. E. Schramm, 'Die Kronen des frühen Mittelalters', in *Herrschaftszeichen und Staatssymbolik: Beiträge zu ihrer Geschichte vom dritten bis zum sechzehnten Jahrhundert*, 3 vols. (Stuttgart, 1954–78), II, 378–417.

[117] Wolfenbüttel, Herzog-August-Bibliothek, MS Guelf. 105 Noviss. 2°, fol. 171v.

[118] J. Fried, 'Königsgedanken Heinrichs des Löwen', *Archiv für Kulturgeschichte* 55 (1973), 312–51; O. G. Oexle, 'Die Memoria Heinrich des Löwen', in *Memoria in der Gesellschaft des Mittelalters*, ed. D. Geuenich and O. G. Oexle, Veröffentlichungen des Max-Planck-Instituts für Geschichte 111 (Göttingen, 1994), pp. 128–77; B. Schneidmüller, 'Kronen im goldglänzenden Buch: Mittelalterliche Welfenbilder und das Helmarshausener Evangeliar Heinrichs des Löwen und Mathildes', in *Helmarshausen: Buchkultur und Goldschmiedekunst im Hochmittelalter*, ed. I. Baumgärtner (Kassel, 2003), pp. 123–46 (pp. 127–36); O. B. Rader, 'Kreuze und Kronen: Zum byzantinischen Einfluss im "Krönungsbild" des Evangeliars Heinrich des Löwen', in *Heinrich der Löwe: Herrschaft und Repräsentation*, ed. J. Fried and O. G. Oexle, Vorträge und Forschungen 57 (Ostfildern, 2003), pp. 199–238 (pp. 205–11).

[119] Schneidmüller, 'Kronen im goldglänzenden Buch', p. 155.

Inauguration and Liturgical Kingship

Plate 3. The 'Coronation Miniature' from the Gospels of Henry the Lion

Liturgical Rituals: Rubrication and Regalia

bride of God, if you serve him faithfully'.[120] Following the bestowal of the ring by the bishop, the virgin received a crown to symbolize her marriage to Christ. This crown (here described as a *torques*), was given as the bishop pronounced the words: 'receive the sign of Christ on your head, that you are made his wife and, if you endure in him, you are crowned in perpetuity'.[121] Both ring and crown were symbols of the virgin's marriage with Christ, a fact that she herself proclaimed by reciting the words: 'my Lord Jesus Christ has joined me with his ring, and adorned me with a crown, like a bride'.[122] Not only was the ring a sign of her marriage contract with Christ, but the crown also embodied that spousal relationship.[123] Without wishing to argue that the parallels between the consecration of queens and nuns should be interpreted as ideologically motivated borrowings, they remain striking and suggest that the coronation of the queen could have associations beyond just the royal. The queen, like the nun, received a ring and a crown as part of her consecration. They were symbols of her royalty, but more than that, they also symbolize, on one level, her union with her husband, upon whom her inauguration was dependent, and, on another level, her union with Christ. For both the nun and the queen, earthly coronation prefigures a heavenly union with the eternal bridegroom, as prayer Q13 makes apparent.

It has become something of a commonplace to see the twelfth century as a period in which devotion to the Virgin reached new heights.[124] Importantly this period also saw the explicit intertwining of nuptial and royal imagery in Marian devotion, which provides a new context for construing the references to crowning within the female inauguration rites. Marian bridal imagery was most closely associated with the celebration of the Assumption of the Virgin (15 August), and, as we shall see, interpretations of this feast changed markedly from the ninth to the twelfth centuries. This reconfirms the suggestion that liturgies, while relatively stable in their contents, were decoded differently due to changes in religious practice and thought external to them. Developments in devotion to the celestial Queen were bound to resonate in terrestrial royal circles, especially when we consider the importance of Mary to the Capetian and Plantagenet dynasties, as well as within the

---

[120] *Le pontifical romano-germanique*, ed. Vogel and Elze, I, 45: 'annulum fidei, signaculum spiritus sancti, ut sponsa Dei voceris, si ei fideliter servieris'.

[121] Ibid.: 'accipe signum Christi in capite, ut uxor eius efficiaris et, si in eo permanseris, in perpetuum coroneris'.

[122] Ibid., I, 46: 'annulo suo subarravit me Dominus meus Jesus Christus, et tanquam sponsam decoravit me corona'.

[123] See Sarah McNamer for a wider discussion of nuns as *Sponsa Christi*. S. McNamer, *Affective Meditation and the Invention of Medieval Compassion* (Philadelphia, 2011), pp. 25–57.

[124] A useful introduction to Marian devotion in the high and late Middle Ages is E. A. Johnson, 'Marian Devotion in the Western Church', in *Christian Spirituality: High Middle Ages and Reformation*, ed. J. Raitt (London, 1987), pp. 392–414.

Empire.[125] Scholars have long stressed the importance of Mary as a role model for queenship, but nuptial symbolism enables, as Laynesmith pointed out, the image of the queen to legitimize kingship too. As we discuss in chapter 3, royal marriage and female consecration provided kings with concrete occasions at which to express their legitimacy and power. The intermingling of nuptial and inaugural imagery in Marian devotion also provided kings with a spouse modelled on the celestial queen, which could only enhance their claims to rule in Christ's image. Bearing fruit by the fifteenth century, I tentatively suggest that the roots were put down in the fertile earth of the twelfth century as part of a post-Gregorian reassertion of royal authority.

The Carolingians had been hesitant about celebrating the Assumption, a feast that was already well established in Byzantium, because it commemorated events that were not found in Scripture. Despite this, the Assumption gradually established itself across the Carolingian empire where, rather than adopting the texts used in the Greek Church, which were considered apocrypha, liturgists turned to a scriptural source, the Song of Songs, in their composition of an acceptable rite.[126] This is rather puzzling, because before the twelfth century there was no formal commentary tradition for reading the Song of Songs as referring to Mary, with Rachel Fulton suggesting that the analogy between the Church, traditionally associated with the Bride in the Song, and Mary only became visible after the fact.[127] In Fulton's view, although the Assumption liturgy draws extensively on biblical material related to marriage and bridal imagery, this is incidental. She might well be right in her judgement of the aims of the creators of this liturgy in the ninth century, but, as Jennifer Dye has argued, the Feast's bridal imagery was widely recognized by the twelfth century.[128]

Of particular relevance to this investigation is an important evolution in the interpretation of the Song of Songs, which provides both a biblical precedent for nuptial crowning (Song of Songs 3. 11) and was used extensively in the liturgy of the Assumption, supplying numerous lessons read throughout the octave of the feast and the texts for many antiphons and responsories proper to the feast itself.[129] While Rupert of Deutz was tradi-

---

[125] Nicholas Vincent has argued that the Plantagenets were just as devoted to Mary as the Capetians. See Vincent, 'King Henry III and the Blessed Virgin Mary'. Veneration of the Virgin was also characteristic of the rulers of the Empire: E.-D. Hehl, 'Maria und das ottonisch-salische Königtum: Urkunden, Liturgie, Bilder', *Historisches Jahrbuch* 117 (1997), 271–310.

[126] R. Fulton, '"Quae est ista ascendit sicut aurora consurgens?": The Song of Songs as the *historia* for the Office of the Assumption', *Mediaeval Studies* 60 (1998), 55–122 (pp. 56–7).

[127] Ibid., p. 70.

[128] Dye, 'The Virgin Mary as *Sponsa*, p. 20.

[129] R. Fulton, *From Judgment to Passion: Devotion to Christ and the Virgin Mary, 800–1200* (New York, 2002), p. 248.

tionally credited with writing the first text that interpreted the Song in a Marian mode, the *Sigillum Beatae Mariae* of the enigmatically named Honorius Augustodunensis is now considered in all likelihood to have been composed earlier, when Honorius was resident at Worcester before his move to Regensburg.[130] The *Sigillum* is essentially a line-by-line commentary on the principal texts used in the Assumption liturgy, including Luke 10. 38–42, the story of Mary and Martha, which was read at the conclusion of Matins, and Ecclesiasticus 24. 11–23, Wisdom personified praising herself, which was read at Vespers as the chapter of the day.[131] The majority of the *Sigillum*, however, is concerned with the Song of Songs and, confronting an exegetical tradition that had interpreted the Song as a dialogue between Christ and the Church, Honorius asserted that anything written about the Church could equally be applied to Mary.[132] Whereas bridal imagery had been peripheral in the ninth-century Assumption celebrations, twelfth-century commentators brought nuptial language to the centre-stage, a development that, as Dye has shown, spread to sermons as well.[133]

This reinterpretation of the Song reverberated in the sphere of the visual arts. As Sandy Heslop has shown, the liturgy for the Assumption was drawn on for one of the most 'radical' iconographic developments of the Romanesque period: the Coronation of the Virgin motif.[134] Heslop demonstrated that this new iconography was developed *c.*1100 as the high point in a cycle of images adorning the newly built chapter house at Worcester, and he links this iconographic innovation to Honorius's presence there.[135] The chapterhouse cycle does not survive, but a transcription of verses from it does survive, leading Heslop to suggest that a similar pictorial cycle surviving in a manuscript dated *c.*1260, now at Eton College, provides a good visual record of the scheme (Plate 4). It is in the roundel at the centre of the manuscript leaf that the coronation image is found, surrounded by other roundels displaying

---

[130] For details of Honorius's career and works see V. I. J. Flint, 'The Career of Honorius Augustodunensis: Some Fresh Evidence', *Revue Bénédictine* 82 (1972), 63–86; V. I. J. Flint, 'The Chronology of the Works of Honorius Augustodunensis', *Revue Bénédictine* 82 (1972), 215–42. The Song of Songs was a popular subject of exegesis in the twelfth century, with surviving commentaries written by Anselm of Laon, Bruno of Segni, Bernard of Clairvaux, Philip of Harveng, Gilbert de la Porree, William of St Thierry, Gilbert of Hoyland, John of Ford, Thomas the Cistercian and Alain de Lille. A. W. Astell, *The Song of Songs in the Middle Ages* (Ithaca, 1995), pp. 8–9.

[131] Fulton, *From Judgment to Passion*, p. 248.

[132] T. A. Heslop, 'The English Origins of the Coronation of the Virgin', *The Burlington Magazine* 147 (2005), 790–7 (p. 792). On the Bride as Church and subsequently Mary see Astell, *The Song of Songs*, pp. 42–72; and E. A. Matter, *The Voice of My Beloved: The Song of Songs in Western Medieval Christianity* (Philadelphia, 1990), pp. 151–77.

[133] Dye, 'The Virgin Mary as *Sponsa*', pp. 21–6.

[134] Heslop, 'The English Origins'.

[135] Heslop, 'The English Origins', p. 792.

Inauguration and Liturgical Kingship

Plate 4. Coronation of the Virgin: Eton College MS 177, fol. 7v

types of the iconography. Earlier visual evidence exists for the motif of an enthroned Mary receiving a crown from an angel or the hand of God.[136] What is radical about this depiction is the manner in which Mary is seated next to Christ and is crowned by him, which is reminiscent of the joint-ruler portraits prevalent in Byzantium.[137] That Christ and Mary are seated together in a chariot and surrounded by the symbols of the four evangelists demonstrates the link to the Assumption. This is the chariot that will carry Christ and Mary up to heaven. As is made explicit in the surrounding verse, this imagery encapsulates both nuptial and regal transformations: 'Betrothed with the dowry of faith and made holy by her virtues the bride is crowned and united to the bridegroom God'.[138] Thus Mary is joined to Christ as his bride at the inauguration of their royal reign of the celestial kingdom.

While this iconography was developed in an ecclesiastical setting at Worcester, within decades the potential of this Marian imagery had been realized in a royal setting, for the earliest surviving representation of the Coronation of the Virgin survives on a capital from Reading Abbey, which was founded by Henry I in 1121. Pauline Stafford has demonstrated that the (re-)foundation of Reading can only be understood in the context of Henry's second marriage to Adeliza of Louvain, following the death of his first wife Matilda of Scotland in 1118 and that of his only legitimate son William in the White Ship disaster of 1120.[139] After the demise of his son Henry quickly sought to remarry with the hope of producing another male heir. Stafford has stressed the extent to which Henry and Adeliza's motives for (re-) founding Reading, which is dedicated to the Virgin, can be understood as penance and purification. The death of the king's only male heir had been interpreted as punishment for the king's own actions, thus penance was required. The new union also needed to be purified, so that a healthy male heir might be forthcoming. It is highly likely that, in accordance with these motives, the marriage and coronation themselves took place on an important Marian celebration: the Feast of the Purification (2 February).[140] The motif of the Coronation of

---

[136] On Coronation of the Virgin iconography see P. Verdier, *La Couronnement de la Vierge: Les origines et le premiers développements d'un thème iconographique* (Montréal, 1980); M.-L. Thérel, *Le Triomphe de la Vierge-Eglise* (Paris, 1984).

[137] Olaf Rader discusses Byzantine joint-ruler portraits in his contribution to the debate surrounding Henry the Lion's Gospel book. See Rader, 'Kreuze und Kronen'. On Western joint-ruler portraits see the doctoral thesis of Erin Barrett: E. G. Barrett, 'Art and the Construction of Early Medieval Queenship: The Iconography of the Joint Royal/Imperial Portrait and the Visual Representation of the Ruler's Consort' (unpublished PhD thesis, Courtauld Institute, University of London, 1997).

[138] Windsor, Eton College Library, MS 177, fol. 7v: 'Dota subarrata fidei meritisque sacrata / Sponsa coronatur sponsoque deo sociatur'.

[139] P. Stafford, '*Cherchez la femme*: Queens, Queens' Lands and Nunneries: Missing Links in the Foundation of Reading Abbey', *History* 85 (2000), 4–27.

[140] J. Dale, 'Inauguration and the Liturgical Calendar in England, France and the Empire, c.1050–c.1250', *Anglo-Norman Studies* XXXVII (2015), 83–98 (pp. 91–4).

the Virgin was thus particularly appropriate in the context. As Stafford has commented, 'what better symbol that the Virgin mother, intercessor *par excellence*, crowned queen by her son, to bring together all the meanings of 1121: queenship, fertility, purity and penance'.[141] 1121 was also about kingship, however, and through his marriage to Adeliza, Henry sought to re-legitimize his own position. The image of the queen directly impacted on the image of her spouse.

Jennifer Dye has pointed to the manifold potential functions of the representation of the Virgin as a bride, arguing that 'language and imagery portraying her as *sponsa* addressed diverse issues within the Christian Church and society at that time. There is no coherent, conscious connecting theme, no consensus of the theology of her bridehood.'[142] Instead, Dye sees the imagery as a 'functional tool that served the varied needs of its users'.[143] Her insight is relevant to this study, because such nuptial Marian imagery has tended to be associated with ecclesiastical rather than secular rulers. Mary Stroll has emphasized how imagery of Maria *Regina* was particularly associated with the papacy and Cecilia Gaposchkin has suggested that the coronation of the Virgin iconography found above the Porte Rouge at Notre-Dame in Paris aimed to confine rather than exalt royal power.[144] The Coronation of the Virgin was a popular subject for architectural sculpture, particularly in Capetian France, where it first adorned the western façade at Senlis, in the late twelfth century.[145] The development of Gothic architecture was once understood as simply a manifestation of growing Capetian power, whereas scholars now recognize that it was driven by a dialogue between competing royal and ecclesiastical ideologies. Donna Sadler, for instance, has suggested that the iconographic programme at Reims cathedral, the traditional site of male inauguration in the French kingdom, embodies an ecclesiastical view of the king's duties, and far from simply exalting royal power provided 'an object lesson in royal behaviour, a carved exhortation to obey the dictates of good kingship'.[146] That Coronation of the Virgin iconography could be used

---

[141] Stafford, '*Cherchez la femme*', p. 26.

[142] Dye, 'The Virgin Mary as *Sponsa*', p. 281.

[143] Ibid.

[144] M. Stroll, 'Maria *Regina*: Papal Symbol', in *Queens and Queenship in Medieval Europe*, ed. A. J. Duggan (Woodbridge, 1997), pp. 173–203; M. C. Gaposchkin, 'The King of France and the Queen of Heaven: The Iconography of the Porte Rouge of Notre-Dame of Paris', *Gesta* 39 (2000), 58–73.

[145] For the suggestion that the image was deployed earlier at Saint-Denis see P. Blum, 'The Lateral Portals of the West Façade of the Abbey Church of St.-Denis: Archaeological and Iconographic Considerations', in *Abbot Suger and Saint-Denis: A Symposium*, ed. P. L. Gerson (New York, 1986), pp. 199–228.

[146] D. Sadler, 'The King as Subject, the King as Author: Art and Politics of Louis IX', in *European Monarchy: Its Evolution and Practice from Roman Antiquity to Modern Times*, ed. H. Duchhardt, R. A. Jackson and D. Sturdy (Stuttgart, 1992), pp. 53–68 (pp. 53–4).

to exalt the power of the church over that of the monarchy does not mean, however, that secular rulers could not make similar claims. Rather than seeing Mary as bride and queen as a purely ecclesiastical symbol we should recognize that a dialogue of competing ideologies lies behind royal and ecclesiastical depictions of the Virgin as *sponsa*.

In conclusion, we return to the inauguration *ordines* themselves. Mary is not prominent in the liturgical texts, but she does appear in two prayers, one in a male context and in one found in the female rite. In prayer K17, found in the Ratold *ordo*, the Cologne *ordo* and in the Second English recension, Mary is, rather prosaically, invoked along with St Peter and St Gregory as a protector of the new monarch.[147] In prayer Q6, which, as we have seen, is found in six of the nine liturgies that include female inauguration, Mary is mentioned soon after the wives of the patriarchs, in an allusion to her role as the mother of Christ. Scholars have seen the Virgin's role in the *ordines* as acting as a model for marriage and fecundity rather than as a model of royalty, especially as she is invoked alongside Sarah, Rebecca, Judith, Esther, Rachel and Leah.[148] Fertility and dynastic concerns are undeniably important aspects of the female *ordines*, but allusions to Mary, who is also invoked for the queen in some *laudes* texts and found in a number of litanies, can be read in a number of ways. By the twelfth century many of the Old Testament figures invoked in the *ordines*, having long been considered as types of the Church, were also seen as types of Mary, including Judith, and Leah and Rachel.[149] In the early thirteenth century Judith was the subject of at least one sermon for the Assumption, which Anne Thayer has seen as 'a fine example of the high medieval transition from ecclesial to Marian exegesis of Old Testament women'.[150] Linking again to Assumption liturgy, Leah and Rachel were seen as types of the sisters Mary and Martha, whose story was read on the feast, and who were themselves types for both the Church and subsequently the Virgin.[151] Finally, Esther was also a type of the Virgin, whose status as queen strengthened her association with Maria *Regina*. Esther's intercession with her royal husband to save the Israelite people foreshadows their eternal salvation at the commencement of Christ's celestial reign alongside his mother Mary.

---

[147] *Ordines Coronationis Franciae*, ed. Jackson, I, 188, 211; *English Coronation Records*, ed. Legg, p. 20.

[148] D. Iogna-Prat, 'La Vierge et les *ordines* de couronnement des reines au IXe siècle', in *Marie: Le culte de la Vierge dans la société médiévale*, ed. D. Iogna-Prat, E. Palazzo and D. Russo (Paris, 1996), pp. 101–7 (p. 107).

[149] On Hrabanus Maurus's commentaries on Judith and Esther in which he describes them as types of *ecclesia* see de Jong, 'Exegesis for an Empress', pp. 88–90.

[150] A. T. Thayer, 'Judith and Mary: Hélinand's Sermon for the Assumption', in *Medieval Sermons and Society: Cloister, City, University*, ed. B. M. Kienzle et al. (Louvain-la-Neuve, 1998), pp. 63–75 (pp. 64–5).

[151] For a discussion of the interpretation of this Gospel reading see Fulton, *From Judgment to Passion*, pp. 259–62.

Esther and Assuerus can therefore be depicted, as they are in *Bible moralisée*, as a prototype for the Coronation of the Virgin.[152]

It is beyond the scope of this study to draw out comprehensively the full resonances of female inauguration liturgies in this new context of heightened Marian devotion, which would require a thorough and in-depth engagement with Marian liturgies, exegesis and sermons. However, it appears to be a fertile subject for further research, especially given the prominence of the Assumption, the concomitant intermingling of royal and nuptial imagery, and well-documented royal devotion to the Virgin. The celestial queen was an obvious model for terrestrial queens, but beyond her royalty, nuptial symbolism enabled her image to strengthen the legitimacy of the king. In the following chapters, we will see some of the very practical ways in which female inauguration was used to strengthen male power, but we should also remain alive to the more ephemeral influences of the female image on concepts of kingship. In her study of the civic pageantry of 1445, which took place between Margaret's marriage and coronation and was thus associated with both, Laynesmith highlighted how reference was made to the parable of the ten virgins, to the wedding feast of Christ the Bridegroom and to the Song of Songs. All these references are encompassed in the *ordines* and enabled the construction of a Marian image for the queen that, through the nuptial transformation, projected a Christ-like image on the king. The moment of marriage and coronation of the royal couple foreshadows the marriage and coronation of Christ and Mary at the inauguration of the heavenly kingdom.

---

[152] Sadler, 'The King as Subject', p. 63, n. 32.

3

Who and Where? Actors, Location and Legitimacy

Roger of Howden provides a detailed description of a procession which arrived at the doors of Westminster Abbey on 3 September 1189.[1] In the vanguard were clerics carrying holy water, crosses, candles and thuribles, closely followed by priors, then abbots, then four barons carrying four golden candlesticks processing amongst the bishops. Godfrey de Lucy and John Marshal followed side by side, Godfrey carrying a felt cap and John a large pair of heavy spurs made of gold. Then came William Marshal, here described as earl of Striguil, with a golden sceptre topped by a cross, accompanied by William FitzPatrick, earl of Salisbury, carrying a golden rod decorated with a golden dove. Then came the triumvirate of David, earl of Huntingdon, John, count of Mortain, and Robert, earl of Leicester, each bearing a sword from the royal treasury. Behind them came six earls and nobles carrying the royal insignia and clothing, then William de Mandeville, count of Aumale, bearing a large and weighty golden crown, decorated with precious stones. Finally came Richard, duke of Normandy, flanked by Hugh, bishop of Durham to his right and Reginald, bishop of Bath to his left. The duke, under a silken canopy, held aloft by four barons, entered the abbey in which he was to be transformed from a duke into a king. His transformation is echoed in the language used by Roger of Howden. Richard arrived at the cathedral as *dux Normanniae*. Following his anointing, crowning and investiture with the objects carried in procession by his barons, he departed Westminster as *dominus rex*. Roger continues his account to tell us that the king swapped his coronation crown for a lighter version and that, 'thus crowned he came to eat, and the archbishops and bishops sat with him on one table, each seated according to his order and dignity. The earls and barons served in the royal household just as their dignities demanded. The citizens of London served in the buttery and the citizens of Winchester in the kitchen.'[2]

Roger's account is suffused with the language of rank.[3] Richard's rank had been enhanced. The churchmen took their places at the king's table according to their order and dignity. The nobles served in the king's

---

[1] Roger of Howden, *Chronica*, ed. Stubbs, III, 9–12.
[2] Ibid., III, 11–12: 'sic coronatus venit prandere; et archiepiscopi et episcopi sederunt cum eo in mensa, unusquisque secundum ordinem et dignitate suam. Comites autem et barones serviebant in domo regis prout dignitates eorum exigebant. Cives vero Lundonienses servierunt de pincernaria, et cives Wintonienses de coquina'.
[3] For a definition of rank see Peltzer, 'Introduction', p. 14.

household according to their dignity. The procession to the abbey was unmistakably a highly choreographed affair with churchmen and nobles assigned roles and positions according to rank, with physical proximity to the king an indication of *Königsnähe*, or power and favour.[4] Even within the groups outlined by Roger there existed internal hierarchies. The three sword bearers, David, earl of Huntingdon, John, count of Mortain, and Robert, earl of Leicester were not of equal rank, for John was the king-elect's brother and his relative importance was shown by the fact that he processed in the middle between the other two sword bearers who were inferior in status to him.[5] Roger outlines the myriad distinct rituals that together constituted Richard's inauguration ceremony. His constant repetition of the word 'then' (*deinde*) in introducing each succeeding ritual element has an almost rhythmical quality, so that we are not just made aware of the order of the ecclesiastical hierarchy within the ceremony, with the aforementioned bishops of Durham and Bath playing subsidiary roles to Baldwin, archbishop of Canterbury, but also of order in its liturgical sense, in the correct and proper ordering of the liturgy. Alas, how frustrating for the historian that Roger's liturgical order does not accord with the surviving twelfth-century English *ordo*, the so-called Third Recension, that includes investiture with the ring, missing in Roger's account, and makes no mention of spurs, which Roger tells us were carried in procession by John Marshal.[6]

This disagreement between the surviving liturgical and narrative sources is entirely typical, and is mirrored in the futility of trying to match, with a few prominent exceptions, items of regalia to descriptions in narrative sources. We might hope that the variety of sources would complement rather than contradict one another, thus enabling the construction of a comprehensive picture, or 'thick description', of an individual inauguration ceremony.[7] The sources, however, do not permit this. Moreover, it is important to recognize that the level of detail in Roger of Howden's chronicle concerning the inauguration of Richard I is highly exceptional. For although Richard Jackson has rightly commented that 'the monarch's inauguration was the greatest and most important ceremony of his reign', the truth is that this

---

[4] That is, William de Mandeville, charged with carrying the crown walked alone and closest to the duke and was Richard's justiciar until his death in November 1189.

[5] Roger of Howden, *Chronica*, ed. Stubbs, III, 9.

[6] Ibid., III, 10. Despite not agreeing with surviving texts of the English Third Recension we should bear in mind that so detailed a description of a liturgical ceremony might well have been composed with the aid of a pontifical. This is certainly the opinion expressed in H. G. Richardson, 'The Coronation in Medieval England: The Evolution of the Office and the Oath', *Traditio* 16 (1960), 111–202 (p. 183).

[7] C. Geertz, 'Thick Description: Toward an Interpretive Theory of Culture', in *The Interpretation of Cultures: Selected Essays*, ed. C. Geertz (New York, 1973), pp. 3–32.

importance is rarely reflected in the source materials.[8] Confining ourselves to English examples for the time being, we have seen that there are only seven surviving manuscript witnesses to the third recension of the inauguration *ordines*: not a large number for a ceremony believed to have been in use for around two centuries. Non-liturgical evidence is hardly more common. Indeed, as Annette Kehnel has recently emphasized, 'the narrative sources are surprisingly uninterested in the issue. Reports of coronations only become fashionable from the fourteenth century onwards.'[9]

The cursory account of Richard's inauguration given by Gervase of Canterbury is, in fact, far more typical of contemporary narrative than Roger's full description. Gervase tells us that Richard

> went to London on 2 September and the following day was crowned in great glory by Baldwin archbishop of Canterbury, with the assistance and cooperation of the bishops of England.[10]

At first glance Gervase's account might appear to add little to our knowledge of monarchical inauguration. Yet this is not the case. In fact, Gervase's economy with words in his description of Richard's inauguration highlights the information that contemporaries considered most important to record. That is: who was involved, what was described as having happened, and where and when an inauguration took place. Instead of lamenting what the sources do not tell us, we should concentrate on what can be gleaned from chronicles, annals and histories. Historians have harvested information from chronicles, collecting descriptions of consecrations that are atypical in their detail. In gathering the grains they have passed over, we shall find that far too many rich kernels have been left unsorted on the threshing-room floor.

Who?

The *Chronica brevi ecclesiae S. Dionysii ad cyclos paschales* has a three-word entry for the year 1059: 'King Philip was ordained (*ordinatur*)'.[11] The chronicler's brevity emphasizes the two key ingredients of all narrative records of monarchical inauguration, coronation or crown-wearings: a king (or emperor)

---

[8] *Ordines Coronationis Franciae*, ed. Jackson, I, 32.
[9] A. Kehnel, 'The Power of Weakness: Machiavelli Revisited', *German Historical Institute Bulletin* 33 (2011), 3–34 (p. 20).
[10] Gervase of Canterbury, *The Historical Works*, ed. W. Stubbs, 2 vols., RS 73 (London, 1879–80), I, 457: 'pervenitque Londoniam iiijo nonas Septembris et in crastino in ingenti gloria coronatus est a Baldwino Cantuariensi archiepiscopo, astantibus et cooperantibus episcopis Angliae'.
[11] *Ex Chronico brevi ecclesiae S. Dionysii ad cyclos Paschales*, ed. L. V. Delisle, RHF 11 (Paris, 1869), pp. 377–8 (p. 377).

and a description of the event, in other words, the 'who' and the 'what'. In this example the Saint-Denis chronicler has pared his description down to the absolute essentials, mentioning only the king, even though the use of the passive verb *ordinatur* alerts us to the fact that there must have been other participants. It is no doubt self-explanatory that a monarch is the central figure in a description, however brief, of his inauguration. But it is worth dwelling on how the king is presented. Descriptions of royal inauguration make the transformative nature of the event explicit, as is made manifest in this particular account in the choice of verb. Philip was 'ordained' king. The account of the inauguration of William the Conqueror found in the *Waltham Chronicle* encapsulates the importance of change in office in recounting that 'the noble duke was consecrated as king'.[12] William had been transformed from a duke into a king. This language finds a parallel in Otto of Freising's account of the elevation of the duke of Bohemia in 1158. Vladislaus II is described as being made king from a duke.[13] Such a modification of office is not confined to the peculiar circumstances of a king being created anew, or the Conquest in which the duke of Normandy assumed the office of king of England for the first time. As we have seen, Roger of Howden, writing over one hundred years after the Waltham chronicler, emphasized the same change in status in the case of Richard I. In a study of the French *Ordo* of 1250, Jacques Le Goff pointed to the importance of the words to be spoken by the archbishop as he anointed the king: 'I anoint you as king' ('ungo te in regem').[14] As Le Goff rightly stressed, '*in* with the accusative indicates an action toward a goal, but also and especially, a consequence, the end of a transformation'.[15] The vast majority of cursory narrative accounts of royal inauguration include the phrase 'in regem', thus echoing the language of the *ordines* and stressing the importance of this change in office.

This catchphrase of royal inauguration finds its imperial counterpart in the phrase 'in imperatorem'. The *Royal Chronicle of Cologne*, for example, describes how in 1220 Frederick II made the journey to Rome, where 'he was received honourably by the Roman pontiff Honorius and the entire senate, on the feast of St Cecilia he was consecrated emperor'.[16] The distinction between the royal

---

[12] *The Waltham Chronicle: An Account of the Discovery of Our Holy Cross at Montacute and Its Conveyance to Waltham*, ed. L. Watkiss and M. Chibnall, OMT (Oxford, 1994), p. 56: 'dux ille nobilis consecratus in regem [est]'.

[13] *Ottonis et Rahewini Gesta Frederici I. Imperatoris*, ed. G. Waitz, *MGH SS Rer. Germ* 46 (Hannover, 1912), p. 183: 'ex duce rex creatur'.

[14] J. Le Goff, 'A Coronation Program for the Age of Saint Louis: The *Ordo* of 1250', in *Coronations: Medieval and Early Modern Monarchic Ritual*, ed. J. M. Bak (Berkeley, 1990), pp. 46–57 (p. 48).

[15] Ibid.

[16] *Chronica regia Coloniensis*, ed. G. Waitz, *MGH SS Rer. Germ* 18 (Hannover, 1880), p. 251: 'ibique a Romano pontifice Honorio et omni senatu honorifice susceptus, in festo sancte Cecilie in imperatorem consecratur'.

and imperial office was widely recognized outside the Empire. William the Breton, chaplain to Philip Augustus of France, explained how the Emperor must first be crowned king in Aachen, before he could be made emperor and that this practice was observed as if a sacrosanct law.[17] Anglo-Norman sources were also aware of the numerous different titles to which the German kings and emperors laid claim. Ralph de Diceto reports Frederick Barbarossa's inauguration as king of Burgundy at Arles in 1178, and goes on to discuss the four different peoples over whom Barbarossa ruled and the four crowns that corresponded to these peoples.[18] He further discourses on the antiquity of the kingdom of Burgundy. It is important that Ralph distinguishes between the kingdoms and that William the Breton recognizes the difference between king and emperor, because one thing that can be very clearly gained from the narrative sources is the sense that what is at stake here is a status-changing ritual. Importantly, however, the change of status is something that is done to the monarch. His role in the transformation is passive and this is reflected either in the use of the passive voice to describe the inauguration, or in the king or emperor being the object of the sentence rather than the subject. Both these techniques are combined in the description of the imperial inauguration of Henry V found in William of Malmesbury:

> the bishop of Ostia anointed him between his shoulders and on his right arm. After this he was led to the altar of the same apostles and in that very place the crown was placed on him and he was consecrated as emperor by the Apostle himself.[19]

The active participants in the event are thus the churchmen who officiate in the inauguration. William of Malmesbury's account allows for the participation of more than one churchman, but it is clear that it is the pope's actions that transformed Henry V from king to emperor. William of Malmesbury took his account from the lost work of David Scottus, bishop of Bangor, whom he considered to have described the event in a way that shone more favourable light on Henry V than was fitting for history.[20] William took particular issue with David's analogy between Jacob wrestling with an angel until he had

---

[17] *Oeuvres de Rigord et de Guillaume le Breton: Historiens de Philippe-Auguste*, ed. H. F. Delaborde, 2 vols. (Paris, 1882–5), I, 301–2.

[18] 'Fredericus imperator Romanus varias regnorum imperio subditorum metas pro varietate linguarum distingues, Longobardos, Baioarios, Austrasios, Burgundiones, diligenter recensuit, et juxta numerum quatuor populorum edoctus est plenius quatuor sibi competere diademata'. Ralph de Diceto, *The Historical Works*, ed. W. Stubbs, 2 vols., RS 68 (London, 1876), I, 427.

[19] William of Malmesbury, *Gesta regum Anglorum*, p. 768: 'unxit eum Hostiensis episcopus inter scapulas et in brachio dextro. Post haec a domino Apostolico ad altare eorundem apostolorum deductus et ibidem imposita sibi corona, ab ipso Apostolico in imperatorem est consecratus'.

[20] Ibid., p. 764: 'magis in regis gratiam quam historicum deceret acclinis'.

wrung a blessing from him (Genesis 32. 22–32), and Henry V's holding the pope in captivity to force him to consecrate him emperor. Having dissociated himself from the ensuing description, William includes what is an unusually detailed account of an inauguration, in his *Gesta regum Anglorum*. What is striking about this account is the extent to which it makes conscious reference to the 'Roman *ordo*'.[21] William, citing David, relates that the king was received at the Silver Gate, a detail also found in the imperial *ordines*, and that the bishop of Ostia then recited the first prayer contained within the ordinal, 'because the bishop of Albano, by whom it ought to have been said if he were present, was absent'.[22] Having been led to the middle of the Rota, the bishop of Porto recited the second prayer 'just as the Roman *ordo* instructs'.[23] The description then continues to include his anointing and coronation, which both took place at the altar of St Peter. David's references to the liturgy are intended to emphasize the liturgical correctness of the inauguration and thereby its legitimacy, highly necessary in the dubious circumstances of 1111.

The majority of accounts make no direct reference to a liturgical *ordo*, but do include the active participant in the inauguration ceremony, if only for the simple reason that it was the celebrant who conferred legitimacy on the event. Richard of Devizes's account of Richard the Lionheart's inauguration is typical here. Richard tells us only that the Lionheart 'was consecrated as king of the English by Baldwin, archbishop of Canterbury'.[24] By contrast, George Garnett has pointed to William of Poitiers's insistence that Harold's anointing was invalid.[25] William of Poitiers wrote that Harold 'was ordained by Stigand, who had not been sacredly consecrated'.[26] In other words, in William of Poitiers's view, the participation of Stigand had rendered Harold's ordination illegitimate, whereas in contrast William I's position was strengthened due to his consecration by Aeldred of York, described as 'a dear archbishop of both holy life and spotless reputation'.[27] There were two issues at stake here. The first is, as identified by Garnett, the issue of the liturgical status of the celebrant. William of Poitiers emphasizes both Aeldred's holding of the archiepiscopal office (in opposition to Stigand who appears without a title) and, secondly, his spotless reputation.

---

[21] Ibid., p. 768.
[22] Ibid., p. 766: 'quoniam Albanus deerat a quo debuisset dici si adesset'.
[23] Ibid., p. 768: 'sicut precipit Romanus ordo'.
[24] Richard of Devizes, *Chronicle of the Time of King Richard the First*, ed. J. T. Appleby (London, 1963), p. 2: 'consecratus est in regem Anglorum a Baldewino archiepiscopo Cantuarie'.
[25] G. Garnett, 'Coronation and Propaganda: Some Implications of the Norman Claim to the Throne of England in 1066', *Transactions of the Royal Historical Society* 5th series 36 (1986), 91–116 (p. 98).
[26] *The Gesta Guillelmi*, ed. Davis and Chibnall, p. 100: 'ordinatus est non sancta consecratione Stigandi'.
[27] Ibid., p. 150: 'archiepiscopus aeque sancta vita carus et inviolata fama'.

There was another important difference between the two churchmen that is equally pertinent. This was that Aeldred was archbishop of York and Stigand (had he been correctly consecrated) archbishop of Canterbury. In William of Poitiers's account we can glimpse a trace of the quarrel between the two archbishoprics over which of them had the right to inaugurate a king.[28] This perhaps explains the stress on Aeldred's holy life and untarnished reputation. It is not enough that he was a legitimately consecrated archbishop. His qualities are also underlined as William of Poitiers strives to legitimize the kingship of the Conqueror.

By the end of the period under consideration in this study, the rights of the archbishops of Canterbury, Reims and Cologne to inaugurate kings in their respective realms were firmly established.[29] Earlier in the period the situation was rather more fluid, particularly in the Empire, where the archbishops of Cologne, Mainz and Trier all claimed the right of inauguration. All three held the initiative at different points in time and, while by the mid-eleventh century Cologne was firmly in the ascendancy, the making of a number of anti-kings continued to provide Mainz and Trier with opportunities to press their claims.[30] In a final attempt to secure the honour for his see, the archbishop of Trier sought to officiate at the inauguration of Conrad III in 1138, when the archbishoprics of Mainz and Cologne were both vacant. His attempt did not meet with success. The archbishop-elect of Cologne objected and ensured that the papal legate, Dietwin, officiated, rather than his archiepiscopal rival.[31] In France and England, earlier custom, by which the archbishops of Reims and Canterbury inaugurated kings, was not translated into rights confirmed by the papacy until the pontificates of Urban II and

---

[28] In England the right to consecrate the king led to frequent quarrels between the archbishops of Canterbury and York, perhaps at their most violent during the Becket conflict, when, on his return from exile, Becket excommunicated all bishops who had taken part in the consecration of Henry the Young King in 1170. R. M. Haines, 'Canterbury versus York: Fluctuating Fortunes in a Perennial Conflict', in *Ecclesia Anglicana: Studies in the English Church of the Later Middle Ages*, ed. R. M. Haines (Toronto, 1989), pp. 69–105 (pp. 79–81).

[29] These established rights do not find their way into the liturgy in this period. They appear in a German liturgy, the so-called *Ordo* of Aachen, in the early fourteenth century, in the fourth recension of the English *ordines* from the late fourteenth century and in France in the Last Capetian *Ordo* from the late thirteenth century. For editions of these texts see *Constitutiones Regum Germaniae*, pp. 384–93; *English Coronation Records*, ed. Legg, pp. 81–112; *Ordines Coronationis Franciae*, ed. Jackson, II, 367–418.

[30] Egon Boshof has comprehensively traced the contours of these developments. E. Boshof, 'Köln, Mainz, Trier – Die Auseinandersetzung um die Spitzenstellung im deutschen Episkopat in ottonisch-salischer Zeit', *Jahrbuch des kölnischen Geschichtsvereins* 49 (1978), 19–48.

[31] Ibid., p. 47.

Alexander III respectively.³² In France, Remigius's baptism and crowning of Clovis was actually used by Hincmar to argue for the primacy of his see, Reims, in the face of a challenge by Sens to his metropolitan rights. This battle for primacy was still raging in the mid-tenth century as Edward Roberts had recently shown in his analysis of the 'longer' will of St Remigius found in Flodoard's *Historia Remensis ecclesiae*.³³

In certain circumstances inauguration was possible without the participation of these figures, but in that event our narrative sources often expand to justify the change. An imperial inauguration was unthinkable without the participation of a pope, hence Henry V's kidnapping of Paschal II. But as we have seen David Scottus was still anxious to explain why the bishop of Ostia said the first prayer in the ceremony, rather than the bishop of Albano. We find similar explanations in other narrative sources. The *Royal Chronicle of Cologne* explains the fact that Archbishop Siegfried of Mainz officiated at the inauguration of Frederick II in 1215, stating that 'at the time the church of Cologne, whose right it was to consecrate the king, was unoccupied by an archbishop'.³⁴ No doubt part of the reason that this information appears in the Cologne account is to protect the archbishop of Cologne's role in the inauguration. But it was also necessary to justify a deviation from the accepted norm. The right to inaugurate a king was fiercely guarded by the three archbishops and histories associated with them always sought to protect their rights. However it was also in a king's best interests to ensure that his inauguration was legitimate. This is where the passive/active vocabulary distinction makes clear the importance of the celebrant.

David Scottus's report of Henry V's imperial inauguration echoed the liturgy in making apparent that archbishops or popes seldom acted without assistance. When additional information is given as to which churchmen supported the celebrant, it is worth noting. In the case of Henry V, we know that the circumstances of his imperial inauguration were not as straightforward as David suggests and that indeed Henry had kidnapped the pope in order to secure the imperial title. In mentioning a co-celebrant, the bishop of Ostia, and in his references to the liturgy, David adds a veneer of legitimacy. A similar approach was taken in describing the inauguration of Louis VI in the anonymous *Historia regum Francorum ab origine gentis ad annum MCCXIV*, written in 1205 and continued until 1214, through which we learn that no fewer than six bishops assisted Archbishop Dalbert of Sens in anointing the new king in 1108:

---

³² For France see Kantorowicz, *Laudes Regiae*, p. 94. For England see *English Coronation Records*, ed. Legg, pp. 43–5.

³³ E. Roberts, 'Flodoard, the Will of St Remigius and the See of Reims in the Tenth Century', *Early Medieval Europe* 22 (2014), 201–30 (pp. 223–8).

³⁴ *Chronica regia Coloniensis*, ed. Waitz, p. 193: 'vacabat enim tunc temporis Coloniensis ecclesia archiepiscopo, cuius iuris erat regem consecrare'.

Actors, Location and Legitimacy

> Thus, with king Philip having died and been buried at the monastery of Fleury, his son Louis, who is called 'the Fat' succeeded him. He was anointed as king by Dalbert archbishop of Sens, and by his co-bishops, namely Galon of Paris, Manasses of Meaux, John of Orléans, Hugh of Nivers, Ivo of Chartres and Humbaud of Auxerre.[35]

The grammar in this account is again worth closer consideration. The bishops were not merely witnesses to the event or part of the audience, but co-celebrants. Louis was anointed as king *by* the archbishop of Sens, and *by* his co-bishops. They were actively involved in transforming Louis into a king. One reason for the naming of the individual bishops was, as with David Scottus, to justify the legitimate nature of what was in fact an exceptional event, in that it did not take place at Reims and that the celebrant was not the archbishop of Reims. In his *Life of Louis the Fat*, Suger includes the same roll-call of six bishops and further mentions the protests of the community at Reims, who arrived too late to stop the inauguration from taking place.[36] Clearly the inclusion of the bishops in these narrative accounts was intended to present ecclesiastical consensus in irregular circumstances.

When, in England, King Stephen wanted to have his son confirmed as his successor, a plan that did not come to fruition, he too sought not just the support of the archbishop of Canterbury, but of other bishops. Gervase of Canterbury tells us that Stephen

> asked the aforementioned archbishop of Canterbury, to whom by the ancient law of the church of Canterbury the coronation of the king of England pertains, and the other bishops whom he had gathered there, that they anoint (*unguerent*) his son Eustace as king and confirm (*confirmarent*) it with their blessing, he grieved very much over their rebuff.[37]

Important here is Gervase's use of plural verbs, *unguerent* and *confirmarent*, through which he makes clear that the bishops were also active celebrants in an inauguration. The use of a plural verb to describe anointing is particularly striking; the royal *ordines* make clear that the actual laying on of hands was the preserve of the archbishop. Even so it seems clear that the other churchmen

---

[35] *Historia regum Francorum ab origine gentis ad annum MCCXIV*, ed. L. V. Delisle, RHF 12 (Paris, 1877), p. 218: 'Defuncto itaque rege Philippo, apud Floriacense monasterium tumulato, Ludovicus filius ejus, qui nominatus est Grossus, successit, qui unctus est in regem a Dalberto Senonensi archiepiscopo, et a suis coepiscopis, videlicet Vallone Parisiensi, Manasse Meldensi, Johanne Aurelianensi, Hugone Nivernensi, Ivone Carnotensi, Humbaudo Autisiodorensi'.
[36] Suger, *Vie de Louis VI le Gros*, ed. H. Waquet (Paris, 1929), p. 86.
[37] Gervase of Canterbury, *The Historical Works*, ed. Stubbs, I, 150: 'Postulans autem a praedicto Cantuariensi archiepiscopo, ad quem de antiquo jure Cantuariensis ecclesiae regum Angliae pertinet coronatio, et caeteris episcopis quos ibidem congregaverat, ut Eustachium filium suum in regem unguerent et benedictione sua confirmarent, repulsam vehementer indoluit'.

were perceived as in some way being involved in the consecration, just as the laying on of hands at an episcopal or archiepiscopal consecration was an entirely communal affair, albeit one governed by a degree of precedence. Beyond the pragmatic seeking for political legitimacy lies a theological explanation. The Holy Spirit descended on the monarch not through the agency of one archbishop, but through the whole community of the Church.

At the time of his inauguration, a king or emperor might already be married, in which case his wife would, more often than not, be made queen or empress in a joint ceremony. This clearly altered the dynamic of the inauguration, which now had a dual rather than a single focus. One thing that is striking in the narrative accounts is the way in which female inauguration is presented as a parallel process. The *Royal Chronicle of Cologne*, for example, describes Henry VI's imperial inauguration at Rome in 1191 thus: 'King Henry was consecrated as emperor at Rome on Easter Monday and his wife Constance was consecrated as empress'.[38] The plural verb *consecrantur* is applied to both Henry and Constance, and the catchphrase 'in imperatorem' finds its female foil in 'in imperatricem'. The phrase 'in reginam' appears in the sources as the royal equivalent. Ralph de Diceto, for example, records that John had Isabella of Angoulême crowned 'as queen (*in reginam*) at Westminster by lord Hubert, archbishop of Canterbury'.[39] We see, then, that the queen or empress was transformed through her inauguration and that identical language was used to express this transformation as was deployed to describe male inauguration.

Even if a king had been married before he ascended the throne, incidences of death and divorce meant that is was not uncommon for another queen to be inaugurated during a king's reign. In this case, the dynamic shifted again, because although the king took part in the ceremony, his role was liturgically subordinate to that of his queen. Following the annulment of his marriage to Eleanor of Aquitaine in 1152, Suger informs us that Louis VII,

> wishing to live according to the divine law, which instructs that man stick to his wife and they might be 'two in one flesh', and in hope of the offspring that might ensue, and that might rule the kingdom of France after him, he joined himself in marriage to Constance, the daughter of the emperor of Spain, and Hugh archbishop of Sens anointed her as queen at Orléans, and with her crowned the king.[40]

---

[38] *Chronica regia Coloniensis*, ed. Waitz, p. 152: 'Heinricus rex... in imperatorem et Constantia, uxor eius, in imperatricem, secunda feria Paschae consecrantur'.

[39] Ralph de Diceto, *The Historical Works*, ed. Stubbs, II, 170: 'in reginam apud Westmonasterium a domino Huberto Cantuariensi archiepiscopo'.

[40] Suger, *Historia Gloriosi regis Ludovici VII, Filii Ludovici Grossi*, ed. L. V. Delisle, *RHF* 12 (Paris, 1877), p. 128: 'volens secundum divinam legem vivere, quae praecipit ut vir adhaereat uxori suae et sint "duo in carne una", propter spem successivae prolis, quae post ipsum regnum Franciae regeret, Constantiam filiam Imperatoris

The distinction Suger makes here is important because it suggests that it was the anointing that made Constance queen. Louis VII could be crowned with his wife, but not anointed, as kingly anointment could not be performed twice. His presence in the ritual makes clear however, that his wife was dependent on him for her office. Thus although liturgically his role was subordinate to that of his wife, the overall effect is that the king became equally the focal point.

In this respect a phenomenon noted by Amalie Fößel in her comprehensive study of queens in the medieval Empire demands further consideration.[41] Fößel brought together a number of instances of a queen being inaugurated before she had even married the king. A prominent example of this is provided by Matilda of England, later wife of the emperor Henry V. Sent from the English court to the Empire in the early spring of 1110, she was received by Henry at Liège before spending Easter with his court at Utrecht.[42] On 25 July her inauguration as queen took place in Mainz, during which she was anointed by Archbishop Frederick of Cologne, while Archbishop Bruno of Trier held her in his arms.[43] Matilda and Henry did not marry until three and a half years later, in January 1114. In 1110 Matilda was too young to marry, but this does not explain her seemingly premature inauguration because, as Fößel's research has shown, it was no isolated event. Amongst other examples, Henry V's mother, Bertha of Savoy, had also been made queen before she married King Henry IV. Her inauguration took place on 29 June 1066 in Würzburg, and she married Henry the following month in Trebur (close to Mainz). Frederick Barbarossa's wife Beatrix is another example of a queen inaugurated before her marriage.[44]

This practice of consecrating a queen before her marriage to a king stands the conventional understanding of queenship on its head. We are accustomed to thinking of a queen as a queen due to her marital relationship to a king. Our evidence from the Empire, however, suggests that in order to marry a king, it was preferable first to be a queen. Fößel offered no justification for this phenomenon and I too lack a concrete explanation. The cursory narrative

---

Hispaniae conjugio sibi junxit: et Hugo Senonensis archiepiscopus Aurelianis eam in reginam inunxit, et cum ipsa regem coronavit'. The phrase 'due in carne una' can be found in a number of biblical passages: Genesis 2. 24; Matthew 19. 5; Mark 10. 8; I Corinthians 6. 16; Ephesians 5. 31.

[41] A. Fößel, *Die Königin im mittelalterlichen Reich: Herrschaftsausübung, Herrschaftsrechte, Handlungsspielräume* (Stuttgart, 2000).

[42] M. Chibnall, *The Empress Matilda: Queen Consort, Queen Mother and Lady of the English* (Oxford, 1991), pp. 24–5.

[43] *The Gesta Normannorum ducum of William of Jumièges, Orderic Vitalis, and Robert of Torigni*, ed. E. M. C. van Houts, 2 vols., OMT (Oxford, 1995), II, 218: 'Desponsatam vero archiepiscopus Coloniensis in festivitate sancti Iacobi Maguntie in reginam consecravit, ceteris coepiscopis assistentibus et precipue archiepiscopo Treverensis, qui eam, dum consecraretur, inter sua brachia reverenter tenuit'.

[44] Fößel, *Die Königin im mittelalterlichen Reich*, pp. 24–7.

accounts from which Fößel has gleaned her data give little away. A practical motive might be suggested by the notorious story of Louis VII's daughter Alice, who spent twenty-five years at the court of Henry II without ever being made an honest woman. Alice was first betrothed to Henry's son Richard, but Henry later apparently considered marrying her to John, before reconfirming to the French king that she would indeed be married to Richard.[45] In the event, the marriage never took place and Richard married Berengaria of Navarre in 1191, justifying the setting aside of Alice to her brother Philip Augustus, king of France following the death of their father Louis VII in 1180, with the assertion that he could not marry her as she had been his father's mistress and had even borne Henry a son.[46] The consecration of, for example, the young Matilda of England soon after her arrival in the Empire in 1110, could thus perhaps be interpreted as a way of ensuring that the agreed marriage would take place and that the kind of scandalous treatment received by Alice several decades later might be avoided.

However, Fößel also identifies several examples where the time period between the inauguration and marriage was far smaller and where the intentions of the parties involved less opaque than the complicated relations between the Capetians and Angevins. For this reason it is necessary to consider this unusual form of pre-emptive queenly consecration in light of the image of queenship we found in the liturgy, for the premature inauguration of a queen was perhaps of symbolic rather than practical importance. Could it be that such a consecration was intended to heighten the association between the future queen and the Virgin Mary? Or does it echo the practice of the consecration of nuns, in which it is made clear that the bestowal of ring and crown were signs of an impending union with Christ should the postulant prove herself worthy? In the *ordo* for the consecration of a nun the bestowal of the ring was accompanied by the condition that the nun will be joined to Christ if she 'serves him faithfully' ('si ei fideliter servieris') and the crown with a similar condition 'if she endures in him' ('si in eo permanseris').[47] In this interpretation, if the queen showed herself worthy, and remained in her consecrated state, she could then be joined in union to the king. Here we would again have a play on the shared imagery of royal and nuptial transformations, that stressed the king's similarity to Christ. These explanations remain speculative, but the very existence of the phenomenon makes clear that there are issues at stake concerning monarchical inauguration that modern historians have yet to appreciate.

---

[45] J. Gillingham, *Richard I* (New Haven, 1999), pp. 77–8, 81–2.
[46] Ibid., p. 142. Richard's assertion is found in Roger of Howden, *Gesta Henrici II et Ricardi I* [formerly attributed to Benedict of Peterborough], ed. W. Stubbs, 2 vols., RS 49 (London, 1867), II, 160: 'sororem tuam non abjicio: sed illam ducere nequeo in uxorem, quia pater meus cognovit eam, generans ex ea filium'.
[47] *Le pontifical romano-germanique*, ed. Vogel and Elze, I, 45–6; McNamer, *Affective Meditation*, pp. 37–8.

Another example of a ceremony in which the king did not play the starring role was the inauguration of a son during a reigning king's lifetime. Perhaps because of the difficulties caused by Henry the Young King's inauguration in 1170, as a flashpoint in the Becket dispute, this event has been treated in English historiography rather as a failed experiment.[48] However, it is clear from narrative sources that contemporaries did not see such inaugurations as being in any way inferior. Ralph de Diceto, for example, reports the Young King's inauguration in a typical way, writing that, 'on 14 June, Henry, first-born son of Henry, the king of England, was consecrated as king at Westminster by Roger, archbishop of York'.[49] Ralph's description of the inauguration of a junior king thus includes all the usual ingredients we find in the brief narrative accounts. It makes no reference to the uniqueness of this event in English history. One difference from queenly inaugurations is that the reigning king is not mentioned as also being crowned or playing a part in the liturgy. However, the sources do make it clear that the reigning king was, unsurprisingly, integral to the elevation of his son. What is perhaps surprising is that on occasion the king seems almost to have usurped the position of the archbishop. Ekkehard of Aura, for example, writes that in 1099, 'Emperor Henry celebrated the nativity of the Lord at Cologne, and on Epiphany at Aachen he made (*fecit*) his younger son king Henry V'.[50] This perhaps has more than an echo of Byzantine practice, for in Constantinople a co-emperor could be crowned by the emperor himself, rather than by the patriarch.[51]

Where?

Most of the brief narrative accounts of royal consecration and coronation inform us of the place where the event occurred. The inclusion of this information demonstrates the importance of location to the consecration ritual. The supremacy of Aachen, Westminster and Reims for royal consecration, as of Rome for the imperial consecration, has long been recognized by historians

---

[48] According to Anne Duggan, 'in the context of the Becket controversy, most observers saw the coronation as a calculated insult to the archbishop of Canterbury, in contempt of whose rights it was performed'. A. J. Duggan [as Heslin], 'The Coronation of the Young King in 1170', *Studies in Church History* 2 (1965), 165–78 (p. 166). The Young King's coronation is also discussed in M. Strickland, *Henry the Young King, 1155–1183* (New Haven, 2016), pp. 78–94.

[49] Ralph de Diceto, *The Historical Works*, ed. Stubbs, I, 338: 'xiiijo kalendas Julii, Henricus, primogenitus filius Henrici regis Angliae, consecratus est in regem apud Westmonasterium a Rogero Eboracensi archiepiscopo'.

[50] Ekkehard of Aura, *Chronica*, ed. G. Waitz, *MGH SS* 6 (Hannover, 1844), p. 210: 'Henricus imperator natalem Domini Coloniae celebravit; in epyphania vero Aquisgrani filium suum iuniorem Henricum quintum regem fecit'.

[51] Nelson, 'Symbols in Context', p. 98.

and it is clear from contemporary accounts that the legitimacy of a consecration could be challenged if it were not carried out by the correct celebrant and in the correct cathedral church. Louis VI's consecration at Orléans, for example, drew protests from the canons of Reims, who, having arrived too late to prevent the ceremony, departed and continued to complain, though Suger tells us, with some satisfaction, that 'whatever they still might say, they achieved nothing useful'.[52] As discussed above, the irregularity of Louis's consecration (he was the only French king in this period to be consecrated away from Reims) is also suggested by the level of detail given about which bishops were present. Departing from the traditional location for royal inauguration precipitated a need to stress the legitimacy of the event in other ways. That the locations of consecration were known outside of their respective realms is made clear in William the Breton's discussion of the consecration of the emperor Frederick II as king of Germany. William recounted that,

> In the time in which the Germans held the dynasty of Empire, this was always observed among them as a custom as if an inviolable law, that the emperor elect could never be crowned by the Roman pope, unless he had first been crowned king at Aachen, and afterwards, having once received the crown in that very place, nothing remained except that he be crowned as emperor of Rome by the highest Pope and this was done on account of the reverence and majesty of Charles the Great, whose body rested in that place.[53]

In describing how the German king must first be crowned in Aachen, William the Breton highlights that Aachen was the burial place of Charlemagne. Indeed, all three royal coronation churches had historical and liturgical associations that increased their importance in legitimizing inauguration. The link between Charlemagne and Aachen was of utmost importance to the German kings in this period. Their coronation church, dedicated to the Blessed Virgin Mary, had been founded by Charlemagne and designed in emulation of the churches of San Vitale in Ravenna and Santa Sofia in Benevento.[54] When the German kings were enthroned, towards the conclusion of the inauguration ceremony, the throne on which they sat was the throne of Charlemagne. The first firm evidence for the use of Charlemagne's throne in the inauguration

---

[52] Suger, *Vie de Louis VI le Gros*, p. 86: 'quicquid tamen dixerint, nichil utile retulerunt'.

[53] *Oeuvres de Rigord et de Guillaume le Breton*, ed. Delaborde, I, 301–2: 'A tempore quo Teutonici obtinuerunt dynastiam imperii, haec semper apud eos consuetudo quasi quaedam lex inviolabiliter observatur, quod electus imperator numquam coronatur a papa Romano, nisi prius fuerit rex coronatus Aquisgrani; et postquam ibidem semel tulerit coronam, nihil restat nisi ut in imperatorem Romae a summo pontifice coronetur; et hoc fit propter reverentiam et majestatem Caroli Magni, cujus corpus requiescit ibidem'.

[54] J. L. Nelson, 'Aachen as a Place of Power', in *Topographies of Power in the Early Middle Ages*, ed. M. de Jong and F. Theuws (Leiden, 2001), pp. 217–37 (p. 220).

of a king at Aachen comes from the 936 inauguration of Otto I.[55] This throne, with its seat originally made from oak believed to have been salvaged from Noah's Ark, was approached by six steps, in accordance with the description of Solomon's throne in I Kings 10. 19.[56] In the twelfth century, in close relation to developments in the English and French realms, association with Charlemagne became increasingly important to the Staufen kings, who sought to reassert themselves in the face of papal hostility.[57] In 1165 Frederick Barbarossa oversaw, with the assent of the anti-pope Paschal III, the canonization of his illustrious predecessor.[58]

In a description of Frederick II's second inauguration, in 1215, it is made clear how important both Aachen and Charlemagne had become. Following the unexpected death of Emperor Henry VI at Messina in 1197, the princes of the Empire had not accepted his infant son, Frederick, as king. Henry had earlier tried to get the position of his son formalized, and to ensure the triumph of hereditary, over elective, kingship in the Empire. Henry was preparing to go on Crusade, and at a court held at Würzburg, in Lent 1196, had made clear that he wished 'that in the kingdom of the Romans, just as in France and other kingdoms, kings might follow one another by hereditary right'.[59] His plans did not come to fruition and on his death different parties of princes elected

---

[55] P. E. Schramm, 'Die Throne des deutschen Königs: Karls des Großen Steinthron und Heinrich IV. Bronzethron', in *Herrschaftszeichen und Staatssymbolik*, I, 336–69 (p. 345).

[56] Ibid., pp. 338–9. Although the throne has long been thought to date from the Ottonian period it has recently been shown to date from c.800. On this re-dating and the broader Solomonic resonances of the German inauguration church see H. Müller et al., 'Pfalz und *vicus* Aachen in karolingischer Zeit', in *Aachen: von den Anfängen bis zur Gegenwart*, 7 vols. (Aachen, 2011–), II, 1–408 (pp. 233–46).

[57] Jürgen Petersohn has linked the canonization of Charlemagne in 1165 to similar developments at St Denis and Westminster and Gesine Oppitz-Trotman has also pointed to close connections between the Plantagenet and Staufer courts in these years. J. Petersohn, 'Saint-Denis – Westminster – Aachen: die Karls-Translatio von 1165 und ihre Vorbilder', *Deutsches Archiv* 31 (1975), 420–54; G. Oppitz-Trotman, 'The Emperor's Robe: Thomas Becket and Angevin Political Culture', *Anglo-Norman Studies* XXXVI (2015), 205–19.

[58] There is a vast literature on Charlemagne's canonization, which has traditionally been interpreted as a politically motivated act, though Knut Görich has recently argued that local Aachen initiative was of great importance. See amongst others L. Vones, 'Heiligsprechung und Tradition: Die Kanonisation Karls des Großen 1165, die Aachener Karlsvita und der Pseudo-Turpin', in *Jakobus und Karl der Große: Von Einhards Karlsvita zum Pseudo-Turpin*, ed. K. Herbers, Jakobus-Studien 14 (Tübingen, 2003), pp. 87–105; O. Engels, 'Des Reiches heiliger Gründer: Die Kanonisation Karls des Großen und ihre Beweggründe', in *Karl der Große und sein Schrein in Aachen*, ed. H. Müllejans (Aachen, 1988), pp. 37–46; K. Görich, 'Karl der Große – ein "politischer Heiliger" im 12. Jahrhundert?', in *Religion und Politik im Mittelalter: Deutschland und England im Vergleich*, ed. L. Körntgen and D. Waßenhoven (Berlin, 2013), pp. 117–55.

[59] 'ut in Romanum regnum sicut in Francie vel ceteris regnis, iure hereditario reges sibi succederent'. *Annales Marbacenses*, ed. H. Bloch, MGH SS Rer. Germ. 9 (Hannover, 1907), p. 68.

his brother, Philip of Swabia, and the Welf Otto IV as rival kings. Following Philip's death in 1208, the young Frederick began to gain ground in Germany and, following further elections in September 1211 and December 1212, he was inaugurated king at Mainz by the archbishop of Mainz. This inauguration was not deemed sufficient, however, and having finally wrested Aachen from the control of Otto IV in 1215, Frederick was 'enthroned [and] solemnly and gloriously consecrated as king'.[60] To be a king in Germany, one had first to sit in Charlemagne's throne in the church of St Mary in Aachen. Frederick also chose this second inauguration (the use of the phrase 'in regem' making clear that this was understood as a constitutive event), as the opportunity to take the Cross.

Reiner of Liège describes how Frederick spent the day subsequent to his inauguration in the coronation church listening to the Crusade being preached. The following day, a Sunday, a solemn mass was celebrated, and

> the king restored the body of holy Charles the Great, which his grandfather Emperor Frederick had released from the earth, to a most noble coffin, which the people of Aachen had woven from gold and silver, and having received a hammer and taken off his cloak, he ... firmly sealed it by driving nails into the shrine.[61]

Charlemagne's splendid shrine is still to be found in the church of St Mary in Aachen. At one end of the shrine Charlemagne is depicted flanked by Pope Leo III and Archbishop Turpin of Reims, under a blessing Christ. The emperor holds a model of the coronation church in his hands. At the opposite end, the Virgin and Child are depicted enthroned and crowned between archangels. The niches along both lengths of the shrine are not filled with saints, as might be expected, but with the royal and imperial successors to Charlemagne, amongst whom Frederick II is numbered. By the very fact that Frederick chose to have a second inauguration and his actions in the ensuing days, Frederick, quite literally, hammered home the importance of Aachen as the resting place of Charlemagne and as the sole legitimate site for male inauguration in the German kingdom.

The French coronation church at Reims, similarly dedicated to the Virgin Mary, also possessed important historical resonances. As the cathedral church of the episcopal see of Reims, it was associated with the baptism of Clovis by St Remigius himself archbishop of Reims at the time of Clovis's baptism. As is well known, the chrism used during the inauguration of the French kings was

---

[60] *Chronica regia Coloniensis*, ed. Waitz, p. 193: 'intronizatus, sollempniter atque gloriose in regem est consecratus'.

[61] *Reineri Annales a. 1066–1230*, ed. G. H. Pertz, *MGH SS* 16 (Hannover, 1859), pp. 651–80 (p. 673): 'rex corpus beati Carlomanni, quod avus suus Fredericus imperator de terra levaverat, in sarcofagum nobillissimum, quod Aquenses fecerant, auro argento contextum reponi fecit, et accepto martello depositoque pallio ... clavos infixos vasi firmiter clausit'.

supposedly that used by Remigius to baptize Clovis and was brought from the nearby abbey of St Rémi for the ceremony.[62] In contrast to the historical claims of Reims and Aachen, Emma Mason suggests that the choice of Westminster as the coronation church in England was, for the most part, pragmatic. Mason points to Edward the Confessor's desire to have a royal presence in London thanks to the city's burgeoning economy and considers Westminster's dedication to St Peter to have been its major attraction for Edward who is said to have had a particular devotion to the saint.[63] As Nicole Marafioti has highlighted, however, with his cultivation of Westminster, Edward was associating himself with a prestigious foundation with conversion-era royal roots, as according to tradition, the first church on the site had been founded by King Æthelbert of Kent in the early seventh century.[64] London's role as the centre of opposition to the Danes in Æthelred II's later years, when Edward himself was a child, might also have made the city attractive to the king.[65] Whatever the initial impetus behind Edward's favouring of Westminster, soon it was his association with the foundation that proved decisive. As early as 1139, an unsuccessful attempt to have the Confessor canonized was supported by King Stephen, himself in need of legitimacy.[66] Edward's saintly status was secured in 1161, and on 13 October 1163, Henry II was present as the Confessor's body was translated into a new shrine.[67]

Just as four years previously, Frederick II had been inaugurated for the first time in a church that was not the traditional site of royal inauguration in the Empire, so too, in 1216, circumstances dictated that Henry III was consecrated in Gloucester rather than Westminster.[68] The church was, like Westminster, dedicated to St Peter, but this correspondence in saintly patronage was not sufficient. Four years later, having regained control of London, Henry III was crowned once more, this time in Westminster. As in the Empire the location of inauguration was an important legitimizing factor for kings

---

[62] On Remigius and the Holy Ampoule see N. Staubach, '"Regia sceptra sacrans": Erzbischof Hinkmar von Reims, der heilige Remigius und die "Sainte Ampoule"', *Frühmittelalterliche Studien* 40 (2006), 79–101.

[63] E. Mason, 'The Site of King-making and Consecration: Westminster Abbey and the Crown in the Eleventh and Twelfth Centuries', in *The Church and Sovereignty: Essays in Honour of Michael Wilks*, ed. D. Wood, SCH Sub 9 (Oxford, 1991), pp. 57–76 (p. 57).

[64] N. Marafioti, *The King's Body: Burial and Succession in Late Anglo-Saxon England* (Toronto, 2014), pp. 40–50.

[65] On the importance of London to Æthelred see S. Keynes, 'The Burial of King Æthelred the Unready at St Paul's', in *The English and their Legacy, 900–1200: Essays in Honour of Ann Williams*, ed. D. Roffe (Woodbridge, 2012), pp. 129–48.

[66] Mason, 'The Site of King-making and Consecration', p. 73.

[67] Ibid., p. 75.

[68] While contingency was clearly behind the choice of Gloucester, it did have established royal credentials, see M. Hare, 'Kings, Crowns and Festivals: The Origins of Gloucester as a Royal Ceremonial Centre', *Transactions of the Bristol and Gloucestershire Archaeological Society* 115 (1997), 41–78.

in England. Matthew Paris only includes a brief account of this second coronation in his *Chronica Majora*, suggesting it did not reach the theatrical heights of Frederick's coronation at Aachen.[69] Evidence from the pipe rolls suggests, however, that similar ideas were at play here. A list of regalia, the earliest surviving full inventory of English royal ornaments, written early in Henry III's reign, mentions golden spurs ('calcaria aurea'). This item has been struck through and the reader is referred to a letter of the king, stating that the golden spurs, which he wore at his first coronation at Westminster ('primam coronacionem nostram apud Westmonasterio'), should be delivered to the Prior of Westminster to finance new work on the chapel of St Mary.[70] It is well documented that the rebuilding of Westminster was integral to the construction of the Plantagenet royal image.[71] Carpenter has further demonstrated how Henry was anxious to finish the rebuilding of the abbey by 13 October 1269, so that Edward the Confessor could be translated to his new shrine on the same liturgical day he had been interred in 1163.[72] By giving an item of regalia used in his coronation to finance the work, Henry III made apparent the link between saint, location and inauguration.

William the Breton also knew that the emperor was crowned in Rome. Unlike Aachen, Rome required no explanation. As the seat of the ancient Roman Empire, home of the papacy and place of Charlemagne's imperial coronation in 800, the necessity of travelling to Rome for imperial inauguration was taken for granted. As we have seen, the site of imperial inauguration was specified in the liturgy, in contrast to the general royal rites of this period. Of the German kings made emperor between 1050 and 1250, all but one were crowned, as the liturgy prescribed, in St Peter's. The exception was Lothar III, who was crowned by Innocent II on 4 June 1133 in the Lateran basilica. The reason for this was simple: the anti-pope Anacletus held the Leonine city, and St Peter's was thus closed to Lothar and Innocent.[73] This event was later commemorated in a mural (no longer extant) in the St Nicholas chapel of the Lateran. The pope's depiction of the emperor, showing the emperor bowing to receive the imperial crown, caused consternation amongst the German bishops, who wrote to Pope Hadrian IV in 1158, petitioning for its removal.[74]

---

[69] Matthew Paris, *Chronica Majora*, ed. Luard, III, 58.

[70] The list of regalia and the accompanying letter are reproduced in *English Coronation Records*, ed. Legg, pp. 54–6. The reference to a first coronation at Westminster is intriguing. Does this suggest that the king thought his coronation at Gloucester invalid, or that he has subsequently been re-crowned at Westminster for a second time, in a festal rather than inaugural context?

[71] See in particular Binski's magisterial study: P. Binski, *Westminster Abbey and the Plantagenets: Kingship and the Representation of Power, 1200–1400* (New Haven, 1995).

[72] D. A. Carpenter, 'Westminster Abbey in Politics 1258–1269', *Thirteenth Century England* VIII (2001), 49–58 (p. 54).

[73] Robinson, *The Papacy, 1073–1198*, p. 447.

[74] Ibid., p. 452.

To be made a king in England, France or the Empire, it was necessary to be inaugurated in Westminster, Reims or Aachen. To become an emperor or empress, a long and hazardous journey to Rome was required. However, if we examine the consecration location of kings' wives, we see that the sites of male royal inauguration did not determine female consecrations.[75] If we take the example of France, Louis VI married Adelaide of Maurienne at Notre-Dame in Paris. Louis VII married Eleanor of Aquitaine in Bordeaux, and she was consecrated, at Christmas 1137, in Bourges. Following his divorce he married Constance at Orléans. Suger recounts in his *Historia gloriosi Regis Ludovici VII* that, 'Hugh, archbishop of Sens anointed her as queen at Orléans and with her crowned the king'.[76] Thus, Louis VII's wife was consecrated in the same location as his father. The marriages of Philip Augustus were likewise conducted away from Reims. According to Roger of Howden, Philip planned to have Isabella of Hainault crowned at Sens following their marriage.[77] However, the coronation was moved to Saint-Denis, on the advice of the Count of Flanders, whose castle at Bapaume provided the venue for the celebration of their nuptials.[78] His second, ill-fated marriage, to Ingebourg of Denmark, took place at Amiens.[79] Louis IX chose Sens for his marriage to Margaret, and William of Nangis specifically mentions that Margaret was anointed queen at the same time.[80] It is thus clear that female consecration was not tied to Reims, and that Saint-Denis, despite its well-documented importance as a royal necropolis for the Capetians, was not favoured as a place of marriage or female consecration.[81] Indeed Saint-Denis was only used by Philip Augustus when, fearing opposition to his marriage, he had to postpone his wedding from Ascension Day to Pentecost and moved

---

[75] Cf. Wolf, 'Königinnen-Krönungen', p. 76.

[76] Suger, *Historia gloriosi regis Ludovici VII*, p. 128: 'Hugo Senonensis Archiepiscopus Aurelianis eam in reginam inunxit, et cum ipsa regem coronavit'.

[77] Roger of Howden, *Chronica*, ed. Stubbs, II, 196–7: 'Deinde statuit Philippus rex Franciae, quod ipse et uxor ejus coronarentur die Pentecostes apud Senonem civitatem: sed per consilium comitis Flandriae anticipavit terminum illum, et fecit se et uxorem suam coronari die Ascensionis apud Sanctum Dionysium ab archiepiscopo Senonensi'.

[78] Gilbert of Mons, *Chronicle of Hainaut*, trans. L. M. Napran (Woodbridge, 2005), pp. 74–5. I am grateful to Laura Napran for drawing Gilbert's account of events to my attention.

[79] *Oeuvres de Rigord et de Guillaume le Breton*, ed. Delaborde, I, 195.

[80] William of Nangis, *Vita Sancti Ludovici regis Franciae*, ed. P.-C.-F. Daunou and J. Naudet, *RHF* 20 (Paris, 1855), p. 322: 'Quam rex paucis diebus revolutis apud Senonensem urbem in uxorem ducens legitimam, ut Francorum dominam et reginam a Galtero, civitatis Senonensis archispiscopo, inungi et regali diademate fecit solemniter coronari'.

[81] It should be noted that until the programme of burials and reinstallations at Saint-Denis in the 1260s queens were not buried there either. K. Nolan, 'The Tomb of Adelaide of Maurienne and the Visual Imagery of Capetian Queenship', in *Capetian Women*, ed. K. Nolan (Basingstoke, 2003), pp. 45–76 (p. 48).

Inauguration and Liturgical Kingship

it from Sens. In France, then, royal marriage and female consecration were not limited to a single location, but could take place in a number of places.

This flexibility gave the Capetians the opportunity to impress their subjects with lavish ceremonial displays that stressed the sacrality of their office, away from their traditional centres of power. The marriage of Louis VII and Eleanor at Bordeaux was a celebration of the (albeit short-lived) joining of the Aquitanian and Capetian houses. Eleanor's consecration and Louis's coronation, at Bourges, at Christmas 1137, was a display of Capetian royal power in a city that had only become part of the royal domain in 1100, when Philip I had purchased it from the vicomte, Eudes Arpin.[82] The ceremony accompanying Philip Augustus's marriage to Ingebourg of Denmark at Amiens was surely designed to enhance royal power in the area, although Philip's abrupt repudiation of his wife probably weakened the desired effect.[83] Amiens and the south-western part of the Vermandois had been added to the royal domain in 1185, but the division of the county of Flanders remained disputed and it was only with the Peace of Arras in 1192 that competing territorial claims were settled.[84] Thus the wedding at Amiens can be seen as an opportunity to confirm royal power in an area that, as John Baldwin has shown, was essential to the development of royal revenues under Philip Augustus.[85]

The site of royal consecration in the German kingdom, Aachen, saw few female consecrations. Instead the German kings also used weddings and female consecration as an opportunity for display in other locations. Henry V had his future wife consecrated at Mainz, on the Feast of St James in 1110, after they had been formally betrothed but before their marriage in 1114, also in Mainz. We know from the account in the anonymous *Kaiserchronik* that their wedding was a splendid affair. It attracted so great a multitude that no one present could count all those in attendance nor keep track of the number of gifts, some sent to the couple from kings and primates and others distributed by the emperor himself.[86] An accompanying miniature suggests that Henry and his new wife both wore crowns at the ensuing feast (Plate 5). Würzburg witnessed the consecration of Bertha of Turin in 1066, and the marriage of Frederick Barbarossa to Beatrix of Burgundy in 1156.[87] Royal weddings in the Empire were most often held in areas in which the king had most power. In

---

[82] R. Branner, *The Cathedral of Bourges and Its Place in Gothic Architecture*, ed. S. Prager Branner (Cambridge, MA, 1989), pp. 8–9.

[83] On historians' approaches to understanding the untangling of this union see D. L. d'Avray, *Dissolving Royal Marriages: A Documentary History, 860–1600* (Cambridge, 2014), pp. 58–61.

[84] G. M. Spiegel, *Romancing the Past: The Rise of Vernacular Prose Historiography in Thirteenth-Century France* (Berkeley, 1995), pp. 36–7.

[85] Baldwin, *The Government of Philip Augustus*, pp. 99–100.

[86] *Frutolfi et Ekkehardi Chronica*, ed. Schmale and Schmale-Ott, p. 262.

[87] *Ottonis et Rahewini Gesta Frederici I. Imperatoris*, ed. Waitz, p. 155: 'proxima dehinc

Plate 5. The wedding feast of Henry V and Matilda of England: Cambridge, Corpus Christi College MS 373, fol. 95v

the case of Frederick II, his 1209 marriage to Constance of Aragon, at Messina, and his 1225 marriage to Isabella of Jerusalem, at Brindisi, provide further evidence of this, or could be seen as the pragmatic choices necessary in such a large realm, with a journey to Aachen, over 1500km to the north, impractical. It seems likely that a combination of political concerns and pragmatism lay behind the choice of location for royal marriage.

Aachen did, however, see two female consecrations in this period, those of Irene Maria and Margaret of Austria. Irene Maria was the wife of Philip of Swabia, and the circumstances of her consecration once again stress the importance of Aachen in legitimizing kingship in the Empire. Following the double election of 1198 Philip had been crowned on 8 September, in Mainz. By 1205, however, Philip's support had grown and plans were made for a second inauguration at Aachen. The king thus travelled to Aachen with his followers and 'in the church of Holy Mary he was raised [to the kingship] by all, and with Maria his wife, he was anointed and consecrated by the archbishop of Cologne'.[88] Seen in the context of the double election of 1198 and Philip's ensuing struggle with Otto IV for power in the Empire, it becomes apparent why Irene was consecrated alongside Philip in Aachen, rather than elsewhere. The double consecration was a statement of Philip's legitimacy and having his wife at his side during the ceremony emphasized that fact. Moreover, Irene Maria was a member of the imperial dynasty of the Angeli, eastern emperors and key players in the recently triumphant Fourth Crusade. She thus became the first Byzantine princess, since Theophanu in the tenth century, either to rule in Germany or to merit a visit to the chief imperial proprietary church of the western empire. The reason for Margaret of Austria's inauguration at Aachen in March 1227 is rather more opaque. Margaret was the wife of Henry (VII), eldest son of Frederick II, who had himself been consecrated in Aachen on 8 May 1222, before their marriage.[89] As Fößel has stressed, Margaret was the first queen since the early Middle Ages to be crowned independently in Aachen.[90] In having his son's wife consecrated at Aachen, Frederick was perhaps making a statement of his intention to unite the Sicilian and German kingdoms, against the wishes of the papacy.[91]

There was a greater correlation between the sites of male and female consecration in England, reflecting both the pre-eminence of Westminster

---

ebdomada in civitate orientalis Franciae Herbipoli regio apparatu, multa principum astipulatione, iuncta sibi Beatrice Reginaldi comitis filia nuptiae celebrat'.

[88] *Chronica regia Coloniensis*, ed. Waitz, p. 219: 'in ecclesia Beatae Mariae; ab omnibus eligitur et a Coloniensi archiepiscopo cum Maria, uxore sua, ungitur et consecratur'.

[89] W. Stürner, 'König Heinrich (VII.): Rebell oder Sachwalter staufischer Interessen?', in *Der Staufer Heinrich (VII.): Ein König im Schatten seines kaiserlichen Vaters*, ed. A. Dörner-Winkler (Göppingen, 2001), pp. 12–42 (p. 16).

[90] Fößel, *Die Königin im mittelalterlichen Reich*, p. 30.

[91] On the politics behind Henry's marriage see Stürner, 'König Heinrich (VII.)', pp. 19–20.

and the established role of Winchester in royal ceremonial. In this period, only Henry I's second wife, Adeliza, and Richard I's wife, Berengaria, were not consecrated at either of these two locations, and in Berengaria's case this was due to her marriage taking place in Cyprus as Richard travelled to the Holy Land on Crusade.[92] In fact, Richard's queen never set foot in England. The narrative sources give us an indication of the opportunity royal marriage provided for displays of largesse. Eadmer tells us of the joyful crowds at Henry and Adeliza's wedding, which took place at Windsor: 'thus the queen was consecrated in the kingdom, and all the people who had assembled had a festal and cheerful day'.[93] Although location was not a legitimizing factor in queenly inauguration in England, it is clear that the English kings made less use of this geographical flexibility.

Another opportunity for the display of royal power was provided by crown-wearings and festal coronations. The nature of these events will be discussed in the following chapter, with the focus here being on the location of such celebrations. The famous formula found in the Anglo-Saxon Chronicle, that William the Conquerer wore his royal crown three times a year, at Easter at Winchester, at Pentecost at Westminster, and at Christmas at Gloucester, has been shown by Martin Biddle not to be the hard and fast rule it was once considered to be.[94] Henry I made gifts to the monks and chanters of these three churches explicitly linking these gifts to his predecessors' practice of wearing their crowns at these locations. However, he celebrated the three great feasts of the year, perhaps wearing his crown, in a number of different locations. In addition to festivals spent at Westminster and Winchester, he celebrated at Windsor, Woodstock, St Albans and Dunstable, amongst others.[95] Tracing where these festivals were celebrated and whether the monarch wore his crown is no simple task.

In a German context, Hans-Walter Klewitz attempted, in 1939, to identify residences favoured by the Ottonians and Salians as places to celebrate the major feasts.[96] As in England, the pattern varies, reflecting both the large size of the Empire, political considerations and personal whims. In any case, it seems unwise to assume that festal coronations were confined to these three feasts. In a charter issued at Regensburg in 1158, Frederick Barbarossa granted

---

[92] On this marriage and its context see J. Gillingham, 'Richard I and Berengaria of Navarre', *Historical Research* 53 (1980), 157–73.
[93] Eadmer, *Historia novorum in Anglia*, in *Eadmeri Historia novorum in Anglia, et Opuscula duo; De vita Sancti Anselmi et quibusdam miraculis ejus*, ed. M. Rule, RS 81 (London, 1965), p. 293: 'regina itaque in regnum consecrata est, et dies festivus et hilaris omni populo qui confluxerat habitus est'.
[94] M. Biddle, 'Seasonal Festivals and Residence: Winchester, Westminster and Gloucester in the 10th to 12th Centuries', *Anglo-Norman Studies* VIII (1986), 51–72.
[95] Ibid., p. 54.
[96] H.-W. Klewitz, 'Die Festkrönung der deutschen Könige', *Zeitschrift der Savigny-Stiftung für Rechtsgeschichte: Kanonistische Abteilung* 28 (1939), 48–96.

the duke of Bohemia the right to wear a circlet on the days that Frederick himself customarily wore his crown. In addition to Christmas, Easter and Pentecost the duke could wear his circlet 'on the feast of St Wenceslas and also St Adalbert, because those solemnities, on account of the fact they are their patrons, are venerated with great reverence and celebration throughout Bohemia'.[97] Otto of Freising recounts that Frederick had been crowned in Regensburg on the Feast of SS Peter and Paul in 1152.[98] In contrast to inaugural coronation, these additional displays were not tied to particular locations.

To conclude this discussion we return to the double election of 1198. As was outlined in the previous chapter, scholars have traditionally supposed that the regalia was of paramount importance in legitimizing a new king in the Empire. In questioning this assumption, Jürgen Petersohn took the struggle between Philip of Swabia and Otto IV as one of his case studies.[99] Petersohn noted that Philip was in possession of the regalia, which he had brought back from Italy during the lifetime of his brother. By contrast, Otto was forced to fabricate new items, such as the *Reichsschwert* discussed earlier, or, Petersohn suggests, to borrow insignia from the English treasury.[100] Otto had, however, two things in his favour. Firstly, he had been consecrated at Aachen. That Philip had tried to prevent this is demonstrated by the fact he had, on hearing of Otto's election, sent three hundred knights to protect the city in early summer 1198. Aachen fell to the Welfs, however, on 10 July, following a siege of about a month. Two days later, Otto IV was inaugurated by the archbishop of Cologne. This was Otto's second advantage, for when Philip was crowned, around two months later, on 8 September, the celebrant was the archbishop of Tarentaise (an Alpine metropolitan with no previous association either with German king-making or German coronations).[101] Following their elections and inaugurations, the two rival kings petitioned the pope for support. Innocent III's decision, publicized in the decretal 'Venerabilem' of 1202, was resounding. He chose Otto IV over Philip of Swabia because

> the aforementioned Duke received coronation and unction neither where he ought nor from whom he ought, the aforemention King though received

---

[97] DD F. I. 201: 'in festivitate sancti Venzelai et sancti Adelberti eo, quod illas sollempnitates propter patronos suos maiori reverentia et celebritate tota Boemia veneretur'.

[98] *Ottonis et Rahewini Gesta Frederici I. Imperatoris*, ed. Waitz, p. 107.

[99] Petersohn, *"Echte" und "falsche" Insignien*, pp. 74–82.

[100] Ibid., pp. 75–6.

[101] Andreas Büttner suggests that the archbishop of Tarantaise presided rather than the archbishop of Trier due to the fact the archbishop of Mainz was absent in the Holy Land and it was not acceptable to the cathedral chapter that another German archbishop of equal rank should consecrate a king in Mainz. Büttner, *Der Weg zur Krone*, I, 67.

each both where he ought (namely Aachen) and from whom he ought (namely our venerable brother N. the archbishop of Cologne), we therefore deem and name not Philip but Otto as king, as justice requires.[102]

Innocent justified his choice of Otto, because the king had been crowned in the right location and by the correct celebrant. The brief entries in chronicles and annals, that have been the focus of this chapter, make clear that it was not only in the Empire, but also in France and England, that celebrant and location were the key signifiers of legitimate inauguration.

---

[102] *Regestum Innocentii III Papae super negotio Romani Imperii*, ed. F. Kempf, Miscellanea Historiae Pontificiae 12 (Rome, 1947), p. 60: 'dux predictus nec ubi debuit nec a quo debuit coronam et unctionem accepit, memoratus vero rex et ubi debuit, videlicet Aquisgrani, et a quo debuit, scilicet a venerabili fratre nostro .. Coloniensi archiepiscopo, recepit utrumque, nos utique non Philippum, sed Ottonem reputamus et nominamus regem, iustitia exigente'.

4

What and When?
Consecration and the Liturgical Calendar

The previous chapter concentrated on two of the four items of information most often found in cursory narrative accounts of royal and imperial inauguration. As has been demonstrated, the location and celebrant were the legitimizing factors in an inauguration, and it is for this reason we so often find the information in the sources. In this period the narrative sources very rarely allude directly to liturgical texts. The case of David Scottus's account, which William of Malmesbury incorporated into his *Gesta regum Anglorum*, is a rare exception. Apart from Roger of Howden's account of Richard I's inauguration, we also find no other description encompassing all the ritual actions and handing over of various items of insignia. This is not to say, however, that the narrative sources are not imbued with liturgical resonances. This chapter is concerned with how writers described royal inauguration with a particular focus on the vocabulary employed. It will be argued that careful consideration of the words used by contemporaries to describe inauguration demonstrates that the rite continued to be understood as intimately related to episcopal consecration.[1] The final piece of information we often find in cursory narrative accounts is the date on which an inauguration took place. In returning to the relative chronology of the medieval period, a host of liturgical references will be uncovered. These resonances point to the conscious manipulation of the liturgy in the construction of images of kingship throughout the period under consideration.

---

[1] The classic study of the links between episcopal and royal consecration is Eichmann, *Königs- und Bischofsweihe*. However, as we saw in chapter 1, the genesis of the act of anointing in the royal right is disputed and his work, which posited a close link between the introduction of unction in royal and episcopal rites, is no longer accepted. See, for example, Nelson, 'Ritual and Reality', p. 334; Angenendt, 'Rex et Sacerdos. Zur Genese der Königssalbung'. On episcopal consecration see M. Andrieu, 'Le sacre épiscopal d'après Hincmar de Reims', *Revue d'histoire ecclésiastique* 48 (1953), 22–73; O. Engels, 'Der Pontifikatsantritt und seine Zeichen', in *Segni e riti nella chiesa altomedievale occidentale*, Settimane di Studio del Centro Italiano di Studi sull' Alto Medioevo, 2 vols. (Spoleto, 1987), II, 707–70.

Consecration and the Liturgical Calendar

What?

Mirroring medieval practice, I have used a number of words in this book to describe the constitutive ceremony in which a king or emperor, queen or empress, was made. In line with current scholarly consensus, I deliberately chose to use the word 'inauguration' in the title of this book. The word 'inauguration' is favoured because, as is apparent from the liturgical texts analysed in earlier chapters, coronation was and is but one action in the making of a king. Scholars stress that the word 'coronation' is insufficient in that it prioritizes the act of crowning over that of anointing, and as will be demonstrated, a coronation in the medieval sense was not in itself a constitutive ceremony. Furthermore, using the word 'coronation' to describe a monarch's inauguration causes us difficulty when discussing crownings that were not constitutive and that took place without an anointing.[2] The word 'inauguration' also has its drawbacks. As Jacques Le Goff has commented, it can be applied to many things, even to something as prosaic as the ceremonial opening of a town hall.[3] The word 'inauguration' thus perhaps fails to capture the status and power-changing nature of royal ceremonial. It is also a word that is never found in the contemporary source material. Nonetheless, its very modernity is of use here. In closely analysing the vocabulary used in the narrative sources we can uncover how contemporaries themselves described royal and imperial 'inaugurations'. By thus taking medieval descriptions on their own terms, we may find ourselves paying closer attention to non-inaugural crownings, once described by Kantorowicz as 'one of the queerest customs of the Middle Ages'.[4]

The vocabulary used to describe monarchical inauguration is varied. Words related to crowning and coronation (the words most often used by modern historians), in fact, represent only a minority of the vocabulary employed. This vocabulary can be divided into five main groups, four of which are relatively cohesive and consist of words related to ordination, to consecration, to unction and to crowning. The fifth consists of a diffuse collection of verbs such as *facere, sublimare, succedere, creare* and *declarare*, amongst others. I have found words related to ordination (*ordinare, ordinatio*) in only three sources: two French ecclesiastical annals, the *Chronica brevi ecclesiae S. Dionysii* and the *Chronica Remensi*, and in the *Gesta Guillelmi* of William of Poitiers.[5] William

---

[2] Liturgical scholars have long recognized the importance of keeping crown-wearings and non-inaugural coronations distinct from coronation as part of the inauguration ritual. See, for example, Nelson, 'Inauguration Rituals', p. 295; C. Brühl, 'Fränkischer Krönungsbrauch und das Problem der "Festkrönungen"', *Historische Zeitschrift* 194 (1962), 265–326; C. Brühl, 'Kronen- und Krönungsbrauch im frühen und hohen Mittelalter', *Historische Zeitschrift* 234 (1982), 1–31.

[3] Le Goff, 'A Coronation Program for the Age of Saint Louis', p. 52.

[4] Kantorowicz, *Laudes Regiae*, p. 92.

[5] *Ex Chronico brevi*, ed. Delisle, p. 377; *Chronica Remensi*, ed. L. Delisle, *RHF* 12 (Paris, 1877), p. 275, 291; *The Gesta Guillelmi*, ed. Davis and Chibnall, p. 150.

twice uses the word as a noun to describe the entire process of inauguration.⁶ It is clear from the fact that in his description he specifies that the archbishop of York both consecrated and crowned the Conqueror, that he intended the word 'ordination' to encompass both acts. Similarly, in both the French annals, though a verb is used, 'ordination' stands for the whole inauguration. Of the terms used to describe inauguration, ordination is the one that most explicitly reflects ideas of office and hierarchy. Moreover, ordination is most often used in an ecclesiastical context, to describe a man being ordained as a priest or bishop.⁷ This sacerdotal parallel perhaps explains why the use of ordination is limited to William of Poitiers (writing soon after the Norman Conquest) and to entries in two sets of monastic annals that were updated as and when events occurred. Thus the latest use I have found of ordination in the context of monarchical inauguration is in a description of the succession of Louis VII in the *Chronica Remensi* in which the entry for the year 1131 reads: 'Pope Innocent celebrated a council at Reims. At the same council the boy Louis was ordained king, following the death of his brother King Philip.'⁸ In the decline of the use of words related to ordination we can perhaps see the effects of the Investiture Controversy on the vocabulary of monarchical inauguration. However, as will be suggested below, language does not remain static and a change in words employed does not necessarily imply a change in understanding.

The most frequently used words are those derived from the closely related verbs *sacrare* and *consecrare*, which are clearly imbued with theological significance. Such words are also used throughout the narrative accounts to denote ecclesiastics ascending to the office of bishop. Thus Eadmer, writing soon after the death of Anselm in 1109, describes William the Conqueror's inauguration as a 'consecration' ('consecratio') and in describing the ceremony in which Anselm became archbishop wrote he 'was sacréd' ('sacratus est').⁹ This parallel usage of 'consecration' and related words to describe monarchical and episcopal inauguration persisted throughout the period under examination. Perhaps the most explicit allusion to the link between monarchical and episcopal inauguration is to be found in Otto of Freising's famous account of Frederick Barbarossa's royal consecration at Aachen in 1152.¹⁰ Otto tells us that,

---

⁶ *The Gesta Guillelmi*, ed. Davis and Chibnall, p. 150: 'Die ordinationi decreto' and 'post celebratam ordinationem'.

⁷ On the use of the words 'ordination' and 'consecration' to describe episcopal inauguration see Schmidt, *'Bischof bist Du und Fürst'*, pp. 348–52.

⁸ *Chronica Remensi*, p. 275: 'Celebratum est Remense concilium a domino Innocentio papa. In eodem concilio ordinatus est Ludovicus puer rex, mortuo fratre suo Philippo rege'.

⁹ Eadmer, *Historia novorum in Anglia*, ed. Rule, RS 81, p. 9.

¹⁰ On Otto's account see S. Dick, 'Die Königserhebung Friedrich Barbarossas im Spiegel der Quellen – kritische Anmerkung zu den "Gesta Friderici" Ottos von Freising', *Zeitschrift der Savigny-Stiftung für Rechtsgeschichte: Germanistische Abteilung* 121 (2004), 200–37.

on the same day in the same church the bishop-elect of Münster, likewise called Frederick, was consecrated as bishop by the same bishops who consecrated the king, so that it was believed that the highest king and priest was taking part in the present rejoicing and this was a prognostication that in one church on one day He saw the unction of two people, who alone are sacramentally anointed by the instruction of the New and Old Testaments and are solemnly called the anointed of the Lord.[11]

Otto thus goes further than drawing a parallel between the two *Christi Domini*, king and bishop, to suggest that it was as if the highest king and priest, that is Christ himself, was present at the celebration. Kantorowicz is perhaps unfair in dismissing Otto for 'clinging to an ideal of by-gone days' in making this claim.[12] It seems unlikely that the twin consecration was a coincidence. Instead it was a carefully choreographed event in which the parallels would have been clear to contemporaries, even if it takes Otto's hyperbole and deliberately contorted language to alert the modern reader to the event's significance.[13] The audience was meant to draw the conclusion that Otto spells out for us: Christ himself approved of Frederick Barbarossa's kingship.

In many of the narratives *consecratio* and connected verbs seem to encompass the whole ceremony. However, while this is often the case, there is some ambiguity in usage. The *Royal Chronicle of Cologne*, for example, reports that Frederick II went to Rome, 'and there he was received honourably by the Roman pontiff Honorius and the entire senate, on the feast of St Cecilia he was consecrated emperor'.[14] Likewise Henry of Huntingdon tells us that Henry I went to London and, 'having promised a longed for improvement of law and custom, he was sacréd there by Maurice, bishop of London'.[15] In these examples, *sacrare* and *consecrare* imply the entire ritual. But on other occasions such sacring words appear in conjunction with a reference to crowning. Roger of Howden, for example, combines consecration and crowning in his descriptions of the inaugurations of Matilda of Scotland, of

---

[11] *Ottonis et Rahewini Gesta Frederici I. Imperatoris*, ed. Waitz, p. 105: 'eadem die in eadem ecclesia Monasteriensis electus, item Fridericus ab eisdem a quibus et rex episcopis in episcopum consecratur, ut revera summus rex et sacerdos presenti iocundiatati hoc quasi prognostico interesse crederetur, qua in una ecclesia una dies duarum personarum, quae solae novi ac veteris instrumenti institutione sacramentaliter unguntur et Christi Domini rite dicuntur, vidit unctionem'.

[12] Kantorowicz, *The King's Two Bodies*, p. 89, n. 6.

[13] This is, of course, echoed in liturgical sources. The *ordines* for royal and episcopal inauguration are found close together in liturgical manuscripts.

[14] *Chronica regia Coloniensis*, ed. Waitz, p. 251: 'ibique a Romano pontifice Honorio et omni senatu honorifice susceptus, in festo sancte Cecilie in imperatorem consecratur'.

[15] Henry of Huntingdon, *Historia Anglorum*, ed. D. Greenway, OMT (Oxford, 1996), p. 448: 'sacratus est ibi a Mauricio Lundoniensi episcopo, melioratione legum et consuetudinum optabili repromissa'.

Henry II, of Henry the Young King and of John.[16] In these examples Roger's sentence structure appears to assign constitutive significance to consecration over crowning. Henry II, was 'crowned and consecrated king' ('coronatus et in regem consecratus').[17] Similarly his eldest son was, 'crowned and consecrated king' ('coronari et in regem consecrari').[18] In such cases it is tempting to see 'consecrating' as a synonym for 'anointing', which, as we have seen, appears with the phrase 'in regem' in the liturgical texts. However, this correlation is not exhibited in all our sources. In the *Historia regum Francorum*, Philip Augustus is described as being both anointed and consecrated ('inungi et in regem consecrari').[19] An examination of the *ordines* makes clear that 'consecration' was the term most frequently used to describe the complete ceremony. Indeed 'here begins the consecration of the king' ('incipit consecratio regis') is the commonly found opening rubric to the liturgical texts.

Words relating to anointing appear frequently in the sources in conjunction with the phrase 'in regem', or its female and imperial counterparts, accentuating the relationship between anointing and consecration, and reflecting the language of the liturgy itself. By contrast, crowning words are only seldom associated with these phrases. If an author mentions both crowning and unction in his account then the 'in regem' is most often associated with unction, only occasionally with both acts.[20] The transformative nature of unction is sometimes stressed by the use of the prefix 'in' to strengthen the word.[21] Thus we read in Rigord that Philip Augustus 'in regem est inunctus',[22] or in Otto of Freising that Conrad III's son Henry Berengar was 'regem inungi ac coronari'.[23] That unction was recognized as the constitutive element in the ritual emerges even more clearly from an examination of descriptions of female inauguration. In the case of a reigning king marrying (a relatively common occurrence), then the king's new wife was usually raised to the office of queen, either at the time of the marriage or in a separate ceremony. Such occasions also provided an opportunity for the king to be crowned. But such coronations were not inaugural. Henry II had his son and namesake made king in 1170. Much to the annoyance of the king of France, the Young

---

[16] Roger of Howden, *Chronica*, ed. Stubbs, I, 156, I, 213, II, 4–5, IV, 90.
[17] Ibid., I, 213.
[18] Ibid., II, 4–5.
[19] *Historia regum Francorum ab origine gentis ad annum MCCXIV*, p. 221.
[20] I have found only two examples of crowning appearing on its own with the phrase *in regem*. These are the description of John's inauguration in William the Breton and Otto IV's inauguration in Rigord. *Oeuvres de Rigord et de Guillaume le Breton*, ed. Delaborde, I, 205; Rigord, *Histoire de Philippe Auguste*, ed. E. Carpentier, G. Pon, and Y. Chauvin, SHM 33 (Paris, 2006), p. 346.
[21] The verb *inungere* (to anoint) should not be mistaken for the more common verb *iniungere* (to enjoin/unite).
[22] Rigord, *Histoire de Philippe Auguste*, p. 128.
[23] *Ottonis et Rahewini Gesta Frederici I. Imperatoris*, ed. Waitz, p. 63.

King's wife Margaret, Louis VII's daughter, was not inaugurated queen at the same time. To appease the French king, another ceremony was arranged two years later. Ralph de Diceto is one of several chroniclers to record both events, and the distinction he draws in his description of the 1172 ceremony is instructive. He writes that 'the archbishop consecrated Margaret queen of England on 27 August at Winchester, and placed the diadem of the kingdom on the head of the king's son'.[24] Margaret was consecrated queen. Henry was merely crowned as he had already been consecrated. Rigord likewise makes the same distinction in his description of Isabella of Hainault being made queen following her marriage to Philip Augustus. According to Rigord, King Philip was crowned for a second time, but Isabella was anointed ('inuncta').[25]

Crowning was an integral part of monarchical inauguration, so it comes as no surprise that words related to crowning and coronation were occasionally used by medieval authors to designate the ceremony in which a king or emperor was made. Their use as the sole identifier is far from universal, although perhaps more evident from the late twelfth century and into the thirteenth century. The increasing prevalence of crowning words in preference to a stress on consecration or unction might perhaps be attributed to clerical writers seeking to undermine the sacrality of the ceremony. Certainly this is the conclusion Andreas Büttner draws. He suggests that the tendency for a shift in these *pars-pro-toto* descriptions from unction to coronation is indicative of a change in perception of the entire ritual, and can be seen as evidence for desacralization.[26] Büttner's knowledge of the sources for the late medieval Empire is unquestionable, but I would suggest that what might well be true of the period after 1250, the main focus of his research, cannot be accepted for the high Middle Ages. As has been demonstrated in relation to the liturgy, the act of coronation and the crown as a symbol were understood on a number of levels. The historical works of Gervase of Canterbury neatly illustrate this point. Writing in the late 1190s, Gervase almost exclusively uses the verb *coronare* in his descriptions of inaugurations. He records in the year 1154, for example, that 'on 19 December Henry, son of Empress Matilda, was crowned king'.[27] Importantly Gervase uses the same vocabulary to describe another, rather different, event: the martyrdom of Thomas Becket. According to Gervase, in the year 1170, 'Saint Thomas ... was crowned in martyrdom'.[28] This second usage serves to remind us, once again, that coronation imagery

---

[24] Ralph de Diceto, *The Historical Works*, ed. Stubbs, I, 352–3: 'archiepiscopus itaque memoratus, xii. kalendas Septembris apud Wintoniam, Margaritam reginam Angliae consecravit, et diadema regni capiti filii regis imposuit'.

[25] Rigord, *Histoire de Philippe Auguste*, pp. 138–40: 'Idem rex Philippus secundo imposuit sibi diadema et tunc inuncta fuit Elisabeth'.

[26] Büttner, *Der Weg zur Krone*, I, 6.

[27] Gervase of Canterbury, *The Historical Works*, ed. Stubbs, I, 159–60: 'sextodecimo kalendas Januarii coronatus est rex Henricus filius Matildis imperatricis'.

[28] Ibid., I, 232: 'Sanctus Thomas ... martirio coronatus est'.

was not confined to monarchical ceremonial and that the more frequent use of crowning words should not be assumed to indicate a devaluing of the rite in the eyes of contemporaries.

Unction and coronation were the two most prominent rituals in inauguration ceremonies, and thus using one or other to designate the entire ceremony is no more than synecdochic. As has been seen, however, monarchs only received unction in an inaugural context, whereas crowning could also be non-inaugural. In modern usage in England, France and Germany 'coronation', 'couronnement' and 'Krönung' are routinely used to describe monarchical inauguration. But this usage is problematic, in that it prejudices the use of the word in other contexts. Because 'coronation' is commonly equated with 'inauguration' we have to use the term *Festkrönung* or 'festal coronation', a nineteenth-century invention, to describe events that contemporaries just termed 'coronations'.[29] This is no mere pedantic point about correct terminology, but an issue of semantic significance. We ignore at our peril the importance of language in the shaping of meaning. It is clear from the manner in which *Festkrönungen* have been studied as some kind of independent phenomenon, and treated, to paraphrase Kantorowicz, as 'queer' customs, that they suffer by the comparison, almost as if the only proper coronation was an inaugural one, and a non-inaugural crowning or crown-wearing somehow an embarrassing throwback. This is not an attitude reflected in the contemporary narrative sources, which are not troubled by the same issue of vocabulary. Otto of Freising's unexceptional account of Frederick Barbarossa's coronation at Regensburg in 1152 is a case in point. He tells us that the king 'entered Bavaria and went to Regensburg, chief city of the Norici, and on the feast of the apostles he was crowned in the monastery of St Emmeram, because the major church had been burned down with several other buildings in the city'.[30]

Historians seeking a medieval ally in their dismissive attitude to non-inaugural coronations might feel they have found one in Henry II of England. Roger of Howden reports two non-inaugural coronations in Henry's reign, one just outside Lincoln at Christmas 1157, and another at Worcester, at Easter 1158. Significantly, following his and Eleanor's crowning at Worcester, Henry and his wife took off their crowns and placed them on the altar,

---

[29] Brühl provides a useful summary of terms used to describe different types of coronations. However, while these terms can certainly be useful in academic discussion we should be cautious before categorizing events that contemporaries did not. At what point or under what circumstances, for example, does a festal coronation (*Festkrönung*) morph into a confirmatory coronation (*Befestigungskrönung*)? Brühl, 'Kronen- und Krönungsbrauch', pp. 2–3.

[30] *Ottonis et Rahewini Gesta Frederici I. Imperatoris*, ed. Waitz, p. 107: 'Baioriam ingreditur ac Ratisponae, Norici ducatus metropoli, in festivitate apostolorum in monasterio sancti Emmerammi – nam maior aecclesia cum quibusdam civitatis vicis conflagraverat – coronatur'.

announcing that they did not want to be crowned again.[31] These actions might have been, as Nicholas Vincent has suggested, 'motivated by a desire to replace the expensive and dispute-ridden ceremony of coronation at the hands of the archbishop of Canterbury with a no less lavish display of alms-giving to the poor'.[32] But Howden specifies that Lincoln was the second time that Henry had been crowned and Worcester the third time, so it would perhaps be better not to speak of 'the abandonment of formal crown-wearings', as if they were a routine occurrence, firstly because Lincoln and Worcester saw coronations rather than crown-wearings and secondly because, according to Howden, such events happened only twice in the first three and a half years of Henry's reign.[33] In any case, a decline in the frequency of crown-wearings seems to have already begun under Henry's grandfather Henry I.[34]

Henry II's coronation at Lincoln on Christmas Day 1157 was perhaps a response to Stephen's crowning in Lincoln at Christmas 1146, although unlike Stephen, as Roger of Howden reports, Henry was crowned outside the city walls.[35] Vincent's suggestion that events at Worcester were a spontaneous attempt to avoid the quarrels that had beset the Lincoln crowning is plausible, but I would suggest there was something else at play here. Henry and Eleanor's actions at Worcester would have been highly choreographed rather than spontaneous. Unfortunately neither Howden nor Ralph of de Diceto, our other witness to the occasion, elaborate on the reason for Henry's behaviour. Perhaps the key lies in a phrase used by Howden. He reports that the royal couple declared that 'they would never again in their lives be crowned'.[36] This phrase leaves open the possibility of coronation in death, a concept, as we have seen, that was applied to saints, such as Thomas Becket. This saintly usage was, moreover, referenced in the *laudes* where the king was described as 'crowned by God' ('a deo coronatus'). It is thus plausible that Henry's action was one driven as much by piety as by ecclesiastical politics and the laying of crowns on the altar at Worcester could perhaps be understood as a votive offering.[37] Whatever the reason, it seems unwise to jump to the conclusion that

---

[31] Roger of Howden, *Chronica*, ed. Stubbs, I, 216: 'ubi cum ad oblationem venirent, desposuerunt coronas suas, et eas super altare obtulerunt; voventes Deo, quod nunquam in vita sua de caetero coronarentur'.

[32] N. Vincent, 'The Court of Henry II', in *Henry II: New Interpretations*, ed. C. Harper-Bill and N. Vincent (Woodbridge, 2007), pp. 278–334 (p. 326).

[33] Ibid.

[34] Biddle, 'Seasonal Festivals and Residence', p. 51.

[35] Roger of Howden, *Chronica*, ed. Stubbs, I, 213. The description of Stephen wearing his crown at Lincoln comes from Henry of Huntingdon, who comments 'duodecimus rex Stephanus anno ad Natale Domini in urbe Lincoliensi diademate regaliter insignitus est, quo regem nullus introire prohibentibus quibusdam supersticiosis ausus fuerat'. Henry of Huntingdon, *Historia Anglorum*, p. 748.

[36] Roger of Howden, *Chronica*, ed. Stubbs, I, 216: 'nunquam in vita sua de caetero coronarentur'.

[37] The practice of making a votive offering by placing a crown on an altar of cross

Henry considered non-inaugural coronation simply too troublesome. That all three of his sons were crowned more than once also suggests that his exploits at Worcester did not put an end to non-inaugural crownings in England.

Henry and Eleanor's actions at Worcester are not recorded in the work of Henry of Huntingdon, who died sometime between 1156 and 1164. Although his *Historia Anglorum* ends with the assertion that 'now a new book must be devoted to a new king', no such book describing the early years of Henry II's reign survives.[38] The third version of his work, written *c*.1140, does, however, include a story that demonstrates that the laying aside of a crown could be interpreted as a pious act in mid-twelfth-century England. In this version of his history, Henry of Huntingdon includes the first description of the now famous story of Cnut commanding the sea not to rise. As is well known, Cnut's words made no difference to the incoming tide, and the king ended up with wet feet. At this point the king cried out 'know all who inhabit the world, that the power of kings is empty and frivolous, nor anyone worthy of the title of king, besides him whose orders the sky, earth and sea obey in everlasting law'.[39] Henry then recounts that the king never again wore his crown but instead 'it was placed for ever above the image of the Lord affixed to the cross in praise of God the great king'.[40] Henry of Huntingdon recorded this story, in which Cnut's setting aside of his crown is presented as an act of great piety, around twenty years before Henry II and his wife set their crowns on the altar at Worcester. That such an idea had contemporary currency nonetheless suggests that we should regard Henry II's act as symbolic not just pragmatic.

Henry II was not the only monarch for whom contemporary evidence points to an eschewal of non-inaugural coronations or crown-wearings. Following a description of Frederick Barbarossa being crowned at Pavia at Easter 1162, the historian Acerbus Morena adds that this was the first such coronation in three years.[41] He writes that Frederick had earlier declared that he would not wear his crown again, until he had conquered Milan.[42] Acerbus's description of this

---

appears to have been more common in the early Middle Ages and is best attested in the Visigothic realm. See Schramm, 'Die Kronen des frühen Mittelalters', pp. 378–9; T. Deswarte, 'Le Christ-roi: Autel et couronne votive dans l'Espagne wisigothique', *Bulletin du centre d'études médiévales d'Auxerre* 4 (2011), 2–9.

[38] Henry of Huntingdon, *Historia Anglorum*, p. 776: 'Et iam regi novo novus liber donandus est. Explicit liber decimus. Hic incipit liber undecimus de Henrico iuniori'.

[39] Ibid., p. 368: 'Sciat omnes habitantes orbem, vanam et frivolam regum esse potentiam, nec regis quempiam nomine dignum, preter eum cuius nutui celum, terra, mare, legibus obediunt eternis'.

[40] Ibid.: 'sed super imaginem Domini que cruci affixa erat, posuit eam in eternum, in laudem Dei regis magni'.

[41] Brühl, 'Kronen- und Krönungsbrauch', p. 10.

[42] *Ottonis Morenae et Continuatorum Historia Frederici I*, ed. F. Güterbock, MGH SS Rer. Germ. N.S. 7 (Berlin, 1930), pp. 158–9: 'Proposuerat enim, quod ipse nunquam coronam sumeret in capite, donec Mediolanum superasset'.

joyful coronation follows directly on from his narrative of the destruction of Milan, and it is worth noting that it is at this point that Acerbus mentions that Frederick has not worn his crown for three years. This fact is not presented in its correct chronological position in the narrative, but appears only after Frederick had destroyed Milan and could thus wear his crown again without breaking his vow. This authorial choice certainly dramatizes the vow and augments the significance of the Pavian coronation. It also suggests that there could perhaps have been other episodes, in which monarchs chose not to wear their crowns for a variety of reasons that went unrecorded. Carlrichard Brühl is absolutely right to stress that there must have been many more coronations and crown-wearings than the sources record. But the reverse is perhaps also true, namely that sometimes kings chose not to wear their crowns or submit to coronation, and that the sources do not always inform us.[43]

Although a number of different words are used to describe the inauguration of a monarch, significantly a verb is almost always used in preference to a noun, i.e. 'coronatus est', or 'coronavit' rather than 'coronatio'. The use of verbal forms is significant because it makes clear that inauguration is a process, a transformation, rather than something static. If a noun is used, either it is paired with a verb, as in the reference to Philip Augustus's inauguration in the *Chronica Remensi*, which states that, in 1179 'the coronation of king Philip at the hands of William, archbishop of Reims, was celebrated',[44] or it refers to the ceremony either before or after it has happened. For example, Richard of Devizes reports that Richard I 'was consecrated king' ('consecratus est in regem').[45] However, in the context of recounting a portent that occurred on that day, that the appropriate bells had not been rung during masses, Richard used the formula, 'on the day of coronation' ('die coronationis').[46] This temporal distinction between the use of nouns and verbs to describe these events can be important, because recognizing it can sometimes help us to distinguish between inaugural ceremonies and non-inaugural coronations or crown-wearings.

Let us consider a short passage from Roger of Howden concerning King Stephen and mentioning a coronation:

> In the year of Grace 1135, on the feast of St Stephen, King Stephen, during whose coronation, it was said, the peace of the Lord was neither said in the mass nor given to the people, held his court in London wearing a diadem.[47]

---

[43] Brühl, 'Kronen- und Krönungsbrauch', p. 10.
[44] *Chronica Remensi*, p. 275: 'Celebrata est coronatio regis Philippi per manum Guillelmi Remensis archiepiscopi'.
[45] Richard of Devizes, *Chronicle*, ed. Appleby, p. 3.
[46] Ibid., p. 4.
[47] Roger of Howden, *Chronica*, ed. Stubbs, I, 189: 'Anno igitur gratiae MoCoXXXoVIo., die Sancti Stephani, diadematus rex Stephanus, curiam suam tenuit apud Lundoniam, in cuius coronatione, ut dicitur, pax Domini ad missam nec dicta fuit nec data populo'.

This is the only mention Roger makes of Stephen's inauguration, and has led some historians to suggest that Stephen's inauguration took place on 26 December 1135, or that Roger has supplied an incorrect date for the inauguration. However a closer evaluation of the passage makes clear that neither of these eventualities is implied by Roger's report. What it tells us is simply that King Stephen appeared crowned at the court he held at London on St Stephen's Day.[48] It then continues to inform us that it was said that the peace had not been handed around at the coronation mass, a rumour repeated by Gervase of Canterbury, amongst others.[49] The noun *coronatio* does not refer back to the first part of the sentence, but to Stephen's inauguration, which we also know from other sources took place on 22 December. Moreover *diadematus* is an adjective qualifying *rex Stephanus*, rather than a passive participle requiring us to supply the verb 'to be'. This is made even clearer by the fact that *rex* appears in the nominative, rather than in the accusative as in the phrase 'in regem', which Howden uses in every other description of an inauguration. Roger has thus not made a mistake in his dating of Stephen's inauguration. In recognizing this, it becomes apparent that his account raises a number of interesting points. Firstly Roger does not actually record Stephen's inauguration; he merely mentions it after the event. This is highly unusual and is perhaps indicative of a certain antipathy to Stephen and a suggestion that his inauguration was unlawful. Secondly it tells us that Stephen appeared crowned at his first royal court, a mere four days after his inauguration. That Stephen felt the need to wear his crown again so soon is suggestive of a desire to emphasize his newly acquired royal status. Finally, Roger states that Stephen wore his crown on St Stephen's Day, rather than Christmas Day as was customary, and in doing so he no doubt sought to draw a parallel between himself and his saintly namesake.[50]

A close reading of these narrative sources has demonstrated the subtlety of vocabulary used to describe elevation to the royal or imperial throne and the difficulties caused by the modern convention of labelling inaugural anointings and crownings as 'coronations', a word contemporaries used frequently to describe non-inaugural ceremonies. Examining the use of constructions using verbs or nouns and active and passive forms is a necessity in decoding whether a chronicler is referring to an inauguration, coronation or crown-wearing. This strikes me as particularly important when we consider ceremonies that are often treated as poor relations to the consecration of a new king following

---

[48] Henry of Huntingdon also suggests Stephen appeared crowned at his first court, although he disagrees with Roger about the date: 'diadematus igitur curiam suam tenuit ad Natale apud Lundoniam'. Henry of Huntingdon, *Historia Anglorum*, p. 702.

[49] Gervase of Canterbury, *The Historical Works*, ed. Stubbs, I, 94–5.

[50] The resonances inherent in saints' days are discussed in the second part of this chapter.

the death of his predecessor. There are two ceremonies of particular significance: the consecration of a new king during the lifetime of his predecessor, and so-called 'festal coronations'. Andrew Lewis has commented upon the complete silence in the source material on the subject of Philip Augustus not having his son consecrated during his own lifetime, something that has been held up as exemplifying the increased strength of the Capetians, who no longer had to consecrate an heir to ensure the succession.[51] Lewis points out that if Philip's inaction was as important as historians have suggested, it would surely have been the subject of discourse by contemporaries.[52] I would suggest that the lack of comment in the sources demonstrates that the consecration of associate kings was considered unexceptional – the sources describe it using exactly the same vocabulary as they describe successional consecration, and make no comment if a king did not have his heir consecrated.

The same is true of non-inaugural coronations, which are certainly not presented as a strange custom. Indeed the sources make clear that it is the anointing that transformed a king-elect into a reigning king in England, France and the Empire. For this reason it would be far better to avoid using 'coronation' to designate the inauguration ceremony, best described as a 'consecration'. The word 'consecration' was most frequently used by contemporaries and reflects much more the transformative nature of the combined rituals of anointing and coronation. It also mirrors the language used to describe the sacrament of episcopal inauguration, a point that it is important to stress. Despite successive popes denying the equivalence of episcopal and royal consecration, the churchmen who wrote chronicles clearly considered them to be of equivalent worth.

When?[53]

Rigord included a story in his *Gesta Philippi Augusti* concerning the postponement of the young prince's consecration from 15 August to 1 November 1179.[54] The mysterious tale of the illness Philip developed after becoming lost in the forest of Compiègne, and his father's visit to the shrine of Thomas Becket in Canterbury to pray for his safe recovery, has understandably intrigued scholars. Less attention, however, has been paid to the importance of the dates, which are stressed by Rigord himself. Rigord twice mentions that the young king should have been consecrated on the feast of the Assumption

---

[51] A. W. Lewis, 'Anticipatory Association of the Heir in Early Capetian France', *The American Historical Review* 83 (1978), 906–27 (p. 906).
[52] Ibid., p. 924.
[53] This section is an edited and abridged version of Dale, 'Royal Inauguration and the Liturgical Calendar'.
[54] Rigord, *Histoire de Philippe Auguste*, pp. 120–8.

of the Virgin, before invoking Mary as a protector of Philip as he wandered through the forest. He also twice mentions that Philip had been born on the feast of Saints Symphorian and Timotheus and remarks thrice that he was eventually consecrated on the feast of All Saints. That Rigord emphasizes the liturgical importance of these dates through repetition indicates that, while the story of Philip's adventure and illness might well bear the imprint of chivalric romance, this was not at the expense of a sacral conception of kingship. By returning to medieval conventions of recording time and considering the evidence provided by royal inauguration and marriage a hitherto overlooked aspect of royal image in this period will be highlighted. In doing so it will be shown that liturgical conceptions of kingship thrived throughout the high Middle Ages.

Diana Greenway has rightly commented that, 'it has been largely through the activity of historians that the passage of time has come to be measured in *dates*'.[55] Indeed, historians are accustomed to reading medieval chronicles in editions in which the chronological information provided in the text is annotated by the date written in the margin or footnotes in the modern manner. Such information is obviously essential for placing events in the correct chronological order, but it also divorces modern readers from the relative chronology practised in this period, in which dates were recorded with reference to saints' days, feasts of the church, regnal years, and years since the birth of Christ, amongst other things.[56] The present was understood as a continuum of biblical history and this is reflected in the manner in which time was recorded. The liturgical calendar was divided according to two systems: the sanctoral cycle of saints' days, and the temporal cycle of moveable feasts and Sunday observations, and this dual cyclicality opens the possibility that dates that to modern eyes do not appear significant were actually imbued with meaning.[57] By returning to medieval methods of reckoning dates, in essence by taking the dates as they are presented in the narrative sources, and considering the liturgical importance that was attributed to particular days and cycles of time we shall uncover an element of monarchical consecration that has previously been camouflaged by the modern convention of recording dates.

---

[55] D. Greenway, 'Dates in History: Chronology and Memory', *Historical Research* 72 (1999), 127–39 (p. 127). Greenway's italics.

[56] There is a vast literature on medieval dating conventions. Good starting points include R. Dean Ware, 'Medieval Chronology: Theory and Practice', in *Medieval Studies: An Introduction*, ed. J. M. Powell, 2nd edn (New York, 1992), pp. 252–77; A. Borst, *The Ordering of Time: From the Ancient Computus to the Modern Computer*, trans. A. Winnard (Chicago, 1993); C. R. Cheney and M. Jones, ed., *A Handbook of Dates for Students of British History*, 2nd edn (Cambridge, 2000).

[57] On liturgical time see A. Angenendt, 'Die liturgische Zeit: zyklisch und linear', in *Hochmittelalterliches Geschichtsbewußtsein im Spiegel nicht historiographischer Quellen*, ed. H.-W. Goetz (Berlin, 1998), pp. 101–15.

Consecration and the Liturgical Calendar

In a seminal article of the 1970s, Hans Martin Schaller declared that consecration dates in the German kingdom were not chosen by chance.[58] He took as his starting point Otto II's German consecration at Aachen on 26 May 961, the date on which Pentecost fell that year, and pointed to the fact that the contemporary *Annales Lobiensis* emphasized the appropriateness of Otto being imbued with the Holy Spirit, on the same day as the Holy Spirit had descended upon the disciples of Christ.[59] Schaller's work has been followed up by a number of German scholars, including Wolfgang Hushner, Michael Sierck and Ernst-Dieter Hehl, and the idea that German rulers timed important events to take place on significant liturgical days has become a commonplace in German medieval scholarship.[60] We can go further, however, than merely noting this phenomenon. As Hehl has elucidated, church feasts were not just days with a festal character on which important royal acts took place, they were bearers of specific content that was made visible in the liturgy and enveloped the event with the feast's meaning.[61] Schaller and his followers concentrated on events within the Empire, but that Philip I of France, in 1059, and Henry III of England, in 1220, also chose to be consecrated and crowned at Pentecost indicates that the symbolism of feast days was appreciated across borders and over a wide timespan. Moreover, in the Anglo-Norman realm there was a further consecration at Pentecost, that of William the Conqueror's wife Matilda in 1068. As queens were fundamental to the production of an heir and images of royalty, it is unsurprising to find that the dates of their marriage and consecration were also carefully chosen. Pentecost was not the only feast that saw consecrations and coronations in more than one kingdom. Other feasts that found favour without geographical constraint included Christmas Day, the feast of the Assumption of the Virgin, and Easter Sunday. This shared utilization of feast days serves to challenge the assumption that there was a significant difference in the nature of sacral self-representation amongst European monarchs.

The choice of consecration date was rarely entirely free, because it was influenced by the death of the previous king, and in the case of the German

---

[58] H. M. Schaller, 'Der heilige Tag als Termin mittelalterliche Staatsakte', *Deutsches Archiv* 30 (1974) 1–24.

[59] *Annales Lobiensis*, ed. G. Waitz, MGH SS 13 (Hannover, 1881), pp. 224–35 (p. 234): 'Dominus noster Otto, aequivocus patris, consors paterni regni asciscitur et septiformi gratia Spiritus sancti donatur in palatio Aquensi, septem ebdomadibus a pascha transactis, die pentecosten et hora qua Spiritus sanctus super discipulos venit, 7. Kalend. Iun., luna 7, anno aetatis suae 7'.

[60] W. Huschner, 'Kirchenfest und Herrschaftspraxis: Die Regierungszeiten der ersten beiden Kaiser aus liudolfingischem Hause (936–983)', *Zeitschrift für Geschichtswissenschaft* 41 (1993), 24–55, 117–34; M. Sierck, *Festtag und Politik: Studien zur Tagewahl karolingischer Herrscher*, Beihefte zum Archiv für Kulturgeschichte 38 (Cologne, 1995); E.-D. Hehl, 'Maria und das ottonisch-salische Königtum'.

[61] Hehl, 'Maria und das ottonisch-salische Königtum', p. 306.

kingdom also by election.[62] But a degree of flexibility was possible and of course in the case of the consecration of an heir with the father still living, the choice was free. Sunday was the favoured day of the week for consecration, a fact mentioned in some of the *ordines* and concomitant with episcopal consecration, which was also supposed to take place on a Sunday.[63] As will be shown, some of the Sundays were imbued with either liturgical or historical significance and were clearly quite deliberate choices, but when a monarch deviated from the norm by being crowned on a weekday it is manifest that there existed specific motives for choosing those days. In the case of William the Conqueror, who was crowned on a Monday, the Monday was Christmas Day, and in the case of John, who was crowned on a Thursday, the Thursday was Ascension Day. Important apostolic feasts were also reasons to deviate from a Sunday, as can be seen in Matilda of England's consecration at Mainz on Monday 25 July 1110 and Frederick II's inauguration at Aachen on Saturday 25 July 1215. 25 July marks the feast of the Apostle James the Great.[64] Henry III of England's consecration at Gloucester following the sudden death of his father King John in 1216 took place on a Monday. There can be no denying that the child's position was weak and that his inauguration took place in unusual circumstances, but it is worth noting that 28 October, as Matthew Paris makes clear in his account, is an apostolic feast: that of Saints Simon and Jude.[65] As will be argued below, aspiring kings could be under political pressure that made speedy inauguration essential, but even in such circumstances, the resonances of the liturgical calendar were exploited where possible to bolster their position. The child-king Henry III needed all the support William Marshal and his associates could muster, including from the apostles. In having the boy inaugurated on the first major feast subsequent to John's death, they sought to enhance this act, which political circumstance prevented them from holding at the traditional site of Westminster, with a halo of liturgical legitimacy.

It appears to have been customary for kings to be consecrated within roughly a month of the death of their predecessor, if they had not already been

---

[62] Schaller, 'Der heilige Tag', p. 5.
[63] Andrieu, 'Le sacre épiscopal', p. 34.
[64] As discussed in the previous chapter, Frederick II also translated Charlemagne's body and took the Cross during the festivities surrounding his 1215 inauguration. The reference to St James therefore takes on additional meaning, as by 1215 the legend that Charlemagne had fought the muslims in Spain at St James's request was well established. On the association between Charlemagne's expedition to Spain and crusading see J. Stuckey, 'Charlemagne as Crusader? Memory, Propaganda, and the Many Uses of Charlemagne's Legendary Expedition to Spain', in *The Legend of Charlemagne in the Middle Ages: Power, Faith and Crusade*, ed. M. Gabriele and J. Stuckey (New York, 2008), pp. 137–52.
[65] Matthew Paris, *Chronica Majora*, ed. Luard, III, 2: 'Coronatur autem rex Henricus iii anno etatis sue XO. In die apostolorum Simon et Jude. XXOVIIIO die in mensis Octobris'.

consecrated, or soon after their election in the case of the German kingdom. Thus it has become usual for historians to see a long gap without a successor being crowned as indicative of strife, and conversely for an apparently quick consecration to be seen as demonstrative of a successor's weak position and anxiety to formalize their rule. In England this interpretation owes much to the situation following William Rufus's death in the New Forest on 2 August 1100 when, despite Henry having a strong claim to the throne, the claim of his eldest brother Robert is often seen by modern historians as having been stronger. Although C. Warren Hollister emphatically rejected the idea of Henry's kingship of England being considered usurpation, the speed with which he assumed the throne has certainly cast a shadow on the interpretation of the early years of his reign.[66] To deny that some pragmatism was involved in the speed of the consecration would be unwise, but there was also a liturgical impetus behind Henry's inauguration on 5 August 1100. Looking beyond the Anglo-Norman realm reinforces this suggestion, because equally short timespans between the death of a predecessor and the inauguration of a new king found in France and in Jerusalem provide illuminating comparisons. In addition, the Empire provides an example of a mere four-day gap between an election and an inauguration. We shall start by looking briefly at the evidence from the Empire and Jerusalem, before turning to consider the inaugurations of Louis VI of France and Henry I of England in greater detail.

In the imperial context, Ernst-Dieter Hehl has forcefully argued that Conrad II's inauguration on 8 September 1024, only four days after his election at Kamba, was not motivated by simple political reasons, for his position was secure, but by a desire to be consecrated on the feast of the Nativity of Mary.[67] Hehl pointed out that the Gospel reading for this feast was the *Liber generationis*, the dynastic tree of Jesus that opens Matthew's account of Christ's life (Matthew 1. 1–16). He develops his argument to show the manner in which the new Salian ruler drew on the dynastic themes of this feast to stress that he ruled in the tradition of the Old Testament patriarchs and kings as Christ's vicar on earth. The kingdom of Jerusalem provides another example of a quick consecration being linked to an important day. Following the death of Amalric I on 11 July 1174, Baldwin IV was made king a few days later on 15 July, which marked the seventy-fifth anniversary of

---

[66] C. W. Hollister, *Henry I* (London, 2001), p. 105. George Garnett has also made the point that, given that William Rufus and Stephen had to cross the Channel before they could be crowned, 'the seventeen- and twenty-one-day periods of interregnum respectively do not reveal much less of a sense of urgency than the three-day one in 1100'. Garnett, *Conquered England*, p. 140.

[67] Hehl, 'Maria und das ottonisch-salische Königtum', p. 272. Cf. S. Weinfurter, 'Idoneität – Begründung und Akzeptanz von Königsherrschaft im hohen Mittelalter', in *Idoneität – Genealogie – Legitimation: Begründung und Akzeptanz von dynastische Herrschaft im Mittelalter*, ed. C. Andenna and G. Melville (Cologne, 2015), pp. 127–37 (pp. 129–31).

the capture of Jerusalem by the First Crusade.[68] This was clearly a day that had great resonance in the Crusader kingdom. 15 July seems to have been established as a feast in Jerusalem within a few years of the fall of the city in 1099; its celebration is first recorded by Baldric of Bourgueil, who wrote the first version of his *Historia Ierosolimitana*, in 1105 before revising it from 1107.[69] In 1149 the Holy Sepulchre, by now the established inauguration church in the kingdom of Jerusalem, was rededicated on the feast, adding another layer to the liturgical importance of the day.[70] Baldwin's leprosy has coloured the interpretation of this event, but as Stephen Lay has stressed there is no evidence to suggest that Baldwin was known to be leprous prior to his taking the throne and in fact his succession appears to have been relatively straightforward, with the nobles who met to discuss a successor to Amalric quickly reaching agreement that his son should be crowned.[71] However, even if his leprosy had not yet manifested itself, Baldwin was still a minor and the swiftness with which he was consecrated is undoubtedly a symptom of the desire of the nobility to avoid political uncertainty. What needs to be recognized, however, was that the rush to crown Baldwin was at least in part motivated by a desire to associate the boy king with the triumphal conquest of Jerusalem and the rededication of Jerusalem's most important church, in which he was crowned.

With these examples in mind, we return to the inaugurations of Henry I and Louis VI, events that took place within a decade of one another and exhibit a number of remarkable similarities. Henry I was consecrated three days after the death of his brother William Rufus on 2 August 1100 and Louis VI only five days after the death of his father Philip I on 29 July 1108. Both consecrations can be described as irregular. Henry I was not consecrated by the archbishop of Canterbury, who customarily crowned a new English king. The archbishop, Anselm, was in exile having clashed with Rufus, and Henry would later write to Anselm to explain why he had not been able to wait for his return, stating that 'enemies were intending to rise up against me and

---

[68] B. Hamilton, *The Leper King and His Heirs: Baldwin IV and the Crusader Kingdom of Jerusalem* (Cambridge, 2000), pp. 41–42.

[69] Baldric of Bourgueil, *Historia Ierosolimitana*, ed. S. Biddlecombe (Woodbridge, 2014), p. 111.

[70] On this feast see S. A. John, 'The "Feast of the Liberation of Jerusalem": Remembering and Reconstructing the First Crusade in the Holy City, 1099–1187', *Journal of Medieval History* 46 (2015), 409–31.

[71] S. Lay, 'A Leper in Purple: The Coronation of Baldwin IV of Jerusalem', *Journal of Medieval History* 23 (1997), 317–23. Oliver Auge has recently suggested that, in any case, a lack of physical integrity might not make a person unfit to rule. See O. Auge, 'Physische Idoneität? Zum Problem körperlicher Versehrtheit bei der Eignung als Herrscher im Mittelalter', in *Idoneität – Genealogie – Legitimation: Begründung und Akzeptanz von dynastische Herrschaft im Mittelalter*, ed. C. Andenna and G. Melville (Cologne, 2015), pp. 39–58.

the people who were mine to govern, and therefore my people did not want to delay it any longer'.[72] Louis VI similarly did not receive consecration at the hands of the primate one would expect. Instead of the archbishop of Reims who, as we have seen, normally officiated at such occasions, Louis was crowned and anointed by the archbishop of Sens, with a number of bishops assisting him. Whereas Henry had at least been consecrated at Westminster, the traditional location for English male inauguration, Louis was consecrated at Orléans rather than Reims, by now the traditional coronation church of the French kings. A letter also survives justifying the speed of Louis's consecration and its irregularity, written not by the king himself but by Ivo of Chartres, who argued that the break from tradition was justified to secure the king's position against the machinations of evil men.[73] It cannot be denied that political expediency played a part in the speed with which these two kings were inaugurated, but the extent to which both events made use of the liturgical calendar to enhance their legitimacy should not be overlooked.

Abbot Suger provides the most detailed description of Louis's inauguration. He explained that following the death of Philip I Louis's succession was somewhat hurried due to the opposition of some 'evil and impious men'. Therefore the archbishop of Sens, with the support of a number of bishops,

> on the day of the invention of the protomartyr Stephen, anointed him with the most holy oil of unction, delivered a mass of thanksgiving and having cast aside his sword of secular knighthood he girded Louis with the ecclesiastical sword for the punishment of malefactors, crowned him with rejoicing with the diadem of the kingdom and also delivered to him most devotedly, with the approval of the clergy and the people, the sceptre and rod with which he must defend the church and the poor and various other royal insignia.[74]

In his *Life* of Louis the Fat, Suger displays little interest in chronology as we would understand it and, in fact, he barely mentions dates at all.[75] That he does here, informing the reader that Louis's consecration took place on the

---

[72] Letter 212: *S. Anselmi Cantuariensis archiepiscopi opera omnia*, ed. F. S. Schmitt, 6 vols. (Edinburgh 1946–91), IV, 109; Anselm of Canterbury, *The Letters of Saint Anselm of Canterbury*, trans. W. Fröhlich, 3 vols. (Kalamazoo 1990–4), II, 162.

[73] Ivo of Chartres's letter has been edited by Christof Rolker. See C. Rolker and M. Schawe, 'Das Gutachten Ivos von Chartres zur Krönung König Ludwigs VI.', *Francia: Forschungen zur westeuropäischen Geschichte* 34 (2007), 146–57.

[74] Suger, *Vie de Louis VI Le Gros*, p. 86: 'Qui in die inventionis sancti prothomartyris Stephani sacratissime unctionis liquore delibutum, missas gratiarum agens abjectoque secularis milite gladio ecclesiastico ad vindictam malefactorum accingens, diademate regni gratanter coronavit necnon et sceptrum et virgam et per hec ecclesiarum et pauperum defensionem et quecumque regni insignia, approbante clero et populo, devotissime contradidit'.

[75] Gabrielle Spiegel has described Suger's text as exhibiting a chronological looseness. G. Spiegel, 'History as Enlightenment: Suger and the *Mos Anagogicus*', in *Abbot*

Feast of the Invention of the Protomartyr Stephen, should alert us to the fact that he wishes to impart more than just chronological information.

Geoffrey Koziol, in an influential essay in which he argued that the chivalric ethos eroded liturgical ideas of kingship, used Suger's description of Louis's inauguration as a prominent example. He discussed the ritual and commented that 'the insignia were the same as in earlier centuries, but their interpretation was not'.[76] Koziol's assertion, however, must be refuted and it is precisely in Suger's reference to a feast of St Stephen that we can see that the opposite is true: that the insignia of kingship were still firmly rooted in liturgical soil. The Feast of the Invention of Stephen on 3 August might at first sight strike one as being considerably less important than his major feast day on 26 December, but in this period the feast commemorating the finding of Stephen's body was also prominent and, in fact, James of Voragine recounts in the *Golden Legend*, written c.1260, that the feast of the finding of his body was celebrated with more gusto than the feast of his martyrdom.[77] In any case, the appropriateness of the king being crowned on a day related to a saint whose name derived from the Greek στέφανος (*stephanos*, meaning crown) would surely not have been lost on an educated churchman like Suger, abbot of a monastery that promoted Greek, not least to strengthen the ties between St Denis and the Pseudo Areopagite.[78] Stephen's name reflects the fact that he was the first to gain a heavenly 'crown of martyrdom' and it is precisely this dual play on the crown as both an item of royal and spiritual insignia that explains the attraction of this feast to Louis and his supporters. Being inaugurated on this feast day enabled Louis to stress the sacrality of his kingship, an emphasis that was entirely necessary given the political situation following his father's death.[79]

Suger and Saint-Denis: A Symposium, ed. P. L. Gerson (New York, 1986), pp. 151–9 (pp. 152–3).

[76] Koziol, 'England, France and the Problem of Sacrality', p. 130.

[77] Jacobi a Voragine, *Legenda Aurea*, ed. T. Graesse (Leipzig, 1845), pp. 461–5; translated in Jacobus de Voragine, *The Golden Legend: Readings on the Saints*, trans. W. G. Ryan, 2 vols. (Princeton, 1993) II, 40–4. On Stephen and his veneration see F. Bovon, 'The Dossier on Stephen, the First Martyr', *Harvard Theological Review* 96 (2003), 279–315.

[78] The art historians Otto von Simson and Erwin Panofsky both highlighted links between Pseudo-Dionysis and Suger's architectural programme at Saint-Denis. Their views have been moderated by Grover Zinn, Jr, who stressed that Suger was not the only twelfth-century ecclesiastic influenced by Pseudo-Dionysian thought: O. von Simson, *The Gothic Cathedral: Origins of Gothic Architecture and the Medieval Concept of Order*, 3rd edn (Princeton, 1988), pp. 103–6; E. Panofsky ed., *Abbot Suger on the Abbey Church of Saint-Denis and its Art Treasures* (Princeton, 1946), pp. 18–25; G. A. Zinn, Jr, 'Suger, Theology, and the Pseudo-Dionysian Tradition', in *Abbot Suger and Saint-Denis: A Symposium*, ed. P. L. Gerson (New York, 1986), pp. 33–40.

[79] In some version of the *laudes* originating in France the king is coupled with St Stephen suggesting that the saint had established royal associations. Kantorowicz, 'Ivories and Litanies', p. 68.

While Abbot Suger's play on words alerts us to the significance of 3 August to Louis's inauguration, no Anglo-Norman historical writer was quite so explicit about Henry I's consecration. The *Chronicle of Battle Abbey*, however, informs us that Henry was consecrated on 'the solemn day of the martyrdom of St Oswald' ('solemni die martirii beati Oswaldi').[80] Being consecrated on the day associated with the most prominent of pre-Conquest royal saints, Oswald, king and martyr, must have been an attractive proposition in the circumstances. The cult of St Oswald was well developed in Norman England as is evidenced by the appearance of his feast day in all but one of the English calendars up to 1100 that survive.[81] He was often invoked in litanies and that his liturgical cult was widespread is indicated from the survival of two distinct masses from the eleventh century.[82] In choosing to be consecrated on Oswald's feast, Henry I invited his identification with this royal saint and indicated that Oswald was his model of kingship. However, there was more than an historical link being made between the new king and his Northumbrian exemplar.

The liturgy for Oswald's feast is dripping with the language of coronation and royal power. The more widely diffused eleventh-century mass proper, represented in a missal from New Minster and in service books belonging to Robert of Jumièges and Wulfstan of Worcester, opens with the following prayer:

> Omnipotent and eternal God who constituted the blessed and pleasing joy of this day in solemn observance of your holy servant Oswald, increase our hearts in your fear and love so that we might celebrate the shedding of holy blood on earth of those we understand in our minds as our united protectors in heaven.[83]

This mass as it survives in written form is very brief and contains no indication of what Psalms or other musical elements would have been included. The prayer makes apparent, however, that the 'shedding of holy blood on earth' refers to both Christ's crucifixion and Oswald's martyrdom and that these two protectors are now united in heaven. Given this connection it is unsurprising that later, fuller surviving offices make abundant use of Psalm 20, a

---

[80] *The Chronicle of Battle Abbey*, ed. E. Searle, OMT (Oxford, 1980), p. 96.
[81] See R. Rushforth, *Saints in English Kalendars Before A.D. 1100*, HBS 117 (Woodbridge, 2008).
[82] A. Thacker, '*Membra Disjecta*: The Division of the Body and the Diffusion of the Cult', in *Oswald: Northumbrian King to European Saint*, ed. C. Stancliffe and E. Cambridge (Stamford, 1995), pp. 97–127 (p. 123).
[83] *The Missal of Robert of Jumièges*, ed. H. A. Wilson, HBS 11 (London, 1896), p. 195: 'Omnipotens sempiterne deus qui huius diei iocundam beatamque laetitiam in sancti serui tui osuualdi sollempnitate consecrasti da cordibus nostris tui timoris karitatisque augmentum ut cuius in terris sancti sanguinis effusionem caelebramus illius in caelo conlata patrocinia mentibus sentiamus'.

praise to God for Christ's exaltation after his Passion. In the Sarum rite, the response to the gradual is drawn from Psalm 20. 4: 'You have set on his head a crown of precious stones.'[84] The theme of coronation is also taken up by the introit: 'You have crowned him with glory and honour and have set him over the works of your hands' (Psalm 8. 6–7).[85]

As in the case of Louis VI's inauguration, the connection between the act of coronation and the liturgical content of the day makes explicit that crowns were objects with far more than mere secular significance. Counter to Koziol's assertion,[86] this item of royal insignia continued to be understood as inherently spiritual in nature. Henry no doubt did need to act with haste to secure the throne following the sudden and mysterious death of his brother Rufus. The extreme rapidity with which he arranged his consecration can, however, be partially explained by a desire to align his exaltation to the kingship with the celebration of Oswald's transition from terrestrial to celestial king. While it cannot be assumed that the Sarum rite represents exactly the liturgy in use at Westminster in 1100, it does make clear the symbolic potential of this feast. The liturgy enabled Henry to stress that his kingship was the will of God, whom himself had placed a crown upon Henry's head. This emphasis on the God-given legitimacy of his kingship served to strengthen Henry's position against the potential opposition of his elder brother Robert. In any case, it seems likely Oswald had established liturgical credentials connecting him to the Anglo-Norman kings. If the versions of the *laudes* sung at Henry's coronation were those included in the Cambridge, Trinity College manuscript of the third recension of the English *ordines*, discussed in chapter 1, then Oswald's name would have once more reverberated around the coronation church.

Given the importance of Marian imagery to the liturgical trappings of royal power it is unsurprising to discover that Marian feasts were particularly favoured by kings in all three realms as days on which to be consecrated or married. This in part reflects a wider shared devotion to the Virgin, but as with other feast days, Marian feasts were not just important days on which such events took place, but liturgical commemorations which shape the way we should understand these royal acts. As we have seen, the inauguration of Philip Augustus was originally intended to have taken place on the Feast of the Assumption of the Virgin before being delayed to the Feast of All Saints. Within the Empire, Frederick Barbarossa's son Henry VI was consecrated on the Assumption in 1169 and Frederick's wife Beatrix was crowned as queen of Burgundy at Vienne on the same day in 1178, a few weeks after Barbarossa had himself been crowned at Arles.[87] In 1193 Philip Augustus's ill-fated wedding

---

[84] *Missale ad usum insignis et praeclarae ecclesiae Sarum*, ed. F. H. Dickinson (Burntisland, 1861), p. 841.
[85] Ibid., p. 840.
[86] See above, p. 148.
[87] On the Arles coronation see J. Fried, 'Friedrich Barbarossas Krönung in Arles

to and coronation with Ingeborg of Denmark took place on the Feast of the Assumption and its vigil. The rather more durable union between Frederick of Sicily and Constance of Aragon also took place on 15 August in 1209. The appropriateness of queens being associated with the pre-eminent Marian feast is straightforward to grasp, although there is a depth to this symbolism that is not immediately apparent. The link between male inauguration and the Feast of Assumption is perhaps more opaque, but as with the inaugurations of Louis VI and Henry I discussed above, Philip Augustus's planned consecration on 15 August and the actual consecration of Henry VI on this day demonstrate, once again, that royal insignia continued to be conceived of in liturgical terms even in the late twelfth century. Psalm 44, which is part of the liturgy for this feast, is invoked in the prayer associated with handing over the sword in royal *ordines* from England, France and the Empire.[88]

That the Assumption was chosen by both Philip Augustus and Frederick of Sicily (later Emperor Frederick II) was no coincidence, but rather a recognition of the potential of this liturgical celebration to enhance the sanctity of their kingship and marriage. The French king's abrupt repudiation of his Danish bride is a good illustration of Philippe Buc's point that rituals could go wrong.[89] However, while recognizing that Philip's actions are demonstrative of the fact that kings could be motivated to act out of a number of reasons, including personal ones, we should not allow his distaste for his new queen to disguise the original intention. Royal marriages were by their very nature political, bringing the king important allies and rich dowries. As generations of scholars have stressed, queens were also fundamental to the production of an heir and thus to the stability of a realm.[90] Such pragmatic considerations are not, however, at odds with a liturgical understanding of kingship and queenship and this is immediately apparent when considering the appropriateness of the Feast of Assumption for royal marriage and the consecration of a new queen. As we saw in chapter 2, the liturgy of this feast was drawn on for one of the most radical iconographical developments of the Romanesque period: the Coronation of the Virgin. It is no coincidence that the earliest surviving representation of the Coronation of the Virgin is found on a capital discovered by George Zarnecki in 1948 and comes from Reading abbey, a foundation closely associated with Henry I and his marriage to his second wife Adeliza of Louvain.[91]

Henry I's son-in-law, the Emperor Henry V, was particularly adept at exploiting the resonances of the liturgical calendar. In 1114 the cathedral city

---

(1178)', *Historisches Jahrbuch* 103 (1983), 347–71.
[88] *English Coronation Records*, ed. Legg, p. 34; *Ordines Coronationis Franciae*, ed. Jackson, I, 209, 259; *Le pontifical romano-germanique*, ed. Vogel and Elze, II, 253.
[89] P. Buc, *The Dangers of Ritual: Between Early Medieval Texts and Social Scientific Theory* (Princeton, 2001), pp. 8–9.
[90] See for example the overview in Parsons, 'Introduction'.
[91] Stafford, '*Cherchez la Femme*', pp. 91–4.

of Mainz witnessed Henry V and Matilda of England marrying amid great splendour. The date chosen for this union of emperor and queen, for as we have seen, Matilda had already been consecrated on the Feast of St James in 1110, was 6 January.[92] The account in the anonymous Latin *Kaiserchronik* makes explicit the liturgical significance of the day, recounting that once the emperor had celebrated Christmas at Bamberg, he travelled to Mainz, where it had been arranged his wedding should take place 'on the approaching epiphany' ('in proxima epiphania').[93] Henry had, himself, been consecrated king on Epiphany 1099 and in marrying Matilda on the same feast day as he had been consecrated fifteen years previously, his marriage appears as a confirmation of his kingship. Moreover, as shall be demonstrated, by choosing 6 January for both his consecration and his marriage, Henry made reference to a smorgasbord of liturgical symbolism, through which he made clear the Christological model for his rule and stressed the sanctity of his marriage.

While Bernard Hamilton is right to point out that there was no special cult of the Magi in Western Europe before the translation of their relics to Cologne in 1164, they were widely represented in the iconography of the Nativity and the attractiveness of being crowned and anointed on the festival celebrating the Three Kings seems clear.[94] Henry thereby identified himself with the New Testament kings who had brought gifts to the Christ Child.[95] However, Henry was making bolder claims than mere equivalence with the Magi. As Robert Deshman elucidated in his classic essay on kingship and Christology in Anglo-Saxon and Ottonian art, the Adoration of the Magi was depicted as a ceremony of the *aurum coronarium*, an ancient Hellenistic rite adopted by the Roman emperors at which citizens of the empire and its subordinate provinces offered gifts.[96] As the name of the ceremony suggests, the gift proffered was a golden crown, a symbol particularly appropriate in the context of an inauguration. Henry thus identified with both the royal gift-givers and with Christ receiving their homage. The liturgy of the feast

---

[92] One often finds 7 January given as the date for their wedding in secondary literature. This was the date included by von Knonau in his chronology of Henry V's reign, but is the result of a misreading of the Chronicle of Ekkehard of Aura. Ekkehard reports that the wedding took place, 'post epiphaniam Domini', but plentiful other evidence suggests this did not mean the day after, as Ekkehard's editor Georg Waitz assumed. G. M. von Knonau, *Jahrbücher des deutschen Reiches unter Heinrich IV. und Heinrich V.*, 7 vols. (Leipzig, 1890–1909) VI, 285; Ekkehard of Aura, *Chronica*, ed. Waitz, p. 247.

[93] *Frutolfi et Ekkehardi Chronica*, ed. Schmale and Schmale-Ott, p. 262.

[94] B. Hamilton, 'Prester John and the Three Kings of Cologne', in *Studies in Medieval History Presented to R. H. C. Davis*, ed. H. Mayr-Harting and R. I. Moore (London 1985), pp. 177–91 (p. 181).

[95] The Magi were first depicted as kings in the Anglo-Saxon Benedictional of Aethelwold and this innovation was soon after adopted in Ottonian Germany. See Deshman, '*Christus rex et magi reges*', pp. 377–81.

[96] Ibid., p. 380.

makes this second facet abundantly clear.[97] The common introit, 'Ecce advenit dominator dominus et regnum in manu eius et potestas et imperium', set the tone for a celebration that incorporates Psalm 71, a prophecy of the coming of Christ and his kingship. The connection between the liturgical celebration of the Epiphany and the liturgical celebration of Henry's consecration ran deeper still. Henry also referenced several other layers of symbolism in the liturgical calendar, and these layers have been obscured by the subsequent dominance of the association of the Epiphany with the Three Kings. 6 January is the day on which two other biblical events were commemorated, both of which held important symbolic connotations for the emperor and his new wife: Christ's baptism in the River Jordan and his first miracle, the turning of water into wine at the wedding at Cana.

Whether the anointing of kings as part of the inauguration ceremony can be linked to baptismal anointing is a matter of much debate, as we have seen. However, the description of Christ's baptism in the Gospel of Matthew makes apparent the link being drawn here. Matthew describes Jesus emerging from the water, the heavens opening and the Holy Spirit descending upon him in the form of a dove (Matthew 3. 16).[98] This link between royal inauguration and the descent of the Holy Spirit echoes the description of the inauguration of Otto II in the tenth-century annals from Lobbes, with which Schaller began his investigation. In the context of Henry's inauguration the commemoration of the homage of the Magi and of Christ's baptism in the day's liturgy influence how his coronation and unction were to be perceived. Interestingly, Christ's baptism was the dominant commemoration observed on 6 January at the court of the Byzantine emperors, where the day was accordingly called the Theophany.[99] Indeed, by the twelfth century there existed a tradition, with sporadic precedents in earlier centuries, of delivering annual panegyrics of the emperor on 6 January.[100] As the living image of Christ, the emperor played an active role in the Theophany celebrations by representing the baptized Christ. Kantorowicz, in an unpublished paper, saw this baptismal symbolism as being central to the Eastern coronation ritual.[101] Rather than the western

---

[97] *Missale Romanum Mediolani 1474*, ed. R. Lippe, 2 vols., HBS, 17, 33 (London 1899–1907), I, 31–2.

[98] Christ's baptism is described in a similar manner in the other Gospels: cf. Mark 1. 9–11; Luke 3. 21–23 and John 1. 29–33.

[99] Acclamations for use during the imperial procession and details of other ceremonial events involving the Byzantine emperor at Epiphany can be found as chapters 3 and 26 in the tenth-century *Book of Ceremonies* compiled and edited by the Byzantine emperor Constantine VII (905–59). Constantine Porphyrogennetos, *The Book of Ceremonies*, trans. A. Moffatt and M. Tall, 2 vols., Byzantina Australiensia 18 (Canberra, 2012), I, 41–3,143–7.

[100] D. Angelov, *Imperial Ideology and Political Thought in Byzantium (1204–1330)* (Cambridge, 2007), p. 31.

[101] Ševčenko, 'Ernst H. Kantorowicz', pp. 286–7.

model provided by Samuel's anointing of David, that placed the churchman above the king he was anointing, in Byzantium the emperor was presented as Christ and the patriarch as John the Baptist.[102] The absence of an anointing in the Byzantine ritual has been seen as the fundamental difference between western and eastern practices. Whereas western kings required the participation of ecclesiastical elites to be crowned, the Byzantine emperors were able themselves to place a crown on their heir's head to make them co-emperor.[103] Whether or not a conscious adoption of Byzantine practice, this symbolism must have been very attractive to Henry V and his father, and in choosing 6 January for his son's consecration, Henry IV emphasized the Christological model for his son's kingship.

The final event celebrated in the liturgy on 6 January demands special attention in the context of royal marriage. At Cana Jesus performed his first miracle by changing water into wine at the ensuing wedding feast. In marrying on this day Henry and Matilda ensured that Christ was, through the liturgy, actually present at their wedding, thereby sanctifying their union and their royal status.[104] That Christ performed his miracle at the wedding feast is perhaps behind the decision of the author of the anonymous *Kaiserchronik* to illustrate his description of the wedding with a miniature of the emperor and his wife crowned and seated side-by-side at their wedding feast (see Plate 5).[105] Henry and Matilda were not the only royal couple to appreciate the symbolism of this day. Almost a century later in 1205 Philip of Swabia, having finally wrested Aachen from the control of Otto IV, was consecrated in the Cathedral of St Mary alongside his wife. The day chosen for this dual consecration was 6 January.

Having shown how Henry V used 6 January for two important events in his reign, I now turn to the temporal cycle of moveable feasts and Sunday observations to uncover the fact that dates, which by modern reckoning do not appear the same, can be shown to be imitative. In England, Stephen was consecrated, according to Gervase of Canterbury's account, 'on the eleventh kalends of January' ('undecimo kalendas Januarii'), or on 22 December.[106] In 1135 22 December fell on the last Sunday in Advent. With this in mind let us turn to Ralph de Diceto's mention of the consecration of Henry II on 19 December 1154. Ralph recorded that it took place 'on the fourteenth kalends

---

[102] Ibid.

[103] Nelson, 'Symbols in Context', pp. 108–10.

[104] The wedding at Cana was the Gospel reading for the second or third Sunday after Epiphany and sermons from these Sundays became important vehicles for marriage preaching at the turn of the twelfth and thirteenth centuries. See D. L. d'Avray, 'The Gospel of the Marriage Feast of Cana and Marriage Preaching in France', in *Modern Questions About Medieval Sermons: Essays on Marriage, Death, History and Sanctity*, ed. N. Bériou and D. L. d'Avray (Spoleto, 1994), pp. 135–53.

[105] Cambridge, Corpus Christi College, MS 373, fol. 95v.

[106] Gervase of Canterbury, *The Historical Works*, ed. Stubbs, I, 94–5.

of January, on the Sunday before the Nativity of the Lord' ('xiiiio kalendas Januarii, die Dominica ante Nativitatem Domini').[107] Ralph's account thus makes clear that although Stephen and Henry II's consecrations did not take place on the same calendar day, they did both occur on the same liturgical day. Contemporaneous consecrations in the German kingdom make clear that this was not just coincidence. Three consecutive kings were consecrated in Lent on Laetare Sunday: Conrad III on 13 March 1138, Henry Berengar as co-king on 30 March 1147, and Frederick I on 9 March 1152. What this repetition means is rather elusive, but the fact that we have the same phenomenon in two kingdoms makes apparent the repetition was not mere chance.

John Gillingham recognized that Henry had chosen the same Sunday as Stephen's coronation, and suggested that he did so 'perhaps to symbolize his position as Stephen's heir'.[108] As we have seen in the case of Henry V getting married on the same day as he had been consecrated years previously, repetition can be understood as confirmation and in the case of repetition of dates by successive kings the idea that it symbolizes rightful succession is persuasive. This is certainly true in the case of Henry Berengar's inauguration in 1147. By having his son crowned and anointed on the same liturgical day as he himself had been elevated to the kingship, the junior king's inauguration appears as both a confirmation of Conrad III's rule and as a way of stressing Henry Berengar was his heir. The case of Frederick Barbarossa's inauguration is rather more complicated. In an insightful article Werner Goez, recognizing that all three German monarchs were crowned on the same liturgical day, tried to use this fact to explain the speed with which Frederick Barbarossa was crowned following Conrad's death (Henry Berengar had predeceased his father, dying in 1150).[109]

Conrad III died at Bamberg on 15 February 1152. Barbarossa was elected king at Frankfurt on 4 March and five days later consecrated at Aachen, meaning that he had to travel the 300km between Frankfurt and Aachen at 'breathtaking speed'. Goez points out that throughout the entire period 911–1254 no other king was inaugurated so swiftly following the death of his predecessor, and he goes on to argue that 9 March 1152 must have been designated for a royal consecration even before the death of Conrad.[110] He suggests that, in the same way Conrad had raised his son Henry to the kingship in preparation for his absence from Germany due to participation in the Second Crusade, Conrad sought to elevate a new co-king to rule Germany while he travelled to Rome to secure the imperial crown finally in 1152.[111] On

---

[107] Ralph de Diceto, *The Historical Works*, ed. Stubbs, I, 298–9.
[108] J. Gillingham, *The Angevin Empire*, 2nd edn (London, 2001), p. 20.
[109] W. Goez, 'Von Bamberg nach Frankfurt und Aachen: Barbarossas Weg zur Königskrone', *Jahrbuch für fränkische Landesforschung* 52 (1992), 61–72.
[110] Ibid., pp. 64–5.
[111] Ibid., p. 67.

the king's unexpected death Frederick had to react quickly to gain support, and in doing so the date for royal election drew close to Laetare Sunday, the day Goez claims had already been earmarked for a consecration in Aachen, necessitating the rush from Frankfurt to Aachen, for it would be seen as a bad omen for the new king if this traditional date was not used.[112]

Goez's assertion that a royal consecration had already been planned for 9 March 1152 is certainly plausible, but the question remains, who was the consecration intended for? Although Conrad's eldest son had died he had another son, Frederick of Rothenburg, whom he could have intended to consecrate king in 1152.[113] It could be that in the German case Barbarossa both symbolically usurped the date of his predecessor's consecration and literally took possession of the day of consecration that had been earmarked for another candidate. In choosing to be consecrated on the same day as Conrad III and Henry Berengar he sought to consciously place himself in the their tradition while at the same time appropriating this tradition for himself. Indeed, Barbarossa returned to Laetare Sunday for another important occurrence in his reign, the 1188 court at Mainz during which he took the Cross.[114] This was not only a way of associating crusading with his consecration, something done even more explicitly by Frederick II in 1215, but we see here more evidence of the exploitation of liturgical resonances. The appropriateness of taking the Cross on the Sunday named after its introit 'Rejoice Jerusalem' could hardly be more apparent. Indeed, in 1250 Henry III of England made exactly the same connection.[115]

We can see the tension between royal and papal imagery when we consider the dates of the imperial inaugurations of those German kings who were elevated to the highest throne in Western Christendom. The first German king to be made emperor during this period was Henry IV, on 31 March 1084, the date on which Easter Sunday fell that year. This suggests that imperial consecrations were also timed to occur on important feast days. Yet it transpires that Henry IV's imperial sacring was an exception and that the remaining six imperial consecrations up to 1250 did not take place on significant liturgical dates, with the exception of the consecration of Henry VI on Easter Monday 1191, an event I have discussed elsewhere.[116] As we saw in the examination of the *ordines*, the fundamental difference between royal and imperial consecration was that in the imperial theatre the pope played a major role. The choice of date for imperial inauguration could not be dictated by the emperor

---

[112] Ibid., p. 70.
[113] This suggestion has recently been accepted by Knut Görich. See Görich, *Friedrich Barbarossa*, pp. 93–7.
[114] I have treated this event more comprehensively in Dale, 'Inauguration and Political Liturgy', p. 197.
[115] Matthew Paris, *Chronica Majora*, ed. Luard, , V, 100–1.
[116] Dale, 'Inauguration and Political Liturgy', pp. 210–12.

alone and was subject to negotiation and it seems that post-Gregorian popes no longer wished to associate imperial inauguration with important liturgical feasts. From the time of Charlemagne's imperial consecration on Christmas Day 800 through to 1084, the emperors had frequently been consecrated on significant church feasts, with a further two Christmas consecrations, three on Easter Sunday, and one each on Pentecost, Candlemas and Ascension Day.[117]

That this eschewal of feast days for the imperial consecration was a papal innovation is indicated by the case of Henry V, as highlighted by Schaller. He saw Henry V's wearing of the imperial crown in Rome on Easter Sunday 1117, and at Pentecost 1118, as attempts to remedy the fact that Henry had been crowned emperor in dubious circumstances on 13 April 1111, an ordinary weekday.[118] That the imperial consecration required the agreement of the pope, in Henry's case forced under duress, meant that the resonances of the liturgical calendar were more difficult to exploit. Henry IV had ensured his imperial consecration took place on Easter Sunday by being consecrated by the anti-pope Clement III rather than by his great adversary Gregory VII. The role of an anti-pope in Henry IV's inauguration is indicative of the fact that Gregorian popes no longer wished to facilitate the drawing of links between royal authority and the liturgical calendar. In fact, Gregory VII and his successors were determined to manipulate the resonances of such feasts to their own advantage. Christmas Day 1075, on which Gregory VII processed through Rome wearing a crown, provides the first evidence for papal crown-wearing, though Schimmelpfennig has suggested that papal crown-wearing might already have been customary in the ninth and tenth centuries.[119] The *Liber Politicus*, a ceremonial compilation completed shortly after Innocent II's return to Rome in 1138 by the canon Benedict and later elaborated by other authors, includes a list of eighteen feasts and holidays on which the pope was to wear his crown.[120] Wearing a crown in Rome on a major church feast was from now on to be the preserve of popes alone.

As we have seen in this chapter, the vocabulary used to describe royal inauguration parallels that to describe episcopal consecration. Where crowning words are used, it should not be assumed that this is a symptom of a diminished royal rite. The crown was no mere secular symbol, and coronation continued to be closely associated with sanctity throughout this period. As in the case of episcopal consecration, royal consecration most often took place on

---

[117] Christmas Day: Charlemagne (800), Otto II (967), Henry III (1046); Easter Sunday: Lothar I (823), Conrad II (1027); Pentecost: Louis II (872); Candlemas: Otto I (967); Ascension: Otto III (996).

[118] Schaller, 'Der heilige Tag', p. 7.

[119] B. Schimmelpfennig, 'Die Bedeutung Roms in päpstlichen Zeremoniell', in *Rom im hohen Mittelalter: Studien zu den Romvorstellung und zur Rompolitik von 10. bis zum 12. Jahrhundert*, ed. B. Schimmelpfennig and L. Schmugge (Sigmaringen, 1992), pp. 7–61 (p. 58).

[120] On the dating and composition of the *Liber Politicus* see Twyman, *Papal Ceremonial*, pp. 24–7.

a Sunday or on a major feast. The situating of royal consecrations on certain feasts was certainly ideologically motivated, as the many examples in this chapter have demonstrated. With the advent of widespread preaching in the twelfth century, knowledge of the content and meaning of such feasts would have permeated, to a greater or lesser extent, most levels of society.[121] That these allusions were not lost, at least on learned contemporaries, is suggested by the writings of the much-maligned Norman Anonymous.[122] As part of his argument for the superiority of royal over episcopal power he wrote that consecration should be considered a royal (rather than episcopal) wedding, 'just as is sung at the Epiphany of the Lord: "today the celestial bridegroom is joined" up until "royal nuptials"'.[123] The Norman Anonymous's late nineteenth-century editor, Heinrich Boehmer, could not identify the antiphon to which the Anonymous referred. Modern research techniques, however, make the discovery straightforward:

> Today the celestial bridegroom is joined to the church, because Christ washes away his sins in the Jordan, the Magi hasten with gifts to the royal wedding and the guests rejoice in wine made from water.[124]

That this antiphon draws together all the events we have seen were celebrated on the Epiphany, demonstrates that the liturgy of feast days could be used to imbue individual events, in this case the inauguration of Henry V in 1099, his marriage to Matilda in 1114 and Philip of Swabia's dual inauguration with his wife Maria in 1205, with potent meaning. It also illustrates that this liturgical imagery could be utilized on a more abstract level, to assert that kingship remained a liturgically defined office on a par with, or even superior to, the episcopal office, though few, perhaps, would have completely accepted the Anonymous's argument.

---

[121] D. L. d'Avray, 'Popular and Elite Religion: Feastdays and Preaching', in *Elite and Popular Religion*, ed. K. Cooper and J. Gregory, Studies in Church History 42 (Woodbridge, 2006), pp. 162–79 (p. 167).

[122] Kantorowicz characterized the Norman Anonymous as the champion of the ideas of four centuries earlier and his analysis has cast a long shadow over this particular text. Kantorowicz, *The King's Two Bodies*, pp. 42–61. Recently scholars have begun to criticize Kantorowicz's approach: S. Airlie, 'A View from Afar: English Perspectives on Religion and Politics in the Investiture Controversy', in *Religion und Politik im Mittelalter: Deutschland und England im Vergleich*, ed. L. Körntgen and D. Waßenhoven (Berlin, 2009), pp. 71–88 (p. 82) and B. Jussen, 'The King's Two Bodies Today', *Representations* 106 (2009), 102–17 (pp. 112–13).

[123] Norman Anonymous, *De consecratione pontificum et regum*, ed. H. Boehmer, *MGH Ldl* 3 (Hannover, 1897), pp. 662–79 (p. 663): 'sicut in Epiphani Domini canitur: "Hodie celesti sponso iuncta est" usque ad "regales nuptias"'.

[124] CANTUS: <http://cantusdatabase.org/node/376438> [accessed 26 September 2016]: 'Hodie caelesti sponso iuncta est ecclesia quoniam in Iordane lavit Christus eius crimina currunt cum muneribus magi ad regals nuptias et ex aquo facto vino laetantur conviuae'.

5

Royal Titles, Anniversaries and their Meaning: The Charter Evidence

Henry of Huntingdon tells us that 'in the year 1100, in the thirteenth year of his reign, King William [II of England] ended his cruel life in a wretched death'.[1] Henry goes on to describe Rufus's many shortcomings as king, concluding that 'whatever was displeasing to God and to those who loved God was pleasing to this king and those who loved him. Nor did they exercise their unspeakable debauchery in secret, but unashamedly in the light of day. He was buried at Winchester on the day after his perdition.'[2] Within days of Rufus's death, his younger brother Henry was consecrated king at Westminster Abbey, on the following Sunday, which as we have seen was the feast of St Oswald, king and martyr. In the absence of the exiled archbishop of Canterbury, the bishop of London officiated, but only after Henry I had 'promised a wished-for amendment of laws and customs'.[3] This 'wished-for amendment' is better known as the 'coronation charter' of Henry I, perhaps the most famous non-liturgical document associated with royal consecration in the central Middle Ages.[4] This being the case, it is striking that no original survives, although there are many manuscript copies from the later twelfth and thirteenth centuries. Henry's coronation charter was a swiftly negotiated agreement to ensure his consecration, necessary due to his brother Robert Curthose's claim to the throne, and the perceived iniquity of his predecessor Rufus. Many of its clauses claim specifically to remedy wrongs committed by Rufus, as is acknowledged in the charter itself.[5] Due to its later importance

---

[1] Henry of Huntingdon, *Historia Anglorum*, pp. 446–7: 'Millesimo centesimo anno, rex Willelmus, tercio decimo regni sui anno, uitam crudelem misero fine terminauit'.

[2] Ibid., pp. 448–9: 'quicquid Deo Deumque diligentibus displicebat, hoc regni regemque diligentibus placebat. Nec luxurie scelus tacendum exercebant occulte, sed ex impudentia coram sole. Sepultus est in crastino perdicionis sue apud Winceastre'.

[3] Ibid: 'melioratione legum et consuetudinum optabili repromissa'.

[4] Candidates for the kingship confirming or granting new laws to negotiate support was not an unusual occurrence in England. Cf. J. Maddicott, 'Edward the Confessor's Return to England in 1041', *English Historical Review* 119 (2004), 650–66; A. Williams, *Æthelred the Unready: The Ill-Counselled King* (London, 2003), pp. 122–6.

[5] 'Henry I's Coronation Charter', ed. R. Sharpe <http://www.earlyenglishlaws.ac.uk/laws/texts/hn-cor/view/#edition,1/translation,1> [accessed 12 December 2016]: 'Et omnes malas consuetudines quibus regnum Anglie iniuste opprimebatur inde aufero, quas malas consuetudines ex parte hic pono'.

as a source used by the barons in the composition of Magna Carta in 1215, it has often been discussed in the context of legal and constitutional history.[6] As with so many English administrative documents, it has become a legal exemplar, hermetically separated from the liturgical context in which it was originally granted. However, while challenging traditional legal-historical approaches to Henry's 'coronation' charter, it is apparent that the focus of this earlier scholarship rightly reflects the importance of the issuance of documents to royal and imperial consecration. Moreover, as shall be demonstrated, the manner in which royal documents were authenticated frequently referred back to the ceremony in which the king had been made monarch. Thus, both the role of documents in the making of kings, and also references to the making of kings embedded in royal documentary practice, speaks for the relevance of an analysis of the charter evidence to a study of inauguration and concepts of kingship.

The text of Henry's 'coronation' charter explicitly links its creation to his being made king. The charter informs the king's new subjects that 'by the mercy of God and common counsel of the barons of the realm of England, I have been crowned king of the same realm'.[7] The charter ends with a witness list and place-date clause, which emphatically links it once again to Henry being made king. The first witness is none other than Bishop Maurice of London, the consecrator, and we learn that the charter was given at Westminster when Henry was crowned.[8] We need, then, to look beyond the detailed clauses in which specific wrongs are righted, to acknowledge the liturgical and performative context in which the document was originally composed.[9] Bishop Stubbs long ago recognized that the charter echoed the three-fold oath of the consecration liturgy, and historians, most recently Judith Green, have often repeated this insight.[10] However, far from encouraging legal historians to consider the charter as the product of liturgical kingship, this has instead led to a liturgical text being dissected and one part of it being treated, in isolation, as a legal document. The promise contained within the

---

[6] See, for example, Hollister, *Henry I*, p. 109.
[7] 'Henry I's Coronation Charter', ed. R. Sharpe <http://www.earlyenglishlaws.ac.uk/laws/texts/hn-cor/view/#edition,1/translation,1> [accessed 12 December 2016]: 'Sciatis me dei misericordia et communi consilio baronum regni Anglie eiusdem regni regem coronatum esse'.
[8] 'Henry I's Coronation Charter', ed. R. Sharpe <http://www.earlyenglishlaws.ac.uk/laws/texts/hn-cor/view/#edition,1/translation,1> [accessed 12 December 2016] 'Apud Westm[onasterium] quando coronatus fui'.
[9] On the issuing of charters as performative acts see G. Koziol, *The Politics of Memory and Identity in Carolingian Royal Diplomas: The West Frankish Kingdom (840–987)*, Utrecht Studies in Medieval Literacy, 19 (Turnhout, 2012), pp. 42–62.
[10] *Select Charters and Other Illustrations of English Constitutional History*, ed. W. Stubbs, 9th edn (Oxford, 1921), p. 116; J. A. Green, '"A Lasting Memorial": The Charter of Liberties of Henry I', in *Charters and Charter Scholarship in Britain and Ireland*, ed. M. T. Flanagan and J. A. Green (Basingstoke, 2005), pp. 53–69 (p. 54).

consecration liturgy has been cut from its natural liturgical stem, and grafted on to the rootstock of early legal texts. Thus we find the promise divorced from its liturgical setting in Felix Liebermann's *Die Gesetze der Angelsachsen*, its inclusion in this canonical tome cementing the oath's status as a legal, rather than a liturgical, text.[11]

Scholarly treatment of the charter issued by Henry I on his day of consecration exemplifies the approach to royal charters that has been prevalent in English scholarship. As David Bates has noted, Anglophone historians are happy to accept the idea of charters as written records but are significantly less familiar with the idea of charters as expressions of power, as found in the work of French historians, such as Olivier Guyotjeannin, Michel Parisse and Benoît-Michel Tock.[12] In English scholarship there has been a tendency to mine texts for detailed information and legal precedents and to discard as irrelevant elements that do not serve the greater historical narrative of bureaucratic development. Given the huge growth in royal documents in England in this period, as famously quantified by Michael Clanchy in his analysis of sealing wax used by the chancery in the reign of Henry III, it is perhaps understandable that historians continue to be preoccupied by the legal transactions and business deals recorded in surviving charters and their copies.[13] As Geoffrey Koziol commented in his vivid study of Carolingian royal diplomas, even though royal documents tend no longer to be seen as analogous to official acts of early modern and modern states, they continue to be consulted most often for incidental evidence.[14]

Charters certainly were legal documents, but they were also considerably more than merely repositories of legal information. Given that it has become a commonplace to recognize that the possession of a charter, royal or otherwise, was no guarantee that one's rights according to the document would be protected suggests that, in any case, charters can hardly be characterized

---

[11] *Die Gesetze der Angelsachsen*, ed. Liebermann, I, 215–17; Recognizing the congealing effects of Liebermann's work on legal history, Patrick Wormald commented that 'since his colossal edition, Anglo-Saxon law has become a statuesque monument to an absorbingly interesting but irretrievably lost past'. P. Wormald, *The Making of English Law: King Alfred to the Twelfth Century* (Oxford, 1999), p. xi.

[12] D. Bates, 'Charters and Historians of Britain and Ireland: Problems and Possibilities', in *Charters and Charter Scholarship in Britain and Ireland*, ed. M. T. Flanagan and J. A. Green (Basingstoke, 2005), pp. 1–14 (p. 2). See, for example, O. Guyotjeannin, J. Pycke, and B.-M. Tock, ed., *Diplomatique Médiévale*, L'atelier du médiéviste, 2 (Turnhout, 1993); M. Parisse, 'Les chartes des évêques de Metz au XIIe siècle: étude diplomatique et paléographique', *Archiv für Diplomatik* 22 (1976), 272–316; B.-M. Tock, *Scribes, souscripteurs et témoins dans les actes privés en France (VIIe–début du XIIe siècle)*, Atelier de recherches sur les textes médiévaux, 9 (Turnhout, 2005).

[13] M. T. Clanchy, *From Memory to Written Record: England 1066–1307*, 2nd edn (Oxford, 1993), p. 59. Clanchy shows that almost ten times as much wax per week was used in the period 1265–71 as had been from 1226–30.

[14] Koziol, *The Politics of Memory*, p. 3.

as being universally legally authoritative.[15] Instead, we need to recognize that medieval charters were political and pious as well as judicial texts.[16] Although royal charters can appear formulaic and repetitive, Koziol has suggested that if we instead consider Carolingian royal diplomas as instruments of power, reading them becomes closer to reading biblical exegesis than legal documentation.[17] Koziol's work on Carolingian royal diplomas was strongly influenced by earlier generations of German-speaking charter scholars, who have long-since rejected the simplistic link between diplomatic history and the history of the state.[18] Famously, Heinrich Fichtenau pioneered the study of political ideas in the *arenga*, his student Herwig Wolfram has worked extensively on royal titles in charters and both have argued that charters can be carriers of political meaning.[19] Peter Rück has built on the work of the Fichtenau school in his analysis of charters as works of art, arguing for the importance of the visual characteristics of documents in expressing royal power, pointing to the impression external characteristics must have made upon a largely illiterate society.[20] The importance of graphic signs, and the 'graphicacy' required to decode them, has been demonstrated by Ildar Garipzanov, whose work focuses on late antiquity and the early Middle Ages.[21] However, English approaches to charter scholarship, with the exception of work by David Howlett, have contrasted with, or perhaps with their continued interest in the medieval English state, merely lagged behind, those of both French and German historians.[22]

---

[15] A. Stieldorf, 'Die Magie der Urkunden', *Archiv für Diplomatik* 55 (2009), 1–32 (p. 28).

[16] B.-M. Tock, 'The Political Use of Piety in Episcopal and Comital Charters of the Eleventh and Twelfth Centuries', in *Negotiating Secular and Ecclesiastical Power*, ed. H. Teunis, A. Wareham and A.-J. A. Bijsterveld, International Medieval Research 6 (Turnhout, 1999), pp. 19–35 (p. 19).

[17] Koziol, *The Politics of Memory*, p. 14.

[18] See Koziol, *The Politics of Memory*, pp. 17–37 for a useful summary of the development of *Diplomatik* and *Urkundenforschung*.

[19] See, for example, H. Fichtenau, *Arenga: Spätantike und Mittelalter im Spiegel von Urkundenformeln*, MIÖG 18 (Graz, 1957); H. Wolfram, *Intitulatio I: Lateinische Königs- und Fürstentitel bis zum Ende des 8. Jahrhunderts*, MIÖG Ergänzungsband 21 (Graz, 1967).

[20] P. Rück, 'Die Urkunde als Kunstwerk', in *Kaiserin Theophanu: Begegnung des Ostens und Westens um die Wende des ersten Jahrtausends*, ed. A. von Euw and P. Schreiner, 2 vols. (Cologne, 1991), II, 311–33. See also Jessica Berenbeim's art-historical study of later medieval English documentary evidence: J. Berenbeim, *Art of Documentation: Documents and Visual Culture in Medieval England* (Toronto, 2015).

[21] I. H. Garipzanov, *Graphic Signs of Authority in Late Antiquity and the Early Middle Ages* (Oxford, 2018); Idem, 'The Rise of Graphicacy in Late Antiquity and the Early Middle Ages', *Viator* 46 (2015), 1–21.

[22] Howlett has drawn attention to the encoded statements found in insular charters before 1066. The charters Howlett analysed lack seals and autograph signatures or signs manual and he argues that they were authenticated instead by infixed devices that were widely understood. After 1066 sealing and autograph signs manual

The Charter Evidence

The extent to which a royal charter, no longer surviving in its original form, and perhaps initially produced in the scriptorium of a beneficiary, can be considered as an expression of royal image, deserves further thought. As Herwig Wolfram recognized in his study of early medieval *intitulatio*, the form of title used in a charter often appears to have been dependent upon who in the circle of the king actually wrote it.[23] This leads to the question of whether charters can really be considered as self-expressive. Wolfram asserts that they can, commenting that in general one can assume that a title would have received the agreement of the person in whose name it was written.[24] If we dissolve the barriers between the work of royal clerks and beneficiaries' scriptoria, it becomes possible to see royal documents as 'products of negotiation', in which the beneficiary sought to produce a charter that met with royal approval.[25] Moreover, as Simon Keynes has demonstrated in his analysis of the 'Dunstan B' charters, royal charters could be issued in the name of the king even when he was absent.[26] Elizabeth Danbury has shown how the earliest illuminated grants in England, dating from the 1250s and 1260s were all for East Anglian beneficiaries. She concludes that the impulse for decoration was beneficiary driven.[27] However, that beneficiaries sought to augment royal documents does not invalidate the importance of such documents in understanding images of royalty. Seeking written authentication of a transaction in their favour, or decorating a charter to impress upon viewers that it carried the weight of royal power, caused beneficiaries to project a conventional image of royal authority. For this reason, it is evident that the sentiments in beneficiary-composed charters could reflect ideas current in royal and imperial circles.

Any study of charters associated with royal consecration is hampered by the difficulties in dating undated documents, by the uneven survival of these documents and by the equally uneven extent to which such charters have been published.[28] In any case, Henry I's charter is practically unique, with

---

became more common and ultimately replaced such structural devices. D. Howlett, *Sealed from Within: Self-authenticating Insular Charters* (Dublin, 1999).

[23] Wolfram, *Intitulatio I*, p. 21. This is an observation David Bates has also made concerning William the Conqueror's charters. *Regesta Regum Anglo-Normannorum: The Acta of William I*, ed. D. Bates (Oxford, 1998), pp. 86–7.

[24] Wolfram, *Intitulatio I*, p. 21.

[25] This is David Bates's description. Bates, 'Charters and Historians of Britain and Ireland', p. 8.

[26] S. Keynes, 'The "Dunstan B" Charters', *Anglo-Saxon England* 23 (1994), 165–93. (p. 185).

[27] E. Danbury, 'The Decoration and Illumination of Royal Charters in England, 1250–1509: An Introduction', in *England and Her Neighbours 1066–1453: Essays in Honour of Pierre Chaplais*, ed. M. Jones and M. Vale (London, 1989), pp. 157–79 (p. 159).

[28] The main published sources consulted have been have been the *Regesta regum Anglo-Normannorum* series, the *Recueil des actes* series and the *MGH Diplomata*

only a handful of surviving royal charters actually datable to the day of a king or queen's consecration. Although so-called 'coronation charters' survive for both Stephen and Henry II, they do not contain direct internal evidence linking them to the kings' consecrations. Neither contains a date clause, nor mentions the king's inauguration. While Henry I's consecrator acted as one of a number of witnesses to his 'coronation charter', the charters of Stephen and Henry II were both witnessed by sole professional administrators. It is only their places of issue, London for Stephen, and Westminster for Henry II, that allows them to be linked to these kings' inaugurations.[29] However, while legally authoritative 'coronation charters' cannot often be identified, it is clear that the issuing of charters was a prominent feature of the initial period of a new monarch's rule, to the extent that Koziol has commented on the 'special place' of Carolingian royal diplomas in the accession of kings, who might have been anointed and crowned but still needed to establish their own networks of power.[30] Similarly, Walter Koch has commented on the fact that at the commencement of Frederick Barbarossa's reign the reuse in documents of word forms and phrases found in the diplomas of his predecessors was a way of presenting the new monarch as a protector of ancient rights.[31] The issuing of royal documents was thus integral to the establishment of a new king's power, and for this reason I have considered a selection of charters, most of which have been dated by scholars to within roughly a year of a king or queen's consecration.

As Herwig Wolfram has rightly commented, 'the whole charter and all of its criteria, both internal and external, can become carriers of political meaning and can contain narrative elements'.[32] In comparing three realms over almost two centuries it is not possible to study these charters in their entirety, and instead several parts of these documents will be compared here.[33] Rather than on the judicial content, my focus is on the political and the pious, and

---

series. These series, often produced over a wide time-span, are inconsistent in their editorial practices. The earliest *Regesta Regum Anglo-Normannorum* volumes do not reproduce the text of documents, for example, while the later collections do. Additionally, the charters of every king and emperor of the period have not yet been published, thus alternative sources have also been consulted and the references for these are provided in the accompanying footnotes.

[29] For Stephen's charter see *Select Charters*, ed. Stubbs, p. 142; 'Henry II's Coronation Charter', ed. N. Vincent, <http://www.earlyenglishlaws.ac.uk/laws/texts/hn2-cor/view/#edition,1/apparatus,1> [accessed 12 December 2016].

[30] Koziol, *The Politics of Memory*, p. 65.

[31] W. Koch, 'Zu Sprache, Stil und Arbeitstechnik in den Diplomen Friedrich Barbarossas', *MIÖG* 88 (1980), 36–69 (p. 43).

[32] H. Wolfram, 'Political Theory and Narrative in Charters', *Viator* 26 (1995), 39–52 (p. 42).

[33] For a breakdown of the different constituent parts of a charter and a summary of scholarly approaches to them see H. Fichtenau, 'Forschungen über Urkundenformeln', *MIÖG* 94 (1986), 285–339.

particularly on the way in which these are manifested at the commencement and conclusion of documents. These are the areas most often associated with visual symbols and are frequently distinguished with the use of different letter forms. In a society in which literacy remained the preserve of the few, these areas of a document were particularly important to the representation of monarchical power. Thus in this chapter invocations and royal titles will be analysed, as will authenticating and dating clauses. The broader physical characteristics of these documents will also be explored through the use of a case study and, in the following chapter, the seals used to validate these documents will also be analysed. *Arengae* will be considered in passing, but it has not been possible to do more than scratch the surface of these rich biblically and liturgically inspired preambles in this chapter. A comprehensive study of *arengae* in the three realms would constitute a book in itself. By drawing attention to some aspects of the charter evidence, however, it will become clear that traces of a Christocentric understanding of royal power can be found in documentary sources in all three realms and that further research of this kind, particularly on English materials of the high medieval period, remains a desideratum.

Protocols

Although no charter survives, we know from Gervase of Reims's memorandum of Philip I of France's consecration that during the ceremony the newly inaugurated king authenticated a charter.[34] Gervase wished, like all ambitious medieval archbishops, to defend and expand the rights of his church and thus ensured that Philip confirmed its possessions 'just as his ancestors did'.[35] Here we see the ease with which a legal transaction could be embedded in royal consecration, that ritual of liturgical kingship *par excellence*.[36] Philip granted his charter, at Pentecost 1059, with his immediate ancestor, his father King Henry I, still living. Following the death of the senior king on 4 August 1060, Philip I issued a number of charters in memory of his father. In the first of these, he gave the farm of Courcelles to the abbey of Saint Denis, where his father had been buried, 'for love of God and the health of my father's soul'.[37] This charter opens with an invocation of the Trinity: 'In the name of the holy

---

[34] *Ordines Coronationis Franciae*, ed. Jackson, I, 232.
[35] Ibid: 'sicut antecessores sui fecerunt'.
[36] The German kings also customarily granted rights to Aachen within a few days of their inauguration. See, for example, the charter of Frederick II issued the day after his 1215 consecration: DD F. II. 316.
[37] *Recueil des actes de Philippe Ier, Roi de France (1059–1108)*, ed. M. Prou and M. H. d'Arbois de Jubainville (Paris, 1908), p. 14 (no. 4): 'pro Dei amore et remedio anime patris mei'.

and indivisible Trinity, namely the Father and Son and Holy Spirit, Amen', alerting us to the fact that, just as charters were not out of place in liturgical ritual, so too liturgical invocations were not excluded from royal charters.[38] As Charles Insley has rightly stressed, charters themselves can be considered as 'quasi-liturgical documents'.[39] The prayer is directly succeeded by the words 'I Philip, by God's grace king of the Franks', this juxtaposition making clear that Philip conceived of himself as making this gift in the name of the Trinity.[40] The king's close relationship with God is further emphasized in the assertion that Philip is king of the Franks, 'by God's grace'.

The *intitulatio* of this charter of Philip I contains the core elements found in the majority of royal charters in this period. That is, the name of the monarch, his office (normally qualified by an ethnic or geographic tag), and the fact that he owes his position to God. Further elaborations were possible, such as the inclusion of prayers and other votive formulae, and additional words and phrases exalting the position of the monarch (*augustus, gloriosus, serenissimus,* etc.). Wolfram has traced the manner in which such royal titles grew from antique roots, specifically the 'public' titles of late antiquity and those of Roman magistrates, nourished by the flourishing of Christian thought under the Carolingians.[41] Wolfram's detailed study recognizes the diverse origins of composite elements in royal titles and thus avoids the pitfall of Jack Autrey Dabbs's flawed and overtly teleological approach to the use of the *Dei gratia* formula.[42] Dabbs's second chapter is misleadingly entitled 'Early use of the *Dei gratia*', when it is actually concerned with ancient Roman formulae.[43] Although Roman conventions clearly influenced later royal titles, *divus* cannot be 'classed as a forerunner of the *Dei Gratia*' purely because 'its position immediately after the first name corresponds to the position of the *Dei Gratia* of later times, and its meaning is closely related'.[44] Not only is the origin of the formula Pauline (I Corinthians 15. 10), but also it was used by ecclesiastics long before it was embraced by Charlemagne.[45] It cannot thus be understood as the Christianization of the Roman *divus*.

---

[38] Ibid: 'In nomine sanctae et individuae Trinitatis, videlicet Patris et Filii et Spiritus Sancti, amen'.

[39] C. Insley, 'Where Did All the Charters Go? Anglo-Saxon Charters and the New Politics of the Eleventh Century', *Anglo-Norman Studies* XXIV (2001), 109–27 (p. 119).

[40] *Recueil des actes de Philippe Ier*, ed. Prou and d'Arbois de Jubainville, p. 14 (no. 4): 'ego Philippus gratia Dei Francorum rex'.

[41] Wolfram, *Intitulatio I*, p. 18.

[42] J. A. Dabbs, *Dei Gratia in Royal Titles* (The Hague, 1971). Fichtenau is scathing in his criticism of this book, calling it the work of a layman, ignorant of specialist literature and possessing limited Latin. Fichtenau, 'Forschungen über Urkundenformeln', p. 295.

[43] Dabbs, *Dei Gratia*, pp. 32–50.

[44] Ibid., p. 39.

[45] H. Fichtenau, '"Dei Gratia" und Königssalbung', in *Geschichte und ihre Quellen:*

Wolfram links the introduction of the *Dei gratia* formula in Carolingian royal titles to the adoption of anointing in the Carolingian consecration ceremony, another reminder of the links between how kings conceived and expressed their authority in written form and the liturgical ceremony in which they were made monarch. Fichtenau has sounded a note of caution here, however, pointing out that the grace formula was used by the Lombard king Agiluf (*c.*600) and by Æthelbald of Mercia (from 716), thus suggesting that linking it to the adoption of anointing is perhaps an over-interpretation of the evidence. In the Carolingian context, he has traced the first royal use of the formula to a letter of Pippin written *c.*765 and has suggested that this usage, in a beneficiary-composed document, demonstrates a new understanding of 'kingship as office'.[46] In doing so he rejected the link, drawn by Walter Ullmann amongst others, between the *Dei gratia* formula and ideas of sovereignty, arguing that it is not appropriate to use the modern concept of sovereignty when describing medieval understandings of royal power.[47] Thus when dukes and earls copied kings by using this formula in their charters we should not talk of them claiming sovereignty but recognize that they were simply mimicking the kings' style and thereby claiming their God-given place in the secular hierarchy, as they would later do by adopting aspects of royal seal iconography.

The widespread usage of the *Dei gratia* formula elicited comment later in the period, with Ludolf of Hildesheim suggesting *c.*1250 that while some princes and dukes could style themselves *Dei gratia*, lesser men should not use the formula. Half a century later an Italian jurist went further, stating that aside from ecclesiastics only emperors and kings should use the style, because only they had been anointed.[48] However, that by *c.*1300, when this pronouncement was made, the formula was linked to unction does not mean that it had been five and a half centuries earlier, when the formula was applied to Pippin. Although the monarchs of England, despite earlier evidence of Anglo-Saxon usage of the formula highlighted by Fichtenau, did not describe themselves as ruling by God's grace at the beginning of the period under consideration here, by the end of the twelfth century they had

---

Festschrift für Friedrich Hausmann zum 70. Geburtstag, ed. R. Härtel (Graz, 1987), 25–35 (p. 30).

[46] Ibid., p. 32.

[47] According to Ullmann, Charlemagne formed the words of St Paul 'into a governmental principle of the first order by means of the adoption of the royal grace formula'. W. Ullmann, *The Carolingian Renaissance and the Idea of Kingship* (London, 1969), p. 45; cf. C. Richter, 'Der Sinn der Dei-gratia-Formel in den französichen und deutschen Dynastenurkunden bis zum Jahre 1000 Untersucht mit besonderer Berücksichtigung der Geschichte dieser Formel von der paulinischen Zeit an' (unpublished PhD thesis, Johann Wolfgang Goethe-Universität Frankfurt am Main, 1974), p. 109.

[48] Fichtenau, '"Dei Gratia" und Königssalbung', p. 33.

long since joined the French and German monarchs in styling themselves kings *Dei gratia*. The formula had been adopted by Henry the Young King, in deliberate imitation of Capetian practice, on the eve of his rebellion in 1173, and was thereafter adopted by his father Henry II.[49]

Klaus Lohrmann has studied the titles of the early Capetians and commented on the qualification of the title *rex* by the ethnic determiner *Francorum* by the reign of Philip I. Lohrmann considered the title in the context of the internal West Frankish political situation, suggesting that by using the ethnic tag, Philip claimed to be king not only of Francia, but also Burgundy and Aquitaine, which had been part of ancient *Gallia*.[50] In the same way, he interprets the emphatic use of the personal pronoun *ego* as signifying that the king could also practise successful princely politics outside the Crown demesne.[51] This use of the personal pronoun is not found in England and Germany, and fell out of favour in France during the reign of Louis VII, a change Lohrmann attributes to a vacancy in the chancery between 1172 and 1179.[52] It seems possible that a strong French monarch no longer sought to vaunt his status above the other French princes and preferred to present himself on the same level as his English and imperial counterparts. Moreover, the tension between the use of the singular personal pronoun in the title and the plural form of verbs in the charter text might well have contributed to the demise of *ego*. With this exception, the titles used by the French kings remained relatively constant under Philip I, Louis VI and Louis VII although there are examples when the base formula, *N. Dei gratia Francorum rex*, was ornamented. Philip I issued three charters in 1092 to the monastery of Saint-Corneille in Compiègne, in which the title 'Philip by God's providence most pious king of the Franks' was used.[53] Lohrmann suggests that this supplies evidence that the king wished to stress his piety following his well-documented marital problems, which had brought his religious devotion into question.[54]

Following Philip's death in 1108, his son Louis succeeded him as king. Louis's first recorded act by charter, the original of which has been lost so that we only know of it from a cartulary copy from the seventeenth century,

---

[49] This is the conclusion of Nicholas Vincent who kindly shared unpublished work with me. See, in due course, the introductory volume to *The Letters and Charters of Henry II*, ed. N. Vincent et al. (Oxford, forthcoming).

[50] K. Lohrmann, 'Die Titel der Kapetinger bis zum Tod Ludwigs VII.', in *Intitulatio III: Lateinische Herrschertitel und Herrschertitulaturen vom 7. bis zum 13. Jahrhundert*, ed. H. Wolfram and A. Scharer, MIÖG Ergänzungsband 29 (Graz, 1988), pp. 201–56 (pp. 210–11).

[51] Ibid., p. 246.

[52] Ibid., p. 254.

[53] *Recueil des actes de Philippe Ier*, ed. Prou and d'Arbois de Jubainville, p. 319 (no. 126): 'Philippus Dei providentia Francorum rex piissimus'.

[54] Lohrmann, 'Die Titel der Kapetinger', p. 224.

was to make a gift to the abbey of Saint-Benoît-sur-Loire for the soul of his father.[55] Saint-Benoît was the church that Philip had chosen for his burial, so an appropriate recipient of a grant for the late king's soul. The cartulary copy begins with the invocation 'In the name of the holy and indivisible Trinity', but it lacks the name of the king or his title. Instead it progresses straight to the text of the charter itself, suggesting it is not an entirely faithful copy of the original. Another charter issued early in the reign, confirming the privilege of immunity to the abbey of Sens, formerly granted by his predecessors Robert the Pious, Henry I and Philip I, opens as follows: 'In the name of the Father and the Son and the Holy Spirit. Amen. I, Louis, by God's grace and divine favour king of the Franks.'[56] The expanded *Dei gratia* formula was copied from the earlier grants of his father and grandfather, but in the circumstances of his irregular consecration, at Orléans by the archbishop of Sens, it seems evident that Louis might have had other reasons to emphasize his divine sanction to rule through the inclusion of this more elaborate form.

There is another example of Louis VI granting a charter with an unusual *intitulatio*, in which the *Dei gratia* formula was replaced by a more elaborate clause, near in time to another royal consecration, this time that of his wife Adelaide in 1115. The charter, surviving in the original, begins: 'In the name of the holy and indivisible Trinity. In Christ's name. I, Louis, by the merciful dispensation of God elevated as king of the Franks.'[57] Particularly noteworthy is the addition to the opening prayer. Having invoked the Trinity, it is made clear that Louis is being most closely associated with one part of the Trinity: the Son, Jesus Christ. This association is strengthened by the charter layout. The first section of the invocation referencing the Trinity stands alone on the top line, whereas the reference to Christ directly precedes Louis's name and title. Louis is identified with God as man. Both the choice of words in the invocation and the visual presentation of this charter convey a Christological image of kingship. Moreover, the king implicitly references his inauguration, which had taken place seven years previously, through the use of the phrase *in regem Francorum sublimatus*. It is probably not a coincidence that the charter records an annual grant of six *solidi* to the monks of Notre-Dame-des-Champs in Paris for the souls of his father, mother and other ancestors.[58] This grant is to be paid on the feast of St Remigius, the French saint most closely associated

---

[55] *Recueil des actes de Louis VI, Roi de France (1108–1137)*, ed. J. Dufour (Paris, 1992), pp. 35–7 (no. 19).

[56] Ibid., p. 41 (no. 21): 'In nomine Patris et Filii et Spiritus Sancti. Amen. Ego Hludovicus, gratia Dei et propitia divinitate Francorum rex'.

[57] Ibid., p. 218 (no. 102): 'In nomine sancte et individue Trinitatis. In Christi nomine. Ego Lucdovicus, Dei dispensante misericordia in regem Francorum sublimatus'.

[58] Ibid.,: 'pro animarum patris mei et matris mee predecessorumque nostrorum remedio, sex solidos, quos nobis unoquoque anno in festi beati Remigii censualiter persolvebant monachi Beate Marie in Canpis, eidem ecclesie in perpetuum cundonaremus [sic]'.

Inauguration and Liturgical Kingship

with royal consecration thanks to his baptismal anointing of Louis's sixth-century royal namesake Clovis I. As we have seen, kings were often crowned again at the time of their marriage, thus Adelaide's consecration could be seen as renewing and strengthening Louis's own royal dignity.

It was usual for new kings to confirm gifts made by their predecessors and Philip Augustus was no exception. As Koziol has stressed, many royal documents, and especially those issued early in a reign, were written in 'active dialogue with past diplomas written for the same institutions'.[59] In 1180, following the death of his father, Philip confirmed Louis VII's gift of one hundred measures of wine each year to the monks of the Holy Trinity at Canterbury.[60] The link to Canterbury is important here, because the charter recounts that Louis VII had travelled to the tomb of Thomas Becket where he had originally made the gift:

> Therefore let it be known to all men present and future that, in admiration of the most blessed martyr Thomas former archbishop of Canterbury, to whose tomb our father proceeded in great devotion for the salvation of our soul and to obtain the health of our body, is granted in alms to the monastery of monks of the Holy Trinity serving God in that place, one hundred measures of wine in Parisian measures to be received each year at the time of the grape-harvest of the castellaria of Poissy.[61]

The reason for Louis's journey had been to pray to the saint for the safe recovery of his heir, Philip, who, shortly before his planned consecration, had fallen ill following a night spent lost in the forest of Compiègne.[62] As a result the future king was unable to be consecrated as planned on the Feast of the Assumption of Mary and the consecration was instead delayed until the Feast of All Saints 1179, by which time Philip's father was himself too ill to play a part in proceedings.

Philip's confirmation of his father's grant of an annuity of wine to the monks of Holy Trinity, Canterbury, opens with the familiar invocation and title: 'In the name of the holy and indivisible Trinity. Amen. Philip, by God's grace king of the Franks.'[63] This is in keeping with the standard openings

---

[59] Koziol, *The Politics of Memory*, p. 2.
[60] *Recueil des actes de Philippe Auguste, Roi de France (1180–1223)*, ed. H. F. Delaborde and E. Berger, 4 vols. (Paris, 1916–79), I, 2–3 (no. 2).
[61] Ibid.: 'Noverint igitur universi presentes pariter et futuri quod, intuitu beatissimi Thome martiris quondam Cantuariensis archiepiscopi, ad cuius tumulum pro salute anime et sanitate corporis impetranda pater noster in multa devotione fuerat profectus, conventui monachorum Sancte Trinitatis ibidem Deo servientium centum modios vini ad mensuram Parisiensem, singulis annis tempore vindemiarum in castellaria Pissaci accipiendos, in eleemosinam concessit'.
[62] Rigord, *Histoire de Philippe Auguste*, pp. 124–6.
[63] *Recueil des actes de Philippe Auguste*, ed. Delaborde and Berger, I, 2–3 (no. 2): 'In nomine sancte et individue Trinitatis. Amen. Philippus Dei gratia Francorum rex.'

The Charter Evidence

used by his predecessor, although by now the personal pronoun *ego* has no place in the king's royal style. Bernd Schneidmüller has pointed to the fact that Philip's title remained constant, despite the fact that he successfully expanded the Crown domain both in westerly and southerly directions, and even though one might have expected to find this expansion of power reflected in an elaboration of the royal style.[64] Schneidmüller explains the lack of addition of other ethnic tags in the same terms that Klaus Lohrmann applied to the early Capetian royal titles, namely that the qualifier *Francorum* already encompassed the people over whom Philip Augustus had now extended his rule. As Schneidmüller concludes, the continuity of the title emphasizes far more the consistency and rigour of a theory of lordship, which kept the king aloof from day-to-day business and instead projected the image of the monarch at the head of a *regnum*, defined both in a legal and geographic manner.[65] Given how other studies have emphasized both the idea of the Franks as a holy people, and the manner in which the term could be used to describe a myriad of ethnic groups, such as crusaders from different areas and kingdoms, I am inclined to agree with Lohrmann and Schneidmüller's assertions of the implicit claim to power outside of the borders of Francia and the royal domain.[66]

With the broad claims of the tag *Francorum*, in contrast to the narrow geographic extent of *Francia* in mind, it is necessary to reassess the pronouncement, first made by Jean Mabillon in the seventeenth century, that the reign of Philip Augustus witnessed a change in the French royal title, in which the ethnic tag was replaced by a geographical one. This change was seen by Percy Ernst Schramm as signalling the move away from the early Germanic *Personenverbandsstaat* to the medieval territorial state and as such has been accorded a significance in political and constitutional history that it does not deserve. Although this discussion might at first sight seem tangential to the concerns of this study, this is not the case, because this shift has been seen as denoting progress towards the formation of the nation state. As we have seen, given the manner in which interpretations of the desacralization of kingship have been embedded in wider narratives of modernization and secularization this supposed shift is actually highly relevant. Importantly, as Bernd Schneidmüller has comprehensively proved, such a change cannot even be securely dated to Philip Augustus's reign. To recognize this it is

---

[64] B. Schneidmüller, 'Herrscher über Land und Leute? Der kapetingische Herrschertitel in der Zeit Philipps II. August und seiner Nachfolger (1180–1270)', in *Intitulatio III: Lateinische Herrschertitel und Herrschertitulaturen vom 7. bis zum 13. Jahrhundert*, ed. H. Wolfram and A. Scharer, *MIÖG* Ergänzungsband 29 (Graz, 1988), pp. 131–62 (p. 134).

[65] Schneidmüller, 'Herrscher über Land und Leute?', p. 134.

[66] On 'Franks' as a broad term see, for example, M. Gabriele, *An Empire of Memory: The Legend of Charlemagne, the Franks, and Jerusalem before the First Crusade* (Oxford, 2011), pp. 22–3.

Inauguration and Liturgical Kingship

necessary to return to the original documents, rather than accept uncritically the work of modern editors.[67] There is an additional problem inherent in the documents themselves, however, as the frequent use of abbreviation means that ambiguity remains. There are two frequently deployed abbreviations, one of which can clearly be expanded as *Francorum*. The other is, however, ambiguous, and could be expanded as either *Francie*, a geographic qualifier, or *Francorum*, the traditional ethnic tag. Schneidmüller argues strongly in favour of expanding the ambiguous abbreviation as *Francorum*, pointing to the fact that whenever a longer form is found in a charter it is either *Francorum* written out in full, or the abbreviation that can only be expanded to *Francorum*. *Francie* is never found in full.[68] He emphasizes that *Francorum rex* is still part of Louis IX's royal style and points to the presence, previously overlooked, of *Francorum* on the seals of Philip Augustus, Louis VIII and Louis IX, and on the regency seal of Louis IX.[69] Schneidmüller also considered the use of ethnic and geographic terms outside of charters, recognizing the difference of usage in Latin and the French vernacular, in which the title *rois de France* is evident from the mid-thirteenth century.[70]

In his otherwise astute discussion of the titles of Philip Augustus and his successors, Schneidmüller makes an uncharacteristic error, seeking to contrast the Capetian ethnic tag with the territorial title used by their Angevin counterparts.[71] As Nicholas Vincent has stressed in his work on the charters of Henry II, determining whether Henry used an ethnic or geographic qualifier is subject to exactly the same issues as Schneidmüller outlined for Philip Augustus. That it to say, the abbreviations are ambiguous.[72] Vincent points out that although some twelfth-century beneficiary-produced documents qualify the king's title through the use of territorial tags, the only expanded title written by a recognized chancery scribe relates to people.[73] If we follow Schneidmüller's lead and consider seal evidence, it is clear that Henry II and his son Richard I continued to use a royal style linked to peoples on their seals and that the use of territorially qualified titles are first witnessed in a great seal inscription in the reign of King John.[74] It seems to me that, as in the Capetian shift from people to territory, we should be on our guard against ascribing too much significance

---

[67] Schneidmüller points out that one finds the same abbreviation expanded differently in different editions of French royal charters. Schneidmüller, 'Herrscher über Land und Leute?', p. 140.
[68] Ibid., p. 147.
[69] Ibid., p. 155.
[70] Ibid., p. 142.
[71] Ibid., p. 144.
[72] N. Vincent, 'Regional Variations in the Charters of King Henry II (1154–89)', in *Charters and Charter Scholarship in Britain and Ireland*, ed. M. T. Flanagan and J. A. Green (Basingstoke, 2005), pp. 70–106 (p. 76).
[73] Ibid.
[74] See below p. 202.

The Charter Evidence

to what was quite possibly simply a linguistic development. Indeed, modern scholars, seeing this change as epitomizing constitutional progression, have vastly exaggerated the distinction between the two forms of title. Popes, for example, addressed letters to the kings of Christendom using both ethnic and geographic titles seemingly indiscriminately, and there is no evidence known to me that Scottish kings, normally diligent imitators of English royal chancery practice, moved away from the traditional title of *rex Scottorum*. Furthermore, such titles were not mutually exclusive. Henry VI of Germany was styled on his seal both 'HEINRICUS DEI GRATIA ROMANORUM IMPERATOR AUGUSTUS' and 'REX SICILIE'. His imperial power was related to a people, the Romans, and his royal power to a territory, Sicily.

In German historiography, the debate has not centred on the difference between ethnic and geographic titles. Instead the focus has been on the nature of the ethnic qualifier, on when it was introduced and why. Territorial titles only appear rarely, as in the case of the German ruler as *rex Sicilie*. Charlemagne had employed ethnic formulas in his titles, but references to the Franks, Lombards and Romans had fallen by the wayside during the reign of Louis the Pious, so that for almost three hundred years, from the reign of Louis 'the German' to that of Henry IV royal and imperial titles most often lack any ethnic qualifier.[75] There were some exceptions to this rule, as Helmut Beumann highlighted in 1981. The term *Romanorum imperator* is found in the reign of Otto II in a diploma issued in southern Italy in 982, and as Beumann elucidated, given Byzantine interest in the south of the peninsula this title should probably be seen as a method of stressing equality with the eastern Emperors.[76] The imperial title is found associated with the Romans more frequently from 996 following the imperial coronation of Otto III.[77] From the turn of the millennium onwards, the imperial title was often associated with the Romans, but the royal title remained absolute. Beumann has pointed to some examples of the royal title being associated with the Romans from the reigns of Henry II to Henry IV, but emphasizes that many of the documents including the Roman royal title were beneficiary produced, and that the title did not become normalized until the reign of Henry V.[78]

By c.1050 the German monarchs routinely, but by no means always,

---

[75] H. Beumann, *Der deutsche König als "Romanorum Rex"* (Wiesbaden, 1981), pp. 7–11.
[76] Ibid., p. 12.
[77] Ibid., p. 13; see also H. Keller, 'Identità romana e l'idea dell' *Imperium Romanorum* nel X e nel primo XI secolo', in *Three Empires, Three Cities: Identity, Material Culture and Legitimacy in Venice, Ravenna and Rome, 750–1000*, ed. V. West-Harling, Seminari internazionale del Centro interuniversitario per la storia e l'archeologia dell'alto mediovo 6 (Turnhout, 2015), pp. 255–82 (pp. 267–71); and W. Huschner, *Transalpine Kommunikation im Mittelalter: Diplomatische, kulturelle und politische Wechselwirkungen zwischen Italien und dem nordalpinen Reich (9.–11. Jahrhundert)* (Hannover, 2003), pp. 333–403.
[78] Beumann, *Der deutsche König*, pp. 66–75.

associated their imperial title with the Romans, but the Roman royal title was still used only sporadically. In the first surviving charter of Henry IV, for example, a confirmation of privileges granted to the monastery of Prüm in December 1056, the boy king is styled 'Henry, king by divine merciful favour'.[79] His mother, acting as regent, likewise used a similar title, this time imperial, without any ethnic tag, in a charter recording a gift made at Speyer in October 1059. Here she is styled, 'Agnes, august empress by divine merciful favour'.[80] Henry IV's first-born son is likewise styled simply as king, without any qualifying tag in two of his three surviving charters. In the final surviving charter from 1097, granting privileges to the cathedral chapter at Cremona, Conrad is styled, 'Conrad, Italian king by divine merciful favour'.[81] In this case the adjective *Italicus* could refer to either a territory or an ethnic group, reminding us that drawing too sharp a distinction is perhaps unwise. In any case, it is clear that it was not necessary to qualify the title *rex* with either an ethnic or geographic determiner, and indeed we find this in the twelfth century too. Lothar III, for example, in his first surviving charter granting immunity and royal protection to the monastery at Rheinau, was styled 'Lothar, king by divine favour and grace', as late as 1125.[82]

The use of the title *Romanorum rex* had, however, become increasingly frequent in the reign of Lothar's predecessor Henry V. In explaining why it took half a century for the royal title to include the ethnic qualifier that had become an established part of the imperial style, Beumann pointed to the general resistance of documentary forms to change.[83] What, then, precipitated the more consistent utilization of the Roman royal title under Henry V? As Brigitte Merta has summarized, the context for the earliest uses of a Roman title under Henry III and Henry IV was Italian. Of eight surviving charters from the two kings' reigns in which the royal or imperial title is qualified by *Romanorum*, seven of them were for Italian or Lombard beneficiaries, with the last a grant to the bishopric of Freising of land near Trieste.[84] As we have seen, it was also in an Italian context that Henry IV's son Conrad was styled *rex Italicus*. However, in the reign of Henry V we find the title *rex Romanorum* used much more extensively in the German as well as Italian kingdom, and for the first time a German seal inscription referring to the monarch as 'king of the Romans'.[85] Merta has traced papal usage of the term *rex Teutonicorum* and suggested that Gregory VII purposely differentiated between the *regnum*

---

[79] DD H. IV. 1: 'Heinricus divina favente clementia rex'.
[80] DD H. IV. Agnes 1:'Agnes divina favente clementia imperatrix augusta'.
[81] DD H. IV. Konrad 5:'Chounradus divina favente clementia rex Italicus'.
[82] DD Lo. III. 1: 'Lotharius divina favente gratia rex'.
[83] Beumann, *Der deutsche König*, p. 75.
[84] B. Merta, 'Die Titel Heinrichs II. und der Salier', in *Intitulatio III: Lateinische Herrschertitel und Herrschertitulaturen vom 7. bis zum 13. Jahrhundert*, ed. H. Wolfram and A. Scharer, *MIÖG* Ergänzungsband 29 (Graz, 1988), pp. 163–200 (p. 185).
[85] See below pp. 202–3 for the Roman royal title being used on seals.

Teutonicorum and the *regnum Italiae* by, for example, recognizing the anti-king Rudolf of Rheinfelden as king in Germany but not in Italy.[86] Henry V did not accept that his power as king was only to be exercised over a people north of the Alps and thus increasingly used the word *Romanorum* in conjunction with his royal title, a word that had previously been associated with imperial power. German historians have aptly dubbed this facet of the Investiture Controversy as *Titelpolitik*, with Beumann emphasizing that the adoption of *Romanorum rex* as the monarch's standard title must be understood against the political circumstances of Henry V's reign.[87]

The political circumstances of Frederick Barbarossa's reign, and this emperor's attempts to renew imperial power in the face of a strong papacy, increasingly powerful imperial princes and the economically dominant Italian communes, also influenced documentary language. This can be seen most clearly in the increasing sophistication of *arengae* under Barbarossa. These statements of the moral, ethical and religious principles of earthly and heavenly kingship preceded the administrative content of a diploma, emphasizing once again that the judicial substance of a royal document was firmly embedded in a mixture of politics and piety.[88] Once dismissed as being composed of stock phrases and therefore of little historical or political worth, the work of Heinrich Fichtenau rehabilitated such preambles as a subject of historical interest, while highlighting the similarity of the language used to that employed in both homilies and inauguration *ordines*.[89] Fichtenau saw a renewal of biblical and liturgical language in the *arengae* of Frederick Barbarossa as an attempt to work against any threat to the spiritual foundations of his office.[90] Interestingly, as Walter Koch has emphasized, this increase in biblical and liturgical vocabulary went hand in hand with the growing use of terms from Roman law and late-antique bureaucracy.[91] Liturgy and law could be, then, complementary rather than incompatible. Koch considers Barbarossa's *arengae* to have reached their high point in the diploma celebrating the canonization of Charlemagne in 1165, before the Roman catastrophe of 1167 thoroughly disrupted the production of documents at the imperial chancery.[92]

The canonization on 29 December 1165 and the associated diploma dated 8 January 1166 have been the subject of much scrutiny. Once considered a purely political act in which a saint's cult was instrumentalized to further the imperial agenda of Frederick Barbarossa, Knut Görich has recently

---

[86] Merta, 'Die Titel Heinrichs II. und der Salier', pp. 185–90.
[87] Beumann, *Der deutsche König*, p. 79.
[88] Koziol, *The Politics of Memory*, p. 59.
[89] Fichtenau, *Arenga*, pp. 19, 30.
[90] Ibid., p. 19.
[91] Koch, 'Zu Sprache, Stil und Arbeitstechnik', p. 61.
[92] Ibid., p. 61.

argued for a more nuanced interpretation, which takes into account factors such as local Aachen traditions and initiatives and the pious motives of the emperor.[93] This is not to deny political motivations, for, as Görich recognizes, we can hardly separate the man Barbarossa from his imperial office, meaning that his actions, pious or otherwise, always had political implications.[94] The pious and the political are both evident in the *arenga* of the canonization diploma, in which Frederick is described as achieving his position at the head of the empire through the ordinance of divine clemency ('divina ordinante clementia'), and in which the exemplary role of Charlemagne as defender of the Church, preserver of the realm, and upholder of law is emphasized.[95] This lengthy diploma, which describes Charlemagne's merits in flowery detail, including his conversion of Germanic tribes and expeditions to Spain and the Holy Land, also incorporates a reference to the role of Henry II of England in securing the Carolingian's canonization.[96]

Scholarship has long placed Charlemagne's canonization in the wider context of twelfth-century royal saint-making with a possible model provided by the canonization of Edward the Confessor a few years earlier.[97] Most recently, Gesine Oppitz-Trotman has situated Henry's support against the backdrop of both the Alexandrine schism and the English king's increasingly bitter conflict with Thomas Becket.[98] Returning to diplomatic, the mention of Henry II invites a comparison between charters issued in his name and the products of Barbarossa's chancery. In stark contrast to the sophisticated *arengae* found in the emperor's diplomas, the charters of his Angevin contemporary lack any kind of liturgically inspired preamble.[99] This is emblematic of a wider divergence between imperial and Angevin chancery practices. Whereas the most common document issued in Frederick's name was a formal privilege, this type of document fell out of use in England in the eleventh century to be replaced by the writ-charter.[100] It must also be

---

[93] Görich, 'Karl der Große'.

[94] Görich, 'Karl der Große', p. 139.

[95] DD F. I. 502: 'Ex quo primitus divina ordinante clementia imperii Romani fastigia gubernanda suscepimus, voluntatis nostrę atque propositi summum desiderium fuit, ut divos reges et imperatores, qui nos precesserunt, precipue maximum et gloriosum imperatorem Karolum quasi formam vivendi atque subditos regendi sequeremur et sequendo pre oculis semper haberemus, ad cuius imitationem ius ęcclesiarum, statum rei publicę incolumem et legum integritatem per totum imperium nostrum servaremus'.

[96] DD F. I. 502: 'sedula peticione karissimi amici nostri Heinrici illustris regis Anglię inducti'.

[97] See, for example, Petersohn, 'Saint-Denis – Westminster – Aachen'.

[98] Oppitz-Trotman, 'The Emperor's Robe'.

[99] A contrast noted by Fichtenau: Fichtenau, *Arenga*, p. 19.

[100] T. Reuter, 'Mandate, Privilege, Court Judgement: Techniques of Rulership in the Age of Frederick Barbarossa', in *Medieval Polities and Modern Mentalities*, ed. J. L. Nelson (Cambridge, 2006), pp. 413–31 (p. 415).

significant that, even allowing for losses, over four times as many royal documents survive from Henry II's Anglo-French realm than endure from Barbarossa's empire.[101] These quantitative and qualitative differences, as Reuter termed them, are demonstrative of genuine disparity, but as we move on to consider eschatocols, we should remember that different instruments can be used to play variations of the same tune.

Eschatocols

The layout of royal documents, especially in France and the Empire, was dynamic. The optical middle point of these solemn documents was normally the authority-bestowing eschatocol. As Peter Rück has described it, the graphic stress is directed from the top to the bottom to the method of legal authentication, thereby breaking through the static plane of the written document.[102] The prominence of the eschatocol is seldom reflected in the layout of charters in modern editions, which perhaps explains why they have been undervalued as arenas for royal self-expression.[103] It is in the eschatocol that we find the kings' authority expressed in words and often visually too, sometimes with a monogram or other graphic symbol.[104] It is to these words and symbols, to witness lists, to dating clauses, to monograms and to seals that the eye is drawn. This effect is significantly less pronounced in post-Conquest English royal charters, which generally lack the dynamic layout and graphic symbols of their continental counterparts.[105] Although often plainer at first sight, it will be shown that English documents reflected at least some of the ideas present in continental charters, for a document's authenticity is its most important characteristic, and the manner in which

---

[101] Ibid., p. 414.
[102] Rück, 'Die Urkunde als Kunstwerk', p. 330.
[103] Manuscript scholars have recently argued that the similar 'dismissal and, in many modern critical editions, deliberate suppression of the "decorative" elements of medieval manuscripts … [is] a symptom of a broader logocentrism that has characterized much of modern European thought and scholarship'. M. P. Brown, I. H. Garipzanov and B. J. Tilghman, 'Introduction: The Role of Graphic Devices in Understanding the Early Decorated Book', in idem, *Graphic Devices and the Early Decorated Book* (Woodbridge, 2017), pp. 1–11 (p. 2).
[104] On the development of monograms and other signs of authority in late antiquity and the early Middle Ages see I. H. Garipzanov, 'Metamorphoses of the Early Medieval *Signum* of a Ruler in the Carolingian World', *Early Medieval Europe* 14 (2006), 419–64.
[105] As David Bates's edition of William I's charters makes clear, a small number of formal diplomas modelled on the Old English diplomatic form were issued in the Conqueror's name. However, the number of extant English diplomas is very small in relation to the number of surviving writs for his reign. Bates, *The Acta of William I*, pp. 68–72.

kings guaranteed this authenticity frequently referred back to the ceremony in which they had been made monarch.

The meaning of dating clauses, with the notable exception of nuanced articles on Scottish royal charters by Dauvit Broun and on Catalan specimens by Michel Zimmermann, has been overlooked by historians, who use them most often only to attempt to date charters using modern chronology, and tend to become frustrated when they do not surrender the necessary evidence.[106] Perhaps it is the formulaic nature of these clauses that has led to their neglect, for, as Broun demonstrated in his analysis of the royal charters of William the Lion and Alexander II of Scotland, these clauses can reveal a great deal about royal image. In consciously avoiding the use of regnal years, the Scottish kings made a 'carefully calibrated statement of the kingship's status', as inferior to that of the Plantagenet kings, whose chancery practice they so often mimicked.[107] In this context, Alexander II's adoption of regnal years, alongside his use of the 'royal we', can be interpreted as a claim to equal status with his southern counterpart.[108] In the Spanish context Zimmermann demonstrated the abrupt change in Catalan dating clauses in 1180, when documents ceased to be dated relative to the reigns of French kings, reflected changed political realities in the Iberian Peninsula.[109] But could it be that regnal years have a significance in and of themselves? As we saw in the previous chapter, modern dating conventions have camouflaged important liturgical allusions. Historians tend to treat relative chronology as an inconvenient system that requires decoding, as the enduring popularity of handbooks such as Cheney's and Grotefend's demonstrate.[110] In his *Manuel de diplomatique*, Arthur Giry devoted almost two hundred pages to describing how different systems of dating can be converted to the modern form, but not one line to what these systems actually mean.[111] Before rushing to run these codes through such handbook ciphers it is worth pausing to see what secrets they reveal in their original form.

---

[106] D. Broun, 'The Absence of Regnal Years from the Dating Clause of Charters of King of Scots, 1195–1222', *Anglo-Norman Studies* XXV (2003), 47–63; M. Zimmermann, 'La datation des documents catalans du IXe au XIIe siècle: un itinéraire politique', *Annales du Midi* 43 (1981), 345–75. Dating charters is a goal that has understandably interested medieval historians. For a number of methodologies, including dating by word-pattern matching, by formulae and vocabulary, by the association of names, and by palaeographic and sigillographic techniques, see the essays in M. Gervers, ed., *Dating Undated Medieval Charters* (Woodbridge, 2000).

[107] Broun, 'The Absence of Regnal Years', p. 57.

[108] Ibid.

[109] Zimmermann, 'La datation des documents catalans', p. 374.

[110] Cheney and Jones, *A Handbook of Dates*; H. Grotefend, *Zeitrechnung des deutschen Mittelalters und der Neuzeit*, 2 vols. (Hannover, 1891). Grotefend is available online thanks to Dr Horst Ruth: <http://www.manuscripta-mediaevalia.de/gaeste/grotefend/grotefend.htm> [accessed 12 December 2016].

[111] A. Giry, *Manuel de diplomatique*, 2 vols. (Paris, 1894), I, 81–275.

The Charter Evidence

Stressing that charters were dated relative to the birth of Christ might strike one as a tedious banality, but perhaps for just that reason, little consideration has been given to this fact. It is taken for granted, as unexceptional, as a method of dating still current today. However, that there is debate over its use in the modern era, with a growing preference for the use of the abbreviations BCE and CE over the traditional Christianity-derived abbreviations BC and AD, should remind us of the centrality of Christ to this system of dating, and that this is not meaningless even today, at least not to the champions of Common Era dating. Medieval documents, dated relative to the birth of Christ, are implicitly positioned within the history of salvation.[112] These are documents that have a role in God's plan for humanity. This role might be a small one, but it is implicit, and I would argue, a role that was understood by the kings themselves, especially those of France and Germany, who opened their charters, 'in the name of the holy and indivisible Trinity'. These were kings using legal documents to carry out the will of God. With this in mind, it should be recognized that the juxtaposition of years since the birth of Christ and regnal years connects regnal years to salvation history. An early charter of Philip I contains a place-date clause, telling us that the charter was 'enacted at Senlis, in the 1050th year of the Lord's incarnation and the first year of King Philip'.[113] King-centred dating is a close relation of Christ-centred dating. Where Christ's birth is commemorated in the phrase *anno dominicae incarnationis*, the king's consecration is remembered in regnal dating.

Sometimes the reference to the king's consecration is more explicit. Louis VI used the phrase 'in the 1109th year of the Lord's incarnation, in the first year of our consecration' in a charter to La Charité-sur-Loire in 1108.[114] Following the consecration of his queen, Louis took the unprecedented step of including her regnal years in dating clauses, concluding one charter 'enacted at Paris, publicly in our palace, in the 1115th year of the incarnation of the Word, in the seventh year of our consecration, in the first year of the consecration of Queen Adelaide'.[115] Louis continued to date documents using both his and his queen's regnal years for the duration of his reign, although not in every charter issued in his name: Marion Facinger counted a total of fifty-five

---

[112] Cf. Pauline Stafford's discussion of the place of Aethelred's 'penitential' charters of the 990s within the history of salvation. P. Stafford, 'Political Ideas in Late Tenth-Century England: Charters as Evidence', in *Law, Laity and Solidarities: Essays in Honour of Susan Reynolds*, ed. P. Stafford, J. L. Nelson and J. Martindale (Manchester, 2001), pp. 68–82 (pp. 70–1).

[113] *Recueil des actes de Philippe Ier*, ed. Prou and d'Arbois de Jubainville, p. 15 (no. 4): 'actum Silvanectis, anno dominicae incarnationis MLXno et regis Philipi primo'.

[114] *Recueil des actes de Louis VI*, ed. Dufour, p. 38 (no. 19): 'anno incarnacionis dominice MCIXmo, anno vero consecracionis nostre primo'.

[115] Ibid., p. 219 (no. 102): 'Actum Parisius, in palacio nostro puplice, anno incarnati Verbi MCXVo, anno nostre cunsecracionis VIIo, primo anno cunsecracionis Adelaidis regine [sic]'.

incidences of Adelaide's regnal year being used in conjunction with Louis's.[116] Given that the days of their consecration were different, their respective regnal years increased unevenly, underscoring the way in which regnal years inherently referenced the specific moment of royal consecration.[117]

For Facinger, whose 1968 study of Capetian queenship remains influential, Adelaide's reign marked the zenith of the queen's position in France. She sketched a trajectory in which in the tenth century the queen was the king's partner in governing with her power increasing into the early twelfth century, after which the monarch's wife slowly disappeared from government, her office undermined by the growth of administration and the dissipation of the former intimacy of court life.[118] Facinger saw Adelaide's prominence in Louis's charters as an important piece of evidence for her thesis, because after Adelaide no French queen was to leave such an imprint on royal documentary practice. As Miriam Shadis has commented, Facinger's study, concluding as it does with the death of Philip Augustus's long-suffering wife Ingebourg of Denmark, avoids her having to fit Blanche of Castile, wife of Louis VIII and mother of Louis IX, into her argument. For Shadis, Facinger's study 'leaves the impression that Blanche of Castile's tenure as queen and queen dowager was anomalous and uninstructive'.[119] Although Blanche does not appear to have played a prominent role during the reign of her husband, she is mentioned in only three of Louis VIII's official charters, Shadis points out that from the time of her marriage in 1200 to the death of her husband in 1226, Blanche produced at least twelve children, leaving limited time for active involvement in administration.[120] That Louis chose his wife to act as regent for his young son suggests, however, that Blanche was not ignorant of the workings of royal government. Shadis also emphasizes that in the reign of Philip Augustus the use of the king's regnal year in non-royal French charters became diminished, which can hardly be interpreted as a weakening of Capetian rule.[121] We should be wary, then, of over-interpreting the absence of later Capetian queens from French royal documents especially given that, as we shall see in the following chapter, queens in all three realms were early adopters of an important innovation in documentary practice: the use of seals by persons other than the king.

---

[116] M. F. Facinger, 'A Study of Medieval Queenship: Capetian France, 987–1237', *Studies in Medieval and Renaissance History* 5 (1968), 3–48 (p. 28).

[117] The precise date of Louis VI and Adelaide's marriage is not known. See A. W. Lewis, 'La date du mariage de Louis VI et d'Adelaïde de Maurienne', *Bibliothèque de l'école des Chartes* 148 (1990), 5–16.

[118] Facinger, 'A Study of Medieval Queenship', pp. 4, 35.

[119] M. Shadis, 'Blanche of Castile and Marion Facinger's "Medieval Queenship": Reassessing the Argument', in *Capetian Women*, ed. K. Nolan (New York, 2003), pp. 137–61 (p. 139).

[120] Ibid., pp. 143, 145.

[121] Ibid, p. 148.

In the German kingdom we also find explicit reference to king-making in dating clauses, which tend to include the indiction number, something not as regularly recorded in French royal documents and indicative of the importance of ancient Rome to imperial self-image. The first surviving charter of Henry IV concludes as follows: 'Given on the 5 December in the 1056th year of the Lord's incarnation, in the ninth indiction, also in the third year of the ordination of lord king Henry, in the first year of his reign, enacted at Cologne, in the name of the Lord, happily Amen'.[122] Here we are provided with two 'regnal' years, one relating to the king's ordination and the other to his attaining power. This distinction is significant, because it appears that a regnal year was not enough. The king's right to rule is related back to his ordination, which occurred while his father was still alive, in addition to the moment he assumed independent control on his father's death. Rather than commemorating solely his assumption of power, this manner of regnal dating purposely refers back to his consecration. The symbolic link between Christ and the German king is also alluded to through the parallel language used to describe the 'year of the Lord's incarnation' and the 'year of the lord king Henry IV's ordination'. Of course for some German kings, those not consecrated in the lifetime of a predecessor, their rule began on the day of their inauguration, and it is perhaps for this reason that we cease to find these events distinguished from one another in later royal charters. A distinction that we do find, however, is that between royal and imperial regnal years. In a charter issued on the day of his wife's imperial consecration in 1167, Frederick Barbarossa authenticated a grant to the archbishop of Cologne, Rainald Dassel, with a dating clause stating that it was the fifteenth year of his royal reign and the thirteenth of his imperial rule.[123] This distinction is consistently demarcated in imperial charters and points to the fact that royal and imperial powers were understood as separate offices.

English royal documents stand apart from those of France and Germany, in that it was not until the reign of Richard I that we regularly find the use of regnal years in charter dating clauses.[124] Despite coming relatively late to the regnal dating party, the Plantagenets clearly understood the potential of the implicit celebration of the day of their consecration in this method of dating. King John, consecrated on 27 May 1199, did not number his regnal years from the ordinal 27th day of that month, instead stressing his piety and the sacrality of his kingship by dating his regnal year from the moveable Feast of the Ascension, which had fallen on 27 May in 1199. This practice might infuriate historians trying accurately to date John's charters, but it also highlights the

---

[122] DD H. IV. 1: 'Data nonas Decembris anno dominicae incarnationis millesimo LVI, indictione VIIII, anno autem domini Heinrici regis ordinationis III, regni I; actum Coloniae; in Dei nomine feliciter amen.'
[123] DD F.I. 532.
[124] Broun, 'The Absence of Regnal Years', p. 48.

extent to which dates were imbued with liturgical significance. Instead of considering John's system of regnal dating as inconvenient, we should be grateful that it so explicitly illustrates the relationship between regnal years and biblical history, a relationship that has often been overlooked. In delineating the different dates used to denote the beginning of a year, Giry singled out Philip Augustus's preferred system of using the moveable feast of Easter as being the most irrational of all the methods used.[125] But in focusing on the disadvantages, presumably for the modern scholar seeking to convert these dates into a form intelligible to modern readers, the inherent meaning in medieval dating is ignored. For condemning dating relative to the celebration of Christ's resurrection as irrational demonstrates a distinct lack of understanding of the theological importance of this biblical event to medieval kings ruling in Christ's image and *Dei gratia*.

I began this section on eschatocols by drawing attention to the layout of royal documents, which is but one of the four visual aspects of such documents that Peter Rück suggests should be considered in any analysis. He further highlights the importance of script, the use of symbols and the employment of different formats, and it is to these features that we shall now turn.[126] These aspects are of course seldom clearly indicated in scholarly editions of charters, although modern information technology has made indicating the presence of a Chrismon or monogram in a document considerably easier. However, despite technological limitations, earlier charter scholars clearly recognized the inherent importance of the appearance of documents, as is evidenced by the later volumes in the *Regesta Regum Anglo-Normannorum* series, in which a number of charters were reproduced in facsimile.[127] Current investment in digital forms of reproduction and the development of scholarly standards for reproducing non-textual features will surely result in an increased awareness of the visual impression made by such documents.[128]

The study of diplomatic has always been closely linked to that of palaeography. Scholars of diplomatic have been reliant on palaeographical techniques to date documents, where a date is not clear from internal textual evidence,

---

[125] Giry, *Manuel de Diplomatique*, I, 110.

[126] Rück, 'Die Urkunde als Kunstwerk', p. 313. Hermann Jung provides a useful historiographical sketch of the study of symbols and signs: H. Jung, 'Zeichen und Symbol: Bestandsaufname und interdiziplinäre Perspektiven', in *Graphische Symbole in mittelalterlichen Urkunden*, ed. P. Rück (Sigmaringen, 1996), pp. 49–66.

[127] *Facsimiles of English Royal Writs to A. D. 1100: Presented to Vivian Hunter Galbraith*, ed. T. A. M. Bishop and P. Chaplais (Oxford, 1957); *Regesta Regum Anglo-Normannorum, 1066–1154: Facsimiles of Original Charters and Writs of King Stephen and the Empress Matilda and Dukes Geoffrey and Henry, 1135–1154.* ed. H. A. Cronne and R. H. C. Davis (Oxford, 1969).

[128] The Text Encoding Initiative (TEI) develops and maintains a standard for the representation of texts in digital form. See <http://www.tei-c.org/index.xml> [accessed 18 December 2016].

and to ascertain whether a document originated, for example, in a royal chancery or the scriptorium of a beneficiary.[129] This interest in script has, however, rarely been extended to the overall visual impact. In his 1957 Lyell lectures at Oxford, Stanley Morison, famous for designing the *Times New Roman* typeface in 1931, sought to explain the development of scripts from the sixth century BC to the present day. Morison's assertion was that all changes in alphabetic lettering in the West were linked to changes in the nature of belief and authority, and he accordingly gave the collection of his published lectures the title *Politics and Script*.[130] His wider conclusion alerts us to the potential of script to convey authority, a quality that is certainly of relevance in a consideration of royal documents. One of the most striking scribal characteristics of royal documents, particularly in France and Germany, is the different treatment afforded to the invocation and royal title. These elements, opening a document, are typically rendered in large letters thereby emphasizing, according to Fichtenau, the distance between the monarch, his officials and everyday existence.[131] Fichtenau further suggested that such treatment would impress upon viewers the sacrality of words issuing from the mouth of the ruler and this is surely linked to the parallel rendering of the sacred invocation. The tall and thin lettering often found in this context is at times difficult to read, but as Peter Rück commented of a script used by popes into the eleventh century that was so difficult to read interlinear transcriptions were also given: 'legibility was secondary when it came to the visualization of power'.[132]

Rück's observation could equally be applied to the monograms, found on French and German royal documents, in which the letters in a ruler's name were amalgamated to form a visual symbol.[133] Here legibility was certainly secondary to the visualization of power. In addition to monograms, the most frequently employed graphic symbols were the cross and Chrismon.[134] That

---

[129] For example, see the study of royal French documents by Françoise Gasparri: F. Gasparri, *L'écriture des actes de Louis VI, Louis VII et Philippe Auguste* (Paris, 1973).

[130] The lectures were posthumously published in revised form in 1972. S. Morison, *Politics and Script: Aspects of Authority and Freedom in the Development of Graeco-Latin Scripts from the Sixth Century B.C. to the Twentieth Century A.D.*, ed. N. Barker (Oxford, 1972).

[131] H. Fichtenau, 'Monarchische Propaganda in Urkunden', in *Beiträge zur Mediävistik: ausgewählte Aufsätze*, 3 vols. (Stuttgart, 1975–86), II, 18–36 (p. 24).

[132] Rück, 'Die Urkunde als Kunstwerk', p. 316. The link between documentary scripts and monumental inscriptions, which also acted as visual symbols of power, has often been noted. See, for example, W. Koch, 'Epigraphik und die Auszeichnungsschrift in Urkunden', in *Documenti medievali greci e latini*, ed. G. de Gregorio and O. Kresten (Spoleto, 1998), pp. 309–26.

[133] O. Guyotjeannin, 'Le monogramme dans l'acte royal français (Xe–début du XIVe siècle)', in *Graphische Symbole in mittelalterlichen Urkunden*, ed. P. Rück (Sigmaringen, 1996), pp. 293–307.

[134] Of these three symbols only the open cross appears in post-Conquest documents in

one of the most common styles of monogram was based on the shape of a cross is indicative of the links between the three symbols. Such symbols were firmly rooted in the text of the charter, as can be seen, for example, in the juxtaposition of Chrismon and invocation.[135] This link between graphic and scribal elements points to the fact that such documents were intended to be both read and seen. In an article on the legal function of graphic symbols in documents, Ruth Schmidt-Wiegand examined illustrations of legal procedures, particularly from the fourteenth century, and highlighted the fact that in images of legal process certain parts of the legal document are drawn most clearly. The parts chosen for special treatment, the opening and closing of the document, are precisely the parts in which graphic signs and symbols appear. Schmidt-Wiegand argues that these images reflect reality and thus the importance contemporaries placed on these graphic symbols.[136]

By way of example, let us consider the visual characteristics of a surviving diploma of the emperor Henry VI, in which he confirms the rights of the citizens of Constance to freedom from taxation by the bishop, Diethelm of Krenkingen, and his successors and their advocates.[137] As one of the major bishoprics in Swabia, Constance had experienced close contact with the Staufer dynasty even before they became monarchs. Duke Frederick II of Swabia, for example, had been present with many other secular and ecclesiastical lords at the celebratory internment of the bones of the recently canonized bishop Conrad on 26 November 1123.[138] At this point in time, Constance was very much an episcopal city, dominated by the bishop and centred on his cathedral and palace. However, the town's geographical position, situated as it is at the point where the Rhine flows out of Lake Constance, meant that

England and even this is rare in comparison with France and Germany. Jane Sayers does not know of any example of a monogram in an English document and points out that although the Chrismon is found in pre-Conquest documents it disappeared after 1066. J. E. Sayers, 'The Land of Chirograph, Writ and Seal: The Absence of Graphic Symbols in English Documents', in *Graphische Symbole in mittelalterlichen Urkunden*, ed. P. Rück (Sigmaringen, 1996), pp. 533–48 (p. 535).

[135] R. Schmidt-Wiegand, 'Die rechtshistorische Funktion graphische Zeichen und Symbole in Urkunden', in *Graphische Symbole in mittelalterlichen Urkunden*, ed. P. Rück (Sigmaringen, 1996), pp. 67–79 (p. 70).

[136] Ibid.

[137] Although the planned editions of Henry VI's *diplomata* are not yet published by the *Monumenta*, a PDF forerunner edition of those already edited is available online at <http://www.mgh.de/datenbanken/urkunden-heinrichs-vi/> [accessed 12 December 2016]. As the numbering of the documents is not yet finalized, the forerunner edition uses those of the *Regesta Imperii*. The diploma under consideration here is BB 253: <http://www.regesta-imperii.de/id/1192-09-24_1_0_4_3_1_319_253> [accessed 12 December 2016].

[138] H. Maurer, 'Die Bischofsstadt Konstanz in staufischer Zeit', in *Südwestdeutsche Städte im Zeitalter der Staufer*, ed. E. Maschke and J. Sydow (Sigmaringen, 1980), pp. 68–94 (p. 68).

there was also a large mercantile community based there. This community was involved in both local and long-distance trade and grew increasingly influential as the century progressed.

In the words of Helmut Maurer, by the end of the Staufer period Constance had been transformed from a *Bischofsstadt* into a *Bürgerstadt*.[139] The increasing intensity with which the Staufer monarchs visited Constance was an important factor in the shift of power from bishop to citizens. Conrad III visited Constance at least twice, and Frederick Barbarossa stayed in the city eight or nine times.[140] As a strategic and convenient stopping point on the route between Germany and Italy, Frederick's frequent sojourns are unsurprising. The importance of the city to imperial–papal relations is demonstrated by the conclusion of the Treaty of Constance between Barbarossa and Pope Eugenius III in 1153. The bishops of Constance remained important advisors to the Staufer, Herman of Arbon (1138–65) enjoyed the confidence of Conrad III and Barbarossa, and Diethelm of Krenkingen would later administer the duchy of Swabia for Philip of Swabia when he was absent in Italy in 1197.[141] However, as in other increasingly wealthy towns across the Empire and, indeed, the continent, the pendulum of power continued to swing from the bishop to the townspeople.

This diploma, given at Liège in September 1192, is illustrative of the changed dynamic of the later twelfth century and is the first time that the king is documented as acting against the interests of the bishop.[142] The diploma states that it was granted following petitions from the city and citizens of Constance, which were heard at Liège, and that the citizens shall henceforth be free from episcopal exactions due to the fact that such a privilege had originally been granted by the seventh-century Merovingian king Dagobert I, who was considered to be the founder of the bishopric.[143] The diploma survives in two engrosments, one original, sealed with wax, is to be found in the Generallandesarchiv in Karlsruhe, the other, which has a golden bull attached, is now in the Rosgartenmuseum in Constance (Plate 6). This copy, which we shall consider here, is a beneficiary-produced document and the fact that it is sealed with a golden bull, presumably financed by the citizens of Constance themselves, demonstrates the importance they attributed to its visual appearance. Indeed, as Bartel Heinemann recognized in the early twentieth century, the beneficiary scribe was careful to mimic the visual

---

[139] Ibid., p. 71.
[140] Ibid., pp. 73–4.
[141] On the involvement of the twelfth-century bishops of Constance in imperial and papal politics see U.-R. Weiss, *Die Konstanzer Bischöfe im 12. Jahrhundert: Ein Beitrag zur Untersuchungen der reichsbischöflichen Stellung im Kräftefeld kaiserlicher, päpstlicher und regional-diözesaner Politik* (Sigmaringen, 1975).
[142] Maurer, 'Die Bischofsstadt Konstanz', p. 81.
[143] DD H. VI. BB 253: 'ex privilegiis et concessione antecessorum nostrorum divorum augustorum regis Dagoberti'.

Inauguration and Liturgical Kingship

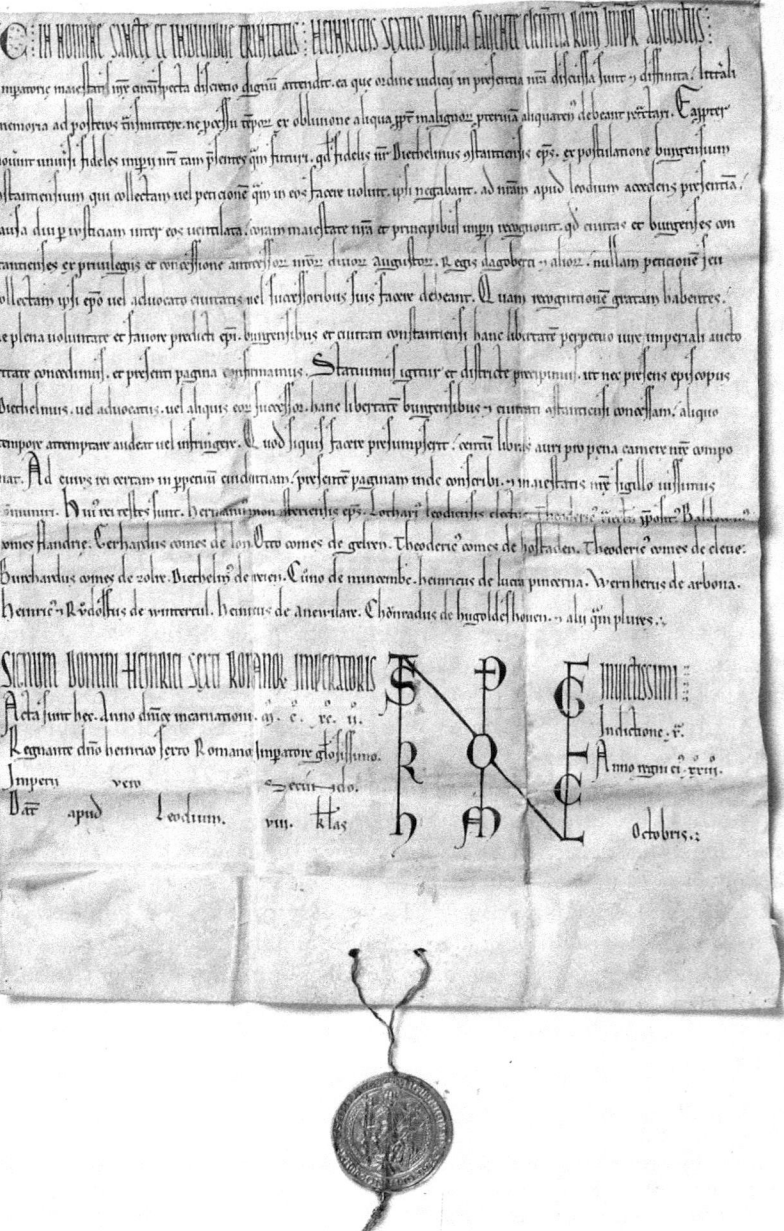

Plate 6. Henry VI's diploma for the citizens of Constance,
source: The Constance Rosgartenmuseum

characteristics of the original, including tracing the monogram and adopting some of the idiosyncrasies of the original chancery scribe, demonstrating the extent to which beneficiary-produced documents can very accurately reflect imperial ideas and pretensions.[144]

The document opens with a Chrismon on the same line as the traditional invocation of the Trinity and the imperial title. The *invocatio* and *intitulatio* stand apart from the body of the document and are distinguished by being written in elongated capitals. The script of the body of the diploma is measured and carefully written. Between each line of text there are generous spaces, into which elegantly drawn ascenders protrude. Within the body of text different sections of the document are signposted by the use of slightly more ornate capital letters. Before the administrative content of the diploma is reached, two lines are given over to an *arenga*, the main text body concludes with a four-line witness list. As with the opening of the document, the eschatocol is similarly distinguished from the body of text, both by its position on the page and, again, by the use of a line of elongated capitals. This line, and the four that follow it, are all broken by the emperor's huge monogram, so that on reading each line one's eyes are drawn to the shapes formed by the letters of the emperor's name. The line of elongated capitals describes the monogram as 'the sign of Lord Henry the sixth, most invincible emperor of the Romans'.[145] That the dating clause is spread over four generously spaced lines of expensive parchment makes clear the importance attributed to this element of an imperial document. In these lines the place of Henry's reign within salvation history is made manifest. The diploma is described as being enacted in the 1192nd year of the Lord's incarnation, the tenth indiction, with Lord Henry VI most glorious emperor of the Romans ruling, in the twenty-third year of his royal rule and the second year of his imperial rule.[146] It is worth noting that Henry's royal rule is calculated from the time of his consecration as co-king during Barbarossa's lifetime, rather than from his assumption of independent power on his father's death.

These visual elements frame the text of the diploma itself and convey, on first glance, the significance of the document they introduce and authenticate, which was surely the aim of the citizens of Constance, in having such an impressive copy of the diploma written and sealed with a golden bull. The diploma itself mentions that the rights within it are made manifest in the

---

[144] B. Heinemann, 'Der Freiheitsbrief Kaiser Heinrich VI. für die Stadt Konstanz vom 24. September 1192: Ein Beitrag zur Diplomatik der Staufenzeit', *Schriften des Vereins für Geschichte des Bodensees und seiner Umgebung* 44 (1915), 50–2.

[145] DD H. VI. BB 253: 'signum domini Henrici sexti romanorum imperatoris invictissimi'.

[146] DD H. VI. BB 253: 'Acta sunt hec anno dominicę incarnationis MCXCIIo, indictione Xa, regnante domino Heinrico sexto Romanorum imperatore gloriosissimo, anno regni eius XXIIIo, imperii vero secundo'.

writing on the page and reinforced by the attached seal of majesty.[147] The design of Henry VI's *bulla* will be discussed in the following chapter, but even without yet decoding the iconography, its visual impact is readily apparent. Andrea Stieldorf has commented that the presence of visual symbols in ruler documents is associated with the opening and, above all, the closure of documents.[148] If we combine this insight with Koziol's observation that the content of invocation, title and preamble in Carolingian royal diplomas stress the 'homology between heavenly and earthly kingship' and that 'the end of the diploma recapitulates the beginning, closing the frame by returning all to God', the fact that the visual elements had a function beyond the merely decorative is made apparent.[149] The visual appearance of royal and imperial documents, in the twelfth century as in the ninth, demonstrates that administration was no mere secular concern.

Graphic symbols such as Chrismon and monogram had either invocatory or corroborative functions, with the monogram in French and German monarchical documents being secondary only to the seal as a guarantor of authenticity.[150] In generally eschewing graphic symbols, with the exception of the occasional use of the open cross, and instead employing the chirograph, final concord and foot of fine, English royal documents stand visually apart from their continental counterparts.[151] In the immediate post-Conquest period diplomas in the Old English style were occasionally issued in the name of William I. Bates has identified eighteen surviving documents in diploma form for thirteen different English beneficiaries, and a further two diplomas with English diplomatic features for continental beneficiaries. Of these twenty diplomas, only six survive as originals or early copies.[152] In Bates's view the surviving documents do not allow for a clear-cut functional distinction to be made between different documentary types, and he suggests that 'the existence of some particularly spectacular diplomas from the early years of the reign is possibly indicative of an understandable wish to record the actions of the new regime in an especially dignified way'.[153]

Jane Sayers sought an explanation for this general absence of graphic symbols in English documents in the 'steady growth of a strong monarchy, based upon a unique (and non-Roman) legal system, [that] kept foreign influence at bay'.[154] In seeing the development of common law as providing the impetus for the difference between on the one hand English and on the

---

[147] DD H. VI. BB 253: 'Ad cuius rei certam in perpetuum evidentiam presentem paginam inde conscribi et maiestatis nostrę sigillo iussimus communiri'.
[148] Stieldorf, 'Die Magie der Urkunden', pp. 18–19.
[149] Koziol, *The Politics of Memory*, p. 59.
[150] Rück, 'Die Urkunde als Kunstwerk', pp. 327–8.
[151] Sayers, 'The Land of Chirograph, Writ and Seal', p. 533.
[152] Bates, *The Acta of William I*, p. 68.
[153] Ibid., p. 72.
[154] Sayers, 'The Land of Chirograph, Writ and Seal', p. 533.

The Charter Evidence

other hand French and German documents, Sayers's work sits firmly in the English legal history tradition discussed earlier. However, her emphasis on the use of seals making graphic symbols redundant seems unsatisfactory, given that these methods of authentication co-existed in the French and German realms. Moreover, foreign influence was hardly 'kept at bay' in English seal design, as will be revealed in the following chapter. Rather than in an English propensity to use seals, the lack of graphic symbols in English documents is better explained by a consideration of the type of documents used (a point also made by Sayers).[155] From the reign of Henry I onwards, English documents developed not from the standard charter formulas, but as a class of instrument derived from the traditions of the Old English writ. We should not see all these documentary types as lacking in visual or performative impact, however. The chirograph, in particular, held more than simply legal significance and, indeed, as with any other document its legal function could be easily ignored or negated, in the case of a chirograph should one of the two parties deny that the other half of the document existed.[156] In Koziol's words, 'the chirograph was an artifactual representation of the reciprocal equality and trust inherent in exchanges and conventions ... while the fact that the parchment had to be divided and distributed was itself a public, ritual demonstration of the equality and mutuality of the convention'.[157] The documentary landscape (*Urkundenlandschaft*) of England certainly appears different from that on the continent, but while recognizing the divergences we should be wary of seeing English royal documents as untarnished by the practices of continental neighbours and thus as an example of English exceptionalism.

This chapter has sought to provide an introduction to the richness of charter evidence and has barely even touched on the written statements of royal majesty found within charter *arengae*, or the religious content often found in sanction clauses. Both due to the uneven publication of royal charters and the sheer number of monarchs under consideration in this monograph a more detailed investigation has not been possible. This survey has shown, nonetheless, that traces of a liturgical and Christocentric understanding of kingship are to be found in royal and imperial documents in this period, whether they were produced by a royal chancery or in the scriptorium of a beneficiary. It cannot be denied that in the issuing of royal documents English practice diverges from French and German. Not only does the English granting of general rights, traditionally linked to the coronation oath by English historians, find no French or German equivalent, despite their kings swearing similar oaths, but English royal documents additionally tend to lack the dynamic visual features of their continental counterparts. These

---

[155] Ibid., pp. 535–6.
[156] Koziol, *The Politics of Memory*, p. 50.
[157] Ibid.

two examples of English variance might be the result of precocious legal and bureaucratic development. Henry II's adoption of the *Dei gratia* formula in 1172 and John's later dating of his regnal year by the Feast of the Ascension nonetheless make clear that the Plantagenet image of kingship was not far removed from that of the Capetians or Staufen. An examination of royal seals will bear out this assertion.

6
Seal Impressions and Christomimetic Kingship

Eadmer describes Henry I's issuing of a 'coronation charter' in his *Historia novorum in Anglia*. He recounts that Henry made promises during his consecration and that he then ordered that 'all these promises confirmed by a solemn oath [were] to be published throughout the kingdom with, by way of a lasting memorial, a written document authenticated by his seal in witness of its validity'.[1] Henry's first seal was two-sided. The obverse depicted him enthroned, clasping items of regalia. On the reverse he was depicted on horseback carrying a banner and shield. By the mid-eleventh century English, French and German kings all used the image of an enthroned monarch on their great seals, and this image was to endure for the rest of the medieval period and beyond. Otto III had been the first Western ruler to be depicted on his seal enthroned in majesty thereby appropriating a previously exclusively religious image for royal purposes.[2] Henry I in France adopted this innovation in 1031 and in England the first surviving royal seal, that of Edward the Confessor, features the enthroned design.[3] That monarchs in all three realms utilized this iconography, in which they presented their kingship as imitating Christ's, is indicative of their shared liturgical and biblical vocabulary. This Christomimetic symbol, used only after consecration, was a visual expression of the transformation wrought by inauguration.

The images of monarchs on seals are often considered stereotyped and unrealistic, raising the question of whether it is valid to apply ideas of self-representation to such images. In moving away from this anachronistic judgement of medieval seal iconography it becomes clear that a lack of realism does not condemn monarchical seals as empty of self-representative qualities. Indeed, as Brigitte Bedos-Rezak has rightly stressed,

---

[1] Eadmer, *Historia novorum in Anglia*, p. 119: 'et haec omnia jurisjurandi interjectione firmata, sub monimento litterarum sigilli sui testimonio roboratarum, per totum regnum divulgatum iri praeceperat'.

[2] B. Bedos-Rezak, 'The King Enthroned, a New Theme in Anglo-Saxon Royal Iconography: The Seal of Edward the Confessor and Its Political Implications', in *Kings and Kingship*, ed. J. T. Rosenthal (New York, 1986), pp. 53–88 (p. 60).

[3] Ibid., pp. 60–1. Although the design itself was new, Catherine Karkov rightly points out that the individual elements of this iconography were largely familiar and established Anglo-Saxon royal attributes. C. E. Karkov, *The Ruler Portraits of Anglo-Saxon England* (Woodbridge, 2004), p. 159.

Inauguration and Liturgical Kingship

realism is, after all, simply a convention, and one that the Middle Ages did not equate or associate with physiognomic likeness. In the charters themselves, authors refer to their seals as their own image, *imago noster*, which reveals that seals and their depictions incorporated elements meaningful to self-representation.[4]

Like the documents they authenticated, seals were carriers of meaning and an important channel of communication between a ruler and his subjects.[5] While anyone seeking an accurate idea of what a king or emperor actually looked like is likely to be disappointed by seal representations, in which monarchs are not portrayed as individuals, this does not mean that the images do not portray particular people.[6] Indeed, the function of a seal was to communicate authority and authenticity in relation to a particular person and particular office, leading Percy Ernst Schramm to comment that the actual meaning of a ruler portrait does not lie in the worth of its portraiture.[7] Rather the meaning lies in its representation of the office of the ruler, with the consequence that portraits on seals have a tendency, like all symbols, to persist in the same form.[8] As in our investigation of the liturgy, however, we should not assume that broad consistency in form indicates a congealing of interpretation.

The seals of the monarchs of England, France and Germany have all been catalogued and the work in this chapter draws on the relevant volumes from the *Corpus des sceaux français du moyen âge* by Martine Dalas and Marie-Adélaïde Nielen, *Die Siegel der deutschen Kaiser und Könige von 751 bis 1806* by Otto Posse, and Alfred Wyon's *The Great Seals of England*.[9] Of these catalogues that by Wyon, which is the oldest, is also the most problematic. Several of the great seals in Wyon's catalogue have been shown to be forgeries linked to Westminster Abbey. T. A. Heslop has commented on how accurate an imitator the Westminster forger was, and he has argued that forged seals can be used as evidence because, 'looked at from the point of view of both the forger and his client, the ideal was to produce a document which would raise

---

[4] B. Bedos-Rezak, 'Medieval Identity: A Sign and a Concept', *The American Historical Review* 105 (2000), 1489–533 (p. 1528).

[5] H. Keller, 'Zu den Siegeln der Karolinger und der Ottonen: Urkunden as "Hoheitszeichen" in der Kommunikation des Königs mit seinen Getreuen', *Frühmittelalterliche Studien* 32 (1998), 400–41 (pp. 400–2).

[6] P. E. Schramm, *Die deutschen Kaiser und Könige in Bildern ihrer Zeit* (Leipzig, 1928), pp. 5–6.

[7] Ibid., p. 11.

[8] Ibid., p. 8.

[9] *Les sceaux des rois et de régence*, ed. M. Dalas, CdS 2 (Paris, 1980); *Les sceaux des reines et des enfants de France*, ed. M.-A. Nielen, CdS 3 (Paris, 2011); *Die Siegel der deutschen Kaiser und Könige von 751 bis 1806*, ed. O. Posse, 5 vols. (Dresden, 1909); A. B. Wyon, *The Great Seals of England: From the Earliest Period to the Present Time, Arranged and Illustrated with Descriptive and Historical Notes* (London, 1887).

no suspicions'.[10] While accepting Heslop's point, this study is confined to a consideration of surviving authentic seals, and in the case of England Wyon's catalogue has thus been mediated by the work of Bishop, Chaplais, Cronne, Davis and Heslop himself.[11] Unfortunately, whereas the seals of queens in France have been systematically catalogued, and seals of the German queens have been studied together by Andrea Stieldorf, the seals of English queens have tended to be considered in isolation in studies of individual queens themselves.[12] Compiled a couple of decades after Wyon's catalogue, the German catalogue is also not without errors, with, for example, Alfred Gawlik identifying a seal of Henry V not included in Posse's volumes.[13] Some inclusions have also been shown to be forgeries, or not to be seals at all. Rainer Kahsnitz's contribution on Staufen seals and bulls to the catalogue for the exhibition *Die Zeit der Staufer* has further augmented the information provided by Posse.[14] The confusing nomenclature of 'first seal' and 'so-called first seal', etc. has been replaced by an alphabetical designation of the seals in the currently accepted chronological order of use. Brief descriptions of, and reference information for, all royal and imperial seals and *bullae* from the period can be found in Appendix 4.[15]

The King in Majesty

As Hagen Keller has elucidated, the Ottonian period was of particular importance in the history of sealing, not least because a picture type, the enthroned ruler, was developed that influenced seal design across western Europe for

---

[10] T. A. Heslop, 'Twelfth-Century Forgeries as Evidence for Earlier Seals: The Case of St. Dunstan', in *St Dunstan: His Life, Time and Cult*, ed. N. Ramsay, M. Sparks, and T. W. T Tatton-Brown (Woodbridge, 1992), pp. 299–310 (pp. 302, 300).

[11] *Facsimiles of English Royal Writs to A. D. 1100*, ed. Bishop and Chaplais; P. Chaplais, 'The Seals and Original Charters of Henry I', *English Historical Review* 75 (1960), 260–75; *English Royal Documents: King John – Henry VI, 1199–1461*, ed. P. Chaplais (Oxford, 1971); T. A. Heslop, 'Seals', in *English Romanesque Art, 1066–1200*, ed. G. Zarnecki, J. Holt and T. Holland (London, 1984), pp. 298–320; *Regesta Regum Anglo-Normannorum, 1066–1154*, ed. Cronne and Davis.

[12] A. Stieldorf, 'Die Siegel der Herrscherinnen – Siegelführung und Siegelbild der "deutschen" Kaiserinnen und Königinnen', *Rheinische Vierteljahrsblätter* 64 (2000), 1–44.

[13] A. Gawlik, 'Ein neues Siegel Heinrichs V. aus seiner Königszeit', in *Geschichte und ihre Quellen: Festschrift für Friedrich Hausmann zum 70. Geburtstag*, ed. R. Härtel (Graz, 1987), pp. 529–36.

[14] R. Kahsnitz, 'Siegel und Goldbullen', in *Die Zeit der Staufer: Geschichte, Kunst, Kultur: Katalog der Ausstellung, Stuttgart 1977*, ed. R. Haussherr and C. Väterlein, 4 vols. (Stuttgart, 1977), I, 17–108.

[15] Unfortunately it has not been possible to include images of all these seals in this volume, but depictions of them can be found by utilizing the catalogue references supplied in Appendix 4.

many centuries.[16] That Christ was depicted in majesty on the reverse of Byzantine bulls provided an obvious iconographic model for the design, but, as Keller argues, the adoption of this motif under Otto III should not be considered solely in the context of imperial–Byzantine relations.[17] We need to remember the context in which seals were used and seen. As discussed in the previous chapter, royal charters can be considered to be quasi-liturgical documents. Charters thus provided a liturgical as well as a diplomatic context in which seal iconography would be decoded. In this way, the rudimentary and monochrome images of the Ottonian rulers on their seals have more in common with the magnificent and colourful depictions of them in liturgical manuscripts than is evident at first sight.[18] As Keller has stressed, for the viewers of Otto III's seals and documents, the analogy between Otto enthroned and Christ in Majesty would have been manifest. Through the adoption of this image, Otto claimed to rule in the image of Christ the King, as his earthly imitator, a sigillographic claim that was taken up enthusiastically by his successors.

In utilizing this Christomimetic image of an enthroned ruler on their great seals, the monarchs of all three realms implicitly referred back to their inauguration during which, after their unction, coronation and the handing over of a number of items of regalia, they had been enthroned. Royal seals in the three realms shared a number of associated iconographical elements. In addition to a full-length figure seated on a throne of varying ornamentation, the figures are all shown wearing a crown or diadem and holding items of regalia. As the original adoption of the German enthroned motif in France and England demonstrates, developments in seal design were not confined to one kingdom or another. Given that seals were portable and designed to travel with the documents they authenticated, this cross-border pollination is to be expected. Harvey and McGuinness have pointed to the fact that 'many archives in medieval Britain – royal, ecclesiastical, aristocratic – will have contained papal and other letters from the Continent bearing seals that may easily have directly influenced design'.[19] This observation can equally be applied to France and the Empire. Thus, Byzantine influence is evident in seals from England and Germany in, for example, the almost contemporaneous introduction of *pendilae* hanging from the crown or diadem from the reign of Henry II in England and Conrad III in Germany. Birds appear as an

---

[16] H. Keller, 'Ottonische Herrschersiegel: Beobachtungen und Fragen zu Gestalt und Aussage und zur Funktion im historischen Kontext', in *Bild und Geschichte: Studien zur politischen Ikonographie*, ed. K. Krimm and H. John (Sigmaringen, 1997) pp. 3–51 (p. 3).

[17] Ibid., pp. 4–5.

[18] As Keller points out, Ottonian seals would have been seen by a far wider audience than the manuscript illuminations. Keller, 'Ottonische Herrschersiegel', pp. 28–9.

[19] P. D. A. Harvey and A. McGuinness, *A Guide to British Medieval Seals* (London, 1996), p. 6.

attribute on a number of English and German seals, and the lily or fleur-de-lys features on royal seals (male or female) from all three realms. A number of seals of Henry IV and Henry V of Germany depict the king seated on a throne decorated with animal heads, a design feature that is also found on the seals of Henry III of England, and on a number of the seals of the French kings. The thrones of the Capetians are ornamented with the heads and feet of lions, which Bedos-Rezak has interpreted as evoking the throne of Solomon, described in I Kings 10. 18–20 as being decorated with lions.[20] Despite the stability of this overall design there are, however, some changes that can give us an insight into developing images of royalty.

That small differences in the design of the enthroned image are important has been emphatically shown by Bedos-Rezak's investigation of the seal design of Louis VII of France.[21] She has convincingly argued that the throne on which Louis is seated represents the throne of the Merovingian King Dagobert, which had recently been restored by Abbot Suger at Saint-Denis, and she suggested that the characteristic X shape of the chair became a symbol of the Capetian monarchy.[22] By being depicted seated on the throne of Dagobert, Louis sought to identify himself with his royal predecessors and he is even portrayed with long flowing locks, which was the fashionable Merovingian hairstyle.[23] In addition to its distinctive X form, Dagobert's throne also had Solomonic associations via its lion head decorations. Given the importance of Charlemagne's throne at Aachen, with its six steps identified by Schramm as an allusion to Solomon's throne, the development of the design of the throne on royal seals in the Empire is worth noting. Earlier German kings and emperors are depicted seated on a bench-like throne. From the time of Conrad III, however, the throne always has a back. In light of Bedos-Rezak's investigation it is worth considering whether this is no longer a generic throne, but a depiction of the throne of Charlemagne at Aachen. Although the decoration is more ornate than on Charlemagne's throne the fact that the back, once adopted, is to be found in almost all subsequent seals argues for this interpretation, as does the fact that this back is normally curved, reflecting both the shape of Charlemagne's throne and the description of Solomon's throne.[24] In contrast to these biblical and historical allusions, the thrones found on English seals are notable not for symbolism but for the increasing intricacy of their design, from a simple bench, such as on the seal of

---

[20] B. Bedos-Rezak, 'Suger and the Symbolism of Royal Power: The Seal of Louis VII', in *Abbot Suger and Saint-Denis*, ed. P. L. Gerson (New York, 1986), pp. 95–103 (p. 96).
[21] Bedos-Rezak, 'Suger and the Symbolism of Royal Power: The Seal of Louis VII'.
[22] Ibid.
[23] Ibid.
[24] I Kings 10. 19: 'et summitas throni rotunda erat in parte posteriori'. The exception is a seal of Otto IV, which is closely related to a seal of Richard I of England, discussed below pp. 200–1.

Edward the Confessor to the ornate gothic throne on Henry III's 'B' seal. This raises an important issue, that sometimes the explanation for design features can lie not in the philosophy of power but in artistic development or in a desire to differentiate one's seal from that of a predecessor.

Bearing in mind Anna Gannon's warning that, we beware of 'the dangers of bending the interpretation of an image to suit one's particular theory', let us turn to another shared element in the enthroned monarch design, the fact that the monarchs all hold items of regalia in both hands.[25] An orb, often topped with a cross, is a feature of all German seals from Otto III's introduction of the enthroned monarch motif and was directly copied from German sources by Edward the Confessor, persisting on English seals up until that of Henry II.[26] By contrast the French rulers are never depicted holding an orb. As we have seen, the orb was not included as an item of regalia to be bestowed on the king in any of the royal liturgies and is found only in the two later imperial *ordines*. However, the fact that the orb was present on both German royal and imperial seals suggests we should not be too definitive in seeing it as an emblem exclusively of imperial rather than royal power. Another attribute, which appears on some German and English seals, is a bird. In the German context the bird is normally interpreted as depicting an eagle, an imperial symbol. In the English tradition it is considered a dove. This is a problematic assertion because the bird is associated with Edward the Confessor, even though the only witness to a bird on his seal is a Westminster forgery, and that the explanation for the presence of the bird on his seal is that it was copied from German seals, in which case surely it should be considered an eagle rather than a dove.[27] William the Conqueror and William Rufus did not adopt the bird motif, but it was readopted by Henry I, Stephen and Henry II.

In her discussion of early Anglo-Saxon coinage, Anna Gannon asked the question, 'is the iconography always unequivocal or can we detect plays and shifts in the layering of meaning, therefore postulating audiences of varying sophistication and multiple roles for the coinage?'.[28] This question seems equally relevant in the context of seals. Is it actually possible or even desirable to identify a particular species of bird? Dolley and Jones were certainly right in challenging the description of the birds on the reverse of one of Edward the Confessor's coin types.[29] Previously the birds had been designated

---

[25] A. Gannon, *The Iconography of Early Anglo-Saxon Coinage: Sixth to Eighth Centuries* (Oxford, 2003), p. 17.

[26] Heslop considers the 'orb and sceptre' image to have been borrowed unchanged from the Ottonians. Heslop, 'Seals', p. 301.

[27] Bedos-Rezak, 'The King Enthroned', p. 63.

[28] Gannon, *The Iconography of Early Anglo-Saxon Coinage*, p. 3.

[29] R. H. M. Dolley and F. E. Jones, 'A New Suggestion Concerning the So-called "Martlets" in the Arms of St. Edward', in *Anglo-Saxon Coins: Studies Presented to F. M. Stenton on the Occasion of His 80th Birthday, 17 May 1960*, ed. R. H. M. Dolley (London, 1961), pp. 215–26.

martlets, but it is clearly anachronistic to apply this heraldic description to tenth-century coinage. Dolley and Jones asserted that the birds should be considered eagles and this interpretation would fit with the suggestion that it is an eagle, adopted from the German model, that is found on his seal.[30] Instead of fixing one meaning for the bird in a German context and another in an English, we should be open to the fact that, especially in this time before the development of rigid rules for heraldry, competing meanings could be implicit in the same symbol at the same time, and that interpretations could change over time, not to mention be interpreted differently by varying audiences. The bird on English seals is a clear example of the same symbol having different meanings in different contexts. For Edward the Confessor the inclusion of a bird on his seal was most likely a reference to the imperial eagle. By the time of the reintroduction of a bird it was a reference to the Confessor himself. The species of the bird was perhaps secondary although later tradition dictated that in an English context birds on items of insignia were doves. Roger of Howden, for example, describes a sceptre topped with a dove in the procession during Richard I's inauguration.[31] By this point doves were associated with the Confessor, an association that Henry III would later exploit more fully.[32] Beyond the Confessor, the dove also symbolized the Holy Spirit, which, as we have seen, was described as taking the form of a dove at the baptism of Christ in Matthew 3. 16.

An item of regalia that only appears as part of the enthroned design on English royal seals, despite its inclusion in liturgies from all three realms, is the sword. Jane Martindale has seen the presence of the sword on seals and tomb effigies as epitomizing the difference between the 'militaristic' self-image of the Anglo-Normans and Angevins and the 'pacific' image the Capetians used on their seals.[33] But the fact that the sword first appeared on the seal of Edward the Confessor, a king not noted for his war-like demeanour, rather undermines any assertion that its presence is linked to the Norman Conquest. Indeed, in the earlier part of this period its inclusion on the seal might well be in imitation of the Confessor, as with the orb topped with a cross and bird discussed in the previous paragraph. In any case, as we have seen, the sword was an item associated with royal consecration and the defence of the church. It also had Davidic associations, which were expressly referenced in the inauguration liturgy through the allusion to Psalm 44.[34] Moreover, Emma Mason, in a discussion of the legendary swords such as Durendal and Excalibur that were connected with the Plantagenet kings,

[30] Ibid., p. 222.
[31] Roger of Howden, *Chronica*, ed. Stubbs, III, 9–10.
[32] Carpenter, 'The Burial of King Henry III, the Regalia and Royal Ideology', p. 441.
[33] J. Martindale, 'The Sword on the Stone: Some Resonances of a Medieval Symbol of Power', *Anglo-Norman Studies* XV (1992), 199–241 (pp. 229–30).
[34] See above pp. 80–7 for the role of the sword in the liturgy.

remarked on the fact that swords used ceremonially and those used in battle were differentiated. King John claimed to possess the sword of Tristan, but in instructions concerning the delivery of his regalia listed separately the sword that was made for his coronation.[35]

That in the context of the enthroned image this sword should be interpreted as of symbolic rather than martial significance is suggested by the seal of Henry the Young King. The Young King is depicted on his seal crowned, enthroned and holding items of regalia. As only two impressions and a fragment of the Young King's seal survive, none of which are in particularly good condition, there is some disagreement as to what exactly the Young King holds, with some seeing an orb topped with a long cross and others a short sceptre in his right hand.[36] What is apparent is that he does not hold a sword in either hand. R. J. Smith has linked this to the fact that the Young King lacked a territorial role and has commented, 'if the sword in the royal seal and on the ducal seal were the symbols of active authority, then the Young King's swordless seal was the sign of an heir in waiting'.[37] Smith's explanation for the lack of sword on the Young King's seal is comparable with Grant Simpson's decoding of a seal from the minority of Alexander III in Scotland.[38] Simpson noted the fact that the seal from Alexander's minority was physically smaller than the great seal of his majority and also had different iconographical elements. Significantly Alexander III does hold a sword, but it rests across his lap, which Simpson interprets as signifying that the child king could not yet actively dispense justice.[39]

All the reigning kings of England, from Edward to John, featured a sword on their great seals. On the 'B' seal of Henry III the sword was replaced with a sceptre, an item of regalia that had appeared on the seals of Richard and John in place of the orb.[40] In his adoption of a sceptre Richard I reintroduced an attribute that had appeared on Edward the Confessor's two-sided enthroned design. He also adopted an item of insignia that had appeared on French and German great seals throughout this period. Sceptres are thus another

---

[35] E. Mason, 'The Hero's Invincible Weapon: An Aspect of Angevin Propaganda', in *The Ideals and Practice of Medieval Knighthood III*, ed. C. Harper-Bill and R. Harvey (Woodbridge, 1990), pp. 121–37 (p. 133).

[36] The Young King's seal is discussed in detail in R. J. Smith, 'Henry II's Heir: The Acta and Seal of Henry the Young King, 1170–83', *English Historical Review* 116 (2001), 297–326 (pp. 304–7).

[37] Ibid., p. 312.

[38] G. G. Simpson, 'Kingship in Miniature: A Seal of Minority of Alexander III, 1249–1257', in *Medieval Scotland: Crown, Lordship and Community: Essays Presented to G. W. S. Barrow*, ed. K. J. Stringer and A. Grant (Edinburgh, 1993), pp. 131–9.

[39] Ibid., p. 136.

[40] Paul Binski has discussed the new design of Henry III's second seal, which was under the express directions of the king. The replacing of the sword with a sceptre was not received positively by contemporaries who interpreted it as fulfilling a prophecy of Merlin. Binski, *Westminster Abbey and the Plantagenets*, pp. 84–6.

iconographical element shared by all three siglliographic traditions, which is unsurprising given that both longer sceptres and shorter rods featured in the inauguration ceremonies in all three realms and were established items of royal regalia. The sceptres and rods are topped with a variety of motifs, including a lily, a cross and a bird. It might be tempting to see such details as representing actual royal insignia, but as should be clear by now, such identifications are seldom sustainable.

As suggested above, small changes to the design of sceptre tops might just reflect a desire to differentiate a seal from that of one's predecessor. However, it is notable that the lily or fleur-de-lys is the only sceptre design that appears on seals from all three realms. This indicates that the meaning of the sceptre lies not solely in its connection with some kind of secularizsed and judicial royal power. The lily was associated with Mary and understood to represent at once both her chastity and her fertility. As such it also had dynastic overtones. Heslop has argued, in the context of seals from ecclesiastical communities dedicated to the Virgin Mary, that the rod should not just be seen as an item of royal regalia, but as a reference to the rod of Jesse and the Incarnation.[41] The sacred associations that Heslop posits for conventual and monastic seals should also not be ruled out in the context of monarchical seals. Seeing lily-topped sceptres on royal seals as purely royal symbols would be to ignore these fertile Marian and dynastic connections. Not only, as we shall see, were there manifest parallels between the seals of royal and ecclesiastical women, but it is also unsurprising to find Marian references in a royal context, given royal interest in, and devotion to, the Virgin.

Marian references are particularly prominent on French royal seals. Philip I and Louis VI are both depicted holding two sceptres. In their right hands they carry a shorter rod topped with three pointed leaves, that Dalas suggests might represent a palm.[42] In their left hands they hold a longer sceptre, topped with a fleur-de-lys. Louis VII's seal saw a further innovation in the use of the fleur-de-lys. The king is no longer depicted with both arms outstretched. Instead his left hand, resting on his knee, grips a sceptre topped by a fleur-de-lys enclosed in a square. His outstretched right arm simply holds a fleur-de-lys. The flower is no longer the decoration on the end of an item of regalia, but a symbol in its own right, stressing the importance of Mary to Capetian images of kingship. Louis VII's pose and insignia were directly copied by Philip Augustus and Louis VIII, whose seal introduced further embellishment to the fleur-de-lys design. Louis IX is similarly depicted, although the lily at the end of his sceptre is no longer surrounded by a square. The edges of Louis IX's tunic are also decorated with a repeating fleur-de-lys design. The reigning kings and emperors in England and France

---

[41] Heslop, 'The Virgin Mary's Regalia and Twelfth-Century English Seals', p. 59.
[42] *Les sceaux des rois et de régence*, ed. Dalas, p. 143.

did not deploy the fleur-de-lys with quite such abandon on their seals, using the flower as a decorative feature on items of insignia rather than as an item of regalia in its own right. However, as we shall see when we turn to queenly seals, overt Marian allusions were not restricted to the Capetians.

The majority of royal seals from England, France and Germany do not have anything in the background, but occasionally there are iconographic elements in the field that demand explanation. Sometimes they appear to be space-fillers or a way of differentiating a seal from the seal of a predecessor or indeed between successive seals of an individual king. Thus, the quartefeuille cross in the field of the seal of Louis VI of France sets it apart from the 'B' seal of his father Philip I, on which it was based, and the 'C' seal of Henry I of England can be distinguished from his earlier two seals due to the addition of two decorative stars or crosses flanking the enthroned king. However, the elements in the field can also convey meaning, and this is surely the case on the seals of Richard I of England. That the features in the field of Richard's seals should not be considered merely to be 'curious emblematic additions' as asserted by Heslop, is suggested by the fact that very similar features appear on the imperial seal of Otto IV.[43]

On his 'A' seal Richard is shown enthroned flanked by a symmetrical arrangement of plant, crescent moon and either a star or small sun.[44] That this might be a sun rather than a star is suggested by the design on his 'B' seal in which Richard is flanked by a crescent moon on the left and a sun on the right. This design finds an exact imitation on the imperial seal of Otto IV, an iconographical borrowing that is indicative of the close relationship between these two monarchs.[45] It has been suggested that Otto IV's seal matrix was in fact made either in England or in the Plantagenet lands on the continent.[46] Rainer Kahsnitz has interpreted the sun and moon as symbols of world-wide dominion (*Weltherrschaft*) that had been occasionally associated with royal rule from Carolingian times.[47] However, the sun and the moon could be seen as an allusion to the Book of Revelation and the breaking of the sixth seal, which saw the sun turn black as sackcloth and the moon red as blood.[48] The design is also reminiscent of Crucifixion miniatures, in which the crucified Christ is often

---

[43] Heslop, 'Seals', p. 304.

[44] The plants have traditionally been considered broom flowers, the flowers from which the Plantagenets are supposed to have drawn their name. For the origin of this name see J. Bradbury, 'Fulk le Réchin and the Origin of the Plantagenets', in *Studies in Medieval History Presented to R. Allen Brown*, ed. C. Harper-Bill, C. J. Holdsworth and J. L. Nelson (Woodbridge, 1989), pp. 27–41 (pp. 40–1).

[45] The son of Henry the Lion and the English princess Matilda, Otto IV had grown up at the Plantagenet court and was supported in his struggle for the Empire by his uncle Richard I of England.

[46] Kahsnitz, 'Siegel und Goldbullen', p. 25.

[47] Ibid.

[48] Revelation 6. 12.

depicted flanked by the sun and moon, sometimes personified and shown mourning. German royal interest in this motif is evidenced in the depiction of an unidentified king on an ivory panel dating from the early twelfth century.[49] On this panel, now part of the Liebieghaus sculpture collection in Frankfurt am Main, a king, who has taken off his crown and placed it on the ground before him, and an abbot kneel on opposite sides at the base of a cross to which Christ is nailed. Christ is flanked by two saints, presumably the Virgin Mary and John the Baptist, and above the arms of the cross are to be found roundels containing personifications of the sun and the moon.

A different iconographical motif sometimes found in depictions of the Crucifixion is the presence of two trees, rather than two saints, flanking the Cross. This variation can be seen in a miniature from the Arundel Psalter, produced in Winchester in the final quarter of the eleventh century.[50] Here the trees represent the two trees of the Garden of Eden; the Tree of Life and the Tree of the Knowledge of Good and Evil. Their presence either side of the Cross can be interpreted as demonstrating that, through Christ's sacrifice, mankind has been redeemed and can once more enter Paradise. With this iconographical motif in mind it is worth re-examining Richard's 'A' seal, on which he is pictured flanked by plants in addition to the two crescent moons and stars/suns. The way the king is depicted with his arms outstretched echoes the cruciform shape of the Cross. Whether we can go so far as to see the designs of Richard and Otto's seals as deliberately presenting these monarchs as analogous to Christ on the Cross remains a matter of conjecture, but the fact that the crescent moon and star motif was often found on Crusader coins in this period, particularly from Tripoli, suggests that these 'curious emblematic additions' were intentional Christological references.[51] Richard the Lionheart's devotion to Crusading requires no introduction, whereas Otto IV's is less well known. Although his insecure position in Germany meant that he never actively took part in a Crusade, Rudolf Hiestand has pointed out that he had not only taken the Cross in private on the day of his consecration as king, but, remembering his unfulfilled vow, he left gifts in his will to pay for others to fight on his behalf for the Holy Sepulchre.[52]

---

[49] This panel, which was originally a book cover, is reproduced as catalogue entry 33 in L. Hegg, S. Heimann and S. Kaufmann, ed., *Die Salier. Macht im Wandel: Katalog* (Munich, 2006), pp. 58–60. It was made in the Maas region and for this reason it has been suggested that the king depicted is Henry IV, who died at Liège in 1106.

[50] London, British Library, Arundel MS 60, fol. 52v. This manuscript is available to view online: <http://www.bl.uk/manuscripts/Viewer.aspx?ref=arundel_ms_60_fs001ar> [accessed 28 November 2017].

[51] J. Porteous, 'Crusader Coinage with Greek or Latin Inscriptions', in *A History of the Crusades: The Impact of the Crusades on Europe*, ed. H. W. Hazard and N. P. Zacour (Madison, 1989), pp. 354–87 (p. 376).

[52] R. Hiestand, 'Kingship and Crusade in Twelfth-Century Germany', in *England and Germany in the High Middle Ages*, ed. A. Haverkamp and H. Vollrath (Oxford, 1996),

A further feature common to the enthroned design from all three realms is the presence of an inscription around the edge of the seal. With the exception of the inscription on William the Conqueror's seal, which comprised two hexameters, the inscriptions are formulaic and link the monarch by title to the peoples or area he claimed authority over, in a fashion consonant with the *intitulatio* discussed in the previous chapter.[53] For example, the seal of Henry I of France bears the inscription HENRICUS DEI GRACIA FRANCORUM REX and that of Henry I of England the inscription HENRICUS DEI GRATIA REX ANGLORUM. Here we see that although the designation *Dei gratia* was not part of the king's title in charters in England until the 1170s, the kings of England had been so proclaimed on their seals since the reign of William Rufus. The French designation REX FRANCORUM remained static throughout this period, as Schneidmüller has emphasized, whereas in contrast in England John began to style himself REX ANGLIE rather than REX ANGLORUM on his seals.[54] It was suggested in the previous chapter that undue attention should not be paid to this shift. Seal evidence confirms this view. The adoption of the shortened territorial form can be linked to John's wish to style himself 'King of England and Lord of Ireland', thus requiring a shortening from *Anglorum* to *Anglie* simply to fit the whole title into one seal inscription. Moreover, we find a much earlier use of the territorial form on a royal seal. The inscription on the seal of Matilda of Scotland reads + SIGILLUM MATHILDIS SECUNDAE DEI GRACIA REGINAE ANGLIE.[55] Here we should not see a tension between Matilda asserting a claim to territorial lordship and the lordship over people claimed by her husband Henry I.

German kings are described as 'rex' on their seals. If the king was crowned emperor a new seal would be issued identifying him as 'imperator augustus'. On his royal seals Henry IV of Germany was referred to as HEINRICUS REX on seal 'A' and HEINRICUS DEI GRATIA REX on seals 'B', 'C' and 'D'. On his imperial seals he is styled HEINRICUS DEI GRATIA TERCIUS ROMANORUM IMPERATOR AUGUSTUS on seal 'A' and HEINRICUS DEI GRATIA III ROMANORUM IMPERATOR AUGUSTUS on seals 'B' and 'C'. Thus, while his emperorship was linked to the Romans, his kingship was not qualified by a people or kingdom. His successor Henry V, however, did link his kingship to a people, and rather than the Germans or *Tuetonici* he related his royal rule to the Romans or *Romani*. As Alfred Gawlik has pointed

---

pp. 235–65 (p. 246). The moon and star/sun also feature on Frederick II's first seal as king of Sicily. Here they could perhaps be interpreted as Frederick appropriating symbols from Otto IV's iconographic canon in order to stress his rightful claim to the throne of Germany as well as Sicily, although it is notable that Frederick also took the Cross in association with his inauguration at Aachen in 1215.

[53] T. A. Heslop, 'English Seals from the Mid-ninth Century to *c*.1100', *Journal of the British Archaeological Association* 132 (1980), 1–16 (p. 10).

[54] Schneidmüller, 'Herrscher über Land und Leute?', p. 155.

[55] Heslop, 'Seals', p. 305.

out, the significance of this innovation is that it is a clear response to papal *Titelpolitik*, that sought to confine Salian rule north of the Alps by designating the German monarch as *Tuetonicorum rex*.[56] As the Staufen expanded their dominions the edge of the seal ceased to be large enough to fit the inscription and it occasionally spills over into the background of the enthroned image. Thus, for example, on the 'B' imperial seal of Henry VI the enthroned king is flanked by the words REX SICILIE in addition to the conventional inscription around the circumference of the seal describing him as HEINRICUS DEI GRATIA ROMANORUM IMPERATOR AUGUSTUS. Following his marriage to Isabella of Jerusalem in 1225, Frederick II had ET REX IERUSALEM added to the field of his existing seal matrix.

Methods of Sealing and Alternative Images

Although the three monarchies shared the Christomimetic enthroned monarch motif, there also existed major differences between the seals of the monarchs of England, France and the Empire, that were related to the methods of sealing used. German royal and imperial seals were both one-sided. However, the German kings and emperors also issued documents with *bullae*, that were two-sided and made at least partially of metal. While we might expect the iconographical division to align with the division between royal and imperial power, it in fact aligns with the division between seals and *bullae*. On attaining the emperorship, the most significant change made to the great seal was to change the inscription, as described above, so that the newly inaugurated emperor was described as such. By contrast to the stability of the enthroned motif on royal seals, the design of the *bullae* was dynamic, with the reverse side most frequently featuring a developing architectural motif representing the city of Rome. In addition, the image of an enthroned monarch, introduced on German seals by Otto III, does not appear on the obverse of *bullae* until the reign of Henry VI. As king of Sicily Frederick II also used two-sided *bullae* that exhibit a huge diversity with regards to the design on the obverse.

The earliest surviving royal seal in England, that of Edward the Confessor, is also two-sided and depicts an enthroned king on both sides, holding different items of regalia. Heslop has commented that, 'in having a two-sided seal [Edward] was competing with the two-sided *bullae* of the Pope and the Byzantine and German emperors'.[57] William the Conqueror continued the practice of using a two-sided seal, but with the innovation of an equestrian portrait appearing on the reverse. This combination of enthroned king and equestrian portrait was mimicked by the kings of Scotland, from Alexander I,

---

[56] Gawlik, 'Ein neues Siegel Heinrichs V. aus seiner Königszeit', p. 534.
[57] Heslop, 'Seals', p. 301.

and uniquely, and briefly, in France during the reign of Louis VII. However, this was an exception as the seals of other French kings were one-sided, albeit that during this period the practice of countersealing with a smaller seal developed in France. These differences were to some extent linked to how the seals were applied to documents. At the beginning of this period, in both France and Germany, seals were attached to the face of documents *en placard* to authenticate them, whereas in England Edward the Confessor sealed his writs as letters patent *sur simple queue*, which meant that two sides of the seal remained visible and could be impressed.[58] Following Louis VII of France's experimentation with sealing patent and a double-sided seal, French royal seals also had two visible sides. Instead of impressing both sides with an image covering the whole surface the French kings began to counterseal with a small seal, which Bedos-Rezak has seen as accelerating the development of the fleur-de-lys as the heraldic emblem of the French monarchy.[59]

Louis VII's double-sided seal showed the king enthroned on the obverse and had an equestrian portrait on the reverse. On the enthroned side the inscription identifies him as king of the French, and on the equestrian side as duke of the Aquitanians. This enthroned/royal and equestrian/ducal identification is found of the majority of the seals of the kings of England and it is often asserted that in the English context the enthroned side depicts the Anglo-Norman rulers in their guise as kings of England, and the equestrian side as dukes of Normandy.[60] This suggestion is supported by the inscription, which proclaims the king DEI GRATIA REX ANGLORUM on the obverse and DUX NORMANNORUM (with the addition of DUX AQUITANORUM ET COMES ANDEGAVORUM when appropriate) on the reverse. That following his father's divorce from Eleanor of Aquitaine, and thus the loss of the ducal title for the Capetian royal house, Philip Augustus reverted to a seal without the equestrian motif lends further credence to this argument. However, not all the English kings could claim to be dukes of Normandy. William Rufus did not and for part of his reign neither could Henry I. Pierre Chaplais has thus claimed that, 'the equestrian side of William Rufus's seal had no particular meaning, since Rufus had no claim to the duchy of Normandy'.[61] However, whilst the equestrian motif was often linked to a ducal position by inscription, to claim that it had no particular meaning when not associated with rule of a duchy is rather too sweeping an assertion.

As with the enthroned image, the choice of regalia on the equestrian side of the great seal is certainly significant. Hagen Keller has seen the first step in the development of Otto III's seal of an enthroned monarch as taking

---

[58] Heslop, 'English Seals from the Mid-ninth Century to *c*.1100', p. 9.
[59] Bedos-Rezak, 'Suger and the Symbolism of Royal Power: The Seal of Louis VII', p. 97.
[60] *English Royal Documents*, ed. Chaplais, p. 2.
[61] Ibid.

place in the reign of his grandfather Otto I.[62] For Keller the enthroned image was made possible by Otto I's decision to replace the traditional Carolingian image of the half figure of a warrior or victor in profile with a frontal half figure and to replace the shield and lance brandished by the military monarch with a sceptre and orb.[63] In the equestrian depiction on the Conqueror's seal we see the return of the military attributes of a shield and lance. Thus, the double-sided majesty/equestrian seal should not just be understood as representing the royal and ducal authority of the Anglo-Norman monarchs. Certainly, this is an aspect of the meaning in the Anglo-Norman context, but the equestrian motif should also be seen as a statement of martial kingship rather than condemned as meaningless when a ducal title is not present. That the Scottish kings imitated the double-sided seals of the English kings, when they made no claim to a duchy, emphasizes that the division is not as clear-cut as is sometimes suggested. On his 'C' seal Henry I was depicted on the equestrian side brandishing a sword, a feature that was to remain, with one exception, a permanent feature of the equestrian design.[64] In contrast to the sword held by the enthroned monarch on the obverse, it seems fair to consider this sword a 'militaristic' symbol. Here is another example of symbols having different meanings in different contexts, even on two sides of the same seal.

The great seals of the German rulers remained single-sided, but the emperors had an alternative to sealing with wax, which was to use double-sided bulls, made either from lead, or wax covered with gold, or occasionally from solid gold. When a metal *bulla* rather than a wax seal should be used does not seem to have been strictly regulated. They tended to be used for ceremonial diplomas and important political deals and, above all, for correspondence with the Holy See.[65] As we saw with the diploma of Henry VI discussed in the previous chapter, beneficiaries might themselves pay for a golden bull to be affixed to an important document. The use of such seals on letters sent to the popes, who also sealed with two-sided metal *bullae*, can be seen as a clear sigillographic statement that the German monarchs considered themselves to be of equal status to the popes. Moreover, the dynamic iconography of the royal and imperial *bullae* drove home this claim. Both surviving royal bulls of Henry IV display the half-figure of the king as a young man in profile. He holds a sceptre topped with a bird (imperial eagle or otherwise) on the obverse; the reverse features a simple architectural motif representing

---

[62] H. Keller, 'Die Siegel und Bullen Ottos III.', in *Europas Mitte um 1000*, ed. H.-M. Hinz and A. Wieczorek (Stuttgart, 2000), pp. 767–73.

[63] Ibid., p. 768.

[64] On his 'C' seal Stephen was depicted with a lance topped with a flag decorated with a cross. This item of regalia is copied from earlier versions of Henry I's seals.

[65] J. Petersohn, *Kaisertum und Rom in spätsalischer und staufischer Zeit* (Hannover, 2010), p. 344.

Inauguration and Liturgical Kingship

Rome.[66] That the architectural representation of Rome is present on both royal and imperial bulls is indicative of the relevance of the city to the German monarchs as kings as well as emperors. Indeed, that royal power was also linked to Rome is made manifest in the rhyming inscription on the reverse of German *bullae*, which reads ROMA CAPUT MUNDI REGIT ORBIS FRENA ROTUNDI. Thus, even before Henry V introduced the title *Romanorum rex* onto the obverse of his seal, the claim to rulership over the Romans was already clearly announced on royal bulls, in a phrase that emphasized the idea of the continuity of the Roman Empire and that had been used since the time of Conrad II.[67]

The city design, which appeared on all the bulls of German kings and emperors, developed throughout this period. Following Henry IV the next known imperial bull with a Rome motif is a bull of Lothar III. On the obverse, the emperor is depicted in half-figure behind the walls of a city. He is crowned and holding items of insignia. On the reverse are diamond shaped walls and a building with five towers. Each tower incorporates one letter of the word 'AUREA' and the word 'ROMA' is found in the gateway, making clear that the city is Rome. Emanuel Klinkenberg has explained how the five towers are characteristics of the New Jerusalem. Four of the towers represent the four corners of the heavenly city, and the fifth tower, in the middle and adorned with a cross, represents Christ.[68] Lothar, depicted within the walls of the eternal city, is thus depicted ruling his terrestrial empire as an analogue of Christ reigning in the heavenly Jerusalem. For the first time on the royal bull of Frederick Barbarossa it is possible to identify an actual building – the Colosseum.[69] On the matrix for Barbarossa's imperial bull, completed before his departure for Rome in 1154, only the inscription was changed. This depiction of an identifiable building from ancient Rome emphasizes the claim of the German monarchs to be the heirs of the Roman emperors. As Jürgen Petersohn has commented, this was a traditional claim, but in depicting an actual historical building on his *bulla* Barbarossa made clear that his claims to the empire were not merely based on a schematic idea, but the real historical

---

[66] Emanuel Klinkenberg has pointed to the similarity in the depiction of Rome on the *bullae* of Henry IV and Pope Victor II (1055–57). E. S. Klinkenberg, 'Romdarstellung auf Kaiser- und Königsbullen, 800–1250', in *Mikroarchitektur im Mittelalter: Ein gattungsübergreifendes Phänomen zwischen Realität und Imagination*, ed. C. Kratze and U. Albrecht (Leipzig, 2008), pp. 225–49 (p. 233).

[67] Ibid., p. 231; Petersohn, *Kaisertum und Rom*, p. 344.

[68] Klinkenberg suggests that Old St Peter's basilica can be identified on Henry IV's bull and the Lateran on Lothar's bull. These are plausible ideas but, following Petersohn's comments about identifying insignia from medieval images, not ones that I think can be accepted as concrete fact. Klinkenberg, 'Romdarstellung auf Kaiser- und Königsbullen', pp. 233–5.

[69] Ibid., p. 235.

Rome, in which buildings such as the Colosseum acted as a witness to the city's antique past.[70]

In choosing an antique motif for the depiction of Rome on all his *bullae*, a motif that was adopted, to all intents and purposes unchanged, by his son Henry VI, Barbarossa made clear that his claim to rule Rome was not dependent on papal approval or coronation. Indeed, in being depicted on the obverse of his bull, as Lothar III had been, as a crowned figure holding items of insignia within the city walls, Barbarossa figuratively took possession of the city and countered papal claims to have a monopoly on the use of these items of regalia within the city walls.[71] Although Henry VI adopted the depiction of the Colosseum from his father's *bullae*, he made a striking change to the design on the obverse. On the obverse of Henry VI's imperial *bulla* he was depicted enthroned in majesty, crowned, wearing ornate robes and clasping a sceptre in his right hand and an orb in his left. This innovation must be understood as an iconographical retaliation to papal claims, in the same way that the emphasis on Rome is demonstrative of the *Titelpolitik* of the popes and German monarchs. Previously, correspondence with the Holy See had not been authenticated with the image of the king or emperor in majesty. In deploying the iconography of Christomimetic kingship on his imperial *bulla*, a practice continued by his successors, Henry VI made clear that despite papal arguments to the contrary, the German kings and emperors perceived themselves as *Christi Domini*, ruling in the image of Christ the King.

Seal usage, at first the sole prerogative of consecrated monarchs, soon spread from the king to other members of the royal family, such as designated kings and to queens, and several differences between the practices of the three monarchies can be identified. In the French context Louis VI seems to have been unique in having a seal as an associated king. His seal was of the equestrian design and bore the legend, SIGILLUM LUDOVICI DESIGNATI REGISI, whereas later prospective kings used seals that were linked to their current territorial lordship rather than their future position as king.[72] The enthroned image was reserved for consecrated kings and symbolized their transformation, thus the motif could not be adopted by kings in waiting. It could be used by associate kings who had been inaugurated, as we saw with the seal of Henry the Young King. However, importantly, the Young King's seal was only one-sided, a clear manifestation of his lack of independent authority. The seal from the minority of Alexander III of Scotland was, by

---

[70] Petersohn, *Kaisertum und Rom*, p. 345.
[71] A claim famously made by Gregory VII in his *Dictatus Papae*.
[72] B. Bedos-Rezak, 'Ritual in the Royal Chancery: Text, Image, and the Representation of Kingship in Medieval French Diplomas (700–1200)', in *European Monarchy: Its Evolution and Practice from Roman Antiquity to Modern Times*, ed. H. Duchhardt, R. A. Jackson and D. Sturdy (Stuttgart, 1992), pp. 27–40 (p. 39); *Les Sceaux des rois et de régence*, ed. Dalas, p. 144.

contrast, two-sided. However, the reverse of the seal does not have the usual equestrian portrait, instead depicting a shield with the royal arms of Scotland, a motif that was also adopted following Alexander's death when the kingdom was ruled by a body of guardians.[73] Nicholas Vincent has highlighted a similar phenomenon in England, pointing to a seal used by Henry III in Gascony in 1253, which had an equestrian figure on one side and a shield of arms on the other.[74] This perhaps provided the model for the shield of arms found on the reverse of the surviving gold bull of Henry's son Edmund as King of Sicily, on which Edmund is described as EDMUNDUS NATUS REGIS ANGLIE ILLUSTRIS. Edmund, whose kingship of Sicily was never a reality, is depicted in the traditional enthroned form on the obverse of this *bulla*. However, Sicilian *bullae*, like those of the German kings and emperors had diverse images on the reverse. Those of Frederick II feature, for example, a castle representing the kingdom, while the reverse of a later bull takes the form of a map.

Henry III's use of a shield of arms was echoed in the development of a separate design for the Exchequer seal. The *Dialogus de Scaccario* suggests that originally a duplicate of the great seal was used, but the earliest surviving impression of an Exchequer seal, from the reign of Edward I, depicts the king mounted on the obverse and has the royal arms on the reverse.[75] As in the case of Alexander III's minority, here the exercise of royal power by people other than the king was indicated in seal iconography by the use of non-personal objects. The iconography of Christomimetic kingship was reserved for the figure of the king himself and was evidently not considered suitable in an institutional context. This use of non-figurative symbolism finds an echo in the French seal of regency of Louis IX. This seal, of which only one cast survives, was used by Louis's regents, Matthew de Vendôme and Simon de Nesle, following the king's departure from Paris on 15 March 1270.[76] On the obverse of the seal a crown is depicted, surmounted with three fleur-de-lys-shaped prongs and decorated with precious stones. The inscription runs + S LUDOVICI DEI GRATIA FRANCORUM REGIS IN PARTIBUS TRANSMARINIS AGENTIS. In keeping with other French royal seals, it is countersealed with a shield adorned with a pattern of fleurs-de-lys. Clearly a crown is being used here as a symbol of royal power, but I would suggest we can identify other resonances, which explain the choice of this symbol. Most simply, the fleur-de-lys prongs,

---

[73] Simpson, 'Kingship in Miniature', p. 137.
[74] N. Vincent, *The Magna Carta* (New York, 2007), p. 25.
[75] The 'royal seal' is mentioned several times by Richard fitz Nigel: *Dialogus de Scaccario*, ed. Amt, 28, 38, 52, 94–6; Harvey and McGuinness, *A Guide to British Medieval Seals*, p. 38. Vincent has pointed to fragmentary Exchequer seals from the reign of Henry III displaying the same devices: Vincent, *The Magna Carta*, p. 25.
[76] *Les Sceaux des rois et de régence*, ed. Dalas, p. 158. Following Louis's death, the two regents continued to use the seal having changed the name in the inscription from Louis to Philip.

in conjunction with the patterned shield counterseal give the symbol Marian associations. More than this, however, the crown on Louis's regency seal makes Christological allusions. The crown is depicted encircled by an architectural motif, echoing the Gothic style of the Sainte-Chapelle, the monument built by Louis to house his most precious relics. This crown is an item of regalia, but one that consciously makes reference to Louis's possession of the Crown of Thorns. The architectural motif has eight niches, with eight being a number associated in architecture with the Temple.[77] Daniel Weiss has drawn attention to the fact that the architectural programme of the Sainte-Chapelle was intended to equate the building with the Temple and hence to draw a further link between the Passion relics and the Ark of the Covenant.[78] In Louis IX's use of a crown on the seal to be used while he was absent fighting for the Holy Land we can see precisely the depth of meaning and the sacred associations that made the crown such an attractive symbol to medieval kings. We should not divorce royal and liturgical resonances: the crown was not a simple secular symbol of state power, but rather a leading motif in the iconographic canon of liturgical kingship.

Queenly Sealing

When Philip Augustus left France to go on the Third Crusade his regents, who were his mother, Adela of Champagne, and Guillaume, the archbishop of Reims, also used a seal of regency. This seal was very similar to Philip's great seal, which he took with him on Crusade.[79] The obverse shows the king enthroned in traditional Capetian style; the most apparent difference from the king's own seal was the counterseal in the form of an eagle. However, the very fact that Philip had a special royal seal of absence made, rather than, for example, empowering the queen dowager's seal, is indicative of the fact that the seals of queens in France were limited to their personal affairs. Bertrada of Montfort was the first French queen to have a seal from c.1115, but significantly this was used in her capacity as a dowager queen, for her personal affairs, rather than for royal matters.[80] Eleanor of Aquitaine was the first

---

[77] Madeline Harrison Caviness has pointed to the importance of this kind of symbolism in medieval art. For example, there are many medieval buildings that viewers claimed to be imitations of the Holy Sepulchre when they varied massively in composition. What was important was less the original form than an essential similarity, which could be numerical or conceptual. Caviness, 'Reception of Images by Medieval Viewers', p. 67.
[78] D. H. Weiss, 'Architectural Symbolism and the Decoration of the Ste.-Chapelle', *The Art Bulletin* 77 (1995), 308–20 (p. 318).
[79] *Les sceaux des rois et de régence*, ed. Dalas, p. 152.
[80] S. M. Johns, *Noblewomen, Aristocracy and Power in the Twelfth-Century Anglo-Norman Realm* (Manchester, 2003), p. 125.

reigning French consort to seal, but she used her seal exclusively in matters concerning the management of her duchy.[81] Bertrada of Montfort and Eleanor of Aquitaine's constrained use of sealing has led, as Kathleen Nolan has commented, to a tendency 'to diminish the significance of reginal use of seals, and to reinforce the private versus public dichotomy that has often been used to marginalize women's authority'.[82] However, it is surely remarkable that, in the early twelfth century, when sealing was not a widespread practice, these women used seals at all. Rather than consider queenly sealing as something diminished by the fact of its distance from the practice of power, we might instead wonder what the depictions of queens on their seals can tell us about the image of royalty.

Susan Johns has indicated some of the issues that arise in any attempt to study female seals, commenting that, 'there is a need to be aware of the ambiguities inherent in female power, the impact of the female life cycle upon that power, and thus the conflicting, and possibly competing, multiple identities and contexts of power'.[83] Bertrada is depicted austerely dressed, standing, wearing a crown and holding a fleur-de-lys in one hand and a bird on her other wrist. This has been interpreted by Nolan as a dowager queen, estranged from court, recalling for strategic purposes her queenship through the use of royal symbols. It is possible, however, to interpret this iconography in a different way. By the time of this seal's production Bertrada had taken the veil at Fontevraud Abbey. In addition to her royal status, the crown could also be seen as alluding to her role as Christ's bride, symbolized in the ceremony in which she became a nun through the bestowal of both a ring and a crown. As we have seen in our discussion of female inauguration liturgies there were striking similarities between the queenly and religious rites and such parallels are also evident in seal design. Moreover, at the time of the production of Bertrada's seal, the fleur-de-lys as an item of insignia in its own right was not a feature of French kingly seals. Rather than focusing on its royal attributes, we might rather think of its Marian associations, which would have made it a particularly appropriate symbol for a member of a community dedicated to the Virgin. In England, the seal of Matilda of Scotland, wife of Henry I, is the earliest surviving seal of a queen. The seal is similar in general to that of her sister-in-law, the abbess of Caen, and depicts the queen standing, crowned and holding a sceptre, topped with a bird, and an orb.[84] These examples remind us of the fact that it is unwise to draw too definite a division between religious and royal imagery.

The seals of queens in England and France had a distinctive 'vesica' shape, which has been seen as a format that emphasizes female identity.[85] However,

---

[81] Bedos-Rezak, 'Ritual in the Royal Chancery', p. 39.
[82] Nolan, 'The Tomb of Adelaide of Maurienne', p. 56.
[83] Johns, *Noblewomen, Aristocracy and Power*, p. 124.
[84] Heslop, 'Seals', p. 305.
[85] Nolan, 'The Tomb of Adelaide of Maurienne', p. 59; Johns, *Noblewomen, Aristocracy*

conventual and monastic seals could also take this form. The reason for the shape is unclear, with the consensus suggesting that it was merely because standing figures required the proportions of the pointed oval. In this period, there are only two examples of a king's seal having this shape and they are both seals of Frederick II. The first, his first seal as king of Sicily, is in direct imitation of the seal of his mother (Constance of Sicily), thereby stressing the dynastic credentials of the boy king. The second is a seal of similar design dating from 1212, on which Frederick is described as REX ROMANORUM ELECTUS.[86] Here the reason for the eschewal of the traditional circular shape of a king's seal is perhaps recognition of the fact that, although he had been elected, until he had been consecrated king Frederick could not be presented as one on his seal.[87] On both these seals Frederick is depicted enthroned, demonstrating that vesica shape and seated figures were not necessarily mutually exclusive.

In contrast to English and French custom, the seals of queens and empresses in the Empire were circular in form. This reflected a difference in iconography for, rather than standing, the German queens and empresses were depicted enthroned. It used to be thought that queenly sealing in Germany was attested to a century before it was found in England and France, but more recent scholarship has actually shown that queenly seal usage only became established in the Empire in the mid-twelfth century. In his catalogue, Posse included a seal for the Empress Kunegunde, the wife of Emperor Henry II, but this is now known to be a late medieval medallion, a trinket associated with Kunegunde's saintly cult.[88] Andrea Stieldorf has examined the evidence for queenly sealing in the Empire and suggests that both Theophanu, wife of Otto II, and Agnes, wife of Henry III, used seals in their role as regents.[89] However, there is no evidence that either of Henry IV's wives sealed in their own right and a seal of Matilda, wife of Henry V, is thus the oldest surviving seal of a German queen.[90] Following Matilda there is no evidence that the wives of Lothar III or Conrad III had seals. Soon after his marriage to Beatrix of Burgundy, Frederick Barbarossa wrote to his former chancellor Wibald of Stablo and asked him to have a seal matrix made for his new wife, and from this time onwards continuous evidence for queenly seal usage survives.[91]

---

and Power, p. 127; E. Danbury, 'Queens and Powerful Women: Image and Authority', in *Good Impressions: Image and Authority in Medieval Seals*, ed. N. Adams, J. Cherry and J. Robinson (London, 2008), pp. 17–24 (p. 17).

[86] *Die Siegel der deutschen Kaiser und Könige*, ed. Posse, V, 27.
[87] Between his use of vesica-shaped seals in Sicily and Germany Frederick had used the traditional circular format in Sicily.
[88] *Die Siegel der deutschen Kaiser und Könige*, ed. Posse, V, 18.
[89] Stieldorf, 'Die Siegel der Herrscherinnen', pp. 2–4.
[90] Ibid., p. 5.
[91] Ibid., p. 11. Josef Deér has suggested that the same goldsmith made Beatrix's seal matrix as made all four of Frederick's matrices and also the arm reliquary that Frederick and Beatrix gave to Aachen on the occasion of Charlemagne's

Significantly, however, this usage seems to have been confined to issuing and sealing documents of a 'private' character, so that Stieldorf speaks of the 'diplomatic abstinence' of German queens, despite their important role in royal government.[92]

The impression of Matilda's seal first survives in England, but was almost certainly deployed in Germany in 1117/18, meaning that its original design should not be seen in the context of the English anarchy but instead within imperial politics.[93] As we do not know what the seals of Theophanu or Agnes looked like, we cannot know whether the design of Matilda's seal was an early twelfth-century innovation or whether it simply followed imperial precedent. However, the enthroned design for queenly seals endured in the Empire for the next two and a half centuries, another indication that Matilda's seal should be considered in an imperial rather than English context. As there was no iconographic precedent for worldly queens being depicted enthroned Stieldorf sees the design as an analogue of the king's seal.[94] She further suggests that in choosing to mimic her husband's enthroned seal rather than the standing seal of her mother, Matilda of Scotland, Matilda demonstrated her enhanced rank. In this interpretation, the queen's seal was thus a way of stressing the higher rank of the German emperors over neighbouring monarchs and their equality with Byzantium.[95]

Despite Matilda's continued use of the enthroned seal after her departure from Germany following the death of her husband, the design had no impact on subsequent queenly seals in England. The unusualness of the seal in an English context has led historians to see this seal as a statement of her claim to English royal authority. Susan Johns, for example, considers the seal to express 'the authority of the state, and [Matilda's] regalia leave this in no doubt: her seal of 1141–42, critical years in the civil war, depicts her enthroned and holding the sceptre – royal insignia designating royal power'.[96] The royal association is, however, but one facet of the imagery here. As Elizabeth Danbury has noted, 'an enthroned, crowned woman on seals after 1100 in England, as in France, almost invariably represented not an earthly sovereign, but the Virgin Mary'.[97] I would argue that this is exactly the connection that the German queenly seals expected the viewer to make. While Stieldorf is absolutely right to point to the lack of iconographic precedent for terrestrial queens being depicted enthroned, the image of celestial queenship was often

---

canonization in 1165. J. Deér, 'Die Siegel Kaiser Friedrichs I. Barbarossa und Heinrichs VI. in der Kunst und Politik ihrer Zeit', in *Festschrift Hans P. Hahnloser*, ed. E. J. Beer, P. Hofer and L. Mojon (Basel, 1961), pp. 47–102 (pp. 54–5, 67).

[92] Stieldorf, 'Die Siegel der Herrscherinnen', p. 10.
[93] Ibid, p. 15.
[94] Ibid, p. 12.
[95] Ibid., pp. 15–16.
[96] Johns, *Noblewomen, Aristocracy and Power*, p. 126.
[97] Danbury, 'Queens and Powerful Women', p. 18.

represented in this manner. Just as the enthroned image of the king, recalling that of Christ in majesty, made clear the king's claims to rule in Christ's image, so the imagery of these female seals made apparent that the terrestrial queen was made in the image of the Queen of Heaven. Stieldorf argues that the seals of the German queens were orientated towards that of their husbands both in their iconography and in their inscriptions and they thus served as a mode of representation for the king too.[98] This interlinking of male and female imagery is precisely why Marian iconography was so attractive to medieval kings, as Laynesmith's work on English queenship in the later Middle Ages has demonstrated.[99]

Although queens in England and France did not adopt the German enthroned motif, their seals abound with Marian symbolism. The fleur-de-lys is found on seals from all three realms, emphasizing that it was not exclusively a Capetian attribute. In the Empire it is to be found on seals belonging to Constance, wife of Henry VI, Maria, second wife of Otto IV, and of Margaret, wife of Henry (VII). In England it is found on the seal of Matilda of Boulogne, wife of King Stephen. John's second wife, Isabella of Angoulême holds a lily rather than the stylized fleur-de-lys. A fleur-de-lys is also to be found on the unusual seal of Henry II's daughter Joanna. Following the death of her first husband William of Sicily, Joanna married the Count of Toulouse. She used a two-sided vesica-shaped seal.[100] On the obverse she is depicted seated and holding a decorated cross and the legend describes her as Duchess of Barr, Countess of Toulouse and Marchioness of Provence. On the other side she is depicted standing, crowned holding a fleur-de-lys. Although she was a queen through her marriage to William, the inscription links her queenship to her father Henry II: +S REGINE IOH'E FILIA QVONDAM h REGIS ANGLORUM.[101] In any case, the deployment of a fleur-de-lys was not the only way to allude to the Virgin. In a study of twelfth-century English seals depicting Mary as a queen, Sandy Heslop has argued that sceptres and rods should not be seen as exclusively royal symbols. Heslop took his evidence from the seals of monastic and cathedral chapters whose churches were dedicated to Mary, and concluded that 'it is on seals … where the attributes are dissociated from queenship that it is most apparent that the rod, for example, is not simply an item of regalia but that it has a prophetic typological significance'.[102] When we find sceptres associated with queenship on royal seals, we should not dissociate them from their inherent Marian symbolism, which would have been apparent to contemporaries. We

---

[98] Stieldorf, 'Die Siegel der Herrscherinnen', pp. 30–1.
[99] Laynesmith, *The Last Medieval Queens*, p. 30.
[100] The matrix for this seal survives and is in the collection of the British Museum (P&E 1897, 5–8, 1&2).
[101] Danbury, 'Queens and Powerful Women', p. 22.
[102] Heslop, 'The Virgin Mary's Regalia and Twelfth-Century English Seals', p. 59.

should see reginal sigillography both making a direct statement about the queen transformed by inauguration and also an indirect statement drawing a parallel with Mary enthroned.

Like the seals of their royal husbands, female seals proclaimed that their owners were queens *Dei gratia*. The use in all three realms of the enthroned majesty design for male seals is demonstrative of the shared imagery of Christomimetic kingship, which presented kings as ruling by the grace of God. Bedos-Rezak has pointed to a metaphor used to explain the idea expounded in Genesis 1. 26–7, of man being created in the image and resemblance of God, in which man is described as a seal impression, imprinted by Christ.[103] That the monarchs of England, France and Germany considered their kingship to be based on their resemblance to Christ and their position as God's representatives on earth, despite opposition from the papacy, is made apparent in the manner in which they impressed their image onto the documents authenticated by their seals and *bullae*. Indeed, Henry VI's adoption of the enthroned motif for his *bulla* is demonstrative of an attempt to stress the Christ-like nature of his kingship, in direct response to papal attempts to assert the inferiority of kings to bishops. The growth of queenly sealing, and the Marian imagery found on queenly seals, particularly within the Empire, can be seen as another facet of a wider response. The imagery on royal and imperial seals played on the multiplicity of associations attached to medieval symbols to present a monarch transformed through inauguration into a Christ-like king whose bride was depicted as the celestial Queen.

---

[103] B. Bedos-Rezak, 'In Search of a Semiotic Paradigm: The Matter of Sealing in Medieval Thought and Praxis (1050–1400)', in *Good Impressions: Image and Authority in Medieval Seals*, ed. N. Adams, J. Cherry and J. Robinson (London, 2008), pp. 1–7 (p. 3).

Conclusion

In a 1982 essay on twelfth-century kings and kingship, Karl Leyser commented that 'the most common characteristic of twelfth-century rulers ... seems to have been chicanery'.[1] Thirty-five years later few scholars would disagree with his assessment that deceit and subterfuge were indeed hallmarks of high medieval kingship. Leyser provides as an example of such deviousness the advice that the Empress Matilda apparently gave to her son Henry II. To paraphrase Walter Map, who disapproved of Henry's man-management techniques, Matilda advised Henry to treat his followers mean to keep them keen.[2] Prone to fits of unspeakable rage, Henry II hardly cuts a figure sympathetic to modern sensibilities.[3] However, like many duplicitous men, Henry could be charming too. This charm was often in evidence in Henry's interactions with his monarchical counterparts. At his obsequious best, the Plantagenet could be a model of humility, stressing his subservience to his Capetian and Hohenstaufen contemporaries in such honeyed terms that it is not just modern historians who doubt his sincerity.[4]

The fawning letter that Henry II sent to Frederick Barbarossa in 1157 has been the subject of much scholarship. Until the 1960s, scholars accepted Henry's flattery at face value and the letter was held up as the ultimate example of the power and influence a medieval German emperor could

---

[1] K. Leyser, 'Some Reflections of Twelfth-Century Kings and Kingship', in *Medieval Germany and its Neighbours 900–1250* (London, 1982), pp. 241–67 (p. 253).

[2] Walter Map, *De nugis curialium*, ed. M. R. James et al., OMT (Oxford, 1983), pp. 478–9.

[3] The importance of the *ira regis* was highlighted by Jolliffe in the 1950s: J. E. A. Jolliffe, *Angevin Kingship*, 2nd edn (London, 1963), pp. 97–109. Jolliffe's work has been mediated by historians interested in the history of emotions. See, for example, the essays in B. H. Rosenwein, ed., *Anger's Past: The Social Uses of an Emotion in the Middle Ages* (Ithaca, 1998).

[4] John Gillingham has commented that using obsequious words was part of Henry's 'habitual style ... a kind of deference that sometimes crossed the line between courtesy and hypocrisy'. J. Gillingham, 'Doing Homage to the King of France', in *Henry II: New Interpretations*, ed. C. Harper-Bill and N. Vincent (Woodbridge, 2007), pp. 63–84 (p. 73). Gillingham has also drawn attention to the fact that a number of Henry's contemporaries, including Thomas Becket and Hubert of Bosham, saw Henry's obsequiousness as a way of tricking the more simple-minded (including Louis VII). See J. Gillingham, 'The Meetings of the Kings of France and England, 1066–1204', in *Normandy and Its Neighbours, 900–1250: Essays for David Bates*, ed. D. Crouch (Turnhout, 2011), pp. 17–42 (pp. 41–2).

exercise over kings in neighbouring lands.[5] It is easy to understand why it became, as Leyser described it, 'the crown-witness for the view that the *imperium* had, if not a direct lordship, at least some kind of indefinable ascendancy over all the *regna*'.[6] Henry, in most deferential terms, claimed that he would do whatever Frederick desired. Except, of course, as Leyser pointed out, Henry refused to do the one thing that Frederick did actually want: for the king to hand over the Hand of Saint James. Brought from Germany to England by Henry's mother the Empress Matilda, the relic was to stay at his grandfather's foundation at Reading. That a relic of the Apostle James was the subject of twelfth-century monarchical diplomacy serves to remind us of the extent to which liturgical and political concerns intermingled. Relics provided a material focus for liturgical ceremonial and, as we have seen in chapters 3 and 4, commemoration of the Apostle James was intertwined with royal ritual within the Empire on more than one occasion. It took on increasing importance in the twelfth century due to James's association with Charlemagne and crusading.[7]

At the peace conference of Montmirail held on Epiphany 1169, at which Henry did homage to Louis VII, the Plantagenet king, according to William of Canterbury, flattered the Capetian monarch by exploiting the liturgical resonances of the feast day.[8] Henry likened his act of homage to Louis to the magi offering gifts to Christ the King.[9] As we have seen, Epiphany was a feast particularly resonant with royal imagery and, although we might well doubt Henry's motives, it is important to recognize that he characterizes Louis's kingship, and by extension his own, as being Christomimetic. As Henry's interactions with his fellow monarchs demonstrate, chicanery and a Christomimetic image of kingship were no more mutually exclusive than were liturgy and law, or liturgy and bureaucracy. Moreover, all three rulers manifestly understood, to some extent, the language of 'political theology', to employ Kantorowicz's term.

---

[5] Both Mayer and Leyser challenged this interpretation: H. E. Mayer, 'Staufische Weltherrschaft? Zum Brief Heinrichs II. von England an Friedrich Barbarossa von 1157', in *Festschrift Karl Pivec*, ed. A. Haidacher and H. E. Mayer, Innsbrucker Beiträge zur Kulturwissenschaft 12 (Innsbruck, 1966), pp. 265–78; K. Leyser, 'Frederick Barbarossa, Henry II and the Hand of St. James', in *Medieval Germany and its Neighbours, 900–1250* (London, 1982), pp. 215–40.

[6] Leyser, 'Frederick Barbarossa, Henry II and the Hand of St. James', p. 217.

[7] Stuckey, 'Charlemagne as Crusader?'.

[8] I thank John Gillingham for bringing this reference to my attention. He has discussed the Montmirail peace conference in Gillingham, 'Doing Homage' and Gillingham, 'The Meetings of the Kings of France and England'.

[9] 'Et ait, "Hac die, domine rex, qua tres reges Regi regum munera obtulerunt" (erat enim dies Epiphaniarum) "me ipsum, natos meos, et terram vestrae commendo custodiae"'. William of Canterbury, *Vita et Passio sancti Thomae*, in *Materials for the History of Thomas Becket*, ed. J. C. Robertson and J. B. Sheppard, 7 vols. (London, 1875–85), I, 73.

Conclusion

The aim of this book has not been, to borrow Timothy Reuter's words, 'to practice a frivolous revisionism by trying to show that German kingship in the high Middle Ages was just like that practiced elsewhere'.[10] The Plantagenets were not simply 'Ottonians with pipe rolls' as others have rightly pointed out.[11] This study has stressed the similarities in the concept of kingship in all three realms, indeed, the very structure of the comparison inherently, and not entirely unintentionally, prioritized the discovery of shared cultural and political impulses.[12] Nonetheless, some differences have also been identified, particularly in diplomatic practice, and no claim has been made about similarities in the exercise of kingship. Shared monarchical imagery did not dictate that political realities were identical. Indeed, Reuter rightly cautioned that the *ordines* 'resemble each other much more than did the polities in which they were used'.[13] However, this study has demonstrated that the *ordines* were not just a static bundle of texts, but also influenced political cultures so that the term 'liturgical kingship' can rightly be used to describe facets of kingship in all three realms. This is not to say that there were not subtle differences in the manner in which the liturgy coloured kingship in the three polities, or indeed during the reigns of successive monarchs within the same realm. While the evidence of the *ordines*, narrative texts and, to an extent, diplomatic materials, points to a shared liturgical framework, this scaffolding could be adapted to national and personal contexts, as we saw in, for example, the saints included in litanies and *laudes*. Indeed, from the mid-thirteenth century the *ordines* in all three realms increasingly incorporated realm-specific details (i.e. the use of the Holy Ampoule in France), which was in part a symptom of the kind of codification of liturgy that the imperial rite had been subjected to in the twelfth century.

I argued in chapters 1 and 2 that the increasingly detailed and prescriptive iterations of the imperial rite were a manifestation of papal attempts to diminish the position of the emperor. Certainly such changes to the imperial rite were interpreted in this way within the Empire, as the famous Besançon incident of October 1157 makes apparent.[14] Frederick rejected Hadrian IV's

---

[10] Reuter, 'The Medieval German *Sonderweg*', pp. 389–90.

[11] A phrase coined by Nicholas Vincent and subsequently discussed by Björn Weiler and Charles Insley: N. Vincent, 'The Pilgrimages', p. 40; B. K. Weiler, 'Review Article: Power and Politics in Medieval History, c.850–c.1170', Early Medieval Europe 16 (2008), 477–93 (p. 490); C. Insley, 'Ottonians with Pipe Rolls? Political Culture and Performance in the Kingdom of the English, c. 900–c.1050', History 102 (2017), 772–86.

[12] Comparative studies tend to fall into two camps: one of which emphasizes similarities and one of which stresses differences. As Nancy Green has commented, 'most comparative projects seem motivated by one approach or the other'. N. L. Green, 'Forms of Comparison', in *Comparison and History: Europe in Cross-National Perspective*, ed. D. Cohen and M. O'Connor (New York, 2004), pp. 41–56 (p. 43).

[13] Reuter, 'The Medieval German *Sonderweg*', p. 410.

[14] Much scholarly ink has been spilled discussing the events at Besançon and, as John Freed has pointed out, whether a scholar is sympathetic to the pope or the emperor

claim, presented by the papal legates Roland, cardinal priest of S. Marco (and later Pope Alexander III), and Bernard, cardinal priest of S. Clemente, that he held the Empire from the pope.[15] In a letter that he deliberately circulated widely within the Empire, and which Rahewin incorporated into the *Gesta Frederici*, Frederick declared:

> With divine power, from which all power in heaven and earth is derived, he has entrusted us, his anointed, the rule of the kingdom and empire and has ordained that the peace of the churches be conserved by the arms of the empire.[16]

The pope, Frederick argued, was not the source of his authority, but God himself. Despite papal attempts to reduce the status of royal unction, Barbarossa describes himself as God's anointed. The vocabulary used to express this sentiment is telling: Frederick is *Christus eius*. He is anointed like Christ and claims to govern the terrestrial empire in imitation of Christ's rule of the celestial kingdom. Frederick also objected to papal attempts to portray the act of imperial coronation as representative of a terrestrial hierarchy. The papal interpretation of coronation was enshrined in a provocative fresco in the Lateran, which depicted Lothar III receiving a crown from Innocent II.[17] Rahewin reports that this image was accompanied by a couplet reading: 'the king comes before the gates, swearing before the honour of Rome / afterwards he is made the Pope's man, from whom he accepts the proffered crown'.[18] The emperor and his vassals did not accept that coronation made the monarch the 'pope's man' and indeed, in their letter to Pope Hadrian in the spring following the court at Besançon the German bishops voiced their disagreement with the image of kingship embodied in this fresco and in the pope's epistle.[19]

---

is often indicative of their own confessional loyalties. See J. B. Freed, *Frederick Barbarossa: The Prince and The Myth* (New Haven, 2016), p. 205.

[15] Much of the outrage has centred on Rainald of Dassel's translation of the word *beneficium* to mean 'fief'. Hadrian would later claim he meant it in the sense of 'good deed'. See the discussion of this word in Freed, *Frederick Barbarossa*, pp. 204–5. Cf. R. L. Benson, 'The Clash at Besançon (October 1157), in *Law, Rulership and Rhetoric: Selected Essays of Robert L. Benson*, ed. L. J. Weber (Notre Dame, 2014), pp. 262–92.

[16] 'Cum divina potentia, a qua omnis potestas in caelo et in terra, nobis Christo eius regnum et imperium regendum commiserit et pacem aecclesiarum imperialibus armis conservandam ordinaverit.' *Ottonis et Rahewini Gesta Frederici*, p. 178.

[17] See Robinson, *The Papacy*, pp. 452–3; A. J. Duggan, '"Totius christianitatis caput": The Pope and the Princes', in *Adrian IV: The English Pope (1154–1159)*, ed. B. Bolton and A. J. Duggan (Aldershot, 2003), pp. 105–55 (pp. 131–2).

[18] *Ottonis et Rahewini Gesta Frederici I. Imperatoris*, p. 177: 'Rex venit ante fores, iurans prius Urbis honores, / Post homo fit papae, sumit quo dante coronam'.

[19] Ibid., pp. 188–9. 'a pictura cepit, ad scripturam pictura processit, scriptura in auctoritatem prodire conatur. Non patiemur, non sustinebimus; coronam ante ponemus, quam imperii coronam una nobiscum sic deponi consentiamus. Picturae deleantur, scripturae retractentur, ut inter regnum et sacerdotiam aeterna inimiciciarum

Conclusion

The Besançon incident highlights two important and related issues: those of the reception and the contestation of inauguration rituals. Indeed, the very concept of ritual has itself been contested in recent decades.[20] However, the medieval actors in inauguration rites were aware of the dangers of ritual well before Philippe Buc reminded modern historians of their potential pitfalls, as Henry VI's reaction to ceremonial innovation at his imperial inauguration demonstrates. In initial negotiations with Clement III to secure the imperial inauguration of his son, Frederick Barbarossa had been adamant that the ceremony should be traditional.[21] When, following Clement's death, Celestine III proffered an orb during the ceremony, Henry withdrew to consult his advisors before accepting it, lest his receiving the orb prejudice his position in some way.[22] Likewise, the two surviving descriptions of Frederick Barbarossa's imperial inauguration, which I have discussed in detail elsewhere, are exemplary witnesses to Buc's warning that 'the written sources in which historians find rituals often can aim at the obfuscation of the ritual act's original meaning and serve polemics more than consensus'.[23] It is no surprise that the version of events found in Otto of Freising's *Gesta Friderici* does not exactly align with that found in Cardinal Boso's *vita* of Hadrian IV.[24] Here we could hardly expect consensus.

In the context of this study it is no coincidence that we find the imperial rite, with its competing participants, to have been contested far more frequently and intensely than the royal rite. Indeed, the relative looseness of the liturgical texts and the lack of detail in the narrative sources concerning royal inauguration is perhaps indicative of the fact that the ritual of royal consecration was

---

monimenta non remaneant.' See the discussion of this cycle of images in A. Eastmond, '"It Began with a Picture": Imperial Art, Texts and Subversion between East and West in the Twelfth Century', in *Subversion in Byzantium*, ed. D. Angelov and M. Saxby (Farnham, 2013), pp. 121–43 (pp. 127–31).

[20] Buc, *The Dangers of Ritual*; G. Koziol, 'Review Article: The Dangers of Polemic: Is Ritual Still and Interesting Topic of Historical Study', *Early Medieval Europe* 11 (2002), 367–88; P. Buc, 'The Monster and the Critics: A Ritual Reply', *Early Medieval Europe* 15 (2007), 441–52; C. Pössel, 'The Magic of Early Medieval Ritual', *Early Medieval Europe* 17 (2009), 111–25.

[21] Robinson, *The Papacy*, p. 512. I discuss Henry VI's imperial inauguration in Dale, 'Inauguration and Political Liturgy', pp. 210–12.

[22] Robinson, *The Papacy*, p. 510. The letters from Frederick and Henry to Clement, stressing the need to follow antique custom, are numbers 323 and 324 in *Frederici I. Constitutiones*, ed. L. Weiland, *MGH Const.* 1 (Hannover, 1893), pp. 191–463 (pp. 461–3).

[23] Dale, 'Inauguration and Political Liturgy', pp. 197–9; P. Buc, 'Text and Ritual in Ninth-Century Political Culture: Rome 864', in *Medieval Concepts of the Past: Ritual, Memory, Historiography*, ed. G. Althoff, J. Fried and P. J. Geary (Cambridge, 2002), pp. 123–38 (p. 126).

[24] *Ottonis et Rahewini Gesta Frederici I. Imperatoris*, ed. Waitz, p. 140; Cardinal Boso, 'Vita Adriani IV', in *Adrian IV: The English Pope (1154–1159). Studies and Texts*, ed. B. Bolton and A. J. Duggan (Aldershot, 2003), pp. 214–33 (pp. 220–3).

generally uncontested. We infrequently have sufficient evidence to construct the kind of Geertzian 'thick description' that normally characterize studies of medieval ritual.[25] But, as we have seen, elements of an inauguration, such as the celebrant and location, could be and were contested. The event itself and its meaning, however, seldom appear to have been called into question. This chimes with Koziol's argument, that churchmen were more likely to dispute their role within a ceremony than to question the efficacy of the ceremony itself.[26] Likewise, a noble might, like a recalcitrant relative at a modern wedding reception, perceive a real or imagined slight in the seating plan for the post-ceremony banquet, but more often than not he still wanted to partake in festivities.[27] There are, of course, exceptions and chief amongst them is the inauguration of Henry the Young King in 1170, an event that was a flash point in the struggle between Henry II and Thomas Becket and which, after the murder of Becket and the rebellions of the Young King, took on additional significance. Most of our evidence for the Young King's inauguration definitely serves polemics rather than consensus, not least the wonderful miniature of his inauguration from the so-called Becket leaves of c.1220–40.[28] The image is made up of two sections.[29] The right-hand section depicts the Young King being crowned by Roger, archbishop of York, with a caption stating that his actions prejudiced the rights of Canterbury.[30] In the left-hand section Henry II is shown slightly hunched and serving his son at the post-inauguration banquet. A figure holds a scroll, which reads 'Behold majesty very much lowered!', implying that Henry II had debased his own position by his actions and especially by willing having his son crowned by the incorrect celebrant.[31]

Should we see the elaboration and increasing specificity of royal liturgies from the mid-thirteenth century onwards as evidence of the contestation of royal inauguration rituals in the later Middle Ages? Answering that question

---

[25] Geertz, 'Thick Description'.
[26] Koziol, 'England, France and the Problem of Sacrality', p. 127.
[27] On feasts see K. Hauck, 'Rituelle Speisegemeinschaft im 10. und 11. Jahrhundert', *Studium Generale* 3 (1950) and G. Althoff, 'Der frieden-, bündnis- und gemeinschaftstiftende Charakter des Mahles im früheren Mittelalter, in *Essen und Trinken in Mittelalter und Neuzeit*, ed. I. Bitsch, T. Ehlert and X. von Ertzdorff (Sigmaringen, 1987), pp. 13–26; As Althoff has pointed out, absence and non-participation were important forms of expression in medieval political communication. G. Althoff, 'The Variability of Rituals in the Middle Ages', in *Medieval Concepts of the Past: Ritual, Memory, Historiography*, ed. G. Althoff, J. Fried and P. J. Geary (Cambridge, 2002), pp. 71–88 (p. 82).
[28] On the historical and art-historical context of these leaves see J. Backhouse and C. de Hamel, *The Becket Leaves* (London, 1988).
[29] London, British Library Loan MS 88, fol. 3r.
[30] Ibid: 'Coronatur rex heinricus iunior per manum rogeri archiepiscopi Eboracensis, in prejudicium ecclesie Cantuariensis'.
[31] Ibid: 'Ecce maiestas nimis inclinata'.

Conclusion

is beyond the scope of this monograph but increasing elaboration does not have to indicate an erosion of liturgical kingship. Indeed, the inclusion of celebrant and location in later *ordines*, for example, merely reflected long-established custom and should be understood in the context of increasing codification and the desire of ambitious archbishops to cement their status and that of their churches within the rite. Clerical participation in royal liturgies was a way of advancing the interests of the clerics themselves and of the institutions they served. While it has not been possible to do justice to the ecclesiastical dimension in this book, it is an area that would certainly benefit from further research. It seems likely that, as the mechanisms of elective monarchy developed within the Empire, the German experience began to diverge from the Anglo-French. Indeed, the 1356 Golden Bull, which outlined the process of election and inauguration in breathtaking detail, was certainly a product of contestation.[32] However, it is important to recognize that what was being disputed was the role of the princes (both ecclesiastical and lay) in the electoral process and the inauguration ceremony: the status of inauguration itself was not at stake and, indeed, Charles IV was as adept at exploiting the resonances of the liturgy as any of his imperial predecessors.

Lay and ecclesiastical participation in inauguration liturgies is closely linked to the issue of reception. Many of Gerd Althoff's most important essays have been bought together in a collection entitled *Inszenierte Herrschaft*, meaning 'staged', or even 'stage-managed' rulership.[33] The performative aspect inherent in this concept presumes an audience, which raises the question of that audience's ritual, liturgical and iconographical literacy. It is important to recognize that the line between audience and participant was blurred. A noble might be present to witness an inauguration, but in being there he was also part of the performance, whether or not he played an active role as, for example, a bearer of regalia in procession. Although it seems sensible to posit varying levels of sophistication in the comprehension of inauguration rituals, the fact that the audience also participated in the event strengthens the assertion that not all of the allusions would have been lost on them. As David d'Avray has asserted, 'liturgy and services tend to make religious thinking concrete'.[34] Witnessing and participating in an inauguration ceremony was itself also a ritual, liturgical and iconographical lesson.

That is not to argue that all the nuances of the inauguration liturgy would have been understood by the entire audience. As with most pedagogical experiences, it is unlikely that all students would have achieved all the desired learning outcomes and unfortunately evidence that would enable an assessment of their understanding does not survive. However, that Henry

---

[32] Büttner, *Der Weg zur Krone*, I, 377–90
[33] G. Althoff, *Inszenierte Herrschaft: Geschichtsschreibung und politisches Handeln im Mittelalter* (Darmstadt, 2003).
[34] d'Avray, 'Popular and Elite Religion, p. 165.

III of England went so far as to ask Robert Grosseteste, bishop of Lincoln, the precise meaning of royal unction, suggests that kings themselves did not always comprehend the exact significance of all elements of the ceremony, even the most important ones.[35] One can recognize importance without full comprehension, however, which explains continued royal interest in unction in the thirteenth century, especially amongst those kings who sought the right to be anointed.[36] The acquisition of this right was doggedly pursued by some, with Henry, bishop of Ostia, commenting in his *Summa Aurea*, written between 1250 and 1261 that 'if anyone wishes to be anointed for the first time, he obtains the rite by petitioning the pope, as the king of the Aragonese does and the king of Scotland insists upon daily'.[37] Unction, it is apparent, was considered a worthy prize, and, moreover, a privilege worth guarding, as Henry III's attempts to prevent the anointing of Scottish kings demonstrates.[38] While Grosseteste stressed in his response to the king's enquiry that, the 'privilege of unction ... does not in any way raise the dignity of a king above, nor even to the level of that of a priest, or give the power to perform any priestly office' such distinctions might well not have been comprehended by the audience at an inauguration.[39] Indeed, as was discussed in chapters 1 and 2, although the act of anointing in the episcopal rite is not now thought to have provided the genesis of royal unction, contemporaries would likely have been struck by the similarities between the rites. Given that episcopal consecration was a more frequently carried out rite and also a significant one attended by lay and ecclesiastical lords, it seems likely that the episcopal rite would have provided the lens through which many present at a royal inauguration would have viewed the royal rite.

As outlined in the introduction, the historiographical traditions of England, France and Germany, although differing in detail, all encompass broad modernization paradigms that have strongly influenced interpretations of high medieval kingship. The long twelfth century has been seen as the pivotal moment of 'desacralization' in the English and German traditions. One of

---

[35] *English Coronation Records*, ed. Legg, p. 67.
[36] Schieffer, 'Die Ausbreitung der Königssalbung'.
[37] 'Si quis de novo inungi velit consuetudo obtinuit qui a papa petatur sicut fecit rex Aragonum et quotidie instat rex Scotiae.' Henry de Susa, *Summa Aurea* (Venice, 1570), p. 57. This reference was first noted in M. Bloch, 'An Unknown Testimony on the History of the Coronation in Scotland', *Scottish Historical Review* 23 (1926), 105–6. For a concise summary of the attempts made by the minority government of Alexander III of Scotland to gain unction and coronation see A. Taylor, 'Historical Writing in Twelfth- and Thirteenth-Century Scotland: The Dunfermline Compilation', *Historical Research* 83 (2010), 228–52, (pp. 246–52).
[38] Taylor, 'Historical Writing', p. 248.
[39] 'hec tamen unccionis prerogativa nullo modo regiam dignitatem prefert aut etiam equiparat sacerdotali aut potestatem tribuit alicuius sacerdotalis officii.' *English Coronation Records*, ed. Legg, p. 67.

the benefits of comparative history, that make its methodological difficulties worth enduring, is the ability to investigate causality.[40] In the case of England and the Empire, a simple comparison of historiographical traditions raised an important issue: that different causes had been identified as having an identical result. In England, law and bureaucracy slowly eroded the sacrality of the monarch, whereas within the Empire sacral kingship met a sudden end at the hands of Gregory VII. This juxtaposition seemed unsatisfactory and, when the French tradition was brought into the mix, things became more unsatisfactory still, for neither law, nor bureaucracy, nor ecclesiastical reform, are considered to have dented Capetian sacrality.

It has been beyond the scope of this study to interrogate the relationship between liturgy and law or liturgy and bureaucracy. However, in demonstrating the continuation of liturgical concepts of kingship in the high Middle Ages it has made manifest that liturgy could thrive within increasingly sophisticated legal and bureaucratic political cultures. In the context of the Empire, Erkens has argued that Roman law actually strengthened ruler sacrality.[41] While it seems unlikely that an investigation of the Angevin experience would evince identical results, given the differences both between Roman Law and English Common Law and also between the legal cultures of the two realms, a wider point can be made: law has a prominent role in the bible and is consequently embedded in the liturgy. As we saw in chapter 1, the model of kingship found in the *ordines* was not a narrow Davidic model, but one encompassing a tradition of Old Testament rulership in which law-giving played a vital role. Indeed, that most prominent of law-givers, Moses, is evoked in prayer K4, which appears in six royal liturgies, and prayer K23, which appears in four royal and four imperial rites. While bureaucracy lacks similar liturgical resonances, our examination of charters and seals pointed to the possibility that aspects of bureaucracy could take place within a liturgical context and thus be considered 'quasi-liturgical'.[42] Of course, much of English, and later French, bureaucracy was what we would consider routine, and not embellished by liturgy. However, routinization does not necessarily equate with 'disenchantment'. Because we tend to see in twelfth-century bureaucracies the origins of modern secular states, it is all too easy to assume that their elaboration signalled the demise of liturgical kingship. However, liturgical ceremonial is tenacious in its survival, even in the democratic

---

[40] This is one of the chief benefits Marc Bloch saw in the comparative method: M. Bloch, 'Pour une histoire comparée des sociétés européenes', *Revue de synthèse historique* 46 (1925), 15–50. Translated into English as 'Towards a Comparative History of European Societies', in *Enterprise and Secular Change*, ed. F. C. Lane and J. C. Riemersma (Homewood, 1953), pp. 494–521. See the discussion of this essay in W. H. Sewell Jr, 'Marc Bloch and the Logic of Comparative History', *History and Theory* 6 (1967), pp. 208–18.
[41] Erkens, 'Der *pia Dei ordinatione rex*', pp. 92–7.
[42] Insley, 'Where Did All the Charters Go?', p. 119.

bureaucracy that is twenty-first century Britain: although the Christomimetic allusion was probably lost on most of his future subjects, in October 2013, Prince George was baptized with water from the River Jordan.

Lazy periodization and the adherence of much of modern scholarship on medieval kingship to overarching teleological narratives of modernization and secularization has led to the privileging of the demise of sacral kingship as an explanatory factor. As Jens Engels pointed out, the imprecision with which scholars use the term 'sacral kingship' tends to a re-mystification of monarchy.[43] Rather than seeing Canossa, law and bureaucracy as signalling the 'disenchantment' of the world, we need to demystify modern scholarly approaches to high medieval kingship. As this study has made explicit, liturgies for inauguration, composed in the Carolingian age and reinterpreted through the centuries, continued to shape concepts of kingship in the high Middle Ages. Liturgies and their interpretation did not remain static. However, liturgy did remain at the heart of the performance of monarchical power in rituals that shaped the political communities of the three realms. When chanters in England, France and the Empire uttered the words 'Christus vincit, Christus regnat, Christus imperat', it was with the conviction that the monarchs they were lauding ruled in the image of Christ the King.

---

[43] Engels, 'Das "Wesen" der Monarchie?', p. 4.

Appendix 1: Editions and Manuscripts of the Selected *Ordines*

The purpose of this appendix is to enable the reader swiftly to find the full texts of the *ordines* referenced in this book and to give an idea of the number of surviving manuscripts. As no critical edition of the English *ordines* exists, all printed works containing readings of individual manuscripts are given and the manuscripts containing witnesses to the English *ordines* are also given in full. As the French, German and imperial *ordines* have all been edited in relatively modern critical editions, only the edition cited in the book and a summary of surviving manuscripts has been included in this appendix. Full details of surviving manuscripts and previous editions of the texts can be found in the relevant critical editions.

English Second Recension (late tenth century)
Alternative names: The Edgar *Ordo*

Editions
1. L. G. Wickham Legg, *English Coronation Records* (London, 1901), 15-21.
2. V. Leroquais, *Les pontificaux manuscrits des bibliothèques publiques de France. Étude et description*, 3 vols. (Paris, 1937), II, 160-4.
3. H. A. Wilson, *The Benedictional of Archbishop Robert*, HBS 24 (London, 1903), 140-7.
4. D. H. Turner, *The Claudius Pontificals*, HBS 97 (London, 1971), 89-95.

Manuscripts
Cambridge, Corpus Christi College, MS 146 (s. x^{ex})
Douai, Bibliothèque municipal, MS 67 (s. xii)
London, British Library, Additional MS 57337 (s. x^{ex}/s. xi^{in})
London, British Library, MS Cotton Claudius A.iii (s. x^{ex}/s. xi^{in})
London, British Library, MS Cotton Vitellius A.vii (s. x^{med})
Paris, Bibliothèque nationale de France, MS lat. 943 (s. x^{ex})
Rouen, Bibliothèque municipale, MS 369 (s. x^{ex})

English Third Recension (twelfth century)
Editions
1. Legg, *English Coronation Records*, 30-9.
2. Turner, *The Claudius Pontificals*, 115-22.
3. H. A. Wilson, *The Pontifical of Magdalen College*, HBS 39 (London, 1910), 89-95.

Manuscripts
Cambridge, Trinity College MS B.II.10 (s. xii^{ex})
Cambridge, University Library MS EE.II.3 (s. xii^{in})
Dublin, Trinity College MS 98 (formerly B.3.6) (s. xii^{in})
London, British Library MS Cotton Claudius A.iii (s. xii^{in})
London, British Library MS Cotton Tiberius B.viii (s. xii^{ex})
Oxford, Bodleian Library Rawlinson MS C.400 (s. xiv^{in})
Oxford, Magdalen College MS 226 (s. xii^{ex})

Royal Ordo from the Romano-Germanic Pontifical (c.950)
Alternative names: Ottonian *Ordo*, Mainz *Ordo*

Edition
Vogel & Elze, *Le pontifical romano-germanique*, I: 246-69.

Manuscript summary
Texts that can be considered as belonging to the PRG tradition are to be found in around fifty manuscripts.

Royal Ordo from Cologne Dombibliothek MS 141 (1000-1050)
Alternative names: *Ordo* of Arras

Edition
Jackson, *Ordines Coronationis Franciae*, I, 201-16.

Manuscript summary
There are two surviving manuscripts, one from the first half of the eleventh century, and one from the fourteenth century.

Ratold Ordo (c.980)
Alternative names: Continental version of the English Second Recension, Fulrad *Ordo*

Edition
Jackson, *Ordines Coronationis Franciae*, I, 168-200.

Manuscript summary
There are twenty surviving manuscripts. The earliest dates from *c*.980 and was copied for Ratold, abbot of Corbie, from whom the *ordo* got its name. One eleventh-century manuscript survives, seven from the twelfth century, a further seven from the thirteenth century, one from the fourteenth century and three from the seventeenth century.

Appendix 1

Ordo of Saint-Bertin (c.1150-1200)
Alternative names: Ordo of Senlis

Edition
Jackson, *Ordines Coronationis Franciae*, I, 240-7.

Manuscript summary
Two manuscripts survive, one from the mid- or late-twelfth century and one from the mid-fourteenth century.

Ordo of 1200 (c.1200)
Alternative names: Compilation of 1200

Edition
Jackson, *Ordines Coronationis Franciae*, I, 248-67.

Manuscript summary
Two thirteenth-century manuscripts of this *ordo* survive, one from the early part of the century and one from the middle.

Imperial Ordo from Cologne Dombibliothek MS 141 (1000-1050)
Alternative names: Ordo of Arras

Edition
Elze, *Die Ordines*, 20-2.

Manuscript summary
There are two surviving manuscripts, one from the first half of the eleventh century and one from the fourteenth century.

Cencius I (c.1100)

Edition
Elze, *Die Ordines*, 22-5.

Manuscript summary
There are ten surviving manuscripts dating from the late-eleventh to the late-thirteenth centuries.

Cencius II (c.1100-1150)
Alternative names: Ordo C, *Ordo* Ia

Edition
Elze, *Die Ordines*, 35-47.

Manuscript summary
There is one surviving late-twelfth-century manuscript and ten copies from the sixteenth and seventeenth centuries.

The Staufen Ordo (late 1100s)
Alternative names: Ordo of 1209, Ordo D (previously considered to be the same as *The Ordo from the Roman Curia*)

Edition
Elze, *Die Ordines*, 61-69

Manuscript summary
There are seven surviving witnesses of this text. Only one survives in a conventional liturgical manuscript, dating from the fourteenth century. The remaining texts are to be found in papal registers and royal and imperial *bullae* and charters, also dating from the fourteenth century.

The Ordo from the Roman Curia (early 1200s)
Alternative names: Ordo of 1209, Ordo D (previously considered to be the same as *the Staufen Ordo*)

Edition
R. Elze, *Die Ordines*, 69-87.

Manuscript summary
This *ordo* was included in the thirteenth-century *Pontifical of the Roman Curia*, that survives in around twenty-four thirteenth- and fourteenth-century manuscripts. The *ordo* can also be found in around another twenty manuscript copies of the curial book of ceremonies from the fourteenth and fifteenth centuries.

Appendix 2: Prayer Formulae Incipits

Male inauguration prayers (K)

K1	Te invocamus domine sancte pater omnipotens aeterne deus
K2	Deus qui populis tuis virtute consulis et amore dominaris
K3	In diebus tuis oriatur omnibus aequitas et iustitia
K4	Omnipotens sempiterne deus creator ac gubernator caeli et terrae
K5	Christe perunge hunc regem in regimen unde unxisti sacerdotes reges
K6	Deus electorum fortitudo et humilium celsitudo
K7	Deus dei filius ihesus christus dominus noster
K8	Accipe anulum signaculum videlicet sanctae fidei
K9	Deus cuius est omnis potestas et dignitas
K10	Accipe hunc gladium cum dei benedictione tibi conlatum
K11	Deus qui prouidentia tua caelestia simul et terrena moderaris
K12	Coronet te deus corona glorie atque iustitiae
K13	Deus perpetuitatis dux virtutem cunctorum hostium victor
K14	Accipe sceptrum regiae potestatis insigne virgam scilicet rectam regni
K15	Omnium domine fons bonorum cunctorumque deus institutor profectuum
K16	Accipe virgam virtutis atque aequitatis qua intellegas mulcere pios
K17	Extendat omnipotens dominus dexteram suae benedictionis
K18	Benedic domine hunc praeelectum principem
K19	Sta et retine amodo statum quem huc usque paterna suggestione tenuisti
K20	Omnipotens det tibi deus de rore caeli et de pinguedine terrae
K21	Benedic domine fortitudinem principis et opera manuum illius suscipe
K22	Benedic domine hunc regem nostrum N. qui regna omnium moderaris
K23	Deus ineffabilis auctor mundi conditor generis humani
K24	Unguantur manus istae de oleo sanctificato unde uncti fuerunt reges
K25	Prospice omnipotens deus serenis optutibus hunc gloriosum regem
K26	Deus qui es iustorum gloria et misericordia peccatorum

K27	Accipe gladium per manus episcoporum licet indignas
K28	Accipe armillas sinceritatis et sapientiae
K29	Accipe pallium quattuor initiis formatum
K30	Deus tuorum corona fidelium qui in capitibus eorum ponis coronam
K31	Accipe regiae dignatis anulum et per hunc in te catholicae fidei signaculum
K32	Benedicat tibi deus custodiatque te
K33	Omnipotens sempiterne deus qui famulum tuum regni fastigio
K34	Deus qui scis genus humanum nulla virtute posse subsistere
K35	Omnipotens sempiterne deus caelestium terrestriumque moderator
K36	Spiritus sancti gratia humilitatis nostrae officio
K37	Accipe coronam regni quae licet ab indignis episcoporum
K38	Exaudi quesumus domine preces nostras
K39	Omnipotens sempiterne deus qui es cunctorum benedictio
K40	Deus in cuius manu corda regum sunt da famulo tuo
K41	Unde unxisti sacerdotes reges et prophetas quatinus iustitiam diligens
K42	Domine deus omnipotens cuius est omnis potestas
K43	Accipe signum gloriae, in nomine patris et filii et spiritus sancti
K44	Deus in cuius manu corda sunt regum inclina at preces humilitatis nostre
K45	Salvum fac servum tuum domine
K46	Actiones nostras quesumus domine aspirando preveni
K47	Accipe gladium ad vindictam malefactorum
K48	Pretende quesumus, domine, famulo tuo dextram celestis auxilii
K49	Benedic domine quesumus hunc principem nostrum N.
K50	Deus pater eterne glorie sit adiutor tuus et protector

Female inauguration prayers (Q)

Q1	Omnipotens sempiterne deus affluentem spiritum tuae benedictionis
Q2	Accipe anulum fidei signaculum sanctae trinitatis
Q3	Deus cuius est omnis potestas et dignitas da famulae tuae N.
Q4	Accipe coronam gloriae honorem iocunditatis splendida ut fulgeas
Q5	Omnium domine fons bonorum et cunctorum dator profectuum
Q6	Omnipotens sempiterne deus fons et origo totius bonitatis
Q7	Deus qui solus habes immortalitatem lucemque habitas inaccessibilem

Q8	Spiritus sancti gratia humilitatis nostrae officio in te copiosa descendat
Q9	Deus tuorum corona fidelium qui in capitibus eorum ponis coronam
Q10	Officio indignitatis nostrae seu congregationis in reginam benedicta
Q11	Adesto domine supplicationibus nostris
Q12	Deus tuorum corona fidelium qui quos ad regnum vocas
Q13	Accipe coronam regalis excellentie, que licet ab indignis episcoporum

Prayers from the mass (M)

M1	Quesumus omnipotens deus ut famulus tuus
M2	Munera domine quesumus oblata santifica
M3	Vere dignum aeterne deus qui es fons inmarcescibilis lucis
M4	Haec domine oration salutaris famulum tuum N.
M5	Omnipotens sempiterne deus caelestium terrestriumque moderator
M6	Deus qui miro ordine universa disponis et ineffabiliter gubernas
M7	Concede quaesumus omnipotens deus his salutaribus sacrificiis placatus
M8	Omnipotens deus qui te populi sui voluit esse rectorem
M9	Haec domine salutaris sacrificii perceptio famuli tui N.
M10	Benedicat tibi dominus custodiatque te et sicut voluit
M11	Deus cuius regnum regnum est omnium seculorum
M12	Sacrificiis domine placatus oblatis pacem tuam
M13	Deus qui est diligentibus te facis cuncta prodesse
M14	Deus regnorum omnium et christiani maxime protector imperii
M15	Suscipe domine preces et hostias ecclesie tue
M16	Deus qui ad predicandum eterni regni evangelium romanum imperium

Appendix 3: Tables of Ritual Elements in the Ordines

This appendix comprises six tables laying out the order of the rituals that together made up the inauguration rite in the different *ordines*. The royal *ordines* are presented side-by-side for ease of comparison. This manner of presentation is not possible for the more detailed imperial liturgies, which are presented individually.

Ritual Elements in the Royal Ordines I

English Second	English Third	PRG	Cologne 141	Cologne 141 (continued)
King	**King**	**King**	**King**	**Queen**
1. entry to church	1. entry to church	1. procession from bedchamber to church	1. procession from bedchamber to church	1. entry to church
2. prostration before altar	2. prostration before altar	2. removal of pallium and weapons	2. regalia placed before altar	2. prostration before altar
3. oath	3. oath	3. prostration before altar	3. interrogation/promise	3. anointing
4. anointing	4. acclamation	4. interrogation/promise	4. congregation asked if they accept king	4. ring
5. ring	5. anointing	5. acclamation	5. prostration before altar	5. crowning
6. sword	6. sword	6. anointing	6. anointing	
7. crowning	7. armillas	7. sword	7. ring	
8. sceptre	8. pallium	8. armillas, pallium and ring	8. sword	
9. virga	9. crowning	9. sceptre and baculum	9. crowning	
10. blessing	10. ring	10. crowning	10. sceptre	
11. designation	11. sceptre	11. blessing	11. virga	
	12. virga	12. enthronement	12. blessing	
	13. blessing	13. kiss of peace	13. enthronement	
	14. kiss of peace		14. oath (read by archbishop)	
	15. enthronement		15. kiss of peace	
Queen	**Queen**	**Mass**		
1. anointing	1. blessing		**Mass**	
2. ring	2. anointing	**Queen**		
3. crowning	3. ring	1. entry to church	**Imperial** (see p. 235)	
	4. crowning	2. blessing		
Mass		3. anointing		
		4. crowning		

Ritual Elements in the Royal Ordines II

Ratold Ordo

Ordo of Saint-Bertin

Ordo of 1200

King

1. interrogation/oath
2. congregation asked if they accept king
3. prostration before altar
4. promise (in 4 MSS)
5. invocation
6. anointing
7. ring
8. sword
9. crowning
10. sceptre
11. virga
12. blessing
13. designation
14. enthronement
15. promise (in 18 MSS)
16. kiss of peace

Mass

Queen

1. entry to church
2. prostration before altar
3. anointing   *(continued in next column)*

Ratold Ordo (continued)

Queen

4. ring
5. crowning
6. sceptre (in 1 MS)

King

1. procession from bedchamber to church
2. removal of pallium
3. prostration before altar
4. interrogation/promise
5. congregation asked if they accept king
6. anointing
7. sword
8. ring
9. sceptre
10. banner
11. crowning
12. blessing
13. enthronement
14. kiss of peace

Mass

King

1. procession from bedchamber to church
2. removal of pallium and weapons
3. prostration before altar
4. interrogation
5. congregation asked if they accept king
6. anointing
7. sword
8. armillas, pallium and ring
9. sceptre and baculum
10. crowning
11. blessing
12. enthronement
13. promise
14. kiss of peace

Mass

Queen

1. entry to church
2. blessing before altar
3. anointing
4. crowning
5. mass

Appendix 3

Ritual Elements in the Earlier Imperial Ordines

Cologne 141

Emperor
1. procession
2. promise
3. prostration
4. anointing
5. crowning

Cencius I

Emperor
1. promise
2. prostration
3. anointing
4. crowning

Ritual Elements in the Ordo Cencius II

Emperor and Empress (integrated with a mass)
1. received by dignitaries at Church of S. Maria Transpadina
2. elect meets pope before bronze doors of S. Maria della Torre
3. kissing of pope's feet
4. withdrawal of queen
5. promise
6. removal of pallium
7. questioning and kisses
8. elect enters S. Pietro
9. queen rejoins husband
10. pope enters S. Pietro
11. blessing
12. interrogation
13. pope dresses in his pontifical garments in the *secretarium*
14. elect led to choir of St. Gregory and dressed in liturgical robes
15. elect led before pope
16. queen fetched by bishop of Ostia and led to altar of St. Gregory
17. pope clothed in planeta and pallium ascends to the altar
18. prostration before altar of elect and queen
19. anointing of elect
20. blessing of queen
21. anointing of queen
22. pope proceeds to altar of St. Maurice followed by elect and queen

Inauguration and Liturgical Kingship

23. crowns moved from altar of St. Peter to altar of St. Maurice
24. ring
25. sword
26. crowning of elect
27. crowning of queen
28. sceptre
29. mass
30. count of palace removes emperor's liturgical footwear and gives him spurs
31. emperor and empress, wearing crowns, led to horses
32. emperor holds stirrup for pope
33. procession with emperor and empress followed by crowned pope
34. on arrival at palace emperor holds stirrup as pope dismounts
35. feasts (empress eats separately with some of the bishops and barons)
36. emperor swears Roman oath on Monte Mario, at the Porta Collina and before the steps of S. Pietro

Ritual Elements in the Staufen Ordo

Emperor (integrated with a mass)
1. procession with dignitaries from Porta Collina to S. Pietro
2. elect dismounts at steps
3. pope emerges from *secretarium*
4. kissing of pope's feet and offering of gifts
5. entry to S. Maria della Torre
6. elect swears oath before altar
7. pope goes to altar of St. Peter
8. elect remains in S. Maria with three bishops and is clothed with imperial insignia
9. elect enters S. Pietro
10. prostration before altar of St. Peter
11. elect proceeds to altar of St. Maurice
12. anointing
13. elect ascends to altar of St. Peter and receives kiss from the pope
14. emperor proceeds to chamber fashioned from wood
15. mass
16. emperor processes to altar
17. crowning
18. orb and sceptre
19. sword
20. emperor returns to wooden chamber
21. emperor takes off crown and cloak
22. kiss of peace
23. emperor holds stirrup for pope

Appendix 3

24. horseback procession to S. Maria Transpadina
25. kiss
26. emperor descends Monte Mario and swears Roman oath

Empress (if present her inauguration follows the emperor's coronation)
1. led to altar before pope
2. crowning
3. return to chamber

Ritual Elements in the Ordo of the Roman Curia

Emperor (integrated with a mass)
1. procession with dignitaries from Porta Collina to S. Pietro
2. elect dismounts at steps
3. pope emerges from private chapel
4. kissing of pope's feet and offering of gifts
5. elect receives a kiss and embrace
6. entry to S. Maria della Torre
7. elect swears oath before altar
8. pope goes to altar of St. Peter
9. elect remains in S. Maria with three bishops and is clothed with insignia
10. elect enters S. Pietro
11. prostration before altar of St. Peter
12. elect proceeds to altar of St. Maurice
13. anointing
14. elect ascends to altar of St. Peter and receives kiss from the pope
15. emperor proceeds to chamber fashioned from wood
16. mass
17. emperor processes to altar
18. crowning
19. sceptre and orb
20. blessing
21. sword*
22. kissing of pope's feet
23. emperor returns to wooden chamber
24. emperor takes off crown and cloak
25. offering of gold to pope
26. kiss of peace
27. emperor holds stirrup for pope
28. horseback procession to S. Maria Transpadina
29. kiss
30. emperor descends Monte Mario and swears Roman oath

Empress (if present her inauguration follows the emperor's coronation)
1. led to altar before pope
2. blessing
3. anointing
4. crowning
5. return to chamber

* An interpolation relates that in some books it is written that the sword should be given before the coronation. The coronation and bestowal of the sceptre and orb are then repeated.

Appendix 4: Brief Descriptions of Royal and Imperial Seals and *Bullae*

The function of this appendix is to provide the reader with brief descriptions of the iconography and inscriptions of royal and imperial seals and *bullae* from the period *c*.1050-*c*.1250 and to point them to the relevant catalogues or literature where fuller descriptions and often reproductions of these seals can be found. As charters and seals have yet to be subject to the kind of digitisation projects that are now commonplace for manuscripts, few of the seals in this appendix can be seen online. A handful of the seals described below have been digitised and when a seal (or its matrix) is available online a link is provided.

References are made to the following catalogues:
Birch, W. de G., *Catalogue of Seals in the Department of Manuscripts in the British Museum*, vol. 1 (London, 1887).
Dalas, M. *Les sceaux des rois et de régence*, CdS 2 (Paris, 1980).
Heslop, T.A. 'Seals' in *English Romanesque Art, 1066-1200*, ed., G. Zarnecki, J. Holt and T. Holland (London, 1984), 298-320.
Kahsnitz, R. 'Siegel und Goldbullen' in *Die Zeit der Staufer*, ed., R. Haussherr and C. Väterlein, 5 vols. (Stuttgart, 1977), IV, 17-108.
Nielen, M.-A. *Les sceaux des reines et des enfants de France*, CdS 3 (Paris, 2011)
Posse, O. *Die Siegel der deutschen Kaiser und Könige von 751 bis 1806*, 5 vols. (Dresden, 1909-13).
Stieldorf, A., 'Die Siegel der Herrscherinnen - Siegelführung und Siegelbild der "deutschen" Kaiserinnen und Königinnen', *Rheinische Vierteljahrblätter* 64 (2000), 1-44.
Wyon, A. B. *The Great Seals of England* (London, 1887).

If a number is given below, it refers to a catalogue entry rather than a page number. In Posse's catalogue of German seals the seals are not numbered sequentially throughout the catalogue. Instead Posse numbers the seals of each monarch individually. When reference is made to secondary literature other than the catalogues listed above, the bibliographic reference is accompanied by a page number.

Where seals are grouped together this is not to imply that they are identical, but that the iconography is broadly similar. For the differences between these seals the reader is referred to the relevant catalogues. R and L are used to refer to the hands of the monarchs depicted on the seal, rather than to sides of the seal itself. Unless otherwise specified, all seals are circular.

Inauguration and Liturgical Kingship

Kings and Queens of England

Edward the Confessor
obverse: enthroned and crowned figure holding an orb (L) and ? (R)
reverse: enthroned and crowned figure holding a sceptre (R) and sword (L)
inscription: + SIGILLUM EADWARDI ANGLORUM BASILEI (both sides)
reference: Heslop, 328
online image: http://www.bl.uk/manuscripts/Viewer.aspx?ref=lfc_ch_xxi_5_ f001r [accessed 24 July 2018]

William I
obverse: mounted figure holding a lance with flag (R) and shield (L)
reverse: enthroned and crowned figure holding a sword (R) and orb with cross (L)
inscription: + HOC NORMANNORUM WILLELMUM NOSCE PATRONUM SI / + HOC ANGLIS REGEM SIGNO FATEARIS EUNDEM
reference: Harvey and McGuinness, *A Guide to British Medieval Seals*, pp. 27-8

William II
obverse: enthroned and crowned figure holding a sword (R) and orb with cross (L), two roundels in field
reverse: mounted figure holding a lance with flag (R) and shield (L)
inscription: + WILLELMUS DEI GRATIA REX ANGLORUM (both sides)
reference: Heslop, 329

Henry I (A)
obverse: enthroned and crowned figure holding an orb with cross and bird (L) and ? (R)
reverse: mounted figure holding a lance with flag (R) and shield (L)
inscription: + HENRICUS DEI GRACIA REX ANGLORUM (both sides)
reference: Wyon, 19-20

Henry I (B)
obverse: enthroned and crowned figure holding an orb with cross and bird (L) and ? (R)
reverse: mounted figure holding a lance with flag (R) and shield (L)
inscription: + HENRICUS DEI GRATIA REX ANGLORUM / + HENRICUS DEI GRATIA DUX NORMANNORUM
reference: Heslop, 330

Henry I (C)
obverse: enthroned and crowned figure holding an orb with cross and bird (L), two stars in field
reverse: mounted figure holding a sword (R) and shield (L)

Appendix 4

inscription: + HENRICUS DEI GRATIA REX ANGLORUM / + HENRICUS DEI GRATIA DUX NORMANNORUM
reference: Wyon, 23-24

Matilda of Scotland
obverse: standing crowned figure holding a sceptre with bird (R) and orb with cross (L), vesica shape
inscription: + SIGILLUM MATHILDIS SECUNDAE DEI GRACIA REGINAE ANGLIE
reference: Heslop, 336

Adeliza of Louvain
Adeliza re-used Matilda of Scotland's seal with a suitably altered inscription.
reference: Heslop, 336

Stephen (A)
obverse: enthroned and crowned figure holding a sword (R) and orb with cross and bird (L)
reverse: mounted figure holding a sword (R) and shield (L)
inscription: + STEPHANUS DEI GRATIA REX ANGLORUM / + STEPHANUS DEI GRATIA DUX NORMANNORUM
reference: Heslop, 331

Stephen (B)
obverse: enthroned and crowned figure holding a sword (R) and orb (L)
reverse: mounted figure holding a sword (R) and shield (L)
inscription: + STEPHANUS DEI GRATIA REX ANGLORUM / + STEPHANUS DEI GRATIA DUX NORMANNORUM
reference: Heslop, 332

Stephen (C)
obverse: enthroned and crowned figure holding a sword (R) and orb with cross and bird (L), one star in field
reverse: mounted figure holding a lance with flag (R) and shield (L)
inscription: + STEPHANUS DEI GRATIA REX ANGLORUM / + STEPHANUS DEI GRATIA DUX NORMANNORUM
reference: Wyon, 27-28

Matilda of Boulogne
obverse: standing crowned figure holding a fleur-de-lys (R) and bird (L), vesica shape
inscription: ... MATILDIS DEI GRATIA
reference: Johns, *Noblewomen, Aristocracy and Power*, p. 203.

Matilda of England
Although the earliest surviving impression of this seal is found in England, Matilda most probably first used this seal in Germany
obverse: enthroned and crowned figure holding a sceptre (R) with hand (L) in front of body
inscription: + MATHILDIS DEI GRATIA ROMANORUM REGINA
reference: Danbury, 'Queens and Powerful Women', p. 18; Stieldorf, 3

Henry II (A)
obverse: enthroned and crowned figure holding a sword (R) and orb with cross and bird (L)
reverse: mounted figure holding a sword (R) and shield (L)
inscription: + HENRICUS DEI GRATIA REX ANGLORUM / + HENRICUS DUX NORMANNORUM ET AQUITANORUM ET COMES ANDEGAVORUM
reference: Wyon, 30-31

Henry II (B)
obverse: enthroned and crowned figure holding a sword (R) and orb with cross and bird (L)
reverse: mounted figure holding a sword (R) and shield (L)
inscription: +, HENRICUS DEI GRATIA REX ANGLORUM / + HENRICUS DUX NORMANNORUM ET AQUITANORUM ET COMES ANDEGAVORUM
reference: Heslop, 333

Henry the Young King
obverse: enthroned and crowned figure holding a sceptre (L) and ? (R)
inscription: + HENRICUS DEI GRATIA REX ANGLORUM
reference: Wyon, 34

Eleanor of Aquitaine
obverse: standing crowned figure holding a bird (L) and ? (R), vesica shape
reverse: same image as obverse
inscription: ALIENOR DEI GRACIA REGINE ANGLORUM DUCISSE NORMAN + / ALIENOR DUCISSE AQUITANORUM ET COMITISSE ANDEGAVOR +
reference: Nielen, 10

Richard I (A)
obverse: enthroned and crowned figure holding a sword (R) and sceptre with flower and cross (L), two plants, moons and stars/suns in field (R and L)
reverse: mounted figure holding a sword (R) and shield decorated with coat of arms (L)

Appendix 4

inscription: + RICARDUS DEI GRATIA REX ANGLORUM / + RICARDUS DUX NORMANNORUM ET AQUITANORUM ET COMES ANDEGAVORUM
reference: Heslop, 334
online image: https://www.siv.archives-nationales.culture.gouv.fr/siv/ media/FRAN_IR_055193/A1_61/FRAN-AEIII_2013_02960 [accessed 24 July 2018]

Richard I (B)
obverse: enthroned and crowned figure holding a sword (R) and sceptre with flower and cross (L), sun and moon in field
reverse: mounted figure holding a sword (R) and shield decorated with coat of arms (L)
inscription: + RICARDUS DEI GRATIA REX ANGLORUM / + RICARDUS DUX NORMANNORUM ET AQUITANORUM ET COMES ANDEGAVORUM
reference: Wyon, 37-38

John
obverse: enthroned and crowned figure holding a sword (R) and sceptre with flower and cross (L)
reverse: mounted figure holding a sword (R) and shield decorated with coat of arms (L)
inscription: + JOHANNES DEI GRATIA REX ANGLIE DOMINUS HIBERNIE / + JOHANNES DUX NORMANNIE ET AQUITANIE ET COMES ANDEGAVIE
reference: Heslop, 335
online images: http://www.bl.uk/manuscripts/Viewer.aspx?ref=add_ ms_4838_f001r [accessed 24 July 2018]
http://magnacarta.cmp.uea.ac.uk/read/original_charters/ Notification_of_the_King_s_permission_for_the_barons_of_London_to_ elect_their_own_mayor [accessed 24 July 2018]

Isabella of Angoulême
obverse: standing crowned figure holding a flower (R) and bird (L), vesica shape
inscription: ISABELLA DEI GRATIA REGINA ANGLIE DOMINA HIBERNIE
reference: Danbury, 'Queens and Powerful Women', p. 20

Henry III (A)
obverse: enthroned and crowned figure holding a sword (R) and sceptre with flower and cross (L)
reverse: mounted figure holding a sword (R) and shield decorated with coat of arms (L)
inscription: + HENRICUS DEI GRATIA REX ANGLIE DOMINUS HIBERNIE

/ + HENRICUS DUX NORMANNIE ET AQUITANIE ET COMES ANDEGAVIE
reference: Wyon, 41-42

Henry III (B)
obverse: enthroned and crowned figure holding a sceptre (R) and orb with elongated cross (L)
reverse: mounted figure holding a sword (R) and shield decorated with coat of arms (L)
inscription: + HENRICUS DEI GRATIA REX ANGLIE DOMINUS HIBERNIE / + HENRICUS DUX NORMANNIE ET AQUITANIE ET COMES ANDEGAVIE
reference: Wyon, 43-44
online image: https://www.siv.archives-nationales.culture.gouv.fr/siv/media/FRAN_IR_055193/A1_3/FRAN-AEIII_S302326N00001 [accessed 24 July 2018]

Henry III (C)
obverse: enthroned and crowned figure holding a sceptre with cross (R) and sceptre with flower (L)
reverse: mounted figure holding a sword (R) and shield decorated with coat of arms (L)
inscription: + HENRICUS DEI GRATIA REX ANGLIE DOMINUS HIBERNIE / + HENRICUS DEI GRATIA REX ANGLIE DOMINUS HIBERNIE DUX AQUITANNIE
reference: Wyon, 45-46

Eleanor of Provence (A)
obverse: standing crowned figure holding a sceptre with cross (R) and sceptre with orb and bird (L), seated lion at base, vesica shape
reverse: shield of arms decorated with three lions hanging from tree with three branches
inscription: ALIANORA DEI GRACIA REGINA ANGLIE DOMINA HYBERNIE / ALIANORA DUCISSA NORMANNIE ET AQUITANIE COMITISSA ANDEGAVIE
reference: Birch, 791

Eleanor of Provence (B)
obverse: standing crowned figure holding a sceptre (R) under a gothic arch, vesica shape
reverse: same as A seal
inscription: ALIANORA DEI GRACIA REGINA ANGLIE / ALIANORA DEI GRACIA DOMINA HIBERNIE ET DUCISSA AQUITANNIE
reference: Birch, 794

Appendix 4

Kings and Queens of France

Henry I
obverse: enthroned and crowned figure holding a virga (R) and sceptre (L)
inscription: HEINRICUS DEI GRATIA FRANCORUM REX
reference: Dalas, 62

Philip I (A)
obverse: enthroned and crowned figure holding a virga (R) and sceptre (L)
inscription: PHILIPUS DEI GRATIA FRANCORUM REX
reference: Dalas, 63

Philip I (B)
obverse: enthroned and crowned figure holding a virga (R) and sceptre (L)
inscription: PHILIPUS DEI GRATIA FRANCORUM REX
reference: Dalas, 64

Bertrada of Montfort
obverse: standing crowned figure holding a fleur-de-lys (R) and bird (L), vesica shape
inscription: SIGILLUM BERTRADE DEI GRACIA FRANCORUM REGINE
reference: Nielen, 5

Louis VI
obverse: enthroned and crowned figure holding a virga (R) and sceptre (L), cross motif in field
inscription: LUDOVICUS DEI GRATIA FRANCORUM REX
reference: Dalas, 66

Adelaide of Maurienne
obverse: standing crowned figure holding a fleur-de-lys (L), this seal is only known from a rough sketch and descriptions from the seventeenth and eighteenth centuries.
reference: Nielen, 6

Louis VII
obverse: enthroned and crowned figure holding a fleur-de-lys (R) and sceptre (L)
reverse*: mounted figure holding a sword (R) and shield (L)
inscription: LUDOVICUS DEI GRATIA FRANCORUM REX / ET DUX AQUITANORUM*
countersealsx: a fantastical creature *or* Diana with the inscription +LODOVICUS REX
reference: Dalas, 67-69

* following his divorce from Eleanor of Aquitaine, the king ceased using the ducal title in 1154. The latest imprint of this reverse design dates from 1153.

× having ceased using the equestrian design on the reverse of his seal, Louis counter-sealed instead

Eleanor of Aquitaine
No surviving seal of Eleanor as Queen of France
reference: Nielen, 10

Constance of Castile
obverse: standing crowned figure holding flowers in both hands, vesica shape
inscription: SIGILLUM REGINE CONSTANCIE
reference: Nielen, 11

Adela of Champagne
obverse: standing crowned figure holding a fleur-de-lys (R) with hand (L) on waist, vesica shape
inscription: + SIGILLUM ADELE DEI GRACIA REGINE FRANCORUM
reference: Nielen, 12

Philip II (A)
obverse: enthroned and crowned figure holding a fleur-de-lys (R) and sceptre (L)
inscription: PHILIPUS DEI GRATIA FRANCORUM REX
counterseal: a fleur-de-lys
reference: Dalas, 70
online image: http://www2.culture.gouv.fr/public/mistral/caran_fr?ACTION=CHERCHER&FIELD_1=REF&VALUE_1=03776 [accessed 24 July 2018]

Philip II (B)
obverse: enthroned and crowned figure holding a fleur-de-lys (R) and sceptre (L)
inscription: PHILIPUS DEI GRATIA FRANCORUM REX
counterseal: a fleur-de-lys
reference: Dalas, 71

Philip II (seal of regency)
obverse: enthroned and crowned figure holding a fleur-de-lys (R) and sceptre (L)
inscription: PHILIPUS DEI GRATIA FRANCORUM REX
counterseal: an eagle
reference: Dalas, 72

Appendix 4

Isabella of Hainault
obverse: standing crowned figure holding a fleur-de-lys (R) and sceptre (L), vesica shape
inscription: +ELIZABEZ DEI GRACIA FRANCORUM REGINA
reference: Nielen, 13
online image (matrix): http://www.britishmuseum.org/research/collection_online/collection_object_details.aspx?objectId=51057&partId=1&searchText=isabella+of+hainault&page=1 [accessed 24 July 2018]

Ingebourg of Denmark
No seal survives although she is known to have had one
reference: Nielen, 14

Louis VIII
obverse: enthroned and crowned figure holding a fleur-de-lys (R) and sceptre (L)
inscription: LUDOVICUS DEI GRATIA FRANCORUM REX
counterseal: a shield patterned with fleur-de-lys
reference: Dalas, 75

Blanche of Castile
obverse: standing crowned figure holding a fleur-de-lys (R) with hand (L) on breast holding cords, six fleurs-de-lys in field, vesica shape
inscription: SIGILLUM BLANCHE DEI GRATIA FRANCORUM REGINE
counterseal: a castle between two fleurs-de-lys with the inscription BLACHA FILIA REGIS CASTELLE
reference: Nielen, 15

Louis IX (A)
obverse: enthroned and crowned figure holding a fleur-de-lys (R) and sceptre (L)
inscription: LUDOVICUS DEI GRATIA FRANCORUM REX
counterseal: a fleur-de-lys
reference: Dalas, 76

Louis IX (B)
obverse: enthroned and crowned figure holding a fleur-de-lys (R) and sceptre (L)
inscription: LUDOVICUS DEI GRATIA FRANCORUM REX
counterseal: a fleur-de-lys
reference: Dalas, 77

Louis IX (seal of regency)
obverse: crown within an architectural border

Inauguration and Liturgical Kingship

inscription: + S LUDOVICI DEI GRATIA FRANCORUM REGIS IN PARTIBUS TRANSMARINIS AGENTIS
counterseal: a shield patterned with fleurs-de-lys
reference: Dalas, 78

Margaret of Provence
obverse: standing crowned figure within a gothic niche supported by two columns holding a sceptre with fleur-de-lys (R) with hand (L) on breast holding cords, vesica shape
inscription: S MARGARETE DEI GRATIA FRANCORUM REGINE
counterseal: a fleur-de-lys with the inscription + AVE MARIA GRACIA PLENA
reference: Nielen, 16

Kings and Emperors and Queens and Empresses of Germany

Henry IV (royal seals A-D)
obverse: enthroned and crowned figure holding a sceptre with bird (R) and orb with cross (L)
inscription: + HEINRICUS REX (A); + HEINRICUS DEI GRATIA REX (B-D)
reference: Posse, Heinrich IV., 1-4

Henry IV (imperial seal A)
obverse: enthroned and crowned figure holding an orb with cross (R) and sceptre with flower (L)
inscription: + HEINRICUS DEI GRATIA TERCIUS ROMANORUM IMPERATOR AUGUSTUS
reference: Posse, Heinrich IV., 7

Henry IV (imperial seals B&C)
obverse: enthroned and crowned figure holding a sceptre with flower (R) and orb with cross (L)
inscription: + HEINRICUS DEI GRATIA III ROMANORUM IMPERATOR AUGUSTUS
reference: Posse, Heinrich IV., 8-9

Henry IV (royal bullae A&B)
obverse: half figure crowned and facing left holding a sceptre with bird (R)
reverse: city gate with three towers
inscription: + HEINRICUS REX / + ROMA CAPUT MUNDI
reference: Posse, Heinrich IV., 6-7

Henry V (royal seal A)
obverse: enthroned and crowned figure holding a sceptre with flower (R) and orb with cross (L)

Appendix 4

inscription: + HEINRICUS DEI GRATIA…
reference: Posse, Heinrich V., 1

Henry V (royal seal B)
obverse: enthroned and crowned figure holding a sceptre with three prongs (R) and orb with cross (L)
inscription: + HEINRICUS DEI GRATIA ROMANORUM QUINTUS REX
reference: Gawlik, 'Ein neues Siegel Heinrichs V.', pp. 529-36

Henry V (imperial seals A & B)
obverse: enthroned and crowned figure holding a sceptre with flower (R) and orb with cross (L)
inscription: + HEINRICUS DEI GRATIA ROMANORUM IIII IMPERATOR AUGUSTUS (A); + HEINRICUS DEI GRATIA IIII ROMANORUM IMPERATOR AUGUSTUS (B)
reference: Posse, Heinrich V., 2-3

Matilda of England
Although the earliest surviving impression of this seal is found in England, Matilda most probably first used this seal in Germany
obverse: enthroned and crowned figure holding a sceptre (R) with hand (L) in front of body
inscription: + MATHILDIS DEI GRATIA ROMANORUM REGINA
reference: Danbury, 'Queens and Powerful Women', p. 18; Stieldorf, 3

Lothar III (royal seals A&B)
obverse: enthroned and crowned figure holding a sceptre with flower (R) and orb with cross (L)
inscription: + LOTHARIUS DEI GRATIA TERCIUS ROMANORUM REX
reference: Posse, Lothar III., 1-2

Lothar III (imperial bulla)
obverse: half figure crowned and facing forward holding a sceptre (L) and encircled by city walls
reverse: five towered building incorporating the legend 'AUREA ROMA'
inscription: + LOTHARIUS DEI GRATIA… /+ ROMA CAPUT MUNDI REGIT ORBIS FRENA ROTUNDI
reference: Posse, Lothar III., 4

Conrad III (royal seal)
obverse: enthroned and crowned figure holding a sceptre with flower (R) and orb with cross (L)
inscription: +CUONRADUS DEI GRATIA ROMANORUM REX II
reference: Kahsnitz, 27

Frederick I (royal seal)
obverse: enthroned and crowned figure holding a sceptre with flower (R) and orb with cross (L)
inscription: + FREDERICUS DEI GRATIA ROMANORUM REX
reference: Kahsnitz, 28

Frederick I (imperial seal)
obverse: enthroned and crowned figure holding a sceptre with flower (R) and orb with cross (L)
inscription: + FREDERICUS DEI GRATIA ROMANORUM IMPERATOR AUGUSTUS
reference: Kahsnitz, 30

Frederick I (royal and imperial bullae)
obverse: half figure crowned and facing forward holding a sceptre (R) and orb with cross (L) and encircled by city walls
reverse: the Colosseum inside circular city walls incorporating the legend 'AUREA ROMA'
inscription: + FREDERICUS DEI GRATIA ROMANORUM REX / + ROMA CAPUT MUNDI REGIT ORBIS FRENA ROTUNDI (inscription altered on imperial *bullae* to reflect different status)
reference: Kahsnitz, 29 and 31

Beatrix of Burgundy
No seal survives although she is known to have had one
reference: Stieldorf, 4

Henry VI (royal seal)
obverse: enthroned and crowned figure holding a sceptre with leaves and flower (R) and orb with cross (L)
inscription: + HEINRICUS DEI GRATIA ROMANORUM REX
reference: Kahsnitz, 32

Henry VI (imperial seal)
obverse: enthroned and crowned figure holding a sceptre with flower (R) and orb with cross (L); 'REX SICILIE' added to field following marriage to Constance of Sicily
inscription: + HEINRICUS DEI GRATIA ROMANORUM IMPERATOR ET SEMPER AUGUSTUS
reference: Kahsnitz, 33

Henry VI (imperial bulla)
obverse: enthroned and crowned figure holding a sceptre with cross (R) and orb with cross (L)

Appendix 4

reverse: the Colosseum inside circular city walls incorporating the legend 'AUREA ROMA'
inscription: + HEINRICUS DEI GRATIA ROMANORUM IMPERATOR AUGUSTUS / + ROMA CAPUT MUNDI REGIT ORBIS FRENA ROTUNDI
reference: Kahsnitz, 34

Constance of Sicily
obverse: enthroned and crowned figure holding a sceptre with fleur-de-lys (R) with hand (L) on breast, vesica shape
inscription: + CONSTANTIA DEI GRATIA ROMANORUM IMPERATRIX SEMPER AUGUSTUS ET REGINA SICILIE
reference: Stieldorf, 5

Philip of Swabia (royal seal)
obverse: enthroned and crowned figure holding a sceptre with cross (R) and orb with cross (L)
inscription: + PHILIPPUS DEI GRATIA ROMANORUM REX ET SEMPER AUGUSTUS
reference: Kahsnitz, 35

Irene Maria
Only a fragment of an impression of her seal survives
reference: Stieldorf, 6

Otto IV (royal seal)
obverse: enthroned and crowned figure holding a sceptre with flower (R) and orb with cross (L)
inscription: + OTTO DEI GRATIA ROMANORUM REX ET SEMPER AUGUSTUS
reference: Kahsnitz, 36

Otto IV (imperial seal)
obverse: enthroned and crowned figure holding a sceptre (R) and orb with cross (L), sun and moon in field
inscription: + DEI GRATIA OTTO ROMANORUM IMPERATOR ET SEMPER AUGUSTUS
reference: Kahsnitz, 39

Otto IV (royal bulla)
obverse: enthroned and crowned figure holding sceptre with cross (R) and orb with cross (L)
reverse: city gate with three towers incorporating the legend 'AUREA ROMA'

Inauguration and Liturgical Kingship

inscription: indecipherable / + ROMA CAPUT MUNDI REGIT ORBIS FRENA ROTUNDI
reference: Posse, Otto IV., 2

Otto IV (imperial bulla)
obverse: enthroned and crowned figure holding a sceptre with cross (R) and orb with cross (L), sun and moon in field
inscription: + DEI GRATIA OTTO ROMANORUM IMPERATOR ET SEMPER AUGUSTUS / + ROMA CAPUT MUNDI REGIT ORBIS FRENA ROTUNDI
reference: Posse, Otto IV., 4

Maria of Brabant (seal)
obverse: enthroned and crowned figure holding a fleur-de-lys (R) and orb (L), sun and moon in field
inscription: + MARIA DEI GRACIA ROMANORUM IMPERATRIX SEMPER AUGUSTA
reference: Kahsnitz, 41; Stieldorf, 7

Frederick II (royal seal A)
obverse: enthroned and crowned figure holding a sceptre with cross (R) and orb with cross (L), 'ET REX SICILIE' in field
inscription: + FRIDERICUS DEI GRATIA ROMANORUM REX ET SEMPER AUGUSTUS
reference: Kahsnitz, 46

Frederick II (royal seal B)
obverse: enthroned and crowned figure holding a sceptre (R) and orb with cross (L)
inscription: +FRIDERICUS DEI GRATIA ROMANORUM REX ET SEMPER AUGUSTUS ET REX SICILIE
reference: Kahsnitz, 48

Frederick II (imperial seal)
obverse: enthroned and crowned figure holding a sceptre (R) and orb with cross (L), 'REX IERUSALEMIAE' added to field following his coronation as king of Jerusalem
inscription: + FRIDERICUS DEI GRATIA IMPERATOR ROMANORUM ET SEMPER AUGUSTUS
reference: Kahsnitz, 50

Frederick II (royal bulla A)
obverse: enthroned and crowned figure holding a sceptre with fleur-de-lys (R) and orb with cross (L), 'ET REX SICILIE' in field

Appendix 4

reverse: large gate tower incorporating the words 'AUREA ROMA' flanked by two smaller towers, small flowers, circles and crosses in field
inscription: + FREDERICUS DEI GRATIA ROMANORUM REX ET SEMPER AUGUSTUS / + ROMA CAPUT MUNDI REGIT ORBIS FRENA ROTUNDI
reference: Kahsnitz, 47

Frederick II (royal bulla B)
obverse: enthroned and crowned figure holding a sceptre with leaves and cross (R) and orb with cross (L)
reverse: large gate tower incorporating the words 'AUREA ROMA' flanked by four smaller towers, encircled by city walls
inscription: + FREDERICUS DEI GRATIA ROMANORUM REX ET SEMPER AUGUSTUS / + ROMA CAPUT MUNDI REGIT ORBIS FRENA ROTUNDI
reference: Kahsnitz, 49

Frederick II (imperial bulla)
obverse: enthroned and crowned figure holding a sceptre with cross (R) and orb with cross (L), 'STUS ET REX SICILIE' in field, Jerusalem added after 1229 coronation
reverse: large gate tower flanked by two smaller towers encircled by city walls that terminated in two further smaller towers
inscription: + FREDERICUS DEI GRATIA ROMANORUM REX ET SEMPER AUGU [STUS] / + ROMA CAPUT MUNDI REGIT ORBIS FRENA ROTUNDI
reference: Kahsnitz, 51
online image: http://www2.culture.gouv.fr/public/mistral/caran_fr?ACTION=CHERCHER&FIELD_1=REF&VALUE_1=AF-02089 [accessed 24 July 2018]

Constance of Aragon
No impression survives, but the design is recorded in a later description
obverse: enthroned and crowned figure holding a sceptre
reverse: mounted figure carrying a harp
inscription: + CONSTANTIA DEI GRATIA REGINA SICILIE, DUCATUS APULIE ET PRINCIPATUS CAPUE / + CONSTANTIA REGINA FILIA ILLUSTRIS REGIS ARAGONENSIUM
reference: Stieldorf, 8

Henry (VII) (royal seal)
obverse: enthroned and crowned figure holding a sceptre with cross (R) and orb with cross (L)
inscription: + HENRICUS DEI GRATIA ROMANORUM REX ET SENPER AUGUSTUS
reference: Kahsnitz, 52

Henry (VII) (royal bulla)
obverse: enthroned and crowned figure holding a sceptre with cross (R) and orb with cross (L)
reverse: large gate tower incorporating the words 'AUREA ROMA' flanked by four smaller towers
inscription: + HEINRICUS DEI GRATIA ROMANORUM REX ET SEMPER AUGUSTUS / ROMA CAPUD MUNDI REGIT ORBIS FRENA ROTUNDI
reference: Kahsnitz, 53

Margaret of Austria
obverse: enthroned and crowned figure holding a sceptre with fleur-de-lys (R) with hand (L) on breast holding cords
inscription: + MARGARETA DEI GRATIA ROMANORUM REGINA ET SEMPER AUGUSTUS
reference: Stieldorf, 10

Bibliography

Manuscripts

Besançon, Bibliothèque municipale, MS 138.
Cambridge, Corpus Christi College, MS 373.
Cambridge, Trinity College, MS B. II. 10.
Cambridge, University Library, MS EE. II. 3.
Cologne, Dombibliothek, MS 139.
Cologne, Dombibliothek, MS 141.
Durham, University Library, MS Cosin V. v. 6.
London, British Library, MS Arundel 60.
London, British Library, MS Cotton Claudius A. III.
London, British Library, MS Cotton Tiberius B. VIII.
London, British Library, MS Harley 863.
London, British Library Loan MS 88.
Paris, Bibliothèque nationale, MS lat. 1246.
Reims, Bibliothèque municipale, MS 343.
Vatican City, Archivio Segreto Vaticano, Registra Vaticana 11.
Windsor, Eton College Library, MS 177.
Wolfenbüttel, Herzog-August-Bibliothek, MS Guelf. 105 Noviss. 2o.
Worcester, Cathedral Library, MS F. 160.

Published Primary Sources

'Aachen *Ordo*', in *Constitutiones Regum Germaniae*, ed. G. H. Pertz, *MGH LL* 2 (Hannover, 1837), pp. 384–93.
Annales Lobiensis, ed. G. Waitz, *MGH SS* 13 (Hannover, 1881), pp. 224–35.
Annales Marbacenses, ed. H. Bloch, *MGH SS Rer. Germ.* 9 (Hannover, 1907).
Anselm of Canterbury, *The Letters of Saint Anselm of Canterbury*, trans. W. Fröhlich, 3 vols. (Kalamazoo, 1990–4).
Baldric of Bourgueil, *Historia Ierosolimitana*, ed. S. Biddlecombe (Woodbridge, 2014).
CANTUS: A Database for Latin Ecclesiastical Chant <http://cantusdatabase.org>.
Cardinal Boso, 'Vita Adriani IV', in *Adrian IV: The English Pope (1154-1159). Studies and Texts*, ed. B. Bolton and A. J. Duggan (Aldershot, 2003), pp. 214–33.
Chronica Regia Coloniensis, ed. G. Waitz, *MGH SS Rer. Germ* 18 (Hannover, 1880).

Bibliography

Chronica Remensi, ed. L. Delisle, *RHF* 12 (Paris, 1877).
The Chronicle of Battle Abbey, ed. E. Searle, OMT (Oxford, 1980).
The Chronicle of Richard of Devizes of the Time of King Richard the First, ed. J. T. Appleby (London, 1963).
The Claudius Pontificals, ed. D. H. Turner, HBS 97 (Woodbridge, 1970).
Constantine Porphyrogennetos, *The Book of Ceremonies*, trans. A. Moffatt and M. Tall, 2 vols., Byzantina Australiensia 18 (Canberra, 2012).
Corpus Iuris Canonici, ed. E. A. Friedberg and A. L. Richter, 2 vols. (Leipzig, 1881).
Dialogus de Scaccario, and Constitutio Domus Regis, ed. E. Amt and S. Church, OMT (Oxford, 2007).
Eadmer, *Historia novorum in Anglia*, in *Eadmeri Historia novorum in Anglia, et Opuscula duo; De Vita Sancti Anselmi et quibusdam miraculis ejus*, ed. M. Rule, RS 81 (London, 1965).
Ekkehard of Aura, *Chronica*, ed. G. Waitz, *MGH SS* 6 (Hannover, 1844).
English Coronation Records, ed. L. G. W. Legg (London, 1901).
English Royal Documents: King John – Henry VI, 1199–1461, ed. P. Chaplais (Oxford, 1971).
Ex chronico brevi ecclesiae S. Dionysii ad cyclos Paschales, ed. L. V. Delisle, *RHF* 11 (Paris, 1869), pp. 377–8.
Facsimiles of English Royal Writs to A.D. 1100: Presented to Vivian Hunter Galbraith, ed. T. A. M. Bishop and P. Chaplais (Oxford, 1957).
Frederici I. Constitutiones, ed. L. Weiland, *MGH Const.* 1 (Hannover, 1893), pp. 191–463.
Friderici I. Diplomata, ed. H. Appelt, R. M. Herkenrath and W. Koch, 5 vols, *MGH DD* 10 (Hannover, 1975–90).
Frutolfi et Ekkehardi chronica necnon anonymi chronica imperatorum, ed. F.-J. Schmale and I. Schmale-Ott (Darmstadt, 1972).
Gervase of Canterbury, *The Historical Works*, ed. W. Stubbs, 2 vols., RS 73 (London, 1879–80).
Die Gesetze der Angelsachsen, ed. F. Liebermann, 3 vols. (Halle, 1903–16).
The Gesta Guillelmi of William of Poitiers, ed. R. H. C. Davis M. Chibnall, OMT (Oxford, 1998).
The Gesta Normannorum ducum of William of Jumièges, Orderic Vitalis, and Robert of Torigni, ed. E. M. C. van Houts, 2 vols., OMT (Oxford, 1995).
Gilbert of Mons, *Chronicle of Hainaut*, trans. L. Napran (Woodbridge, 2005).
Heinrici IV. Diplomata, ed. D. von Gladiss and A. Gawlik, 3 vols., *MGH DD* 4 (Hannover, 1941–78).
'Henry I's Coronation Charter', ed. R. Sharpe <http://www.earlyenglishlaws.ac.uk/laws/texts/hn-cor/view/#edition,1/translation,1>.
'Henry II's Coronation Charter', ed. N. Vincent <http://www.earlyenglishlaws.ac.uk/laws/texts/hn2-cor/view/#edition,1/apparatus,1>.

Bibliography

Henry of Huntingdon, *Historia Anglorum*, ed. D. Greenway, OMT (Oxford, 1996).
Henry de Susa, *Summa Aurea* (Venice, 1570).
Historia regum Francorum ab origine gentis ad annum MCCXIV, ed. L. V. Delisle, *RHF* 12 (Paris, 1877).
Jacobus de Voragine, *The Golden Legend: Readings on the Saints*, trans. W. G. Ryan, 2 vols. (Princeton 1993).
―――, *Legenda Aurea*, ed. T. Graesse (Leipzig, 1845).
The Leofric Missal, ed. N. A. Orchard, 2 vols., HBS 114 (Woodbridge, 2002).
The Letters and Charters of Henry II, ed. N. Vincent et al. (Oxford, forthcoming).
Lotharii III. Diplomata nec non et Richenzae Imperatricis Placita, ed. E. von Ottenthal and H. Hirsch (Berlin, 1927).
Matthew Paris, *Chronica Majora*, ed. H. R. Luard, 7 vols, RS 57 (London, 1872–80).
The Missal of Robert of Jumièges, ed. H. A. Wilson, HBS 11 (London, 1896).
Missale ad usum insignis et praeclarae ecclesiae Sarum, ed. F. H. Dickinson (Burntisland, 1861).
Missale Romanum Mendiolani 1474, ed. R. Lippe, 2 vols., HBS 17, 33 (London 1899–1907).
Mittelalterliche Schatzverzeichnisse I: von der Zeit Karls des Großen bis zur Mitte des 13. Jahrhunderts, ed. B. Bischoff (Munich, 1967).
Norman Anonymous, *De consecratione pontificum et regum*, ed. H. Boehmer, *MGH LdL* 3 (Hannover, 1897), pp. 662–79.
Oeuvres de Rigord et de Guillaume le Breton: Historiens de Philippe-Auguste, ed. H. F. Delaborde, 2 vols. (Paris, 1882–5).
Ordines Coronationis Franciae: Texts and Ordines for the Coronation of Frankish and French Kings and Queens in the Middle Ages, ed. R. A. Jackson, 2 vols. (Philadelphia, 1995–2000).
Die Ordines für die Weihe und Krönung des Kaisers und der Kaiserin, ed. R. Elze, *MGH Fontes Iuris* 9 (Hannover, 1960).
Ottonis et Rahewini Gesta Frederici I. Imperatoris, ed. G. Waitz, *MGH SS Rer. Germ.* 46 (Hannover, 1912).
Ottonis Morenae et Continuatorum Historia Frederici I, ed. F. Güterbock, *MGH SS Rer. Germ. N.S.* 7 (Berlin, 1930).
Le pontifical romano-germanique du dixième siècle, ed. C. Vogel and R. Elze, 3 vols. (Vatican City, 1963–72).
Ralph de Diceto, *The Historical Works*, ed. William Stubbs, 2 vols., RS 68 (London, 1876).
Recueil des actes de Louis VI, Roi de France (1108–1137), ed. J. Dufour (Paris, 1992).
Recueil des actes de Philippe Auguste, Roi de France (1180–1223), ed. H. F. Delaborde and E. Berger, 4 vols. (Paris, 1916–79).
Recueil des actes de Philippe Ier, Roi de France (1059–1108), ed. M. Prou and M. H. d'Arbois de Jubainville (Paris, 1908).

Regesta Regum Anglo-Normannorum, 1066–1154: Facsimiles of Original Charters and Writs of King Stephen and the Empress Matilda and Dukes Geoffrey and Henry, 1135–1154, ed. H. A. Cronne and R. H. C. Davis (Oxford, 1969).
Regesta Regum Anglo-Normannorum: The Acta of William I, ed. D. Bates (Oxford, 1998).
Regestum Innocentii III Papae super negotio Romani Imperii, ed. F. Kempf, Miscellanea Historiae Pontificiae 12 (Rome, 1947).
Die Register Papst Innocenz' III., ed. O. Hageneder, A. Sommerlechner and H. Weigl, 13 vols. (Vienna, 1964–2015).
Reineri Annales a. 1066–1230, ed. G. H. Pertz, *MGH SS* 16 (Hannover, 1859), pp. 651–80.
Rigord, *Histoire de Philippe Auguste*, ed. E. Carpentier, G. Pon and Y. Chauvin, SHM 33 (Paris, 2006).
Roger of Howden, *Chronica magistri Rogeri de Houedene*, ed. W. Stubbs, 4 vols, RS 51 (London, 1870)
———, *Gesta Henrici II et Ricardi I* [formerly attributed to Benedict of Peterborough], ed. W. Stubbs, 2 vols., RS 49 (London, 1867).
S. Anselmi Cantuariensis archiepiscopi opera omnia, ed. F. S. Schmitt, 6 vols. (Edinburgh 1946–91).
Les sceaux des reines et des enfants de France, ed. M.-A. Nielen, CdS 3 (Paris, 2011).
Les sceaux des rois et de régence, ed. M. Dalas, CdS 2 (Paris, 1980).
Select Charters and Other Illustrations of English Constitutional History, ed. W. Stubbs, 9th edn (Oxford, 1921).
Die Siegel der deutschen Kaiser und Könige von 751 bis 1806, ed. O. Posse, 5 vols. (Dresden, 1909).
Suger, *Historia Gloriosi regis Ludovici VII, Filii Ludovici Grossi*, ed. L. V. Delisle, *RHF* 12 (Paris, 1877).
———, *Vie de Louis VI le Gros*, ed. H. Waquet (Paris, 1929).
Urkunden Heinrichs VI., ed. H. Appelt and B. Pferschy-Maleczek <http://www.mgh.de/datenbanken/urkunden-heinrichs-vi/>.
Walter Map, *De nugis curialium*, ed. M. R. James et al., OMT (Oxford, 1983).
The Waltham Chronicle: An Account of the Discovery of Our Holy Cross at Montacute and Its Conveyance to Waltham, ed. L. Watkiss and M. Chibnall, OMT (Oxford, 1994).
William of Canterbury, *Vita et Passio sancti Thomae*, in *Materials for the History of Thomas Becket*, ed. J. C. Robertson and J. B. Sheppard, 7 vols. (London, 1875–85), I, 1–136.
William of Malmesbury, *Gesta regum Anglorum*, ed. M. Winterbottom, R. M. Thomson and R. A. B. Mynors, 2 vols., OMT (Oxford, 1998).
William of Nangis, *Vita Sancti Ludovici regis Franciae*, ed. P.-C.-F. Daunou and J. Naudet, *RHF* 20 (Paris, 1855).
Wyon, A. B., *The Great Seals of England: From the Earliest Period to the Present Time, Arranged and Illustrated with Descriptive and Historical Notes* (London, 1887).

Bibliography

Secondary Works

Airlie, S., 'A View from Afar: English Perspectives on Religion and Politics in the Investiture Controversy', in *Religion und Politik im Mittelalter: Deutschland und England im Vergleich*, ed. L. Körntgen and D. Waßenhoven (Berlin, 2009), pp. 71–88.

Althoff, G., *Family Friends and Followers: Political and Social Bonds in Early Medieval Europe*, trans. C. Carroll (Cambridge, 2004).

———, 'Der frieden-, bündnis- und gemeinschaftstiftende Charakter des Mahles im früheren Mittelalter, in *Essen und Trinken in Mittelalter und Neuzeit*, ed. I. Bitsch, T. Ehlert and X. von Ertzdorff (Sigmaringen, 1987), pp. 13–26.

———, 'Friedrich von Rothenburg: Überlegungen zu einem übergagenen Königssohn', in *Festschrift für Eduard Hlawitschka zum 65. Geburtstag* (Kallmünz, 1993), pp. 307–16.

———, *Inszenierte Herrschaft: Geschichtsschreibung und politisches Handeln im Mittelalter* (Darmstadt, 2003).

———, 'The Variability of Rituals in the Middle Ages', in *Medieval Concepts of the Past: Ritual, Memory, Historiography*, ed. G. Althoff, J. Fried and P. J. Geary (Cambridge, 2002), pp. 71–88.

———, *Spielregeln der Politik im Mittelalter: Kommunikation in Frieden und Fehde* (Darmstadt, 1997).

Andrieu, N., 'Le sacre épiscopal d'après Hincmar de Reims', *Revue d'histoire ecclésiastique* 48 (1953), 22–73.

Angelov, D., *Imperial Ideology and Political Thought in Byzantium (1204–1330)* (Cambridge, 2007).

Angenendt, A., *Kaiserherrschaft und Königstaufe* (Berlin and New York, 1984).

———, 'Die liturgische Zeit: zyklisch und linear', in *Hochmittelalterliches Geschichtsbewußtsein im Spiegel nicht historiographischer Quellen*, ed. H.-W. Goetz (Berlin, 1998), pp. 101–15.

———, 'Rex et Sacerdos: Zur Genese der Königssalbung', in *Tradition als historische Kraft: Interdiziplinäre Forschungen zur Geschichte des früheren Mittelalters*, ed. N. Kamp and J. Wollasch (Berlin, 1982), pp. 100–18.

———, 'Vor und nach Canossa: rex et sacerdos', in *Canossa: Aspekte einer Wende*, ed. W. Hasberg and H.-J. Scheidgen (Regensburg, 2012), pp. 141–50.

Appelt, H., 'Friedrich Barbarossa und das römische Recht', *Römische Historische Mitteilungen* 5 (1962), 18–34.

Astell, A. W., *The Song of Songs in the Middle Ages* (Ithaca, 1995), pp. 8–9.

Auge, O., 'Physische Idoneität? Zum Problem körperlicher Versehrtheit bei der Eignung als Herrscher im Mittelalter', in *Idoneität – Genealogie – Legitimation: Begründung und Akzeptanz von dynastische Herrschaft im Mittelalter*, ed. C. Andenna and G. Melville (Cologne, Weimar and Vienna, 2015), pp. 39–58.

Backhouse, J., and C. de Hamel, *The Becket Leaves* (London, 1988).
Bak, J. M., 'Introduction: Coronation Studies – Past, Present, and Future', in *Coronations: Medieval and Early Modern Monarchic Ritual*, ed. J. M. Bak (Berkeley, 1990), pp. 1–15.
Baldwin, J. W., *The Government of Philip Augustus: Foundations of French Royal Power in the Middle Ages* (Berkeley, 1986).
Baldwin, P., 'Comparing and Generalizing: Why All History is Comparative, Yet No History is Sociology', in *Comparison and History: Europe in Cross-National Perspective*, ed. D. Cohen and M. O'Connor (New York, 2004) pp. 1–22.
Barratt, N., 'Finance and the Economy in the Reign of Henry II', in *Henry II: New Interpretations*, ed. C. Harper-Bill and N. Vincent (Woodbridge, 2007), pp. 242–56.
———, 'The Revenue of King John', *English Historical Review* 111 (1996), 835–55.
Barrett, E. G., 'Art and the Construction of Early Medieval Queenship: The Iconography of the Joint Royal/Imperial Portrait and the Visual Representation of the Ruler's Consort' (unpublished PhD thesis, Courtauld Institute, University of London, 1997).
Bartlett, R., 'Heartland and Border: The Mental and Physical Geography of Medieval Europe', in *Power and Identity in the Middle Ages: Essays in Honour of Rees Davies*, ed. H. Pryce and J. Watts (Oxford, 2007), pp. 23–36.
———, *The Making of Europe: Conquest, Colonization and Cultural Change, 950–1350* (Princeton, 1993).
Bates, D., 'Charters and Historians of Britain and Ireland: Problems and Possibilities', in *Charters and Charter Scholarship in Britain and Ireland*, ed. M. T. Flanagan and J. A. Green (Basingstoke, 2005), pp. 1–14.
Bedos-Rezak, B., 'In Search of a Semiotic Paradigm: The Matter of Sealing in Medieval Thought and Praxis (1050–1400)', in *Good Impressions: Image and Authority in Medieval Seals*, ed. N. Adams, J. Cherry and J. Robinson (London, 2008), pp. 1–7.
———, 'The King Enthroned, a New Theme in Anglo-Saxon Royal Iconography: The Seal of Edward the Confessor and Its Political Implications', in *Kings and Kingship*, ed. J. T. Rosenthal (New York, 1986), pp. 53–88.
———, 'Medieval Identity: A Sign and a Concept', *The American Historical Review* 105 (2000), 1489–533.
———, 'Ritual in the Royal Chancery: Text, Image, and the Representation of Kingship in Medieval French Diplomas (700–1200)', in *European Monarchy: Its Evolution and Practice from Roman Antiquity to Modern Times*, ed. H. Duchhardt, R. A. Jackson and D. Sturdy (Stuttgart, 1992), pp. 27–40.
———, 'Suger and the Symbolism of Royal Power: The Seal of Louis VII', in *Abbot Suger and Saint-Denis*, ed. P. L. Gerson (New York, 1986), pp. 95–103.

Benson, R. L., 'The Clash at Besançon (October 1157), in *Law, Rulership and Rhetoric: Selected Essays of Robert L. Benson*, ed. L. J. Weber (Notre Dame, 2014), pp. 262–92.

———, 'The Gelasian Doctrine: Uses and Transformations', in *La notion d'autorité au Moyen Âge: Islam, Byzance, Occident*, ed. G. Makdisi, D. Sourdel and J. Sourdel-Thomine (Paris, 1982), pp. 13–44.

Benson, R. L., and J. Fried, ed., *Ernst Kantorowicz: Erträge der Doppeltagung Institute for Advanced Study Princeton / Johann Wolfgang Goethe-Universität Frankfurt*, Frankfurter Historische Abhandlungen 39 (Stuttgart, 1997).

Berenbeim, J., *Art of Documentation: Documents and Visual Culture in Medieval England* (Toronto, 2015).

Beumann, H., *Der deutsche König als "Romanorum Rex"* (Wiesbaden, 1981).

Biddle, M., 'Seasonal Festivals and Residence: Winchester, Westminster and Gloucester in the 10th to 12th Centuries', *Anglo-Norman Studies* VIII (1986), 51–72.

Binski, P., *Westminster Abbey and the Plantagenets: Kingship and the Representation of Power, 1200–1400* (New Haven, 1995).

Blezzard, J., S. Ryle and J. Alexander, 'New Perspectives on the Feast of the Crown of Thorns', *Journal of the Plainsong and Mediaeval Music Society* 10 (1987), 23–47.

Bloch, M., 'Pour une histoire comparée des sociétés européenes', *Revue de synthèse historique* 46 (1925), 15–50.

———, *Les rois thaumaturges: études sur le caractère surnaturel attribué à la puissance royale particulièrement en France et en Angleterre* (Strasbourg, 1924).

———, *The Royal Touch: Sacred Monarchy and Scrofula in England and France*, trans. J. E. Anderson (London, 1973).

———, 'Towards a Comparative History of European Societies', in *Enterprise and Secular Change*, ed. F. C. Lane and J. C. Riemersma (Homewood, 1953), pp. 494–521.

———, 'An Unknown Testimony on the History of the Coronation in Scotland', *Scottish Historical Review* 23 (1926), 105–6.

Blum, P., 'The Lateral Portals of the West Façade of the Abbey Church of St.-Denis: Archaeological and Iconographic Considerations', in *Abbot Suger and Saint-Denis: A Symposium*, ed. P. L. Gerson (New York, 1986), pp. 199–228.

Bobrycki, S., 'The Royal Consecration *Ordines* of the Pontifical of Sens from a New Perspective', *Bulletin du centre d'études médiévales d'Auxerre* 13 (2009), 131–42.

Bojcov, M. A., 'Warum pflegten deutsche Könige auf Altären zu sitzen?', in *Bilder der Macht in Mittelalter und Neuzeit: Byzanz – Okzident – Rußland*, ed. O. G. Oexle and M. A. Bojcov (Göttingen, 2007), pp. 243–314.

Borgolte, M., *Europa entdeckt seine Vielfalt 1050–1250* (Stuttgart, 2002).

———, 'Mediävistik als vergleichende Geschichte Europas', in *Mediävistik im 21. Jahrhundert: Stand und Perspektiven der internationalen und interdiziplinären Mittelalterforschung*, ed. H.-W. Goetz and J. Jarnut (Munich, 2003), pp. 313–23.

———, 'Perspektiven europäischer Mittelalterhistorie an der Schwelle zum 21. Jahrhundert', in *Das europäische Mittelalter im Spannungsbogen des Vergleichs: Zwanzig internationale Beiträge zu Praxis, Problemen und Perspektiven der historischen Komparatistik*, ed. M. Borgolte (Berlin, 2001), pp. 13–27.

Borst, A., *The Ordering of Time: From the Ancient Computus to the Modern Computer*, trans. A. Winnard (Chicago, 1993).

Boshof, E., 'Köln, Mainz, Trier – Die Auseinandersetzung um die Spitzenstellung im deutschen Episkopat in ottonisch-salischer Zeit', *Jahrbuch des kölnischen Geschichtsvereins* 49 (1978), 19–48.

Bouman, C. A., *Sacring and Crowning: The Development of the Latin Ritual for the Anointing of Kings and the Coronation of an Emperor before the Eleventh Century* (Groningen, 1957).

Bovon, F., 'The Dossier on Stephen, the First Martyr', *Harvard Theological Review* 96 (2003), 279–315.

Bradbury, J., 'Fulk le Réchin and the Origin of the Plantagenets', in *Studies in Medieval History Presented to R. Allen Brown*, ed. C. Harper-Bill, C. J. Holdsworth and J. L. Nelson (Woodbridge, 1989), pp. 27–41.

Brand, P., 'Henry II and the Creation of the English Common Law', in *Henry II: New Interpretations*, ed. C. Harper-Bill and N. Vincent (Woodbridge, 2007), pp. 215–41.

Branner, R., *The Cathedral of Bourges and Its Place in Gothic Architecture*, ed. S. Prager Branner (Cambridge, MA, 1989).

Brooks, N. P., 'The Career of St Dunstan', in *St Dunstan: His Life, Times and Cult*, ed. N. Ramsey, M. Sparks and T. Tatton-Brown (Woodbridge, 1992), pp. 1–24.

Broun, D., 'The Absence of Regnal Years from the Dating Clause of Charters of King of Scots, 1195–1222', *Anglo-Norman Studies* XXV (2003), 47–63.

Brown, E. A. R., '"Franks, Burgundians, and Aquitanians" and the Royal Coronation Ceremony in France', *Transactions of the American Philosophical Society* 82 (1992), 1–189.

Brown, M. P., I. H. Garipzanov and B. J. Tilghman, 'Introduction: The Role of Graphic Devices in Understanding the Early Decorated Book', in idem, *Graphic Devices and the Early Decorated Book* (Woodbridge, 2017), pp. 1–11.

Brückmann, J., 'English Coronations, 1216–1308: The Edition of the Coronation *Ordines*' (unpublished PhD thesis, University of Toronto, 1964).

———, 'The *Ordines* of the Third Recension of the Medieval English Coronation Order', in *Essays in Medieval History Presented to Bertie Wilkinson*, ed. T. A. Sandquist and M. R. Powicke (Toronto, 1969), pp. 99–115.

Bibliography

Brühl, C., 'Fränkischer Krönungsbrauch und das Problem der "Festkrönungen"', *Historische Zeitschrift* 194 (1962), 265–326.

———, 'Kronen- und Krönungsbrauch im frühen und hohen Mittelalter', *Historische Zeitschrift* 234 (1982), 1–31.

Buc, P., *L'ambïguité du livre* (Paris, 1994).

———, *The Dangers of Ritual: Between Early Medieval Texts and Social Scientific Theory* (Princeton, 2001).

———, 'The Monster and the Critics: A Ritual Reply', *Early Medieval Europe* 15 (2007), 441–52.

———, 'Text and Ritual in Ninth-Century Political Culture: Rome 864', in *Medieval Concepts of the Past: Ritual, Memory, Historiography*, ed. G. Althoff, J. Fried and P. J. Geary (Cambridge, 2002), pp. 123–38.

Büttner, A., *Der Weg zur Krone: Rituale der Herrschererhebung im spätmittelalterlichen Reich*, 2 vols. (Ostfildern, 2012).

Cantor, N., *Inventing the Middle Ages: The Lives, Works and Ideas of the Great Medievalists of the Twentieth Century* (New York, 1991).

Carpenter, D. A., 'The Burial of King Henry III, the Regalia and Royal Ideology', in *The Reign of Henry III* (London, 1996), pp. 427–62.

———, 'Westminster Abbey in Politics 1258–1269', *Thirteenth Century England* VIII (2001), 49–58.

Cassidy, R., 'The 1259 Pipe Roll' (unpublished PhD thesis, King's College London, 2012).

Caviness, M. H., 'Reception of Images by Medieval Viewers', in *A Companion to Medieval Art: Romanesque and Gothic in Northern Europe*, ed. C. Rudolph (Oxford, 2006), pp. 65–85.

Chaplais, P., 'The Seals and Original Charters of Henry I', *English Historical Review* 75 (1960), 260–75.

Cheney, C. R., and M. Jones, ed., *A Handbook of Dates for Students of British History*, 2nd edn (Cambridge 2000).

Chibnall, M., *The Empress Matilda: Queen Consort, Queen Mother and Lady of the English* (Oxford, 1991).

Clanchy, M. T., *From Memory to Written Record: England 1066–1307*, 2nd edn (Oxford, 1993).

Cohen, M., *The Sainte-Chapelle and the Construction of Sacral Monarchy: Royal Architecture in Thirteenth-Century Paris* (Cambridge, 2015).

Collins, R., 'Julian of Toledo and the Royal Succession in Late Seventh-Century Spain', in *Early Medieval Kingship*, ed. P. H. Sawyer and I. Wood (Leeds, 1977), pp. 30–49.

Cowdrey, H. E. J., 'The Anglo-Norman *Laudes Regiae*', *Viator* 12 (1981), 37–78.

Cramer, P., *Baptism and Change in the Early Middle Ages* (Cambridge, 1993).

Dabbs, J. A., *Dei Gratia in Royal Titles* (The Hague, 1971).

Dale, J., 'Inauguration and the Liturgical Calendar in England, France and the Empire, c.1050–c.1250', *Anglo-Norman Studies* XXXVII (2015), 83–98.

———, 'Inauguration and Political Liturgy in the Hohenstaufen Empire, 1138–1215', *German History* 34 (2016), 191–213.

Danbury, E., 'The Decoration and Illumination of Royal Charters in England, 1250–1509: An Introduction', in *England and Her Neighbours 1066–1453: Essays in Honour of Pierre Chaplais*, ed. M. Jones and M. Vale (London, 1989), pp. 157–79

———, '"Domine Salvum Fac Regem": The Origin of "God Save the King" in the Reign of Henry VI', *The Fifteenth Century* X (2011), pp. 121–42.

———, 'Queens and Powerful Women: Image and Authority', in *Good Impressions: Image and Authority in Medieval Seals*, ed. N. Adams, J. Cherry and J. Robinson (London, 2008), pp. 17–24.

Davies, R. R., 'The Medieval State: The Tyranny of a Concept?', *Journal of Historical Sociology* 16 (2003), 280–300.

d'Avray, D. L., 'Comparative History of the Medieval Church's Marriage System', in *Das europäische Mittelalter im Spannungsbogen des Vergleichs: Zwanzig internationale Beiträge zu Praxis, Problemen und Perspektiven der historischen Komparatistik*, ed. M. Borgolte (Berlin, 2001), pp. 209–22.

———, *Dissolving Royal Marriages: A Documentary History, 860–1600* (Cambridge, 2014).

———, 'The Gospel of the Marriage Feast of Cana and Marriage Preaching in France', in *Modern Questions About Medieval Sermons: Essays on Marriage, Death, History and Sanctity*, ed. N. Bériou and D. L. d'Avray (Spoleto, 1994), pp. 135–53.

———, 'Popular and Elite Religion: Feastdays and Preaching', in *Elite and Popular Religion*, ed. K. Cooper and J. Gregory, *Studies in Church History* 42 (Woodbridge, 2006), pp. 162–79.

Dean Ware, R., 'Medieval Chronology: Theory and Practice', in *Medieval Studies: An Introduction*, ed. J. M. Powell, 2nd edn (New York, 1992), pp. 252–77.

Deér, J., 'Die Siegel Kaiser Friedrichs I. Barbarossa und Heinrichs VI. in der Kunst und Politik ihrer Zeit', in *Festschrift Hans P. Hahnloser*, ed. E. J. Beer, P. Hofer and L. Mojon (Basel and Stuttgart, 1961), pp. 47–102.

de Jong, M. B., 'Exegesis for an Empress', in *Medieval Transformations: Texts, Power, and Gifts in Context*, ed. E. Cohen and M. B. de Jong (Leiden, 2001), pp. 69–100.

de Lubac, *Medieval Exegesis: Volume I, The Four Senses of Scripture*, trans. M. Sebanc (Grand Rapids, 1998).

Deshman, R., '*Christus rex et magi reges*: Kingship and Christology in Ottonian and Anglo-Saxon Art', *Frühmittelalterliche Studien* 10 (1976), 367–405.

Deswarte, T., 'Le Christ-roi: Autel et couronne votive dans l'Espagne wisigothique', *Bulletin du centre d'études médiévales d'Auxerre* 4 (2011), 2–9.

Dick, S., 'Die Königserhebung Friedrich Barbarossas im Spiegel der Quellen – kritische Anmerkung zu den "Gesta Friderici" Ottos von Freising',

Zeitschrift der Savigny-Stiftung für Rechtsgeschichte: Germanistische Abteilung 121 (2004), 200–37.

Dolley, R. H. M., and F. E. Jones, 'A New Suggestion Concerning the So-called "Martlets" in the Arms of St. Edward', in *Anglo-Saxon Coins: Studies Presented to F. M. Stenton on the Occasion of His 80th Birthday, 17 May 1960*, ed. R. H. M. Dolley (London, 1961), pp. 215–26.

Duggan, A. J., [as Heslin], 'The Coronation of the Young King in 1170', *Studies in Church History* 2 (1965), 165–78

———, ed., *Queens and Queenship in Medieval Europe* (Woodbridge, 1997).

———, '"Totius christianitatis caput,": The Pope and the Princes', in *Adrian IV: The English Pope (1154–1159)*, ed. B. Bolton and A. J. Duggan (Aldershot, 2003), pp. 105–55.

Dumville, D. N., 'Kingship, Genealogies and Regnal Lists', in *Early Medieval Kingship*, ed. P. H. Sawyer and I. Wood (Leeds, 1977), pp. 72–104.

Dye, J. M., 'The Virgin Mary as *Sponsa c.*1100–*c.*1400' (unpublished PhD thesis, University College London, 2001).

Eastmond, A., '"It Began with a Picture": Imperial Art, Texts and Subversion between East and West in the Twelfth Century', in *Subversion in Byzantium*, ed. D. Angelov and M. Saxby (Farnham, 2013), pp. 121–43.

Eichmann, E., *Königs- und Bischofsweihe* (Munich, 1928).

Elze, R., 'Der Liber Censuum des Cencius (Cod. Vat. lat. 8486) von 1192 bis 1228', in *Päpste – Kaiser – Könige und die mittelalterliche Herrschaftssymbolik: Ausgewählte Aufsätze*, ed. B. Schimmelpfennig (London, 1982), pp. 251–70.

Engels, J. I., 'Das "Wesen" der Monarchie? Kritische Anmerkungen zum "Sakralkönigtum" in der Geschichtswissenschaft', *Majestas* 7 (1999), 3–39.

Engels, O., 'Der Pontifikatsantritt und seine Zeichen', in *Segni e riti nella chiesa altomedieval occidentale*, Settimane di Studio del Centro Italiano di Studi sull' Alto Medioevo, 2 vols. (Spoleto, 1987), II, 707–70.

———, 'Des Reiches heiliger Gründer: Die Kanonisation Karls des Großen und ihre Beweggründe', in *Karl der Große und sein Schrein in Aachen*, ed. H. Müllejans (Aachen, 1988), pp. 37–46.

Enright, M. J., *Iona, Tara, and Soissons: The Origin of the Royal Anointing Ritual* (Berlin, 1985).

Erdmann, C., *Forschungen zur politischen Ideenwelt des Frühmittelalters*, ed. F. Baethgen (Berlin, 1951).

Erkens, F.-R., *Herrschersakralität im Mittelalter: Von den Anfängen bis zum Investiturstreit* (Stuttgart, 2006).

———, 'Der "pia Dei ordinatione rex" und der Krise sakral legitimierter Königsherrschaft in spätsalisch-frühstaufischer Zeit', in *Vom Umbruch zur Erneuerung?: Das 11. und beginnende 12. Jahrhundert. Position der Forschung* (Munich, 2006), pp. 71–101.

———, '"Sicut Esther Regina": Die westfränkische Königin als *consors regni*', *Francia* 20 (1993), 15–38.

Facinger, M. F., 'A Study of Medieval Queenship: Capetian France, 987–1237', *Studies in Medieval and Renaissance History* 5 (1968), 3–48.

Fichtenau, H., *Arenga: Spätantike und Mittelalter im Spiegel von Urkundenformeln*, MIÖG 18 (Graz, 1957).

———, '"Dei Gratia" und Königssalbung', in *Geschichte und ihre Quellen: Festschrift für Friedrich Hausmann zum 70. Geburtstag*, ed. R. Härtel (Graz, 1987), 25–35.

———, 'Forschungen über Urkundenformeln', *MIÖG* 94 (1986), 285–339.

———, 'Monarchische Propaganda in Urkunden', in *Beiträge zur Mediävistik: ausgewählte Aufsätze*, 3 vols. (Stuttgart, 1975–86), II, 18–36.

Flint, V. I. J., 'The Career of Honorius Augustodunensis: Some Fresh Evidence', *Revue Bénédictine* 82 (1972), 63–86.

———, 'The Chronology of the Works of Honorius Augustodunensis', *Revue Bénédictine* 82 (1972), 215–42.

Foreville, R., 'Le sacre des rois anglo-normands et angevins et le serment du sacre (XI–XIIe siècles)', *Anglo-Norman Studies* I (1978), 49–63.

Fößel, A., *Die Königin im mittelalterlichen Reich: Herrschaftsausübung, Herrschaftsrechte, Handlungsspielräume* (Stuttgart, 2000).

Freed, J. B., *Frederick Barbarossa: The Prince and The Myth* (New Haven, 2016).

Fried, J., *Canossa: Entlarvung einer Legende: eine Streitschrift* (Berlin, 2012).

———, *Die Entstehung des Juristenstandes im 12. Jahrhundert: Zur sozialen Stellung und politischen Bedeutung gelehrter Juristen aus Bologna und Modena* (Cologne and Vienna, 1974).

———, 'Friedrich Barbarossas Krönung in Arles (1178)', *Historisches Jahrbuch* 103 (1983), 347–71.

———, 'Königsgedanken Heinrichs des Löwen', *Archiv für Kulturgeschichte* 55 (1973), 312–51.

———, 'Der Pakt von Canossa: Schritte zur Wirklichkeit durch Erinnerungsanalyse', in *Die Faszination der Papstgeschichte: Neue Zugänge zum frühen und hohen Mittelalter*, ed. W. Hartmann and K. Herbers (Cologne, 2008), pp. 133–98.

Fulton, R., *From Judgment to Passion: Devotion to Christ and the Virgin Mary, 800–1200* (New York, 2002).

———, '"Quae est ista ascendit sicut aurora consurgens?": The Song of Songs as the *historia* for the Office of the Assumption', *Mediaeval Studies* 60 (1998), 55–122.

Gabriele, M., *An Empire of Memory: The Legend of Charlemagne, the Franks, and Jerusalem before the First Crusade* (Oxford, 2011).

Gannon, A., *The Iconography of Early Anglo-Saxon Coinage: Sixth to Eighth Centuries* (Oxford, 2003).

Gaposchkin, M. C., 'The King of France and the Queen of Heaven: The Iconography of the Porte Rouge of Notre-Dame of Paris', *Gesta* 39 (2000), 58–73.

Bibliography

——, *The Making of Saint Louis: Kingship, Sanctity and Crusade in the Later Middle Ages* (Ithaca, 2008).
Garipzanov, I. H., *Graphic Signs of Authority in Late Antiquity and the Early Middle Ages* (Oxford, 2018).
——, 'Metamorphoses of the Early Medieval *Signum* of a Ruler in the Carolingian World', *Early Medieval Europe* 14 (2006), 419–64.
——, 'The Rise of Graphicacy in Late Antiquity and the Early Middle Ages', *Viator* 46 (2015), 1–21.
Garnett, G., *Conquered England: Kingship, Succession, and Tenure, 1066–1166* (Oxford, 2007).
——, 'Coronation and Propaganda: Some Implications of the Norman Claim to the Throne of England in 1066', *Transactions of the Royal Historical Society* 5th s. 36 (1986), 91–116.
——, 'The Third Recension of the English Coronation *Ordo*: The Manuscripts', *Haskins Society Journal* 11 (1998), 43–71.
Garrison, M., 'The Franks as the New Israel? Education for an Identity from Pippin to Charlemagne', in *The Uses of the Past in the Early Middle Ages*, ed. Y. Hen and M. Innes (Cambridge, 2002), pp. 114–61.
Gasparri, F., *L'écriture des actes de Louis VI, Louis VII et Philippe Auguste* (Paris, 1973).
Gathagan, L. L., 'The Trappings of Power: The Coronation of Mathilda of Flanders', *Haskins Society Journal* 13 (1999), 21–39.
Gawlik, A., 'Ein neues Siegel Heinrichs V. aus seiner Königszeit', in *Geschichte und ihre Quellen: Festschrift für Friedrich Hausmann zum 70. Geburtstag*, ed. R. Härtel (Graz, 1987), pp. 529–36.
Geertz, C., 'Centers, Kings and Charisma: Reflections on the Symbolics of Power', in *Culture and its Creators: Essays in Honor of Edward Shils*, ed. J. Ben-David and T. N. Clark (Chicago, 1977), pp. 150–71.
——, 'Thick Description: Toward an Interpretive Theory of Culture', in *The Interpretation of Cultures: Selected Essays*, ed. C. Geertz (New York, 1973), pp. 3–32.
Gerson, P. L., ed., *Abbot Suger and Saint-Denis* (New York, 1986).
Gervers, M., ed., *Dating Undated Medieval Charters* (Woodbridge, 2000).
Gillingham, J., *The Angevin Empire*, 2nd edn (London, 2001).
——, 'Conquering Kings: Some Twelfth-Century Reflections on Henry II and Richard I', in *Warriors and Churchmen in the High Middle Ages: Essays Presented to Karl Leyser*, ed. T. Reuter (London, 1992), pp. 163–78.
——, 'Doing Homage to the King of France', in *Henry II: New Interpretations*, ed. C. Harper-Bill and N. Vincent (Woodbridge, 2007), pp. 63–84.
——, 'Elective Kingship and the Unity of Medieval Germany', *German History* 9 (1991), 124–35.
——, 'The Meetings of the Kings of France and England, 1066–1204', in *Normandy and Its Neighbours, 900–1250: Essays for David Bates*, ed. D. Crouch (Turnhout, 2011), pp. 17–42.

———, *Richard I* (New Haven, 1999).
———, 'Richard I and Berengaria of Navarre', *Historical Research* 53 (1980), 157–73.
Gilsdorf, S., *The Favor of Friends: Intercession and Aristocratic Politics in Carolingian and Ottonian Europe* (Leiden, 2014).
Giry, A., *Manuel de diplomatique*, 2 vols. (Paris, 1894).
Goez, W., 'Von Bamberg nach Frankfurt und Aachen: Barbarossas Weg zur Königskrone', *Jahrbuch für fränkische Landesforschung* 52 (1992), 61–72.
Görich, K., *Friedrich Barbarossa: Eine Biographie* (Munich, 2011).
———, 'Karl der Große – ein "politischer Heiliger" im 12. Jahrhundert?', in *Religion und Politik im Mittelalter: Deutschland und England im Vergleich*, ed. L. Körntgen and D. Waßenhoven (Berlin, 2013), pp. 117–55.
Grant, L., *Abbot Suger or Saint-Denis: Church and State in Early Medieval France* (London, 1998).
Green, J. A., '"A Lasting Memorial": The Charter of Liberties of Henry I', in *Charters and Charter Scholarship in Britain and Ireland*, ed. M. T. Flanagan and J. A. Green (Basingstoke, 2005), pp. 53–69.
Green, N. L., 'Forms of Comparison', in *Comparison and History: Europe in Cross-National Perspective*, ed. D. Cohen and M. O'Connor (New York, 2004), pp. 41–56.
Greenway, D., 'Dates in History: Chronology and Memory', *Historical Research* 72 (1999), 127–39.
Grotefend, H., *Zeitrechnung des deutschen Mittelalters und der Neuzeit*, 2 vols. (Hannover, 1891).
Guerry, E., *Crowning Paris: King Louis IX, Archbishop Cornut, and the Translation of the Crown of Thorns*, Transactions of the American Philosophical Society (Philadelphia, forthcoming).
Guyotjeannin, O., 'Le monogramme dans l'acte royal français (Xe–début du XIVe siècle)', in *Graphische Symbole in mittelalterlichen Urkunden*, ed. P. Rück (Sigmaringen, 1996), pp. 293–307.
Guyotjeannin, O., J. Pycke and B.-M. Tock, ed., *Diplomatique Médiévale*, L'atelier du médiéviste, 2 (Turnhout, 1993).
Hack, A., *Das Empfangszeremoniell bei mittelalterlichen Papst-Kaiser-Treffen* (Cologne, 1999).
———, 'Zur Herkunft der karolingischen Königssalbung', *Zeitschrift für Kirchengeschichte* 110 (1999), 170–90.
Haines, R. M., 'Canterbury versus York: Fluctuating Fortunes in a Perennial Conflict', in *Ecclesia Anglicana: Studies in the English Church of the Later Middle Ages*, ed. R. M. Haines (Toronto, 1989), pp. 69–105.
Hallam, E. M., 'Royal Burial and the Cult of Kingship in France and England, 1060–1330', *Journal of Medieval History* 8 (1982), 359–80.
Hamilton, B., *The Leper King and His Heirs: Baldwin IV and the Crusader Kingdom of Jerusalem* (Cambridge, 2000).
———, 'Prester John and the Three Kings of Cologne', in *Studies in Medieval*

Bibliography

History Presented to R. H. C. Davis, ed. H. Mayr-Harting and R. I. Moore (London 1985), pp. 177–91.

———, 'Women in the Crusader States: The Queens of Jerusalem (1100–1190)', in *Medieval Women*, ed. D. Baker (Oxford, 1978), pp. 143–74.

Hare, M., 'Kings, Crowns and Festivals: The Origins of Gloucester as a Royal Ceremonial Centre', *Transactions of the Bristol and Gloucestershire Archaeological Society* 115 (1997), 41–78.

Harvey, P. D. A., and A. McGuinness, *A Guide to British Medieval Seals* (London, 1996).

Haskins, C. H., *The Renaissance of the Twelfth Century* (Cambridge, MA, 1927).

Hauck, K.,'Rituelle Speisegemeinschaft im 10. und 11. Jahrhundert', *Studium Generale* 3 (1950).

Haupt, H.-G. and J. Kocka, 'Comparative History: Methods, Aims, Problems', in *Comparison and History: Europe in Cross-National Perspective*, ed. D. Cohen and M. O'Connor (New York, 2004), pp. 23–40

Hausmann, F., *Reichskanzlei und Hofkapelle unter Heinrich V. und Konrad III.* (Stuttgart, 1956).

Hegg, L., S. Heimann and S. Kaufmann, ed., *Die Salier. Macht im Wandel: Katalog* (Munich, 2006).

Hehl, E.-D., 'Maria und das ottonisch-salische Königtum: Urkunden, Liturgie, Bilder', *Historisches Jahrbuch* 117 (1997), 271–310.

Heinemann, B., 'Der Freiheitsbrief Kaiser Heinrich VI. für die Stadt Konstanz vom 24. September 1192: Ein Beitrag zur Diplomatik der Staufenzeit', *Schriften des Vereins für Geschichte des Bodensees und seiner Umgebung* 44 (1915), 50–2.

Hen, Y., 'Key Themes in the Study of Early Medieval Liturgy', in *T&T Clark Companion to Liturgy*, ed. A. Reid (London, 2015), pp. 73–92.

Heslop, T. A., 'The English Origins of the Coronation of the Virgin', *The Burlington Magazine* 147 (2005), 790–7.

———, 'English Seals from the Mid-ninth Century to c.1100', *Journal of the British Archaeological Association* 132 (1980), 1–16.

———, 'Seals', in *English Romanesque Art, 1066–1200*, ed. G. Zarnecki, J. Holt and T. Holland (London, 1984), pp. 298–320.

———, 'Twelfth-Century Forgeries as Evidence for Earlier Seals: The Case of St. Dunstan', in *St Dunstan: His Life, Time and Cult*, ed. N. Ramsay, M. Sparks and T. W. T Tatton-Brown (Woodbridge, 1992), pp. 299–310.

———, 'The Virgin Mary's Regalia and Twelfth-Century English Seals', in *The Vanishing Past: Studies of Medieval Art, Liturgy and Metrology Presented to Christopher Hohler*, ed. A. Borg and A. Martindale (Oxford, 1981), pp. 53–63.

Hiestand, R., 'Kingship and Crusade in Twelfth-Century Germany', in *England and Germany in the High Middle Ages*, ed. A. Haverkamp and H. Vollrath (Oxford, 1996), pp. 235–65.

Hoffmann, H., *Buchkunst und Königtum im ottonischen und frühsalischen Reich*, 2 vols. (Stuttgart, 1986).

———, 'Canossa – eine Wende?', *Deutsches Archiv* 66 (2010), 535–69.
Hollister, C. W., *Henry I* (London, 2001).
Hollister C. W., and J. W. Baldwin, 'The Rise of Administrative Kingship: Henry I and Philip Augustus', *The American Historical Review* 83 (1978), 867–905.
Howlett, D., *Sealed from Within: Self-authenticating Insular Charters* (Dublin, 1999).
Huneycutt, L. L., 'Intercession and the High Medieval Queen: The Esther Topos', in *Power of the Weak: Studies on Medieval Women*, ed. J. Carpenter and S.-B. MacLean (Champaign, IL, 1995), pp. 126–46.
———, *Matilda of Scotland: A Study in Medieval Queenship* (Woodbridge, 2003).
Huschner, W., 'Kirchenfest und Herrschaftspraxis: Die Regierungszeiten der ersten beiden Kaiser aus liudolfingischem Hause (936–983)', *Zeitschrift für Geschichtswissenschaft* 41 (1993), 24–55, 117–34.
———, *Transalpine Kommunikation im Mittelalter: Diplomatische, kulturelle und politische Wechselwirkungen zwischen Italien und dem nordalpinen Reich (9.–11. Jahrhundert)* (Hannover, 2003).
Insley, C., 'Ottonians with Pipe Rolls? Political Culture and Performance in the Kingdom of the English, c. 900–c.1050', *History* 102 (2017), 772–86.
———, 'Where Did All the Charters Go? Anglo-Saxon Charters and the New Politics of the Eleventh Century', *Anglo-Norman Studies* XXIV (2001), 109–27.
Iogna-Prat, D., 'La Vierge et les *ordines* de couronnement des reines au IXe siècle', in *Marie: Le culte de la Vierge dans la société médiévale*, ed. D. Iogna-Prat, E. Palazzo and D. Russo (Paris, 1996), pp. 101–7.
Isabella, G., 'Das Sakralkönigtum in Quellen aus ottonischer Zeit: unmittelbarer Bezug zu Gott oder Vermittlung durch die Bischöfe', *Frühmittelalterliche Studien* 44 (2010), 137–52.
Jackson, R. A., *Vive le roi: History of the French Coronation from Charles V to Charles X* (Chapel Hill, 1984).
Jobson, A., ed., *English Government in the Thirteenth Century* (Woodbridge, 2004).
John, S. A., 'The "Feast of the Liberation of Jerusalem": Remembering and Reconstructing the First Crusade in the Holy City, 1099–1187', *Journal of Medieval History* 46 (2015), 409–31.
Johns, S. M., *Noblewomen, Aristocracy and Power in the Twelfth-Century Anglo-Norman Realm* (Manchester, 2003).
Johnson, E. A., 'Marian Devotion in the Western Church', in *Christian Spirituality: High Middle Ages and Reformation*, ed. J. Raitt (London, 1987), pp. 392–414.
Jolliffe, J. E. A., *Angevin Kingship*, 2nd edn (London, 1963).
Jung, H., 'Zeichen und Symbol: Bestandsaufname und interdiziplinäre Perspektiven', in *Graphische Symbole in mittelalterlichen Urkunden*, ed. P. Rück (Sigmaringen, 1996), pp. 49–66.

Bibliography

Jussen, B., 'The King's Two Bodies Today', *Representations* 106 (2009), 102–17.
Kantorowicz, E., 'Ivories and Litanies', *Journal of the Warburg and Courtauld Institutes* 5 (1942), 56–81.
——, *The King's Two Bodies: A Study in Mediaeval Political Theology*, 2nd edn (Princeton, 1997).
——, *Laudes Regiae: A Study in Liturgical Acclamations and Medieval Ruler Worship* (Berkeley, 1942).
Kahsnitz, R., 'Siegel und Goldbullen', in *Die Zeit der Staufer: Geschichte, Kunst, Kultur. Katalog der Ausstellung, Stuttgart 1977*, ed. R. Haussherr and C. Väterlein, 4 vols. (Stuttgart, 1977), I, 17–108.
Karkov, C. E., *The Ruler Portraits of Anglo-Saxon England* (Woodbridge, 2004).
Kasten, B., 'Krönungsordnungen für und Papstbriefe an mächtige Frauen im Hochmittelalter', in *Mächtige Frauen? Königinnen und Fürsten im europäischen Mittelalter (11.–14. Jahrhundert)*, ed. C. Zey, Vorträge und Forschungen 81 (Ostfildern, 2015), pp. 249–306.
Kauffmann, C. M., *Biblical Imagery in Medieval England 750–1550* (London, 2003).
Kehnel, A., 'The Power of Weakness: Machiavelli Revisited', *German Historical Institute Bulletin* 33 (2011), 3–34.
Keller, H., 'Identità romana e l'idea dell' *Imperium Romanorum* nel X e nel primo XI secolo', in *Three Empires, Three Cities: Identity, Material Culture and Legitimacy in Venice, Ravenna and Rome, 750–1000*, ed. V. West-Harling, Seminari internazionali del Centro interuniversitario per la storia e l'archeologia dell'alto medioevo 6 (Turnhout, 2015), pp. 255–82.
——, 'Ottonische Herrschersiegel: Beobachtungen und Fragen zu Gestalt und Aussage und zur Funktion im historischen Kontext', in *Bild und Geschichte: Studien zur politischen Ikonographie*, ed. K. Krimm and H. John (Sigmaringen, 1997) pp. 3–51.
——, 'Die Siegel und Bullen Ottos III.', in *Europas Mitte um 1000*, ed. H.-M. Hinz and A. Wieczorek (Stuttgart, 2000), pp. 767–73.
——, 'Zu den Siegeln der Karolinger und der Ottonen: Urkunden as "Hoheitszeichen" in der Kommunikation des Königs mit seinen Getreuen', *Frühmittelalterliche Studien* 32 (1998), 400–41.
Keynes, S., 'The Burial of King Æthelred the Unready at St Paul's', in *The English and their Legacy, 900–1200: Essays in Honour of Ann Williams*, ed. D. Roffe (Woodbridge, 2012), pp. 129–48.
——, 'The "Dunstan B" Charters', *Anglo-Saxon England* 23 (1994), 165–93.
Kjær, L., 'Food, Drink and Ritualised Communication in the Household of Eleanor de Montfort, February to August 1265', *Journal of Medieval History* 37 (2011), 75–89.
Klewitz, H.-W., 'Die Festkrönung der deutschen Könige', *Zeitschrift der Savigny-Stiftung für Rechtsgeschichte: Kanonistische Abteilung* 28 (1939), 48–96.
Klinkenberg, E. S., 'Romdarstellung auf Kaiser- und Königsbullen,

800–1250', in *Mikroarchitektur im Mittelalter: ein gattungsübergreifendes Phänomen zwischen Realität und Imagination*, ed. C. Kratze and U. Albrecht (Leipzig, 2008), pp. 225–49.

Koch, G., *Auf dem Wege zum Sacrum Imperium: Studien zur ideologischen Herrschaftsbegründung der deutschen Zentralgewalt im 11. und 12. Jahrhundert* (Cologne, 1972).

Koch, W., 'Epigraphik und die Auszeichnungsschrift in Urkunden', in *Documenti medievali greci e latini*, ed. G. de Gregorio and O. Kresten (Spoleto, 1998), pp. 309–26.

———, 'Zu Sprache, Stil und Arbeitstechnik in den Diplomen Friedrich Barbarossas', *MIÖG* 88 (1980), 36–69.

Körntgen, L., 'Herrscherbild im Wandel – Ein Neuansatz in staufischer Zeit?', in *BarbarossaBilder: Entstehungskontexte, Erwartungshorizonte, Verwendungszusammenhänge*, ed. K. Görich and R. Schmitz-Esser (Regensburg, 2014), pp. 32–45.

———, 'Der Investiturstreit und das Verhältnis von Religion und Politik im Frühmittelalter', in *Religion und Politik im Mittelalter: Deutschland und England im Vergleich* (Berlin, 2013), pp. 89–115.

———, *Königsherrschaft und Gottes Gnade: Zu Kontext und Funktion sakraler Vorstellungen in Historiographie und Bildzeugnisse der ottonisch-frühsalischen Zeit* (Berlin, 2001).

———, '"Sakrales Königtum" und "Entsakralisierung" in der Polemik um Heinrich IV.', in *Heinrich IV.*, ed. G. Althoff, Vorträge und Forschungen 69 (Ostfildern, 2009), pp. 127–60.

Koziol, G., 'England, France and the Problem of Sacrality in Twelfth-Century Ritual', in *Cultures of Power: Lordship, Status and Power in Twelfth-Century Europe*, ed. T. N. Bisson (Philadelphia, 1995), pp. 124–48.

———, *The Politics of Memory and Identity in Carolingian Royal Diplomas: The West Frankish Kingdom (840–987)*, Utrecht Studies in Medieval Literacy, 19 (Turnhout, 2012).

———, 'Review Article: The Dangers of Polemic: Is Ritual Still an Interesting Topic of Historical Study', *Early Medieval Europe* 11 (2002), 367–88.

Kuder, U., 'Die Ottonen in der ottonischen Buchmalerei: Identifikation und Ikonographie', in *Herrschaftsrepräsentation im ottonischen Sachsen*, ed. G. Althoff and E. Schubert, Vorträge und Forschungen 46 (Sigmaringen, 1998), pp. 137–234.

Lapidge, M., *Anglo-Saxon Litanies of the Saints*, HBS 106 (Woodbridge, 1991).

Lay, S., 'A Leper in Purple: The Coronation of Baldwin IV of Jerusalem', *Journal of Medieval History* 23 (1997), 317–23.

Laynesmith, J. L., *The Last Medieval Queens: English Queenship 1445–1503* (Oxford, 2004).

Le Goff, J., 'A Coronation Program for the Age of Saint Louis: The *Ordo* of 1250', in *Coronations: Medieval and Early Modern Monarchic Ritual*, ed. J. M. Bak (Berkeley, 1990), pp. 46–57.

———, *Saint Louis* (Paris, 1996).
Le Goff, J., et al., *Le sacre royal à l'époque de Saint Louis* (Paris, 2001).
Lendinara, P., 'Forgotten Missionaries: St Augustine of Canterbury in Anglo-Saxon and Post-Conquest England', in *Hagiography in Anglo-Saxon England: Adopting and Adapting Saints' Lives into Old England Prose (c.950–1150)*, ed. L. Lazzari, P. Lendinara and C. di Sciacca (Barcelona, 2014), pp. 365–497.
Levison, W., 'Die mittelalterliche Lehre von den beiden Schwerten', *Deutsches Archiv* 9 (1952), 14–42.
Lewis, A. W., 'Anticipatory Association of the Heir in Early Capetian France', *The American Historical Review* 83 (1978), 906–27.
———, 'La date du mariage de Louis VI et d'Adelaïde de Maurienne', *Bibliothèque de l'école des Chartes* 148 (1990), 5–16.
Leyser, K., 'Frederick Barbarossa, Henry II and the Hand of St. James', in *Medieval Germany and its Neighbours, 900–1250* (London, 1982), pp. 215–40.
———, *Rule and Conflict in an Early Medieval Society: Ottonian Saxony* (London, 1979).
———, 'Some Reflections of Twelfth-Century Kings and Kingship', in *Medieval Germany and its Neighbours 900–1250* (London, 1982), pp. 241–67.
Licence, T., 'The Cult of St Edmund', in *Bury St Edmunds and the Norman Conquest*, ed. T. Licence (Woodbridge, 2014), pp. 104–30.
Lohrmann, K., 'Die Titel der Kapetinger bis zum Tod Ludwigs VII.', in *Intitulatio III: Lateinische Herrschertitel und Herrschertitulaturen vom 7. bis zum 13. Jahrhundert*, ed. H. Wolfram and A. Scharer, MIÖG Ergänzungsband 29 (Graz, 1988), pp. 201–56.
Maddicott, J., 'Edward the Confessor's Return to England in 1041', *English Historical Review* 119 (2004), 650–66.
Marafioti, N., *The King's Body: Burial and Succession in Late Anglo-Saxon England* (Toronto, 2014).
Martindale, J., 'The Sword on the Stone: Some Resonances of a Medieval Symbol of Power', *Anglo-Norman Studies* XV (1992), 199–241.
Mason, E., 'The Hero's Invincible Weapon: An Aspect of Angevin Propaganda', in *The Ideals and Practice of Medieval Knighthood III*, ed. C. Harper-Bill and R. Harvey (Woodbridge, 1990), pp. 121–37.
———, 'The Site of King-making and Consecration: Westminster Abbey and the Crown in the Eleventh and Twelfth Centuries', in *The Church and Sovereignty: Essays in Honour of Michael Wilks*, ed. D. Wood, Studies in Church History Subsidia 9 (Oxford, 1991), pp. 57–76.
Matter, E. A., *The Voice of My Beloved: The Song of Songs in Western Medieval Christianity* (Philadelphia, 1990).
Maurer, H., 'Die Bischofsstadt Konstanz in staufischer Zeit', in *Südwestdeutsche Städte im Zeitalter der Staufer*, ed. E. Maschke and J. Sydow (Sigmaringen, 1980), pp. 68–94.
Mayer, H. E., 'Das Pontificale von Tyrus und die Krönung der lateinischen

Könige von Jerusalem: zugleich ein Beitrag zur Forschung über Herrschaftzeichen und Staatssymbolik', *Dumbarton Oaks Papers* 21 (1967), 213–30.

———, 'Staufische Weltherrschaft? Zum Brief Heinrichs II. von England an Friedrich Barbarossa von 1157', in *Festschrift Karl Pivec*, ed. A. Haidacher and H. E. Mayer, Innsbrucker Beiträge zur Kulturwissenschaft 12 (Innsbruck, 1966), pp. 265–78.

Mayer-Pfannholz, A., 'Die Wende von Canossa: Eine Studie zum Sacrum Imperium', *Hochland* 30 (1933), 385–404.

Mayr-Harting, H., *Ottonian Book Illumination: An Historical Study*, 2 vols. (London, 1991).

McNamer, S., *Affective Meditation and the Invention of Medieval Compassion* (Philadelphia, 2011).

Mentzel-Reuters, A., 'Die goldene Krone: Entwicklungslinien mittelalterlicher Herrschaftssymbolik', *Deutsches Archiv* 60 (2004), 135–82.

Merta, B., 'Die Titel Heinrichs II. und der Salier', in *Intitulatio III: Lateinische Herrschertitel und Herrschertitulaturen vom 7. bis zum 13. Jahrhundert*, ed. H. Wolfram and A. Scharer, MIÖG Ergänzungsband 29 (Graz, 1988), pp. 163–200.

Molyneaux, G., 'Did the English Really Think They Were God's Elect in the Anglo-Saxon Period?', *Journal of Ecclesiastical History* 65 (2014), 721–37.

Morison, S., *Politics and Script: Aspects of Authority and Freedom in the Development of Graeco-Latin Scripts from the Sixth Century B.C. to the Twentieth Century A.D.*, ed. N. Barker (Oxford, 1972).

Müller, H., et al., 'Pfalz und *vicus* Aachen in karolingischer Zeit', in *Aachen: von den Anfängen bis zur Gegenwart*, 7 vols. (Aachen, 2011–), II, 1–408.

Nelson, J. L., 'Aachen as a Place of Power', in *Topographies of Power in the Early Middle Ages*, ed. M. de Jong and F. Theuws (Leiden, 2001), pp. 217–37.

———, 'The Earliest Surviving Royal *Ordo*: Some Liturgical and Historical Aspects', in *Authority and Power: Studies on Medieval Law and Government Presented to Walter Ullmann on his Seventieth Birthday*, ed. B. Tierney and P. Linehan (Cambridge, 1980), pp. 29–48.

———, 'Inauguration Rituals', in *Politics and Ritual in Early Medieval Europe* (London, 1986), pp. 283–307.

———, 'Kingship and Empire', in *The Cambridge History of Medieval Political Thought c.350–c.1450*, ed. J. H. Burns (Cambridge, 1988), pp. 211–51.

———, 'Liturgy or Law: Misconceived Alternatives?', in *Early Medieval Studies in Memory of Patrick Wormald*, ed. S. Baxter et al. (Aldershot, 2009), pp. 433–50.

———, 'The Lord's Anointed and the People's Choice: Carolingian Royal Ritual', in *The Frankish World 750–900* (London, 1996), pp. 99–132.

———, 'The Rites of the Conqueror', *Anglo-Norman Studies* IV (1982), 117–32.

———, 'Ritual and Reality in the Early Medieval *Ordines*', in *Politics and Ritual in Early Medieval Europe* (London, 1986), pp. 329–39.

———, 'Rituals of Royal Inauguration in Early Medieval Europe' (unpublished PhD dissertation, University of Cambridge, 1967).

———, 'Symbols in Context: Rulers' Inauguration Rituals in Byzantium and the West in the Early Middle Ages', in *The Orthodox Churches and the West*, ed. D. Baker, Studies in Church History 13 (Oxford, 1976), pp. 97–119.

Niederkorn, J. P., 'Zu glatt und daher verdächtig? Zur Glaubwürdigkeit der Schilderung der Wahl Friedrich Barbarossas (1152) durch Otto von Freising', *MIÖG* 115 (2007), 1–9.

Noble, T. F. X., 'Introduction', in *European Transformations: The Long Twelfth Century*, ed. T. F. X. Noble and J. van Engen (Notre Dame, 2012), pp. 1–16.

Nolan, K., 'The Tomb of Adelaide of Maurienne and the Visual Imagery of Capetian Queenship', in *Capetian Women*, ed. K. Nolan (Basingstoke, 2003), pp. 45–76.

Oexle, O. G., 'Die Memoria Heinrich des Löwen', in *Memoria in der Gesellschaft des Mittelalters*, ed. D. Geuenich and O. G. Oexle, Veröffentlichungen des Max-Planck-Instituts für Geschichte 111 (Göttingen, 1994), pp. 128–77.

Opfermann, B., *Die liturgischen Herrscherakklamationen im Sacrum Imperium des Mittelalters* (Weimar, 1953).

Oppenheimer, F., *The Legend of the Ste. Ampoule* (London, 1953).

Oppitz-Trotman, G., 'The Emperor's Robe: Thomas Becket and Angevin Political Culture', *Anglo-Norman Studies* XXXVII (2015), 205–19.

Oschema, K., *Bilder von Europa im Mittelalter* (Ostfildern, 2013).

Panofsky, E., *Abbot Suger on the Abbey Church of Saint-Denis and its Art Treasures* (Princeton, 1946).

Parisse, M., 'Les chartes des évêques de Metz au XIIe siècle: étude diplomatique et paléographique', *Archiv für Diplomatik* 22 (1976), 272–316.

Parkes, H., *The Making of Liturgy in the Ottonian Church: Books, Music and Ritual in Mainz, 950–1050* (Cambridge, 2015).

———, 'Questioning the Authority of Vogel and Elze's *Pontifical romano-germanique*', in *Understanding Medieval Liturgy: Essays in Interpretation*, ed. S. Hamilton and H. Gittos (Farnham, 2016), pp. 75–101.

Parsons, J. C., 'The Intercessionary Patronage of Margaret and Isabella of France', *Thirteenth Century England* VI (1997), 145–56.

———, 'Introduction: Family, Sex, and Power: The Rhythms of Medieval Queenship', in *Medieval Queenship*, ed. J. C. Parsons (Stroud, 1994), pp. 1–14.

———, 'The Queen's Intercession in Thirteenth-Century England', in *Power of the Weak: Studies on Medieval Women*, ed. J. Carpenter and S.-B. MacLean (Champaign, IL, 1995), pp. 147–77.

Peltzer, J. 'Introduction', in *Princely Rank in Late Medieval Europe: Trodden Paths and Promising Avenues*, ed. T. Huthwelker, J. Peltzer and M. Wemhöner (Ostfildern, 2001), pp. 11–25.

Petersohn, J., *"Echte" und "falsche" Insignien im deutschen Krönungsbrauch des*

Mittelalters?, Sitzungsberichte der wissenschaftlichen Gesellschaft an der Johann-Wolfgang-Goethe-Universität Frankfurt am Main 30 (Stuttgart, 1993).

———, *Kaisertum und Rom in spätsalischer und staufischer Zeit* (Hannover, 2010).

———, 'Saint-Denis – Westminster – Aachen: die Karls-Translatio von 1165 und ihre Vorbilder', *Deutsches Archiv* 31 (1975), 420–54.

———, 'Über monarchische Insignien und ihre Funktion im mittelalterlichen Reich', *Historische Zeitschrift* 266 (1998), 47–96.

Plassmann, A., 'The King and His Sons: Henry II's and Frederick Barbarossa's Succession Strategies Compared', *Anglo-Norman Studies* XXXVI (2014), 149–66.

Porteous, J., 'Crusader Coinage with Greek or Latin Inscriptions', in *A History of the Crusades: The Impact of the Crusades on Europe*, ed. H. W. Hazard and N. P. Zacour (Madison, 1989), pp. 354–87.

Pössel, C., 'The Magic of Early Medieval Ritual', *Early Medieval Europe* 17 (2009), 111–125.

Rader, O. B., 'Kreuze und Kronen: Zum byzantinischen Einfluss im 'Krönungsbild' des Evangeliars Heinrich des Löwen', in *Heinrich der Löwe: Herrschaft und Repräsentation*, ed. J. Fried and O. G. Oexle, Vorträge und Forschungen 57 (Ostfildern, 2003), pp. 199–238.

Reuter, T., 'All Quiet Except on the Western Front? The Emergence of Pre-modern Forms of Statehood in the Central Middle Ages', in in *Medieval Polities and Modern Mentalities*, ed. J. L. Nelson (Cambridge, 2006), pp. 432–58.

———, 'The "Imperial Church System" of the Ottonian and Salian Rulers: A Reconsideration', in *Medieval Polities and Modern Mentalities*, ed. J. L. Nelson (Cambridge, 2006), pp. 325–54.

———, 'The Making of England and Germany, 850–1050: Points of Comparison and Difference', in *Medieval Polities and Modern Mentalities*, ed. J. L. Nelson (Cambridge, 2006), pp. 284–99.

———, 'Mandate, Privilege, Court Judgement: Techniques of Rulership in the Age of Frederick Barbarossa', in *Medieval Polities and Modern Mentalities*, ed. J. L. Nelson (Cambridge, 2006), pp. 413–31.

———, 'The Medieval German *Sonderweg*? The Empire and Its Rulers in the High Middle Ages', in *Medieval Polities and Modern Mentalities*, ed. J. L. Nelson (Cambridge, 2006), pp. 388–412.

———, '*Velle Sibi Fieri in Forma Hac*: Symbolic Acts in the Becket Dispute', in *Medieval Polities and Modern Mentalities*, ed. J. L. Nelson (Cambridge, 2006), pp. 167–90.

Reynolds, S., 'The Historiography of the Medieval State', in *Companion to Historiography*, ed. M. Bentley (London, 1997), pp. 117–38.

———, 'There were States in Medieval Europe: A Response to Rees Davies', *Journal of Historical Sociology* 16 (2003), 550–5.

Richardson, H. G., 'The Coronation in Medieval England: The Evolution of the Office and the Oath', *Traditio* 16 (1960), 111–202.
——, 'The English Coronation Oath', *Speculum* 24 (1949), 44–75.
——, 'The English Coronation Oath', *Transactions of the Royal Historical Society* 4th s. 23 (1941), 129–58.
Richter, C., 'Der Sinn der Dei-gratia-Formel in den französichen und deutschen Dynastenurkunden bis zum Jahre 1000 Untersucht mit besonderer Berücksichtigung der Geschichte dieser Formel von der paulinischen Zeit an' (unpublished PhD thesis, Johann Wolfgang Goethe-Universität Frankfurt am Main, 1974).
Ridyard, S. J., *The Royal Saints of Anglo-Saxon England: A Study of West Saxon and East Anglian Cults* (Cambridge, 1988).
Roach, L., 'Penance, Submission and *deditio*: Religious Influences on Dispute Settlement in Later Anglo-Saxon England (871–1066)', *Anglo-Saxon England* 41 (2012), 343–71.
Roberts, E., 'Flodoard, the Will of St Remigius and the See of Reims in the Tenth Century', *Early Medieval Europe* 22 (2014), 201–30.
Robinson, I. S., *Authority and Resistance in the Investiture Contest: The Polemical Literature of the Late Eleventh Century* (Manchester, 1978).
——, *The Papacy, 1073–1198: Continuity and Innovation* (Cambridge, 1990).
Rogge, J., *Die deutschen Könige im Mittelalter: Wahl und Krönung* (Darmstadt, 2006).
Rolker C., and M. Schawe, 'Das Gutachten Ivos von Chartres zur Krönung König Ludwigs VI.', *Francia: Forschungen zur westeuropäischen Geschichte* 34 (2007), 146–57.
Rollason, D., 'St Oswald in Post-Conquest England', in *Oswald: Northumbrian King to European Saint*, ed. C. Stancliffe and E. Cambridge (Stamford, 1995), pp. 164–77.
Rosenwein, B. H., ed., *Anger's Past: The Social Uses of an Emotion in the Middle Ages* (Ithaca, 1998).
Rück, P., 'Die Urkunde als Kunstwerk', in *Kaiserin Theophanu: Begegnung des Ostens und Westens um die Wende des ersten Jahrtausends*, ed. A. von Euw and P. Schreiner, 2 vols. (Cologne, 1991), II, 311–33.
Ruehl, M., '"In this Time without Emperors": The Politics of Ernst Kanotorowicz's *Kaiser Friedrich der Zweite* Reconsidered', *Journal of the Warburg and Courtauld Institutes* 63 (2000), 187–242.
Rumble, A. R., 'From Winchester to Canterbury: Ælfheah and Stigand – Bishops, Archbishops and Victims', in *Leaders of the Anglo-Saxon Church from Bede to Stigand*, ed. A. R. Rumble (Woodbridge, 2012), pp. 165–82.
Rushforth, R., *Saints in English Kalendars Before A.D. 1100*, HBS 117 (Woodbridge, 2008).
Sadler, D., 'The King as Subject, the King as Author: Art and Politics of Louis IX', in *European Monarchy: Its Evolution and Practice from Roman*

Antiquity to Modern Times, ed. H. Duchhardt, R. A. Jackson and D. Sturdy (Stuttgart, 1992), pp. 53–68.

Saur, M., 'Königserhebung im antiken Israel', in *Investitur- und Krönungsrituale: Herrschaftseinsetzungen im kulturellen Vergleich*, ed. M. Steinicke and S. Weinfurter (Cologne, 2005), pp. 29–42.

Sayers, J. E., 'The Land of Chirograph, Writ and Seal: The Absence of Graphic Symbols in English Documents', in *Graphische Symbole in mittelalterlichen Urkunden*, ed. P. Rück (Sigmaringen, 1996), pp. 533–48.

Scales, L., *The Shaping of German Identity: Authority and Crisis, 1245–1414* (Cambridge, 2012).

Schaller, H. M., 'Der heilige Tag als Termin mittelalterliche Staatsakte,' *Deutsches Archiv* 30 (1974), 1–24.

Schieffer, R., 'Die Ausbreitung der Königssalbung im hochmittelalterlichen Europa', in *Die mittelalterliche Thronfolge im europäischen Vergleich*, ed. M. Becher, Vorträge und Forschungen 84 (2017), pp. 43–79.

———, '"Mediator cleri et plebis": Zum geistlichen Einfluß auf Verständnis und Darstellung des ottonischen Königtums', in *Herrschaftsrepräsentation im ottonischen Sachsen*, ed. G. Althoff and E. Schubert, Vorträge und Forschungen 46 (Sigmaringen, 1998), pp. 345–61.

Schimmelpfennig, B., 'Die Bedeutung Roms in päpstlichen Zeremoniell', in *Rom im hohen Mittelalter: Studien zu den Romvorstellung und zur Rompolitik von 10. bis zum 12. Jahrhundert*, ed. B. Schimmelpfennig and L. Schmugge (Sigmaringen, 1992), pp. 7–61.

Schmidt, A., *'Bischof bist Du und Fürst': Die Erhebung geistlicher Reichsfürsten im Spätmittelalter –Trier, Bamberg, Augsburg* (Heidelberg, 2015).

Schmidt-Wiegand, R., 'Die rechtshistorische Funktion graphische Zeichen und Symbole in Urkunden', in *Graphische Symbole in mittelalterlichen Urkunden*, ed. P. Rück (Sigmaringen, 1996), pp. 67–79.

Schneidmüller, B., 'Außenblick für das eigene Herz: Vergleichende Wahrnehmung politischer Ordnung im hochmittelalterlichen Deutschland und Frankreich', in *Das europäische Mittelalter im Spannungsbogen des Vergleichs: Zwanzig internationale Beiträge zu Praxis, Problemen und Perspektiven der historischen Komparatistik*, ed. M. Borgolte (Berlin, 2001), pp. 315–38.

———, 'Canossa – Das Ereignis', in *Canossa 1077 – Erschütterung der Welt: Geschichte, Kunst und Kultur am Aufgang der Romanik*, ed. C. Stiegemann and M. Wemhoff (Munich, 2006), pp. 36–46.

———, 'Herrscher über Land und Leute? Der kapetingische Herrschertitel in der Zeit Philipps II. August und seiner Nachfolger (1180–1270)', in *Intitulatio III: Lateinische Herrschertitel und Herrschertitulaturen vom 7. bis zum 13. Jahrhundert*, ed. H. Wolfram and A. Scharer, MIÖG Ergänzungsband 29 (Graz, 1988), pp. 131–62.

———, 'Kronen im goldglänzenden Buch: Mittelalterliche Welfenbilder und das Helmarshausener Evangeliar Heinrichs des Löwen und Mathildes',

Bibliography

in *Helmarshausen: Buchkultur und Goldschmiedekunst im Hochmittelalter*, ed. I. Baumgärtner (Kassel, 2003), pp. 123–46.

Schramm, P. E., *Die deutschen Kaiser und Könige in Bildern ihrer Zeit* (Leipzig, 1928).

———, *A History of the English Coronation*, trans. L. G. Wickham Legg (Oxford, 1937).

———, 'Die Kronen des frühen Mittelalters', in *Herrschaftszeichen und Staatssymbolik: Beiträge zu ihrer Geschichte vom dritten bis zum sechzehnten Jahrhundert*, 3 vols. (Stuttgart, 1954–78), II, 378–417.

———, 'Die *Ordines* der mittelalterlichen Kaiserkrönung: Ein Beitrag zur Geschichte des Kaisertums', *Archiv für Urkundenforschung* 11 (1930), 285–390.

———, '*Ordines*-Studien II: Die Krönung bei den Westfranken und den Franzosen', *Archiv für Urkundenforschung* 15 (1938), 4–55.

———, 'Die Throne des deutschen Königs: Karls des Großen Steinthron und Heinrich IV. Bronzethron', in *Herrschaftszeichen und Staatssymbolik: Beiträge zu ihrer Geschichte vom dritten bis zum sechzehnten Jahrhundert*, 3 vols. (Stuttgart, 1954–78), I, 336–69.

Schroll A.-L., and E. Reversi, ed., *Brief und Kommunikation im Wandel: Medien, Autoren und Kontexte in den Debatten des Investiturstreits* (Cologne, 2016).

Schulze-Dörrlamm, M., *Das Reichsschwert*, Römisch-germanisches Zentralmuseum Forschungsinstitut für Vor- und Frühgeschichte 32 (Sigmaringen, 1995).

Ševčenko, I., 'Ernst H. Kantorowicz (1895–1963) on Late Antiquity and Byzantium', in *Ernst Kantorowicz: Erträge der Doppeltagung Institute for Advanced Study, Princeton/Johann Wolfgang Goethe-Universität, Frankfurt*, ed. R. L. Benson and J. Fried, Frankfurter Historische Abhandlungen 39 (Stuttgart, 1997), pp. 274–87.

Sewell Jr, W. H., 'Marc Bloch and the Logic of Comparative History', *History and Theory* 6 (1967), 208–18.

Shadis, M., 'Blanche of Castile and Marion Facinger's "Medieval Queenship": Reassessing the Argument', in *Capetian Women*, ed. K. Nolan (New York, 2003), pp. 137–61.

Sharpe, R., 'The Setting of St Augustine's Translation, 1091', in *Canterbury and the Norman Conquest: Churches, Saints and Scholars, 1066–1109*, ed. R. Eales and R. Sharpe (London, 1995), pp. 1–13.

Sierck, M., *Festtag und Politik: Studien zur Tagewahl karolingischer Herrscher*, Beihefte zum Archiv für Kulturgeschichte 38 (Cologne, 1995).

Simpson, G. G., 'Kingship in Miniature: A Seal of Minority of Alexander III, 1249–1257', in *Medieval Scotland: Crown, Lordship and Community: Essays Presented to G. W. S. Barrow*, ed. K. J. Stringer and A. Grant (Edinburgh, 1993), pp. 131–9.

Sluga, G., 'The Nation and the Comparative Imagination', in *Comparison and History: Europe in Cross-National Perspective*, ed. D. Cohen and M. O'Connor (New York, 2004), pp. 103–14.

Smith, J. A., 'The Earliest Queen-Making Rites', *Church History* 66 (1997), 18–35.
Smith, R. J., 'Henry II's Heir: The Acta and Seal of Henry the Young King, 1170–83', *English Historical Review* 116 (2001), 297–326.
Spiegel, G., 'History as Enlightenment: Suger and the *Mos Anagogicus*', in *Abbot Suger and Saint-Denis: A Symposium*, ed. P. L. Gerson (New York, 1986), pp. 151–9.
———, *Romancing the Past: The Rise of Vernacular Prose Historiography in Thirteenth-Century France* (Berkeley, 1995).
Stafford, P., 'Charles the Bald, Judith and England', in *Charles the Bald: Court and Kingdom*, ed. M. T. Gibson and J. L. Nelson, 2nd edn (Aldershot, 1990), pp. 139–53.
———, '*Cherchez la femme*: Queens, Queens' Lands and Nunneries: Missing Links in the Foundation of Reading Abbey', *History* 85 (2000), 4–27.
———, 'The Laws of Cnut and the History of Anglo-Saxon Royal Promises', *Anglo-Saxon England* 10 (1981), 173–90.
———, 'Political Ideas in Late Tenth-Century England: Charters as Evidence', in *Law, Laity and Solidarities: Essays in Honour of Susan Reynolds*, ed. P. Stafford, J. L. Nelson and J. Martindale (Manchester, 2001), pp. 68–82.
Staubach, N., '"Regia sceptra sacrans": Erzbischof Hinkmar von Reims, der heilige Remigius und die "Sainte Ampoule"', *Frühmittelalterliche Studien* 40 (2006), 79–101.
Stiegemann C., and M. Wemhoff, ed., *Canossa 1077 – Erschütterung der Welt: Geschichte, Kunst und Kultur am Aufgang der Romanik*, 2 vols. (Munich, 2006).
Stieldorf, A., 'Die Magie der Urkunden', *Archiv für Diplomatik* 55 (2009), 1–32.
———, 'Die Siegel der Herrscherinnen – Siegelführung und Siegelbild der "deutschen" Kaiserinnen und Königinnen', *Rheinische Vierteljahrsblätter* 64 (2000), 1–44.
Strayer, J. R., *On the Medieval Origins of the Modern State* (Princeton, 1970).
Strickland, M., *Henry the Young King, 1155–1183* (New Haven, 2016).
Stroll, M., '*Maria Regina*: Papal Symbol', in *Queens and Queenship in Medieval Europe*, ed. A. J. Duggan (Woodbridge, 1997), pp. 173–203.
Struve, T., 'Die Rolle des römischen Rechts in der kaiserlichen Theorie vor Roncaglia', in *Gli inizi del diritto pubblico: L'età de Frederico Barbarossa: legislazione e scienza del diritto*, ed. G. Dilcher and D. Quaglioni (Bologna, 2007), pp. 71–99.
———, 'Die Salier und das römische Recht: Ansätze zur Entwicklung einer säkularen Herrschaftstheorie in der Zeit des Investiturstreites', *Akademie der Wissenschaften Mainz: Abhandlung der Geistes- und Sozialwissenschaftlichen Klasse* 5 (1999), 7–89.
———, Die Stellung des Königtums in der politischen Theorie der

Salierzeit', in *Die Salier und das Reich*, ed. S. Weinfurter, 3 vols. (Sigmaringen, 1991), III, 217–44.

Stuckey, J., 'Charlemagne as Crusader? Memory, Propaganda, and the Many Uses of Charlemagne's Legendary Expedition to Spain', in *The Legend of Charlemagne in the Middle Ages: Power, Faith and Crusade*, ed. M. Gabriele and J. Stuckey (New York, 2008), pp. 137–52.

Stürner, W., 'König Heinrich (VII.): Rebell oder Sachwalter staufischer Interessen?', in *Der Staufer Heinrich (VII.): Ein König im Schatten seines kaiserlichen Vaters*, ed. A. Dörner-Winkler (Göppingen, 2001), pp. 12–42.

Taylor, A., 'Historical Writing in Twelfth- and Thirteenth-Century Scotland: The Dunfermline Compilation', *Historical Research* 83 (2010), 228–52.

Thacker, A., 'Cults at Canterbury: Relics and Reform under Dunstan and his Successors', in *St Dunstan: His Life, Times and Cult*, ed. N. Ramsey, M. Sparks and T. Tatton-Brown (Woodbridge, 1992), pp. 221–45.

———, '*Membra Disjecta*: The Division of the Body and the Diffusion of the Cult', in *Oswald: Northumbrian King to European Saint*, ed. C. Stancliffe and E. Cambridge (Stamford, 1995), pp. 97–127.

Thayer, A. T., 'Judith and Mary: Hélinand's Sermon for the Assumption', in *Medieval Sermons and Society: Cloister, City, University*, ed. B. M. Kienzle et al. (Louvain-la-Neuve, 1998), pp. 63–75.

Ther, P., 'Beyond the Nation: The Relational Basis of a Comparative History of Germany and Europe', *Central European History* 36 (2003), 45–73.

Thérel, M.-L., *Le Triomphe de la Vierge-Eglise* (Paris, 1984).

Tock, B.-M., 'The Political Use of Piety in Episcopal and Comital Charters of the Eleventh and Twelfth Centuries', in *Negotiating Secular and Ecclesiastical Power*, ed. H. Teunis, A. Wareham and A.-J. A. Bijsterveld, International Medieval Research 6 (Turnhout, 1999), pp. 19–35.

———, *Scribes, souscripteurs et témoins dans les actes privés en France (VIIe–début du XIIe siècle)*, Atelier de recherches sur les textes médiévaux 9 (Turnhout, 2005).

Töpfer, B., 'Tendenzen der Entsakralisierung der Herrscherwürde in der Zeit des Investiturstreites', *Jahrbuch für Geschichte des Feudalismus* 6 (1982), 164–71.

Twining, E., *European Regalia* (London, 1967).

Twyman, S., *Papal Ceremonial at Rome in the Twelfth Century*, HBS Subsidia 4 (Woodbridge, 2002).

Ullmann, W., *The Carolingian Renaissance and the Idea of Kingship* (London, 1969).

———, *The Growth of Papal Government in the Middle Ages: A Study in the Ideological Relation of Clerical to Lay Power* (London, 1955).

———, *Principles of Government and Politics in the Middle Ages* (London, 1966).

———, 'Schranken der Königsgewalt im Mittelalter', *Historisches Jahrbuch* 91 (1971), 1–21.

van Deusen, N., '*Laudes Regiae*: In Praise of Kings, Medieval Acclamations, Liturgy and the Ritualization of Power', in *Procession, Performance, Liturgy and Ritual*, ed. N. van Deusen (Ottawa, 2007), pp. 83–118.
van Houts, E. M. C., 'Cnut and William: A Comparison' (forthcoming).
Verdier, P., *La Couronnement de la Vierge: Les origines et le premiers développements d'un thème iconographique* (Montréal, 1980).
Vincent, N., 'The Court of Henry II', in *Henry II: New Interpretations*, ed. C. Harper-Bill and N. Vincent (Woodbridge, 2007), pp. 278–334

———, 'King Henry III and the Blessed Virgin Mary', in *The Church and Mary*, ed. R .N. Swanson, Studies in Church History 39 (Woodbridge, 2004), pp. 126–46.

———, *The Magna Carta* (New York, 2007).

———, 'The Pilgrimages of the Angevin Kings of England 1154–1272', in *Pilgrimage: The English Experience from Becket to Bunyan*, ed. C. Morris and P. Roberts (Cambridge, 2002), pp. 12–45.

———, 'Regional Variations in the Charters of King Henry II (1154–89)', in *Charters and Charter Scholarship in Britain and Ireland*, ed. M. T. Flanagan and J. A. Green (Basingstoke, 2005), pp. 70–106.

———, 'Stephen Langton, Archbishop of Canterbury', in *Étienne Langton, prédicateur, bibliste, théologien*, ed. L.-J. Bataillon et al., Bibliothèque d'histoire culturelle du Moyen Âge 9 (Turnhout, 2010), pp. 51–126.

———, 'The Strange Case of the Missing Biographies: The Lives of the Plantagenet Kings of England 1154–1272', in *Writing Medieval Biography: Essays in Honour of Professor Frank Barlow*, ed. D. Bates, J. Crick and S. Hamilton (Woodbridge, 2006), pp. 237–57.

———, 'Twelfth and Thirteenth-Century Kingship: An Essay in Anglo-French Misunderstanding', in *Les ideés passent-elles La Manche? Savoirs, representation, pratiques (France-Angleterre, Xe–XXe siècles)*, ed. J.-P. Genêt and F.-J. Ruggiu (Paris, 2007), pp. 21–36.
von Knonau, G. M., *Jahrbücher des deutschen Reiches unter Heinrich IV. und Heinrich V.*, 7 vols. (Leipzig, 1890–1909).
von Simson, O., *The Gothic Cathedral: Origins of Gothic Architecture and the Medieval Concept of Order*, 3rd edn (Princeton, 1988).
Vones, L., 'Heiligsprechung und Tradition: Die Kanonisation Karls des Großen 1165, die Aachener Karlsvita und der Pseudo-Turpin', in *Jakobus und Karl der Große: Von Einhards Karlsvita zum Pseudo-Turpin*, ed. K. Herbers, Jakobus-Studien 14 (Tübingen, 2003), pp. 87–105.
Waitz, G., *Die Formeln der deutschen Königs- und der römischen Kaiser-Krönung vom zehnten bis zum zwölften Jahrhundert* (Göttingen, 1872).
Warner, D. A., 'Comparative Approaches to Anglo-Saxon and Ottonian Coronations', in *England and the Continent in the Tenth Century: Studies in Honour of Wilhelm Levison (1876–1947)*, ed. D. Rollason, C. Leyser and H. Williams (Turnhout, 2010), pp. 275–92.

———, 'Reading Ottonian History: The "Sonderweg" and Other Myths', in

Bibliography

Challenging the Boundaries of Medieval History: The Legacy of Timothy Reuter, ed. P. Skinner (Turnhout, 2009), pp. 81–114.
Watts, J., *The Making of Polities: Europe, 1300–1500* (Cambridge, 2009).
Webster, P., *King John and Religion* (Woodbridge, 2015).
Weiler, B. K. U., *Henry III of England and the Staufen Empire, 1216–1272* (Woodbridge, 2006).
———, 'The King as Judge: Henry II and Frederick Barbarossa as Seen by Their Contemporaries', in *Challenging the Boundaries of Medieval History: The Legacy of Timothy Reuter*, ed. P. Skinner (Turnhout, 2009), pp. 115–40.
———, *Kingship, Rebellion and Political Culture: England and Germany, c.1215–c.1250* (Basingstoke, 2007).
———, 'Review Article: Power and Politics in Medieval History, c.850–c.1170', *Early Medieval Europe* 16 (2008), 477–93.
———, 'Suitability and Right: Imperial Succession and the Norms of Politics in Early Staufen Germany', in *Making and Breaking the Rules: Succession in Medieval Europe, c.1000–c.1600*, ed. F. Lachaud and M. Penman (Turnhout, 2008), pp. 71–86.
Weinfurter, S., 'Canossa als Chiffre: von den Möglichkeiten historischen Deutens', in *Canossa: Aspekte einer Wende*, ed. W. Hasberg and H.-J. Scheidgen (Regensburg, 2012), pp. 124–40.
———, *Canossa: Die Entzauberung der Welt* (Munich, 2006).
———, 'Idoneität – Begründung und Akzeptanz von Königsherrschaft im hohen Mittelalter', in *Idoneität – Genealogie – Legitimation: Begründung und Akzeptanz von dynastische Herrschaft im Mittelalter*, ed. C. Andenna and G. Melville (Cologne, 2015), pp. 127–37.
———, 'Sakralkönigtum und Herrschaftsbegründung um die Jahrtausendwende: Die Kaiser Otto III. und Heinrich II. in ihren Bildern', in *Bilder erzählen Geschichte*, ed. H. Altrichter (Freiburg im Breisgau, 1995), pp. 47–104.
Weiss, D. H., 'Architectural Symbolism and the Decoration of the Ste.-Chapelle', *The Art Bulletin* 77 (1995), 308–20.
Weiss, U.-R., *Die Konstanzer Bischöfe im 12. Jahrhundert: Ein Beitrag zur Untersuchungen der reichsbischöflichen Stellung im Kräftefeld kaiserlicher, päpstlicher und regional-diözesaner Politik* (Sigmaringen, 1975).
Wickham, C., 'Problems in Doing Comparative History', in *Challenging the Boundaries of Medieval History: The Legacy of Timothy Reuter*, ed. P. Skinner (Turnhout, 2009), pp. 5–28.
Wild, B. L., 'The Empress's New Clothes: A Rotulus Pannorum of Isabella, Sister of King Henry III, Bride of Emperor Frederick II', *Medieval Clothing and Textiles* 7 (2011), 2–31.
———, 'Royal Finance Under King Henry III, 1216–72: The Wardrobe Evidence', *Economic History Review* 65 (2012), 1380–1402.
Williams, A., *Æthelred the Unready: The Ill-Counselled King* (London, 2003).
Wolf, G., 'Königinnen-Krönungen des frühen Mittelalters bis zum Beginn

Bibliography

des Investiturstreits', *Zeitschrift der Savigny-Stiftung für Rechtsgeschichte: Kanonistische Abteilung* 76 (1990), 62–88.

Wolfram, H., *Intitulatio I: Lateinische Königs- und Fürstentitel bis zum Ende des 8. Jahrhunderts*, MIÖG Ergänzungsband 21 (Graz, 1967).

———, 'Political Theory and Narrative in Charters', *Viator* 26 (1995), 39–52.

Wormald, P., *The Making of English Law: King Alfred to the Twelfth Century* (Oxford, 1999).

Zey, C., '"Imperatrix, si venerit Romam...": Zu den Krönungen von Kaiserinnen im Mittelalter, *Deutsches Archiv* 60 (2004), 3–52.

Zimmermann, M., 'La datation des documents catalans du IXe au XIIe siècle: un itinéraire politique', *Annales du Midi* 43 (1981), 345–75.

Zinn, Jr, G. A., 'Suger, Theology, and the Pseudo-Dionysian Tradition', in *Abbot Suger and Saint-Denis: A Symposium*, ed. P. L. Gerson (New York, 1986), pp. 33–40.

Index of Biblical References

Genesis 1. 26–7   214
Genesis 27. 28–9   50
Genesis 32. 22–32   109–10

Exodus 23. 20–3   54

Judges 8. 22–3   49

I Samuel 8   50
I Samuel 10. 1   50
I Samuel 15. 23   50
I Samuel 16. 1–14   59
I Samuel 17. 49–51   52

I Kings 1. 45   55
I Kings 2. 2–3   57
I Kings 10. 18–20   119, 195

Judith 13. 8–10   52

Esther 2. 17   52

Psalm 8. 6–7   150
Psalm 19. 9   56
Psalm 20   149–50
Psalm 44   82, 151
Psalm 71   153
Psalm 88. 14–15   57
Psalm 109   80

Song of Songs 3. 11   98

Ecclesiasticus 24. 11–23   99

Isaiah 40. 3   54

Malachi 3. 1   53

Matthew 1. 1–16   49, 145
Matthew 3. 16   153
Matthew 11. 10   54
Matthew 19. 3–11   92
Matthew 22. 1–14   94
Matthew 25. 1–13   94

Mark 1   54
Mark 1. 9–11   153 n.97

Luke 3. 21–23   153 n.97
Luke 7. 27   54
Luke 7. 36–50   75 n.31
Luke 10. 38–42   99

John 1. 29–33   153 n.97
John 12. 1–8   75 n.31
John 21. 15   55

Ephesians 5. 22–33   92

Hebrews 1. 8   80

General Index

Numbers in **bold** indicate that there is an illustration on that page

Aachen 109, 117–20, 122, 124, 126, 128, 129, 154–6, 176, 195
Aachen Gospels 16
Abraham, biblical figure 48, 49, 50, 66, 89, 91
Acerbus Morena 138–9
Adalbert, saint 128
Adelaide of Maurienne, wife of Louis VI 123, 169, 170, 179–80, 245
Adela of Champagne, wife of Louis VII 209, 246
Adelheid of Italy, wife of Otto I 90
Adeliza of Louvain, wife of Henry I 101–2, 127, 151, 241
administrative kingship 2–4, 10, 12–3, 14, 25, 160
Adrian IV *see* Hadrian IV, pope
Aeldred, archbishop of York 110–11
Ælfheah *see* Alphege, archbishop of Canterbury
Æthelbald, king of Mercia 167
Æthelbert, king of Kent 121
Æthelwulf, king of Wessex 31, 49
Agiluf, king of the Lombards 167
Agnes of Poitou, wife of Henry III 174, 211, 212
Ahasuerus *see* Assuerus, biblical figure
Alexander I, king of Scotland 203
Alexander II, king of Scotland 178
Alexander III, king of Scotland 198, 207, 208
Alexander III, pope 112, 218
Alice, daughter of Louis VII 116
Alphege, archbishop of Canterbury 65–6
Amalric I, king of Jerusalem 145–6
Anglouême, Sacramentary of 31
anointing *see* unction
anticipatory succession *see* associate inauguration
Anselm, archbishop of Canterbury 52, 66, 132, 146
arenga 162, 165, 175–6, 187, 189
Arles 109, 150
Arundel Psalter 201

Assuerus, biblical figure 52, 104
associate inauguration 111 n.28, 113, 117, 132, 134–5, 141, 220
Augustine, archbishop of Canterbury 65

Baldric of Bourgeil 146
Baldwin IV, king of Jerusalem 145–6
Baldwin, archbishop of Canterbury 106, 107, 110
baptism 29–30, 54, 77, 78, 112, 120, 153, 170, 197
Beatrix of Burgundy, wife of Frederick Barbarossa 115, 124, 150, 211, 250
Becket Leaves 220
Berengaria of Navarre, wife of Richard I 116, 127
Bertha of Savoy, wife of Henry IV 115, 124
Besançon incident 217–9
bishop of Ostia, role in imperial and papal inauguration 26, 70, 71, 109, 110, 112
bishops, consecration of 29, 30, 36, 76–7, 88, 114, 130, 132, 133, 141, 144, 157–8, 222
Blanche of Castile, wife of Louis VIII 180, 247
Bruno, archbishop of Trier 115
byzantine influence on western rites 28, 55 n.117, 117, 153–4

Cana, wedding at *see under* Marriage
Canossa 11, 15–18, 224
Canterbury 65–6, 170
Celestine III, pope 219
Charlemagne 60, 118, 120, 122, 157, 166, 173, 175, 216
 canonization 119, 175–6
 throne of 118, 120, 195
Charles the Bald, king of the Franks 32, 91
chrismon 182–4, 187, 188
Christ *see* Jesus Christ
Clement III, anti-pope 157
Clement III, pope 219

286

General Index

Clovis, baptism of 33, 75 n.28, 112, 120–1, 170
Cnut, king of Denmark, England and Norway 138
Conrad, bishop of Constance 184
Conrad, son of Henry IV 174
Conrad II, king of Germany, emperor 145, 157 n.116, 206
Conrad III, king of Germany 111, 134, 155–6, 185
  seal 194, 195, 249
Constance (town) 185–7
Constance of Aragon, wife of Frederick II 90, 126, 151, 253
Constance of Castile, wife of Louis VII 114–5, 123, 246
Constance of Sicily, wife of Henry VI 114, 211, 213, 250, 251
coronation *see also* crowns 28, 31, 72, 94, 95, 131, 136, 153, 218
  festal 127–8, 136–41
  nuptial symbolism 87, 92, 97–8, 104, 116
  of emperors 26–7, 59, 60, 69, 70, 71, 72, 78–80, 110
  of empresses 88–9, 90, 93–4
  of kings 78–80, 89
  of queens 88–9, 92, 93–4, 97
  of the Virgin *see under* Mary (Blessed Virgin)
crosses 70, 72, 75, 105, 138
  in documents 183–4, 188
  on seals 196, 197, 198, 199, 200, 201, 206, 213
crowns *see also* coronation 79, 80, 84, 88–9, 95, 138, 150, 152, 157, 218
  of martyrdom 60, 148
  of thorns 57
  on seals 194, 208–9, 210
  symbolising the realm 78
  the *Reichskrone* 78–9
crusades and crusading 3, 119, 120, 126, 127, 146, 155, 156, 201, 209, 216

Dagobert I, king of the Franks 185, 195
Dalbert, archbishop of Sens 112–3
David, biblical figure 29, 48–52, 55, 56, 66, 154, 197
David, earl of Huntingdon 105
David Scottus, bishop of Bangor 26–7, 109–10, 112, 113, 130
diadems *see also* crowns 52, 95, 135, 139, 147

in the liturgy 79, 80
on seals 194
dei gratia 182, 214
  in charters 168, 169, 190
  origins of 166–7
  on seals 173, 202, 203, 204, 208
Diethelm of Krenkingen, bishop of Constance 184–5
Dietwin, papal legate 111
Doppelkönigtum 120, 126, 128–9
Dunstan, archbishop of Canterbury 65–6

Eadmer of Canterbury 127, 132, 191
Edgar, king of England 66
Edmund, king and martyr 64–5
Edmund, son of Henry III 208
Edward the Confessor, king of England 121
  canonization and cult 122, 176
  seal 191, 196–7, 198, 203, 204
Ekkehard of Aura 117, 152 n.91
enthronement *see also* thrones 47, 118, 120, 194
Eleanor of Aquitaine, wife of Louis VII and Henry II 114, 123, 124, 136–8, 204
  seal 209–10, 242
Eleanor of Provence, wife of Henry III 244
elective kingship 7-8, 56, 119–20, 126, 128, 144, 145, 211, 221
Ermengild, saint 64
Ermenilda, saint 65
Ermentrude, wife of Charles the Bald 32, 51, 90, 91
Esther, biblical figure 51–2, 103–4
Eustace, son of Stephen 113
Eugenius III, pope 185
Eutropia, saint 58
exchequer 4, 208

feast days 141–58
  All Saints 142
  apostolic feasts 124, 128, 144, 152, 216
  Ascension 56, 123, 144, 157, 181, 190
  Christmas 123, 124, 127, 128, 136, 137, 140, 143, 144, 157
  Easter 56, 115, 127, 128, 136, 138, 143, 156, 157, 182
  Epiphany 117, 152, 153–4, 158, 216
  Laetare Sunday 54, 155–6

287

General Index

Pentecost 56, 90, 123, 127, 128, 143, 157, 165
marian feasts 97–99, 101, 103, 104, 141, 143, 145, 150–1, 157, 170
Festkrönung see festal *under* coronation
fleurs-de-lys *see also* lilies 195, 199–200, 204, 208, 210, 213
Frederick, archbishop of Cologne 115
Frederick I Barbarossa, king of Germany, emperor 8, 17, 84 n.79, 109, 119, 127–8, 136, 138–9, 164, 175, 181, 185, 215–6, 217–8
  royal inauguration 132–3, 155–6
  imperial inauguration 219
  marriage 115, 124
  seals and bulls 206, 211
Frederick II, duke of Swabia 184
Frederick II, king of Germany, emperor 7, 22, 165 n.36,
  royal inauguration 112, 118, 119–20, 122, 144
  imperial inauguration 90, 108, 133
  marriages 126, 151
  seals and bulls 202 n.52, 203, 208, 211
Frederick, duke of Rothenburg 156

Gabriel, archangel 58
Galon, bishop of Paris 113
Gellone, Sacramentary of 31
Gervase of Canterbury 107, 113, 135, 140, 154
Gideon, biblical figure 49
Godfrey de Lucy, bishop of Winchester 105
Goliath, biblical figure 52
Goscelin of Saint-Bertin 65
Gloucester 121, 127, 144
Gregory the Great, pope 40, 44, 65, 71, 103
Gregory VII, pope 15, 19, 157, 174, 207 n.71, 223

Hadrian IV, pope 122, 217–8, 219
Henry, bishop of Ostia 222
Henry I, king of England 12, 13, 15, 52, 127, 189, 204, 210
  inauguration 133, 145, 146–7, 149–50, 151
  'coronation charter' 46, 159–61, 163, 164, 191
  marriages 101–2, 127, 151
  seals 191, 196, 202, 205
Henry I, king of France 165, 169, 202
Henry II, king of England 14, 15, 116, 121, 136–8, 164, 176, 177, 213, 215–6, 220
  inauguration 134, 135, 155
  seals 194, 200
  titles 168, 172, 190
Henry II, king of Germany, emperor 173, 211
Henry III, king of England 12, 156, 161, 221–2
  inauguration 121–2, 143, 144
  seals 195, 196, 197, 198, 208
Henry III, king of Germany, emperor 174, 211
Henry IV, king of England 91
Henry IV, king of Germany, emperor 15, 18–9, 117, 181, 211
  imperial inauguration 156, 157
  marriages 115
  titles 173, 174, 202
  seals and bulls 195, 202, 205, 206
Henry V, king of Germany, emperor 7, 151, 211
  royal inauguration 117, 151–4, 158
  imperial inauguration 26, 109–10, 112, 157
  marriage 87, 115, 124, **125**, 151–4, 158
  titles 173, 174, 175, 202
  seals 193, 195, 206
Henry (VI), king of Germany *see* Henry Berengar
Henry VI, king of England 56
Henry VI, king of Germany, emperor 24, 119, 184–7, 213
  royal inauguration 150, 151
  imperial inauguration 114, 156, 219
  diploma of 184–5, **186**, 187–8
  titles 173, 203
  seals and bull 173, 188, 203, 205, 207, 214
Henry VII, king of Germany, emperor 77
Henry (VII), king of Germany 126, 213
Henry Berengar 134, 155, 156
Henry of Huntingdon 133, 138, 140 n.48, 159
Henry the Lion, duke of Saxony and Bavaria 95, **96**
Henry the Young King, son of Henry II of England 168
  inauguration 111 n.28, 117, 134–5, 220
  seal 198, 207

288

General Index

Herman of Arbon, bishop of Constance 185
Hincmar, archbishop of Reims 32, 51, 112
Holofernes, biblical figure 52
Holy Ampoule 75, 78, 217
Honorius III, pope 69 n.3, 90, 108, 133
Honorius Augustodunensis 99
Hubert, archbishop of Canterbury 114
Hugh, archbishop of Sens 114, 123
Hugh, bishop of Durham 105
Hugh, bishop of Nivers 113
Humbaud, bishop of Auxerre 113

inauguration rights of Canterbury, Reims and Cologne 111, 112, 117 n.48, 147, 220
Ingebourg of Denmark, wife of Philip II Augustus 123, 124, 180, 247
Innocent II, pope 84 n.79, 122, 132, 157, 218
Innocent III, pope 72–3, 76, 82 n.65, 128–9
Investiture Controversy 2, 15–19, 26, 83, 88, 132, 175
Irene Maria, wife of Philip of Swabia 126, 251
Isaac, biblical figure 50, 89
Isabella of Anglouême, wife of John 114, 213, 243
Isabella of Hainault, wife of Philip II Augustus 123, 135, 247
Isabella of Jerusalem, wife of Frederick II 126, 203
Ivo, bishop of Chartres 113, 147

Jacob, biblical figure 50, 51, 89, 109
James the Great, apostle 124, 144, 152, 216
Jesus Christ 29, 45, 49, 58, 64, 72, 81, 87, 99, 103, 120, 133, 142, 143, 145, 152, 169, 179, 181–2, 206, 216, 218, 224
  as Bridegroom 91, 93–4, 97, 98, 101, 104, 116, 158, 210
  as Heavenly King 103, 104, 175, 188
  baptism of 54, 55 n.117, 143, 153–4, 158, 197
  crucifixion of 149–50, 200–1
  in majesty 16, 191, 194, 207, 213–4
John, bishop of Orléans 113
John, king of England 114, 116, 182, 190
  as Count of Mortain 105, 106
  inauguration 134, 144, 181
  titles 172, 202
  seal 172, 198, 202
John Marshal 105
John the Baptist 54, 154, 201
Joshua, biblical figure 48, 49, 66
Judith, wife of Æthelwulf 31, 32, 50, 90
Judith, biblical figure 51–2, 103
Julian of Toledo 29

Kaiserchronik (Latin) 26, 124, **125**, 152, 154
kissing rituals 47, 71–2

Lanfranc, archbishop of Canterbury 66
laudes 53, 58–66, 85–7, 89, 93, 103, 137, 150, 217
law 3, 10, 15, 46, 160–1, 175, 176, 216, 224
  English Common law 2, 14, 188, 223
  Old Testament law 54
  Roman law 15, 17, 18, 175, 223
Leah, biblical figure 51, 89, 91, 103
Leo III, pope 120
lilies *see also* fleurs-de-lys 195, 199, 213
Lincoln crown-wearing 136–7
litanies 26, 53, 57–8, 60, 65, 68, 103, 149, 217
Lothar III, king of Germany, emperor 84 n.79
  imperial inauguration 122, 218
  titles 174
  seals and bull 206–7
Louis IV of Wittelsbach, king of Germany, emperor 77
Louis VI, king of France 7, 179–80
  inauguration 112–3, 118, 145–9, 150, 151
  marriage 123, 124
  title 168, 169
  seal 199, 200, 207
Louis VII, king of France 116, 216
  inauguration 132
  marriages 114–5, 123
  title 168, 170
  seal 195, 199, 204
Louis VIII, king of France 180
  marriage 123
  title 172
  seal 199
Louis IX, king of France 7, 12, 57, 180
  title 172
  seals 199, 208–9

289

General Index

Louis 'the German', king of the East Franks 173
Louis the Pious, king of the Franks 173
Louis the Stammerer, king of the Franks 32
Ludolf of Hildesheim 167

Mainz 87, 115, 120, 124, 126, 144, 152, 156
magi *see* three kings
Manasses, bishop of Meaux 113
manuscript miniatures 19, 24
Margaret, wife of Henry the Young King 134–5
Margaret of Anjou, wife of Henry IV 91, 104
Margaret of Austria, wife of Henry (VII) 126, 213, 254
Margaret of Provence, wife of Louis IX 123, 248
Mary (Blessed Virgin) 58, 68, 87, 89, 116, 118, 142, 199, 201, 209, 210, 213, 214
  as Bride 97–104
  as Queen 91, 97, 103, 212, 213
  Coronation of the Virgin 99, **100**, 101–3, 151
  marian feasts *see under* feast days
Mary and Martha, biblical figures 99, 103
marriage 87–104
  liturgy for 22, 88, 92–3
  symbolism of 51, 97, 98
  feasts 94, 104, 124, **125**
  wedding at Cana 153, 154, 158
Matilda of Boulogne, wife of Stephen 213, 241
Matilda of England, daughter of Henry I, wife of Henry V 87, 135, 215, 216
  inauguration in Germany and marriage to Henry V 115, 116, 124, **125**, 144, 152–4, 158
  seal 211, 212, 242, 249
Matilda of England, daughter of Henry II **96**, 200 n.45
Matilda of Flanders, wife of William I 58, 90, 143
Matilda of Scotland, wife of Henry I 50, 101, 133, 202, 210, 241
Matthew de Vendôme 208
Matthew Paris 7, 122, 144
Maurice, bishop of London 133, 160
Maurice, saint 69, 71, 84–5

sword of *see under* swords
Maurilius, saint 58
Michael, archangel 58
modernization paradigms 1–2, 11, 15, 17, 171, 222, 224
monograms 177, 182, 183–4, 187–8
Monty Python 1, 7
Moses, biblical figure 48, 49, 66, 223

Nathan, biblical figure 55–6
Norman Anonymous 158
Notre-Dame, Paris 102, 123
nuns, consecration of 95–7, 116

oaths *see also* promises 44, 46–7, 66, 68, 72, 160–1, 189, 191
orbs 219
  in the liturgy 81, 83 n.73
  on seals 196, 197, 198, 205, 207, 210
ordines 22, 27–8, 30–2, 33–8
  Cencius I 38, 45–6, 69, 71, 73
  Cencius II 38, 44, 45–6, 59–61, 68, 69, 70, 71, 77, 81, 84, 88, 89, 93
  English Second Recension 36, 40, 46, 55, 57, 71, 75, 81, 83, 88, 103
  English Third Recension 36–7, 40, 46, 48, 49, 51, 57, 61, 70, 73, 76, 89, 93, 106, 107, 150
  Erdmann *Ordo* 90
  Ermentrude *Ordo* 32, 51, 90
  Imperial *Ordo* from Cologne Dombibliothek, MS 141 38, 71, 93
  Judith *Ordo* 31–2, 50, 51
  Leofric *Ordo* 31, 36
  Ordo of 1200 37, 40, 47, 48, 49, 58, 66, 76, 92–3,
  Ordo of 1250 76, 82 n.66, 84 n.76, 92 n.109
  Ordo from the Roman Curia 38, 61, 68, 71, 77, 79, 81–3, 85, 93
  Ordo of Saint-Bertin 37, 44–5, 57, 58, 70, 75, 81, 93
  Ratold *Ordo* 34, 37, 40, 47, 51, 55, 57, 80, 81, 83, 88, 103
  Royal *Ordo* from Cologne Dombibliothek, MS 141 37, 55, 57, 73, 75, 93, 103
  Royal *Ordo* from the Romano-Germanic Pontifical (PRG) 37, 38, 40, 44, 46–7, 48, 49, 53, 57, 58, 76, 80
  Staufen *Ordo* 38
Orléans 118, 123, 147, 169

General Index

Oswald, king and martyr 64, 65, 149–50, 159
Otto I, king of Germany, emperor 90, 119, 205
Otto II, king of Germany, emperor 143, 153, 173, 211
Otto III, king of Germany, emperor 16, 173, 191, 194, 196, 203, 204
Otto IV, king of Germany, emperor 120, 126, 154, 213
  royal inauguration 85, 128–9
  seals and bulls 195 n.24, 200–1
Otto, bishop of Freising 8, 108, 128, 132–3, 134, 136, 219

Paschal II, pope 26, 112
Paschal III, anti-pope 119
Pavia 138–9
Peter, saint 45–6, 55, 66, 82, 103, 121, 128
  altar of 71, 81–2, 84, 110
  basilica of 26, 59, 69–71, 122
Peter of Eboli 24
Philip, son of Louis VI of France 132
Philip I, king of France 113, 124, 146–7, 168–9, 179
  inauguration 107–8, 143, 165
  titles 166
  seals 199, 200
Philip II Augustus, king of France 12–3, 109, 116, 141, 142, 150, 170, 180, 182
  inauguration 134, 139
  marriages 123–4, 135, 150–1
  titles 171–2
  seals 199, 204, 209
Philip of Swabia, king of Germany 120, 185
  royal inauguration 126, 128–9, 154, 158
pipe rolls 12, 13, 14, 25, 122, 217
Pippin, king of the Franks 29, 30, 48, 167
pontificals 34–5, 53, 92
promises *see also* oaths 28, 45–7, 173–4, 191
prostration 57, 68

Rachel, biblical figure 51, 89, 91, 93, 103
Raphael, archangel 58
Ralph de Diceto 109, 114, 117, 135, 137, 154–5
Reading Abbey, re-foundation of 101, 151, 216
Rebecca, biblical figure 51, 89, 91, 93, 103

Recceswinth, Visigothic king 29
Reginald, bishop of Bath 105
Reims 37, 38, 58, 102, 111, 112, 113, 117–8, 120–1, 123, 132
Remigius, saint 30, 58, 112, 120–1
Reiner of Liège 120
relics 57, 70, 152, 209, 216
Richard I, king of England 84 n.76, 181
  inauguration 105–7, 108, 110, 130, 197
  marriage 116, 127
  titles 172
  seals 198, 200–1
Richard fitz Nigel, bishop of London 4, 208 n.75
Richard of Devizes 110, 139
Rigobert, saint 58
Rigord 134, 135, 141–2
rings 26, 83, 87, 88, 95–7, 106, 116, 210
Robert, earl of Leicester 105, 106
Robert I, duke of Normandy 145, 150, 159
Robert Grosseteste, bishop of Lincoln 222
Robert of Jumièges, missal of 149
Robert the Pious, king of France 169
rods *see* sceptres
Roger, archbishop of York 117, 220
Roger of Howden 105–7, 108, 123, 130, 133–4, 136–7, 139–40, 197
Rome 59, 84, 117, 122, 123, 157, 181
  image on seals 203, 206–7
rubrication of liturgical manuscripts 23, 38, 66, 68–78, 80–2, 89, 134
Rupert of Deutz 98–9

sacral kingship 1–2, 3, 11–20
Sacramentary of Anglouême, *see* Anglouême, Sacramentary of
Sacramentary of Gellone *see* Gellone, Sacramentary of
Saint-Denis 13, 29, 123, 148, 165
Sainte-Chapelle 57, 209
Samuel, biblical figure 29, 48, 49–50, 154
Sarah, biblical figure 51, 89, 91, 93, 103
Saul, biblical figure 29, 49–50
sceptres 105, 147, 197
  in the liturgy 40, 42, 80, 81, 83, 88
  on seals 198–9, 205, 207, 210, 212, 213
Siegfried, archbishop of Mainz 112
Sinicius, saint 58
Sixtus, saint 58
spurs 84, 85, 105, 106, 122

291

Solomon, biblical figure 48, 49, 55–6, 66, 119, 195
Sonderweg 11, 17
Song of Songs 98–9, 104
Stephen, king of England 113, 121, 137, 164
   inauguration 139–40, 154–5
   seals 196, 205 n.64, 213
Stephen, protomartyr 147–8
Stephen, pope 29
Stigand, archbishop of Canterbury 110–1
strator, German emperors performing role as 84 n.79
Suger, abbot of Saint-Denis 7, 13, 113, 114–5, 118, 123, 147–9, 195
swords 1, 105, 106, 147
   of St Maurice 85, **86**, 87
   in the liturgy 80–3, 151
   on seals 197–8, 205

Te Deum 25, 56, 57, 77
ten virgins, parable of 94, 104
Theophanu, wife of Otto II 126, 211, 212
three kings 152–3, 158, 216
Titelpolitik 173–5, 203, 207
Thomas Becket, archbishop of Canterbury 64, 111 n.28, 117, 135, 137, 141, 170, 176, 215 n.4, 220
thrones *see also* enthronement
   of Charlemagne 118–9, 120, 195
   of Dagobert 195
   of Solomon 119, 195
   in the liturgy 40, 42
   on seals 191, 193–5, 196
Turpin, archbishop of Reims 120

unction 6–7, 19, 27, 72, 78, 92, 94, 95, 131, 134–36, 141, 167, 218, 167, 222
   baptismal 29–30, 153, 170
   episcopal *see* bishops, consecration of
   of emperors 26, 44, 69, 70, 71, 72–3, 85, 109–10
   of empresses 77
   of kings 40, 44, 70, 72–6, 108, 110, 113, 115, 133, 147, 153, 222

   of queens 77–8, 114, 123
   Old Testament models for 30, 48, 50, 55–6, 154
   origins of 28–32

Vladislaus II of Bohemia 108
virga *see* sceptres
virgins, consecration of *see* nuns, consecration of

Walter Map 215
Wamba, Visigothic king 29
weddings and wedding symbolism *see* Marriage
Wenceslas, saint 128
Westminster 117, 121–3, 126–7, 144, 147
White Ship disaster 101
William, archbishop of Reims 139
William I, king of England 15, 58, 124, 143, 188
   inauguration 34, 36, 90, 108, 110, 132, 144
   seal 196, 202, 203
William II, king of England 145, 146, 159
   seal 196, 202, 204
William de Mandeville, count of Aumale 105, 106 n.4
William FitzPatrick, earl of Salisbury 105
William of Canterbury 216
William of Malmesbury 26, 109–10, 130
William of Nangis 123
William of Poitiers 90, 110, 111, 131–2
William of Sicily 213
William Marshal, earl of Pembroke 105, 144
William the Breton 109, 118, 122
William the Lion, king of Scotland 178
Winchester 127
Worcester chapter house 99–101
Worcester crown-wearing 136–8
Wulfstan of Worcester 149
Würzburg 115, 119, 124

Zadok, biblical figure 48 n.84, 55, 56

www.ingramcontent.com/pod-product-compliance
Lightning Source LLC
Chambersburg PA
CBHW051602230426
43668CB00013B/1947